Shaped for Service

Shaped for Service
Ministerial Formation and Virtue Ethics

PAUL W. GOODLIFF

☙PICKWICK *Publications* · Eugene, Oregon

SHAPED FOR SERVICE
Ministerial Formation and Virtue Ethics

Copyright © 2017 Paul W. Goodliff. All rights reserved. Except for brief quotations in critical publications or reviews, no part of this book may be reproduced in any manner without prior written permission from the publisher. Write: Permissions, Wipf and Stock Publishers, 199 W. 8th Ave., Suite 3, Eugene, OR 97401.

Pickwick Publications
An Imprint of Wipf and Stock Publishers
199 W. 8th Ave., Suite 3
Eugene, OR 97401

www.wipfandstock.com

PAPERBACK ISBN: 978-1-4982-9123-1
HARDCOVER ISBN: 978-1-4982-9125-5
EBOOK ISBN: 978-1-4982-9124-8

Cataloguing-in-Publication data:

Names: Goodliff, Paul.

Title: Shaped for service : ministerial formation and virtue ethics / Paul W. Goodliff.

Description: Eugene, OR : Pickwick Publications, 2017 | Includes bibliographical references and index(es).

Identifiers: ISBN 978-1-4982-9123-1 (paperback) | ISBN 978-1-4982-9125-5 (hardcover) | ISBN 978-1-4982-9124-8 (ebook)

Subjects: LSCH: Clergy—Training of. | Virtue.

Classification: BV4020 .G66 2017 (print) | BV4020 .G66 (ebook)

Manufactured in the U.S.A.   02/15/17

To Gill, my wife and unfailing encourager,
and the members of those churches that have called me to be
their minister: in Streatham, London; Stevenage, Hertfordshire;
and Abingdon, in the county of Oxfordshire.

Contents

Preface | ix
Acknowledgments | xi
Introduction: Ministerial Formation and Virtue Ethics | xv

Part One: Formation and Virtue Ethics

1. Formation for Ministry | 3
2. History and Landscape | 28
3. Virtue Ethics and Practitioners | 42
4. Creation, Eschaton, and the Formation and the Practice of Ministry | 56

Part Two: Models of Ministerial Formation

5. Formation and Wisdom | 73
6. Focused Discipleship | 94
7. Ministerial Formation as Apprenticeship | 110

Part Three: Forming the Person

8. Intellectual Formation | 125
9. Spiritual Formation | 138
10. Character Formation | 165

Part Four: Forming the Practices of Ministry

11. Formation of the Practitioner | 179
12. Forming the Liturgist | 187
13. The Formation of Pastoral Integrity | 194
14. Ministry as Guidance | 210
15. Ministry as Mission | 230
16. Forming the Preacher | 244
17. Forming the Administrator | 257
18. Forming the Leader | 270

Bibliography | 291
General Index | 303
Ancient Document Index | 309

Preface

This book explores the ways in which virtue ethics, with its focus upon the development of practices that shape a life, offers an overarching way of understanding the formation of ministers of the church. The language of formation has come to dominate much ministerial training, replacing earlier designates such as theological education or training. Formation signifies the shaping of the whole of life to the goal or end of godly and fruitful ministry, with character and spirituality as important as the acquisition of skills for the competent undertaking of the tasks of ministry, and the growth in understanding of the fields of knowledge appropriate for ministry (such as theology, biblical studies, pastoral psychology, and missiology), if not more so.

The shaping of such a life requires multiple modes of pedagogy, and not just the traditional lecture-hall delivery of knowledge or the field placement practice of ministerial roles, such as preaching and pastoral visiting. There is still plenty of room for the passing on of knowledge through a lecture, seminar or private study, but to this default mode of delivery of formation should be added apprenticeship, mentoring, supervision of practice, and awareness of the great significance in the personal journey of faith and growth in spirituality.

Because the delivery of formation takes place on a variety of ways, I decided that a range of approaches within the confines of the written word might offer a richer way of exploring formation and ministry than simply the mainstay of theological writing: the argumentation of theological discourse. So, as well as some personal narrative and story (present not simply out of egotism, although something of that might be detected, but as an example of how important is the life story of the minister-in-training or ordinand), I have used on a number of occasions analysis of paintings or music. The images that I refer to have not been reproduced here, but all are readily available online through access to the worldwide web. Using a search tool should readily bring up the image referred to in, sometimes, multiple versions on many sites. Thus, reading this book with a tablet, computer, or smartphone to hand is recommended (or if using the e-book option, switching to your search tool). To reproduce the images in full color reproduction would have increased the expense of producing the book (and therefore its cost) and so I trust that readers will be glad that I have considered their pocket, as well as their eyesight, for the size of reproduction available to a laptop, or larger tablet, exceeds that of images matching the page size of 15 x 23 cm of this book. It also facilitates an enlarged view of aspects of any picture, and at times this repays the effort involved.

Acknowledgments

It is tempting to say that a book with such a long gestation demands the acknowledgment of the role played by all who have formed me in ministry, and so any list is bound to be selective. However, it is possible to identify a few significant players, to whom my thanks will ever be due. Two of the three most influential ministers are now dead: the vicar of the parish church in Patcham where my family worshiped when I was a teenager, and under whose preaching I came to faith and first sensed a call to pastoral ministry, E. Garston-Smith; and the minister at the first Baptist church I joined, in Streatham, South London, and where that call came to practical expression—Douglas McBain. Their influence is beyond calculation, and in many ways I was formed to be the kind of minister that I am through having seen aspects of ministry as they practiced it. The third influential minister is still very much alive, and for nine years I was his associate at Streatham Baptist Church—Douglas McBain's successor, Mike Wood. Here I saw ministry at much closer quarters, and while Mike's generosity of spirit and deeply committed pastoral ministry allowed me to be my own man, I also learned so much about ministry under his wise apprenticeship.

The three contemporaries who have traveled with me as we exercised Baptist ministry for over thirty years have played a very significant role, not least in challenging and encouraging me. So, thank you Geoff Colmer, Colin Norris, and Martin Taylor. Since the mid-1980s we have met regularly, and for the past few years dreamed into being *The Order for Baptist Ministry*, which we hope goes some way to form spiritual depth in ministers new and old.

The book was started when I was still Head of Ministry at the Baptist Union, and gratitude to my colleagues in the Ministry Team there is due in abundance, especially to Viv O'Brien, whose support over ten years as my deputy team leader was unfailing and rich. Upon leaving that post the Baptist Union funded some writing time during which a major part of this work was completed, and so I want to express my appreciation of that support. Latterly in that post, John Rackley was a much-respected colleague and friend as Moderator of the Baptist Union's Ministerial Recognition Committee, and in John I saw how pastoral ministry, generous orthodoxy, and spiritual depth could combine to great effect.

Some early chapters first saw the light of day as papers presented to the Spurgeon's College Post-graduate seminar, and I am grateful to Nigel Wright, whose offer of an associate research fellowship at Spurgeon's College I gladly accepted, for making that seminar available to me, and to his successor as Principal, Roger Standing, for continuing the deal. A most helpful seminar to explore the theme of the book was organized by Jim Purves in 2015, who, when I was Head of Ministry, was my opposite number in the Baptist Union of Scotland: a post he continues to fill. I am appreciative of his kindness and hospitality in organizing this, amongst many of other examples of the virtues exhibited in his life.

Most recently, as part-time Minister of Abingdon Baptist Church in Oxfordshire, an historic church established in 1650, but with a heart for renewal of its life in the twenty-first century, I have been able to test some of the material in the book as, once again, I find myself serving as a working local pastor (although, I daresay, they did not realize it). My colleague there, Stephen Millard, has been an unfailingly supportive friend and co-pastor, and I want to say thank you to him too.

There have been opportunities to play a small part in ministerial formation at Spurgeon's College, London; Regent's Park College, Oxford; Bristol Baptist College and Trinity College, Bristol, where I teach sacramental theology to the combined Anglican and Baptist ministerial cohort with my colleague at Trinity, Paul Roberts; and with the largely Pentecostal ministerial students at the University of Roehampton, West London. My thanks to those students and colleagues on the faculties there. I must also acknowledge the friendship and encouragement of Paul Beasley-Murray, who invited me to teach at Spurgeon's College for a year shortly after my ordination, and with whom I was involved in founding both the *Richard Baxter Institute for Ministry* (now *Ministry Today*) and, more recently, *The College of Baptist Ministry*. Paul's passion for professional and godly ministry stands as an example of much that this book commends.

The contribution to my intellectual development made by the John Colwell—friend, fellow *Order for Baptist Ministry* founder, and fellow Old Varndeanian—cannot go unacknowledged either. Much of the material in this book has been forged in dialogue with John, and though we were at the same school for at least a year (John being older, we did not realize it until many years later) it was John's attempts to begin to teach me Greek when I first joined the staff at Streatham Baptist Church, and the instilling in me of the first glimmerings of a love of systematic theology, that joined our life's pathways. John's fingerprints might be detected at various points in the book, and always for the good.

But by far the most important thanks must go to my wife Gill, who has encouraged me in this project even as she developed her own interests as a university lecturer. At my lowest point over the past two years she was relentlessly encouraging and positive, assured me that God had something yet for me to do by way of service of Christ and his church, and proved me wrong when I doubted her. I would not have completed this book without that support, and I cannot begin to express my thanks to her adequately. "Thank you" must suffice.

Introduction

Ministerial Formation and Virtue Ethics

The nature of leadership in the church has always been contentious, but perhaps the questions that surround its character and purpose have never been so starkly put. For a few, an improvement in the quality of its leadership is the answer to most of the church's woes, while for others "leadership" is a taboo subject, promising little but a wholesale capitulation to the spirit of the age: secular, commercial and shallow. This book draws upon a range of ideas to construct an understanding of the preparation of men and women for the leadership of the church, construed as "formation" for Christian ministry. I take a less sanguine view of the merits of adopting secular and managerial models for the leadership of the church than many, but I do not underestimate the importance of formation for ministry as of key significance in the future growth (or even survival) of the church in the West.

Formation for ministry is a holistic understanding of the processes engaged in the preparation of men and women for ministry. It is the shaping of a whole life that is of concern here, not merely the imparting of knowledge or the acquiring of skills. It is a development of character, spirituality, ministerial skills, and growth in knowledge with understanding that is the task of the church in preparing such for the leadership, care, and service of its congregations, and the advancement of its mission.

The overarching framework I have adopted is that of virtue ethics, especially as mediated through the work of Alasdair MacIntyre, but along the way I will incorporate supporting structures to this argument from the work of the educational and psychological theorist, Leo Vygotsky, and its derivative: "communities of practice." The opening chapter lays those particular foundations. I will also place this within a narrative of the changing nature of the task of the preparation of ministers for their roles within the church, tracing the story from apprenticeship to education, to training, and most recently, to formation. I do so in this opening chapter.

Subsequently we will continue to explore in Part 1 the history of theological education and formation, and then turn to describing virtue ethics and in particular, that version espoused by one of its foremost exponents, Alasdair MacIntyre. Finally, in Part 1, in the theological framework for ministerial formation, an outworking of the narrative of creation, eschaton and redemption, we give the overarching framework for the origins and goals of ministry. In Part 2 three ways of approaching ministerial formation will be discussed: ministry (i) as wisdom, (ii) as a form of focused discipleship, and (iii) ministry formation as a type of apprenticeship. Here are other models of ministerial formation that will give this argument's primary model of virtue ethics, a thicker resonance. In Part 3 we will analyze within a virtue ethics framework the formation of the minister's intellect, spirituality, and character, before turning in Part 4 to the practices of ministry as the roles through which formation takes place: the minister as liturgist, pastor, spiritual guide, and resident theologian, missioner, preacher, administrator, and leader. These final two parts give substance to the oft-used trio of overlapping circles of knowing, being, and doing that combine together in formation.

It is my hope that this book might be of interest and guidance to those whose task it is to prepare others for ministerial office. In addition, I hope that this book provides a map for those undergoing ministerial formation, and assist them in understanding quite what is going on in the processes to which they have submitted themselves in response to the call of God to serve him and his people. It is not intended to be a course in ministerial formation, nor a manual for any who might misunderstand that ministerial formation can be achieved in some kind of "self-help" way (although some might argue that ministry at times is a form of disorder that might benefit from its own self-help guide). Rather, this is an extended exploration of a way to understand formation for ministry, or rather the formation of ministers, as a communal and ecclesial process that seeks to create "the good" minister, in the sense of the one who personally embodies the practices of the church, and in whom the church might place its confidence and trust.

It is written from the perspective of a British Baptist, and I cannot but reflect my cultural and ecclesial presuppositions and prejudices, although I hope it has a wider currency than just addressing British Baptists. I have exercised pastoral ministry in two local churches for seventeen years during the period 1982 to 1998, and again, most recently, from 2015. After 1998 I offered regional oversight or episcope for five years and during the past decade held the post of national leadership within the Baptist Union of Great

Britain for ministry (variously Head of Ministry Department and Ministries Team Leader). Within this latter responsibility I have worked closely with our denominational theological colleges through a period of great change, and while I have only briefly held a staff position within a college, I have taught occasionally at a number, and am presently associate research fellow at Spurgeon's College in London, where many years ago I was educated/trained and, perhaps even "formed" for ministry, and been a visiting lecturer at two or three institutions. I have also seen the quality and caliber of my colleagues in ministry on a regional, then national canvas, and have been generally impressed by what I have seen: dedicated, hard-working, and godly men and women, whose pastoral ministry and leadership has borne fruit in countless ways. I have also seen too often the damage that failure in ministry causes, both to individuals and to their church communities. That failure can be moral, when conduct that brings the gospel and the church into disrepute is perpetrated, often with profound self-delusion and harm. But it can also be a failure of capability and competence by those who are morally stable, but otherwise rather inadequate practitioners of ministry, and equally a failure in sustaining ministry through sheer overextension and burnout. My conviction is that if we take the formational process, and a virtue-ethics conception of it, more seriously, we might reduce the frequency of either kind of failure, and in a day of ever-increasing public scrutiny of our failures, and cynicism about the church, such a trajectory is vital.

I am convinced that a variety of approaches to this theme enriches its understanding, and so together with the familiar tools of description, argument, and analysis, I utilize discussion of visual images from pictorial art from time to time, together with something of my own story, which could be rather grandly described as auto-ethnography, or simply narrative theology. This is a deliberate strategy since formation for ministry also encapsulates a rich variety of approaches, from the imparting of information through traditional means (lectures, reading, and so forth), to the development of self-knowledge and self-critical reflection on practice and, at least in the formation of liturgists, the use of musical and visual imagery. In a small way I hope this mixed approach reflects the varied nature of ministry formation itself.

PART ONE

Formation and Virtue Ethics

1

Formation for Ministry

This is a book about Christian ministry and its formation. Thousands of people each year embark upon this adventure, seeking to prepare themselves, or be prepared by others, to serve the worldwide church as its ministers, and about two thousand of those do so in Britain. What is this role, or rather, vocation, they envisage they will fulfil, and just how can a woman or a man be formed to serve Christ and his church? There are plenty of people who think that a little sanctified common sense will suffice, and in an age where it is assumed that "anybody can" (a common subtext in educational vernacular), the idea of the robust, challenging, and transformative process that ministerial formation should be is often met with mild suspicion or outright hostility. It smacks too much of a professionalized elite, withholding arcane information from others. The French postmodernist philosopher Foucault has popularized the notion that the acquisition of all knowledge is a bid for power, and the clergy are supposed to be no different.

This is especially true when theological educators begin to build the curriculum comprising areas for study considered essential in every ministerial education: learning the biblical languages, studying the Fathers, grasping the breadth of church history (notably that of the tradition to which each belongs), acquiring knowledge of philosophy, pastoral psychology, systematic theology or dogmatics, Christian ethics, biblical studies, and contemporary culture. There is much else besides deemed essential by special interest groups. Those engaged in urban mission think every ministerial student should be taught its principles, while their rural counterparts are equally passionate about their context. Church planters see their calling as the future of the church, so all students must be exposed to pioneer situations, and experience of overseas mission is obviously beneficial in a global world for a church with a global mission. If every aspect were included I guess theological education and ministerial formation would last seven or eight years, not the two to four it currently occupies (Roman Catholics excepted).

Brian Harris, writing of a conversation with theological educators from around the world, gathered at a Lausanne Forum for World Evangelization working group in 2004, describes the various components of an adequate theological education, and concludes,

> It highlights the difficult task facing all theological educators. Their training is expected to produce Hebrew, Greek and Patristic scholars who are capable of ensuring that all in leadership positions have police and working-with-children checks while they rapidly plant growing churches filled with new converts eager to be disciples as they worship in contemporary and contextually relevant ways.[1]

For many Protestants such training seems excessively academic, while Catholics will have their own prejudices about what a good priest needs to know and do, and reading the Old Testament in Hebrew is probably not on the list. One approach to ministerial formation is, therefore, the minimalist approach, and this currency is all-too widespread in its circulation. The emphasis is upon basic skills acquisition for ministry, with a minimum of academic knowledge, just sufficient to preach an interesting sermon liberally laced with humorous stories. All of this could be acquired at the hands of an experienced and effective practitioner, so the necessity of a dedicated theological institution is avoided, with all of its expensive delivery costs and capital investment in buildings and resources, as well as the delay in getting hands-on experience and beginning to "do ministry."

Another concern is the relationship of the curriculum, be it academic or practical, to the wider church that its products—pastors and ministers—are being called to serve. Such is the pressure upon theological colleges and seminaries from their academic validating bodies (generally in Britain a University generous enough to validate external Higher Education institutes) that sometimes the prime task of forming ministers can become subservient to maintaining the partnership with the academy. So, theological curricula can reflect the concerns of the academy (and those who teach it, who wish to maintain their credibility within the academy) rather than the concerns of the churches that receive the ministers they commend. In addition, all of this can hide the mistake of forming "useful" ministers for a church eager to be seen as contributing to society, rather than truthful

---

1. Harris, "Defining and Shaping."

ministers with a passion for the church to first of all be itself. Stanley Hauerwas and William H. Willimon write (albeit into the North American scene),

> When seminaries do not get direction from congregations, they will go their own way—usually the wrong way. Our seminaries still arrange their curricula as if the world had not changed. In imitation of the secular university systems they aspire to be accepted by, our seminaries offer future pastors a mix of a little this, and a little that, psychology here, organizational management there, a little Bible, a little ethics. After all, we don't want our pastors to be narrow-minded or ignorant; in other words, we want them to be fully conversant in all aspects of modern American culture. Our curriculum is structured to produce people who can help the church continue to "serve the world" by putting a vaguely Christian tint upon the world's ways of salvation.[2]

A basic question must be, therefore, what is formation for? I am not arguing for an uneducated ministry, or a poorly trained ministry: far from it. But I am asking the question whether the current strategies of the churches for their survival are working: whether a great deal of our social action, designed to make the churches seem acceptable to a secular and multi-faith society, actually brings people to faith in Christ and deep conformity to his way and image. If the church is a faintly religious voluntary arm of social services, all well and good. And that *is* how the prevailing political culture wants the church to be: useful to its own agendas, but subservient. Woe betide if it speaks prophetically about the reasons why those services are necessary in the first place. That is "meddling in politics" when it should be "saving souls." But the church is something else entirely: it is the community of Christ crucified; a "colony of heaven" residing here on earth; a people formed by Scripture and sacrament to worship Jesus Christ as Lord, and reject the pretensions of Caesar to the lordship of human lives, be that Augustus Caesar of the first century, or the many Caesars of our own day. Such are the claims of the nation state for our absolute allegiance, or the gods of the international bond markets and their addiction to economic growth as our masters. If the church is truly to be the church of Jesus Christ, then it needs ministers who have been formed, not just as educated professionals, but as perceptive and courageous prophets and compassionate and confident pastors.

I may seem critical of the current approach to ministerial formation (and indeed, to an extent, I am) but I have been partly the product of such

---

2. Hauerwas and Willimon, *Resident Aliens*, 115.

an approach. Having been a schoolmaster for four years following University, I was appointed Full-time Elder at a large charismatic Baptist church in South London. I had no formal theological education, and no senior staff colleagues initially (thank God for the appointment of my senior colleague nine months into the role), and faced major pastoral challenges from day one following a visit by John Wimber to the church during the weekend that preceded my first day in post. To say it was high octane, high-risk ministry is no exaggeration. I am not sure whether I am more impressed by the trust that this church placed in me or appalled by the sheer folly of what they thought they were doing in calling such a young and inexperienced pastor!

By the time, two years later, when I finally started at theological college (which had not really figured in my original plan—my arrogance was breath-taking), I had considerable experience of ministry, but little grounding in knowledge beyond that of a reasonably well-discipled Christian. Four years later I was a probationer Baptist minister, with a voracious appetite for theology, and a rather more "formed" minister. I guess the most one might say was that this was an appropriate pathway for me, but not one that I would entirely endorse for most. The church was large enough to hold a very green and young minister, and most do not have that context in which to learn their craft.

As will become evident, if I am critical of the minimalist approach, I am also critical of the current normal delivery of formation. Where a two to four year course at seminary or theological college is considered sufficient, I believe this is inadequate. There needs to be a recognition that formation begins long before embarking upon a college course, and that it continues long after the course has been completed. Indeed, life-long learning has become *de rigueur* amongst many professions, and life-long formation is the reality for all ministry. Brian Harris notes,

> In an ideal world, those sensing a call to ministry, would, like the early disciples, leave their nets and embark upon their new life. In the real world, a much longer delay is often inevitable. While this might cause frustration, it can be a very constructive period. A local church alert to the ministerial call of one of their members can provide invaluable in-house training. Where seminaries offer flexible training, it is also possible to undertake some training via part time or distance options. It is often wise to first put one's toe in the water before making the full body plunge. Pity those who have resigned career and sold house only to arrive at seminary to find that they cannot stop yawning through the Greek class. The seminary should not view itself in isolation from the local church. Both have key roles to play

in ministerial training and formation, and it is as well for the partnership to begin as early as possible.³

The Baptist Union of Great Britain's 2014 *Review of Selection and Formation* of ministers, which I initiated in my capacity as its then Ministries Team Leader, and then wrote its Report (although I left that post before its full implementation) took a similar approach, recommending,

> Other denominations selection processes seem far less hurried than ours, and there is some virtue in slowing our own process. For instance, in The Church of England the work of the Diocesan Director of Ordinands (DDO) to support the candidate and prepare them for the selection conference is much more intense than our own Regional Ministers routinely provide. It is not intended that to the already very full work-load of Regional teams a new and time-consuming task be added, but rather that, while Regional Ministers continue to provide the initial information and interview, the continuing support for the candidate be given to two figures: (i) pastoral support to be expected from their sending church (or network or association) in the form of a named pastoral accompanier throughout the selection and initial formational process, and (ii) a post similar to that of the DDO be created (we suggest naming this person The Association Selection Advisor, ASA) so that in the months that lead up to a Ministerial Recognition Committee (MRC), and in the months that follow a successful candidature before a college course is commenced, the person may be given greater opportunity to grow in their understanding of the nature and challenges of ministry, and where appropriate prepare for college spiritually, intellectually and/or emotionally and psychologically. For instance, for some candidates a deepening (indeed, perhaps, the establishment) of an appropriate raft of spiritual disciplines might be necessary, while for others some introductory reading and intellectual preparation might be valuable. It is recognized that this is profoundly counter-cultural in its ethos. We recommend (R8) that the posts of named pastoral accompaniers for candidates and Association Selection Advisor be established.
>
> 1.2.1 MRCs should indicate to a successful candidate that they should not embark upon formal training at college before completing a pre-collegiate formation period of at least 12 months' duration, normally in their home church while continuing in current employment, in order to continue formation process with the ASA. It is better to enter college prepared for

3. Harris, "Defining and Shaping," 159.

the rigors of formation, albeit a little delayed, than to hurry the process and struggle. If the candidate has existing experience of being in pastoral charge for at least two years prior to attending the association MRC, then the requirements for a pre-collegiate formational period would normally be waived. The experience would have provided it sufficiently. Colleges would be expected to advise candidates accordingly, and only admit ministers-in-training once an adequate pre-collegiate formational process had been fulfilled.[4]

A recognition that ministerial formation is a much more extensive process than simply the period in college or seminary, and as such begins long before a call is heard, and continues long after ordination, while also intensifying the core of the formational process while at college, seems to me important.

However the duration and place of formation is conceived, the bigger questions are "What is formation for and how is it accomplished?" These are questions also asked in that Baptist Union Report, and which in a much fuller way I shall attempt to answer in this book. I do so by utilizing the lens of virtue ethics, and applying this to every aspect of ministerial formation. But first, while this book focuses upon ministerial formation, its prior question must be what is ministry?

I begin by reference again to that Baptist Union Report. For over ten years until 2014 I led the team at the Baptist Union of Great Britain that had oversight of its ministers and ministry. Towards the end of that time I was involved in initiating a review of ministerial selection and formation, and, on behalf of the Steering Group for that Review, I wrote its Report. This went out to consultation as I stepped down. It was the last piece of policy development that I was engaged with, and in the preamble to that Report I wrote the following:

> *"I feel a presence, a reverence humming within me that was and is difficult to articulate."*
>
> This description of what it might be like to sense that a life has been captured by the call of Christ, a call to serve him and his church, ably voices the inner conviction which lies at the heart of ministry, often so difficult to articulate, yet profoundly experienced. We use language like vocation, or calling to frame it; offer Scripture to justify it and explain it; use language like captured, constrained and held to express how it feels to be caught

---

4. Draft 6.1 *Report of the Review of Selection, Formation, Funding and CMD*, Baptist Union of Great Britain, 2014, n.p., 11–12.

by such a calling; perhaps we run away from it, like Jonah on his way to Tarshish, or rush into it without submitting to the proper "stature of waiting." However, we handle it, ministry is not simply a job we employ some people to do on behalf of those others, the majority of the church whose time, inclination or ability is in such short supply that they will find someone else and pay them instead. It is, rather, deeply rooted in the conviction that God is involved in this human endeavor, his call is mediated through the wisdom and discernment of the churches, and it is his Spirit that is most significantly at work. It might come as a surprise to know that the person who wrote that epigraph was Jane Fonda.[5]

There followed a longer section describing what ministry is and is not, and this reflects the interplay between ministry expressed in both inherited and pioneer church:

In beginning to identify the kind of ministry that the current and future contexts require, we have looked to both the inherited tasks and character of ministry, and those insights developed from pioneering and global perspectives. We have recognized that ministry is as much about the kind of person exercising it as the tasks through which ministry is expressed. We have sought to track a path away from the equally foolish notions that "anybody can do ministry" (as if a modicum of common sense might suffice to equip a person to lead and pastor the flock of Christ), and an unhealthy professional elitism, that withdraws behind a cloak of esoteric language and practice detached from the everyday discipleship that ministry is meant to exemplify.

We have been aware of those siren voices that always threaten to tempt the ministry away to shipwreck and ruin: from the latest management fad that promises seven steps to a growing church, utterly devoid of any sense of a cross to be carried, to the gaudy prizes of success built upon mere consumer preference.

Amongst the distortions of ministry that we have sought to avoid are the unaccountable entrepreneur, for whom the congregation is little more than the body which funds the minister to do whatever he or she wants, building their own empire rather than the life of the local congregation, and is resistant to challenge and calls for accountability. Its polar opposite, the compliant minister who is merely the chaplain to the congregation, fails to bring the prophetic edge to ministry, and attempts at all costs to please the congregation. One is the cuckoo in the nest, with the congregation as the poor host parent attempting

---

5. Ibid., 1.

to feed the monster in its midst, while the other is the mother, continually attempting to feed an open-mouthed chick that should have been finding its own food long ago.

Another parody of effective ministry is the sole minister who holds all ministry to themselves, and seems incapable of releasing others to grow in their own gifts, for fear of imperfection, perhaps; or their polar opposite, the minister who fails to bring any leadership or vision of their own, simply following where the herd wanders, and who allows "hired hands" to lead the sheep by means of management dogma or too close an attention to "the bottom line."

Ministry is not meant to reflect a clericalising of religion, whereby we select a heroic few to live, on our behalf, a life of sacrificial discipleship that the many are reluctant to embrace. True, ministry has often functioned like this, and church has in every age relied upon those who it sets apart to be what it aspires to, but fails in the main, to reach: the martyrs of the early centuries, the monastic communities at their rigorous best, the celibate priest or over-worked pastor, for whom the dictum of the congregation "Lord, you keep him humble, and we'll keep him poor" is still too real to be entirely funny.[6] Yet we are

---

6. Cf. P. Goodliff, "Baptist Futures, Networks," paper presented to BUGB Council March 2012: "It must be recognized also that Baptists have been tempted to enact a dichotomy between the unholy congregant and the holy professional, at least as unhelpful as the Catholic separation of the ordinary secular Christian and those for whom there are expectations of greater piety and holiness of life. There the Religious, or the clergy are called to a life of holiness, while ordinary Catholics go about their life without such demanding expectations. In other words, while most of us are sinners, for a few the expectation is of sainthood. The Baptist model in fact has attempted to make saints of all the members of the church, even if this is no longer really practiced with any vigor. This need not require a fundamental rejection of the recognition of ministry (as perhaps McClendon suggests as he rejects 'a set-apart ministry of those who work for God while others work for themselves, and not a flock of secular 'callings . . . tended by a shepherd with a religious calling . . . but a *people set apart*,' where, 'Every member is called to discipleship; baptism . . . is commissioning to this ministry; thus it occupies the place ordination must in churches that celebrate a "clergy"' (McClendon, *Systematic Theology. Doctrine*, 2:369), but it does place the ministry of the few called to the ministry of word and sacrament firmly within the context of the discipleship of all. Every member in the Gathered Church is called to holiness of life and a vocation to discipleship, even if those called to ministry are also called to exemplify that calling so that they in particular might be examples to the flock. Here is the way in which the sainthood of all recognizes the saintliness of some, those who are called to a life set apart in order that they might present every member complete. We might express that alternatively, the ministry of all is enabled by the ministry of some, the gifts of Ephesians 4:11 are to equip the saints for the work of service and ministry."

convinced that ministry should not reflect such an ideology, for all are called to be disciples and to serve his world.

If that is what ministry is meant not to look like, how should it be portrayed instead? Overall, we see ministry as gifted leadership that, by "equipping the saints" (Ephesians 4:12) enables the church to be truly itself: a prophetic and missional community engaged in the acts of the risen Christ, called to a living and profound worship of God and, living under the Scriptures in the power of the Holy Spirit, bearing the fruit of that one Spirit, who is always the Spirit of the risen Christ and the gift of the Father. Where such ministry is offered, we should expect there to be growth in the life of the church: both growth in holiness and spiritual vitality, and a sharing of the gospel that produces fruit. To such leadership God calls women and men from all conditions and cultures, and the church sets them apart by ordination and commissioning to a life lived in service of that calling. Not everyone is so called, and such are the demands of courage, determination, intellect, heart and will in living out that way of life, that the church searches for those of proven ability to fulfil that calling. Of course, even for the ablest of women or men, it is only ever by God's Spirit that anything truly eternal can be accomplished, yet God uses the character, gifts and abilities placed at his disposal as the agency by which Christ does indeed build his church. So selection will pay attention to those human qualities, and seek to enhance and develop them through formation and training, and encourage their sustenance by prayer and longing. A recommendation from the Formation Working Group asked for an articulation of ministerial virtues, to accompany the already-agreed ministerial competencies and the broad agreement around what a minister ought to be expected to know (ministerial comprehensions, one might say). While we may describe them in various ways, those virtues will include courage, humility and obedience; perseverance and self-control, patience and compassion, and above all, the virtue of love (Col 3:12–14).

Ministry embraces pastoral care of the people of God, and leadership in the mission of the church. It is a ministry that offers leadership, while avoiding a contractual obligation that such an offering must be accepted. In this way, it is reflective of the ministry of the Chief Shepherd, whose "sheep hear my voice" (John 10:4), and who "lays down his life for the sheep" (John 10:15). The much over-worked phrase "servant leadership" is most often employed to describe the marks of such leadership. Ministry embraces the gifts of the risen Christ that Paul distinguishes in Ephesians 4 (pastor, teacher, prophet, evangelist and apostle) and is characterized by a devotion to "the Word and to prayer" (Acts 6:4), held in balance with an active fulfilment of the tasks that comprise the practice of ministry. It serves both inherited church (perhaps most urgently and needful by challenging it) and pioneers new ways of expressing church; it both cares for the people of God and reaches out to those yet to be found, and those who may be the never-found, alike; and it lives out the Word in the parlor, the pantry and the pew before it ever declaims it from the pulpit.[7]

Above all, we saw ministry as the living out in a consistent and loving way what it means to be a woman or man of God. Meet a minister, and in some way you should encounter Christ, and catch "the whiff of Jesus" (to use a memorable phrase from Glen Marshall).

That is a beginning, at least, in answering this question, "what is ministry?" or its associated question "what is ministry for?" It is gifted leadership that enables the church to be truly itself, enabling its mission and caring for its community. It is servant leadership that recognizes the gifts of the many and seeks to develop and enable them for the good of the whole. It is prophetic leadership that challenges the church and the world with the good news of Christ and the call to live a life of discipleship. It is wise leadership that draws upon the whole council of God in shaping, with others, the path the church must tread. Above all, it is "virtuous" leadership, embodying first in itself what it subsequently calls the whole church to be and to do. If ministers are under-shepherds of the one Good Shepherd, Jesus Christ, the Lord of the Church, then they, too, must be "good" in two ways. First good in the sense of effective, professional, accomplished. Good in the sense that one might say of an accomplished pianist, "John is a very good musician." However, that very good musician might also be a serial philanderer,

---

7. We toyed with ideas of ministry from such varied images as the electrician (who attends to the wiring so that everything is connect to the mains, and who ensures that a new extension is connected to the original home); to the midwife (who assists at the birth of a new life, but is not the mother, and who, following intensive support, has a decreasing engagement as the mother and child become self-sufficient); to the weather forecaster (who makes calculated assessments of what the climate will be like in the near future) or the occupant of the crow's nest (who sees further than those on deck, so has a wider vision); and to the apprentice-master (who takes unskilled people and enables them to become skilled practitioners in the life of faith and discipleship). We wondered if ministers were cooks, preparing nutritional meals for their congregations; building inspectors, who ensured the foundations were strong enough; or ambassadors, who represent another state in a foreign land, and embody its values and characteristics, speaking both their own language and the language of the foreign country where they are placed.

devious, and deceptive in their private life and relationships. It does not, in their case, detract from their musicianship. It cannot be so for ministers. Another, more significant, understanding of "good" must be applied: that of moral propriety, personal integrity, and godly character. The "good minister" is both proficient at the tasks of their calling, and righteous in their living–to use a word often on the lips of the Psalmist. The thesis of this book is that in both senses of that word, virtue ethics and its outworking is the best model to apply in seeking to enable proficiency and deepen character and spirituality. The next chapter explores in greater detail what is meant by virtue ethics, and why and how it might be helpfully applied. Meanwhile, let me continue to describe what ministry is and what shape it takes. As in so many other answers to this question, I will do so by means of metaphor.[8] The first is drawn from music, the second and third from the visual arts. A feature of the way in which this book will examine formation is to refer to the arts, as I have already suggested in the introduction. This is in part because of a conviction that formation itself is much more than a cerebral acquisition of knowledge, and that a varied approach will deliver formation more deeply: the book, therefore, mimics the approach I will advocate, within the limits of a book, of course. The tangential approach afforded by looking at paintings or listening to music is itself a kind of formation, a meditative and even prayerful consideration. I shall argue throughout for an approach that is deeper than often is the case, and the careful attention to a painting or the listening to music is an expression of that approach. It is also, partly, because this conveys my own interests, and if that has itself a hint of self-indulgence, then perhaps the reader will forgive this: I believe it pays dividends in broadening the approach to our analysis, coming at the issues from a different perspective.

The Art of Fugue

I want first to liken the character of ministry and the formation of ministers to a piece of music. Bach's final monumental work in the medium of the fugue, *Die Kunst der Fuge*, *The Art of Fugue*, will suffice for illustration. This is not an arbitrary choice, for Johann Sebastian Bach is the Christian

---

8. Together with the classic metaphor of shepherd, pastor, a common way of describing ministry in the recent past has been as a profession. Russell analyzed this from the perspective of the Church of England and the development of the professions in the nineteenth century: Russell, *The Clerical Profession*. Others have emphasized its relationship to the laity: Pickard, *Theological Foundations for Collaborative Ministry*; while Thompson and Thompson have explored ministry as a mindful interaction between God, the church, and the minister: *Mindful Ministry*.

composer *par excellence,* and it was that extraordinary German theologian and pastor of the Confessing Church, Dietrich Bonhoeffer, writing to his friend Eberhard Bethge from prison in Berlin on 23rd February 1944, who noted that,

> The important thing today is that we should be able to discern from the fragment of our life how the whole was arranged and planned, and what material it consists of. For really there are some fragments that are only worth throwing into the dustbin ... and others whose importance lasts for centuries, because their completion can only be a matter for God, and so they are fragments that must be fragments—I am thinking of, e.g., of the art of fugue. If our life is but the remotest reflection of such a fragment, if we accumulate, at least for a short while, a wealth of themes and weld them into a harmony in which the great counterpoint is maintained from start to finish, so that at last, when it breaks off abruptly, we can sing no more than the chorale, *Vor deinen Thron tret' ich allhier,* we will not moan the fragmentariness of our life, but rather rejoice in it.[9]

This is a work whose importance has lasted for centuries, and Bonhoeffer refers to its sudden unfinished character. The final fugue is left incomplete in the published edition: it just dies on the page mid-exposition, just as Bonhoeffer's life was ended so suddenly under the hangman's noose in Flossenburg on 9th April 1945. Ministry seems something like this: fragments, some of which are only fit for the rubbish, but others that last, a very few, perhaps, far beyond the life of the minister. Those fragments are woven into a larger counterpoint whose theme is given by the Christian gospel, and each section a fresh variation on the one great theme.

The Art of Fugue is Bach's great tour de force, its theme Bach's own[10] and composed in the early 1740s until around 1745, by which time Bach was sixty. It has fugues of all sorts (fourteen in all), some simple, others inverted, double, triple and quadruple of great inventiveness and complexity, together with four canons. Yet the theme is always present; sometimes obviously so, at other times more obscure. Bach was considered "old fashioned" by this stage of his life, and it may be that "In this rather austere, abstract

---

9. Bonhoeffer, *Letters and Papers from Prison,* 135–36.

10. The third subject of the final fugue, Contrapunctus XIV, a four-voice triple fugue, is based on the German musical notation of BACH (Bb – A – C – B, in German, H) which had led to some speculation that Bach was writing the work at his death. Almost certainly this was a transcribing error, not a compositional one, as Bach was preparing for publication a text that was already over five years old.

work it could well be that Bach was setting down models of his fugal art, for a generation that no longer cherished it."[11]

Perhaps this book on formation and virtue ethics also has something of this tenor about it. Ministry as I shall be describing it, and the formation of those who are called to it in particular, places itself firmly in a tradition that seems old fashioned to some, those enamored of all things "emerging" and "fresh." The personal demands of it seem too great, the theme too unvarying, the complexity in effectively exercising such ministry seems bewildering. Yet, a quarter of a millennium later, Bach's *The Art of Fugue* remains a towering achievement, a lasting fragment of a Christian culture, where easier, less demanding music has been consigned to the land-fill of history. Similarly, the core traditional ministry tasks have stood the test of time, and the heart of what it is to be a minister likewise.

It is a vision of such challenge, such beauty and such Kingdom fruitfulness that I want to set out. To those who limit the preparation of those entering Christian ministry to an academic education, or even training in the skills and tasks of ministry, I want to say "not enough." It is the preparation of men and women as living symbols of the gospel, embodying in their lives and actions the very character of Christ that we should aspire to. This is an unashameably sacramental understanding of ministry: the minister is not simply tasked to fulfil certain functions, even if those functions are representative of the church, but to live a life through which the gracious presence of Christ by His Spirit might be encountered. True this is mediated through the actions of pastoral care and prayer, proclamation of the faith, and leadership of the church; evangelism, and liturgical presidency; but that is not the essence of what ministry is.

Remaining with Bonhoeffer and music, Jeremy Begbie explores how Bonhoeffer uses the metaphor of polyphony and the *cantus firmus* in another letter to Bethge:

> There is always the danger that intense love may cause one to lose what I might call the polyphony of life. What I mean is that God wants us to love him eternally with our whole hearts – not in such a way as to injure or weaken our earthly love, but to provide a kind of *cantus firmus* to which the other melodies of life provide the counterpoint ... Where the *cantus firmus* is clear and plain, the counterpoint can be developed to its limits.[12]

What Bonhoeffer envisages is,

---

11. Stacie and Latham, *The Cambridge Music Guide*, 203.
12. Bonhoeffer, *Letters and Papers from Prison*, 162.

a polyphonous kind of life for the church in the world, a rich life shot through with joy (a persistent theme in his writings). It is a life of "worldliness" – not the worldliness of the secularist, denying God, nor the worldliness of a certain kind of aesthete, fleeing responsibility, but a fully down-to-earth kind of Christian life that can include free "aesthetic existence" (friendship, art, etc.) while also being ethically alert and responsible.[13]

The calling of Christian ministry, like *The Art of Fugue*, has one common theme: the good news of Christ and all that flows from it in the glorious depth and richness of the Christian faith. This theme will be expressed in different ways. In Bach's work it is sometimes inversed, sometimes its cadence is altered, and there is plenty of variation and diversity in its expression, yet the same theme is discerned everywhere. There are different voices that contribute to each contrapunctus, with four of them contributing most often. So, the multi-voiced character of ministry is echoed in this music. Ministry works as different voices interact with one another: the voice of Scripture, and the voice of the wider culture; the voice of the minister's experience and the voice of the wisdom of the tradition which that ministry inhabits; the voice of the academy and the voice of the public square, the pulpit and the parlour; the voices of private prayer and public proclamation.

As Bonhoeffer noted, this rich polyphony is only secure "as long as the cantus firmus is kept going."[14] Similarly ministry is only secure as long as the "deposit of faith" remains the undying theme and ground: the gospel, the Christian tradition, and the orthodox faith. David Moseley states it like this, "the cantus firmus of our love for God orders and brings coherence to the multidimensional and fragmentary nature of contrapuntal human life."[15] Jeremy Begbie explains further, about the idea of the Spirit's work as enabling polyphony:

> Bonhoeffer uses the image to speak of the relation between our love of God and the loves and desires that shape the rest of our lives. But we could also use it to speak of the relation of Jesus Christ to his church and to the world, and us to one another. Christ crucified and risen is the cantus firmus, the rumor of wisdom at the heart of things. The Spirit takes human lives and weaves them into a polyphony around this cantus firmus. Moreover, by extension we could say: Christ lives in the polyphony

---

13. Begbie, *Resounding Truth*, 161.
14. Bonhoeffer, *Letters and Papers*, 163.
15. Moseley, "'Parables' and 'Polyphony,'" 259.

of the Trinity, and by the Spirit we are granted, through him, a share in this Trinitarian "enchantment."[16]

Time is what enables music to be realized: it has its own pace, and cannot be hurried without ridiculous distortion. One could say that time is what prevents all the notes of Bach's *The Art of Fugue* being played at once, and getting the pace right is essential to the interpretation of a piece. Similarly, a theme of this book is the necessity for an unhurried formation for ministry. We live in such a frantic world, conscious that the pace of life is ever increasing. Children are hurried from one extra-curriculum activity to the next, filling their time so that the essential childhood quality of boredom is avoided. Teenagers are bombarded by the media of communication: the smart phone constantly chattering. The working person is seemingly available 24/7 on email and expected to be in contact for work at all hours, while everyone seems to be expected to work more productively and for longer. One of the defining characteristics of the age is its hurried activism, already glimpsed perhaps a century before by W. H. Davies in his poem of 1911, *Leisure*, "What is this life if, full of care, / We have no time to sit and stare." A rather romantic notion of the pastoral life, no doubt, but even in the golden haze of the Edwardian period the technological developments that would enable the frenzied modern existence were already present: rapid and mass transportation, electronic communication and mass production of consumer durables. The scene was set, anticipating the great disruption of the First World War, and the globalized society.

Listening to a piece of music like *The Art of Fugue*, or looking at a great painting like Piero della Francesca's *The Baptism of Christ* of the mid fifteenth century (as we shall do in a second metaphor), requires of us the time to "sit and stare." It cannot be hurried, although it can be diminished to background musak, a form of aural wallpaper, or the hurried glimpse that skims across the surface of things. Ministry too requires this slow and deliberate attention, not least in the very heart of the ministry which lies somewhere in the careful attention to God and to others. Formation will require similar pacing, slowing down the process when everything about the wider culture, about funding and about the church, even, echoes the siren voices of productivity, cost-effectiveness and our obsession with growth.

---

16. Begbie, *Resounding Truth*, 269–70. He notes that the image of polyphony has been much used in contemporary Trinitarian thought, for instance, by Ford, *Self and Salvation: Being Transformed*, 245–59; and Cunningham, *These Three Are One: The Practice of Trinitarian Theology*, chap. 4.

The Baptism of Jesus

The second metaphor is drawn from a painting that now hangs in London's National Gallery, *The Baptism of Jesus* by Pierro della Francesca. Painted in San Sepolcro in either 1440,[17] or thereabouts (or, less likely, about 1455[18]) it was part of a triptych altar piece, with the two wings painted possibly by Matteo di Giovani later than *The Baptism*. It was designed for the Camaldulite Abbey church of St John the Evangelist in San Sepolcro, according to Ginzburg[19] and the National Gallery's own Guide[20]. We will explore in some detail the meaning in this painting, and proceed then to its application to ministry. Here, I will argue, the painting reflects ministry as gift, and the painting is subject to hermeneutic interpretation.

The picture is in many ways simple: Christ is central, baptized by effusion by the Baptist, with a choir of three angels to the left and another candidate getting ready to the right hand background. The elder citizens of Jerusalem are walking away in the background on a perfect spring day. Above, the Spirit descends, and rays of golden light descend upon Christ. It is believed that above the painting in its original setting della Francesca had panted a depiction of the Father. Are the angels bystanders or active participants? There is a sense of calm, yet also something uncanny, a brooding atmosphere, with angels frozen as if caught in a camera. Christ seems preoccupied with some inner awareness of what is happening. He is, in some sense, withdrawn. Indeed, the stillness of the waters of the Jordan, here transposed to the Tiber at San Sepolcro, echo the perfect stasis of this moment. The legend was that the Jordan reversed its flow at Jesus' baptism, and here that still point between the flow and its reversal is captured.[21]

---

17. The dating based upon iconographic features that relate the context of the picture to the Council of Florence of 1439, is consistent with that on exclusively stylistic grounds. With the figures in the background identified as Byzantine priests, and the three angels depicting the concord between East and West, soon broken five years later, Tanner sees the work as symbolic of this brief rapprochement between the fractured East and West Churches. Tanner, "Concordia in Piero della Francesca's Baptism of Christ." Clark suggests, similarly, that "This is Piero before he had been to Rome." Clark, *Piero della Francesca*, 13.

18. According, for instance, to Lavin, who suggests it was commissioned for the church of Santa Maria della Pieve, the only church in San Sepolcro where baptism was performed until 1518. Lavin, *Piero della Francesca*, 81. Similarly, Bertelli dates it soon after 1451, Bertelli, *Piero della Francesca*, 54.

19. Ginsburg, *The Enigma of Piero*, 11.

20. Langmuir, *The National Gallery Companion Guide*, 82. The National Gallery acquired it in 1861.

21. Cf. Bertolli, *Piero della Francesca*, 55. Lavin, *Piero della Francesca*, 86.

In the landscape the straight road leads to San Sepolcro itself, nestling in its volcanic crater valley. The tree that shares the foreground, almost another baptismal candidate itself, is a Mediterranean walnut. This is highly symbolic. San Sepolcro's valley was called the valley of the walnut, Val di Nocea, and so it locates the sacred site as none other than della Francesca's home town. The walnut, always a symbol of fertility, also was a symbol of the crucifixion. Its hard outer casing, the wood of the cross, its soft inner kernel, the flesh of the Savior. So the waters of baptism are over-shadowed by the passion.

The Tiber itself has become the Jordan, with exquisite reflections of the sky and landscape in its still waters. The other candidate is either putting on his baptismal garment (putting on Christ) or stripping off his old clothes (stripping off of vice) and the image is deliberately ambiguous. Did della Francesca hide the candidate's head deliberately, symbolizing the struggle to believe, the ambiguity of revelation? Probably not, but it nonetheless speaks of the way in which at baptism it is not what we think that matters, so much as that in the sheer physicality of getting wet (in Baptist practice, thoroughly wet all over), God does something beyond our ability to fully comprehend.

The angels have colored wings and clasp hands. They are ambiguously male/female. Undoubtedly beautiful, the swell of the central angel's breast is neither a female breast nor a muscular male chest, but the breast of an angel. Clasping hands was a sign of marriage and covenant,[22] although these angels are not married. In this iconography, Christ is the Bridegroom, the Church the Bride of Christ, and the angels present were known as the Friends of the Bridegroom. Some contend that they represent the three angels who met Abraham under the oak tree at Mamre, and the colors represent the Trinity: blue for the Father (the left hand angel with a jewel on his head), white for the Spirit in the center and red for the Son.[23] The right hand angel (Son) wears a garland of victory in his head, the Spirit, a crown. Either way, della Francesca is drawing upon complex and multi-faceted Medieval theology, and placing it in the context of his home town, whence the commission to paint the picture had come.

The figures in the background could also be the Three Magi, with their Byzantine costume. One of them is pointing to the sky. The date of celebrating Epiphany, the feast of Christ's baptism, 6th January, was also the

---

22. Ginsburg, *The Enigma of Piero*, 5, citing Tanner, "Concordia in Piero della Francesca's Baptism of Christ." Tanner sees the context as the religious concord between the churches of West and East ratified at the Council of Florence of 1439. Lavin argues that the hand clasp is a symbol of marriage, alluding to the Wedding at Cana.

23. In accordance with the symbolism proposed by Innocent III on the founding of the Order of the Holy Trinity.

feast of the Wedding at Cana and the liturgy included the reading of Psalm 72:10, the kings of Tarshish and the Isles will bring gifts, referring to the Magi, in Medieval thought. So, in his imagery, della Francesca has pointed to the three events celebrated on the 6th January: the baptism of Christ, the wedding of Cana (and thus the marriage of the Bride the Church and her groom, the Lord) and the journey of the magi.

Ministry reflected in this picture is primarily a matter of giftedness. The baptism of Jesus, and especially the reception of the Spirit, reflects the essential 'charismatic' character of ministry: ministry is exercised out of the gift of the Spirit, and this giftedness turns the ordinary into the extraordinary, just as water was turned into wine at Cana. The visit of the Magi points to the response of the human to the gift of Christ, the bringing of gifts laid at his feet. Ministry is a matter of gift exchange, and in that exchange the human takes on the dimension of the holy and the divine.

The story of the baptism of Jesus as told by the evangelists is shocking. What on earth is Jesus doing here, standing with the other penitents in Jordan's muddy waters? John seems as shocked as we are, as if to say, "Surely, you should be baptizing me, Jesus? You've got it the wrong way round?" As we read on in the gospels we discover that "getting it the wrong way round" is the usual response of both disciples, and opponents alike, so we might forgive John for his mistake. We would all make it too, and still do. The disciples expect a military revolution to throw out the Roman overlords. Peter expects Jesus to take the road that avoids the cross, and finds himself numbered amongst Satan's partners for doing so. The disciples think that leadership and power go together, so that the greatest will exercise the power of government in the coming kingdom.

But Jesus says leaders must be servants: children are our models. The extravagant wastefulness of a life-time's savings in an alabaster jar poured out on Jesus is a beautiful thing. Rules are made to serve people not people made to serve rules, so go ahead and munch on some wheat when you are peckish on a Sabbath, or heal a disfigured fellow when the rules forbid it. Ministers do just the same, because we too get things upside down, and inside out. We get hung up over things that do not matter, and avoid the greater challenge. We mistake servanthood and leadership, strutting our stuff like some second-rate CEO, and get busy, busy, busy, when what God wants is our devotion. So, listening out for the voice in these gospel stories is important if men and women are to be ministers, rather than just do ministerial things.

The way of discipleship is the way of obedience, and Jesus takes this way first at his baptism. This is also true for ministry. With all of our talk of leadership and vision, strategy and competence, the very heart of Christian ministry is humble obedience to the way of Christ, going his way because he has walked there first. The sense here is not of some semi-divine human demiurge, but of a human life lived anointed by the Spirit in obedience to the Spirit's leading. Jesus demonstrates that he is the victorious Son of God by being the humble servant; he is the obedient Son, and we are called to live after that pattern. That way we fulfil righteousness.

It is the coming of the Spirit that empowers that life for the man Jesus of Nazareth. He is able to be obedient because he is anointed by the Spirit, not because he somehow has divine blood flowing through his veins! This opens up the extraordinary possibility that in the power of that same Spirit we too might do the works of the Father . . . but only as we go his way, and in an imperfect expression. The foundational ministerial virtue is humility, and its obverse, the besetting sin of ministers, is pride and arrogance. If ministry is firstly "gift", then attributing its effectiveness to our own abilities is mistaken. The belief that we are there to lead, and the church must therefore follow uncritically; the arrogant confidence in our own inviolability, so that, believing our own publicity, we are taken unawares when temptation sneaks up on us and nibbles our defenses away: these are the dangers that ministers face.

All the Evangelists in their accounts of the baptism of Jesus focus the attention of the reader upon the descent of the Spirit and the heavenly voice. The early sermon in Acts 10:37–38 recalls how Jesus' mission "began from Galilee after the baptism which John preached, how God anointed Jesus of Nazareth with the Holy Spirit and with power." The early Christians understood Isaiah 61:1 to have been fulfilled in Jesus, and he himself understands this in the Lukan narrative. Jesus here becomes the anointed one, the Messiah, the Christ, and the anointing is of the Spirit. The first disciples saw in this personal and semi-public event–the dove visible, the voice audible–the beginnings of his mission as Messiah. And Jesus saw himself in that way too. He hinted at it sufficiently for them to come to believe that he was Spirit-inspired. His own sense of his mission crystallized from this point.

This is not to say that Jesus became the Messiah at this point, or was adopted as the divine Son of God then. He was that from the beginning. Did Jesus experience a commissioning, a call, at this point? It is entirely possible. Did something change then? Yes. Did Jesus think he was the second person in the Holy Trinity, begotten of the Father before all worlds? Probably not. Nonetheless, the Trinitarian iconography of della Francesca's *Baptism* reminds us that the church's identifying of the baptism of Jesus as a moment of Trinitarian revelation is clear.

If ministers stand where Jesus stood, open to the anointing of the Spirit as he was, they too can hear the voice declare that they are beloved and that

God delights in them. They can hear, time and again confirmed, the call of God that holds them true to the way of Christ. They too, then, understand that ministry is all about following Jesus, being obedient to his will, rather than slaves to their own self-interest. That way will also shoulder a cross.

The Crucifixion of St Peter

And shouldering a cross brings us to a second picture that is our third metaphor for ministry: ministry as focused, and cross-bearing, discipleship. Instead of the many portrayals of the crucified Christ, I want to visit a portrayal of the death by crucifixion of the Apostle Peter. Painted as one of a pair (the other is the *Conversion of St Paul*) it was commissioned by a rich Papal banker, Monsignor Tiberio Cerasi for his burial chapel in Santa Maria del Popolo, Rome, in July 1600, from the star painter of his generation, Michaelangelo Merisi, known as Caravaggio (from his home town). Cerasi was keen for the work to be completed, sensing his own approaching death. St Paul and St Peter were closely associated with Rome, their heads reputedly preserved at St John Lateran, their bodies buried beneath the high altar at St Peter's.[24] The two paintings by Caravaggio, facing one another on the side walls of the chapel, were accompanied by another, also commissioned by Cerasi from the other pre-eminent painter in Rome, one who was fifteen years Caravaggio's senior, Annibale Carracci. He was responsible for the painted altarpiece in the chapel, *The Assumption of the Virgin*. The style of this was pure, sweet High Renaissance, "Swathed in drapery the color of a summer's sky, arms outspread, and expression of beatific serenity on her perfectly round face, Carracci's Virgin Mary rises from the tomb like an ecstatic doll."[25] It represents stylistically everything Caravaggio was opposed to. Like its counterpart, *The Conversion of St Paul*, *The Crucifixion of St Peter* is tense, dynamic, vernacular, and intuitive. Both figures are cruciform in pose: St Paul prone, blinded, meets the risen crucified Christ as if on a cross himself in a pose of spiritual empathy, while St Peter is literally crucified, albeit, according to legend, upside down.

Caravaggio shows Peter already nailed to the cross, half raised up yet transfixed by the nails, he tenses against the pain, stomach muscles tight. He looks away (in its situation in the chapel, he looks towards the altar) and understands that his own salvation is achieved, not by his death, but by Christ's. The three executioners strain to raise the cross: in the foreground the stooping figure braces his back against the cross, while the figure at the

24. Graham-Dixon, *Caravaggio*, 211.
25. Ibid., 212.

top of the painting pulls on the rope that raises the bottom of the cross to its upside down configuration. The third figure pulls at the same wooden base to aid his companion. None of their faces are seen clearly (only the face of the figure on the left, grasping the base and with it Peter's legs, is seen at all, and then in shadow) and they wear working men's clothes. They "grunt and sweat under the burden of his weight, grimly immersing themselves in the practical business of hoisting up a human body nailed to a cross."[26] The perspective is close, so that we are drawn into the scene, which threatens to spill out of the canvas into the space we occupy. This is gritty real life, devoid of the elegance and transcendence of the Mannerism epitomized in Carracci's altar piece, with its costly blues (the Virgin's cloak is painted in expensive ultramarine, as specified by Cerasi, with an eye on the verdict of posterity, and in no mind to be thought of as a cheapskate). Caravaggio's palette is composed of earth colors—ochre, umber, carbon black—and when he does use ultramarine, as his patron requested, it is reduced to a muddy green in the cloak of the crucified Peter lying crumpled in the bottom right hand corner. Much about this painting by Caravaggio, as also its counterpart on the opposite wall, is proletarian, poor. As Graham-Dixon remarks, "As a parting gesture to his rival, as if to stress the disdain for Carracci's brand of vapid magnificence, Caravaggio contrived a cunning insult: the rump of St Paul's proletarian carthorse is pointedly turned towards Carracci's Assumption of the Virgin."[27] However, what Caravaggio loses in color by way of a subdued palette (dull compared to Carracci's reds, yellows and golden light) he makes up for in the contrast between the dark background and the flood of light upon Peter. Where Carracci has an evenly diffused light, Caravaggio brilliantly uses *chiaroscuro*, the dramatic lighting of the subject against a dark ground that resembles a theatrical stage.

If the meaning of della Francesca is found in a hermeneutic of Medieval belief and legend, the meaning of the Caravaggio is all about the structure. Not that the della Francesca *Baptism* is unstructured. Far from it: it is a perfectly geometric composition, utilizing the square and circle. It is what gives the picture a great deal of its stillness. The Caravaggio, however, is all tension and energy, with triangles dominating the overall diagonally-biased cruciform composition. The backs of the two figures to the right of the third form one large diagonal, from bottom left to top right, while Peter's legs, torso and left arm give shape to its cross piece, sloping from middle left of the canvas towards the bottom right. Within this overall structure, triangles repeat: the bent leg of the crouching executioner, and the arc of his right

26. Ibid., 218.
27. Ibid., 220.

arm and the cross beam; the heads of the other two executioners and Peter's own; and the dark, brooding, background is etched out from the light cast upon Peter and his executioners in shapes that are broadly triangular.

Is it too much to see in this interaction between cross and triangle, with all of the energy of the action to raise the crucified Apostle, the two great themes of Christian theology: redemption by Christ upon the cross wrought by the One-in-Three? Behind human action and seeming evil there is a deeper purpose, just as in the passion of Christ. In the words of the Patriarch Joseph, making sense in later life of his betrayal by his brothers: you meant it for evil, but God meant it for the good of many people. (Genesis 50:20).

The whole picture, however, draws your attention to one point: the face of an old man, the eyes rheumy, the cheek lined with age and weather, the expression one of pain and longing, "the still point around which the visible effort pivoted."[28] This is the only face we really see, the face of a man facing death, in all of its cruel agony, without glamour or transcendence. There is more tension in this face than in the bulging veins of the executioner's hands, or the tightened muscles of crouching figure. There is no charming assumption about to happen here: just death in its inevitability. Yet, beyond it, does Peter see something of his welcoming Lord, here at the end of life, as Paul sees the same Jesus at the moment of his conversion, blinded by too much reality, in the picture on the opposite wall of the chapel?

This depiction of an old man facing death takes us immediately back to the words of Jesus following his stinging rebuke of the younger Peter, still known as Simon then. Peter had gone from the glow of acclamation and the light of revelation ("Blessed are you, Simon son of Jonah! For flesh and blood has not revealed this to you, but my Father in heaven. And I tell you, you are Peter, and on this rock I will build my church . . . " Matt 16:17–18) to the darkness and opprobrium of "Get behind me Satan." (Matt 16:23)—all in the space of a couple of minutes. Jesus then tells all the disciples what following him will mean: deny yourself, take up a cross and follow, lose your life to gain it (Matt 16:24–26) Here is Peter discovering literally the truth of this vocation.

Ministry is above all focused discipleship, a life of cross-shaped obedience, of cross-bearing following, of losing a life otherwise chosen in order to gain a richer life. Formation must in no small way prepare men and women to encompass disappointment, bear other's disloyalty, carry other's pain and suffering, and sometimes share it. It must be a life that ensures the first task of the church (which is, as Stanley Hauerwas insists, learning to be the

---

28. Robb, *M*, 164.

church, and not the world), is borne through that long obedience in the same direction. Too often ministry is portrayed with a sheen of glamour about it, with the approval of the crowd and the ease of a self-directed life. This is ministry on the cheap: shallow, thin, and time-serving. It is ministry that fails to distinguish between the institution and the call to discipleship, especially when the institution lives in fear of the world, and anxious not to disturb its quiet irrelevance to the powers of press or politics. Caravaggio's Peter reminds us that ministry turns the world's values upside down, even as Jesus did, so that death becomes life, and too-close a clinging to the rights and privileges of this life issues all-too easily in death. Sometimes ministry means '"when you grow old, you will stretch out your hands, and someone else will fasten a belt around you, and take you where you do not wish to go." (He said this to indicate the kind of death by which he would glorify God). After this he said to him, 'Follow me.'" (John 21:18–19) Caravaggio's Peter reminds us that there is a wounded-ness about ministry that no set of legal employment rights can protect us from, and far from an unwelcome evil, to be avoided at all costs, it might just be the arena of God's deepest glory. Ministry imagined as Carracci's *Assumption*—colorful, glorious, sunny, carried on the wings of angels amidst general adulation—is the stuff of fantasy. Ministry as seen in Caravaggio's Peter is the stuff of hidden glory and true discipleship. We form men and women to expect the former at our peril: but form them to live the latter, and the church lives true to itself and its Lord.

Through the rigor of academic study, we can educate ministers, so that they grasp firmly what they need to know. Through practice and apprenticeship, we can train ministers in the skills they require, be that pastoral care, preaching or leading a congregation in its worship. But formation is about character, following Jesus Christ, and growth in wisdom. Ministry has its essential knowledge base, and requires the skillful application of the tasks that shape its routines. There can be no effective ministry without these. Yet, at its heart, ministry is about more than just education and training can provide: it is about a life given in service of Christ and his people, a way of living in integrity and with an integration of "doing" and "being," and "knowing" that we might describe as growing in goodness and godliness. This is what people recognize when they remember fondly a "good minister", and it is the development of the virtues that gives particular shape to this goodness. This book argues that virtue ethics provides a way of understanding precisely what happens in the growth of *who* a minister is, alongside what it is they *do*. And to virtue ethics we turn in the next chapter.

In the first part we lay foundations for an understanding of formation in terms of the overarching story of creation and redemption, ministry as wisdom, as apprenticeship, and as focused discipleship. The second part explores four dimensions of the virtues: intellectual, spiritual, ethical, and practice. The third part pays closer attention to core practices of ministry: liturgist, missioner, preacher, pastor, leader, spiritual guide, and resident theologian. It is my hope that not only those whose task it is to assist the formation of ministers will find this approach helpful, but also those who are curious to know quite what it is they have embarked upon, what all this education, training and formation is shaping them for. In this approach I have combined a sense of the academy and the cell: it is neither exclusively an academic analysis of a virtue ethics approach to ministerial formation (though I hope it is in part just such) nor a "how to" approach to ministerial training. Its *métier* is located in both the seminar room and the prayer room, for it is precisely in the interweaving of mind, character, spirit, and action that ministry is constituted. Indeed, it has been the dislocation of the academy from the practice of the worshipping and praying community that has delivered an earlier means of preparing men and women for ministry, against which so-called mixed-mode means of formation have reacted. These formational modes of delivery have largely supplanted "theological education," seen as a largely cerebral process of gaining knowledge, and replaced it with varying combinations of training and formation. I welcome this, even if I am critical of some expressions of this move. Yet, I am still uneasy, and that uneasiness lies in a conviction that we still have not moved far enough in securing the core of what we do as shaping the character and spirituality of those preparing to serve the churches. The default to the examinable, the assessable and the measurable is all-too seductive in a culture obsessed with league tables and quality assurance in all levels of educational practice. What lies at the heart of ministry is not easily susceptible to measurement, to grading, and to the assessment of competence. Of course, much in the formation of ministry is: the academy is well-able to assess learning and award examination success, and the training establishment is suited to developing skills and shaping practices. Much of what develops character and spirituality will be a by-product of these aspects of formation, and mostly seminaries and theological colleges have relied upon this happening without too great an intentionality about it. However, with the lens of virtue ethics as our guide, I hope that this most important dimension of ministerial formation: the development of the person as a man or woman of God, will take a greater significance, and move center-stage. The church longs for such ministers, and mostly candidates for ministry aspire to be such. In the challenging times the church faces, at least in the West, and in Britain in particular, aspiration to be such with a dose of holy luck is too random a process. A renewed focus upon deliberately finding the ways to achieve such formation, to shape such ministers is now an urgent task.

2

History and Landscape

Men and women have been formed as ministers since the beginnings of the church. One could view the Pastoral Epistles as, in part, instruction in the good practice of ministry. However, the widespread formal and intentional education, training and formation of ministers is a relatively recent phenomenon in the church, and even at the beginning of the last century it was by no means universal, as the example of the formation of Archbishop Randall Davidson portrays.

The formation of this early twentieth century Archbishop, Randall Davidson illustrates a pattern for Anglican clergy from one strata of society. Schooled at Harrow, with Brooke Fosse Westcott as his housemaster (latterly Regius Professor of Divinity at Cambridge and New Testament scholar[1]) his formation began at school, and he had wished to be "ultimately ordained" for as long as he could remember. He went up to Trinity, Oxford in 1867, although his health there was very fragile following an accidental shooting prior to University that very nearly killed him. He collapsed at his Final examinations, and graduated with a Third. He looked back upon them as a disappointment and failure. After a year's travels he was effectively apprenticed to Dr. Charles Vaughan, Master of the Temple (the legal area between the Strand and the Thames in London). Vaughan had started training young men for the ministry while Vicar of Doncaster, and his pattern in London was to offer rooms in and around The Temple, assign them districts where the parochial clergy oversaw their practical work, and with guided reading, and lectures delivered by himself, educated these apprentices. Bell describes Vaughan as "an excellent scholar, a good parish priest, and above all a remarkable expositor and preacher."[2] These studies continued from 1872–74, and Davidson was ordained on March 1st 1874.

1. Cf. Westcott, *The Epistle to the Hebrews*.
2. Bell, *Randall Davidson*, 28.

His apprenticeship continued as curate at Dartford, Kent, first under the High churchman Canon Bowlby, then, for the majority of his time there, under F.S. Dale, an Evangelical. At no time was Davidson at any theological college, although they certainly existed, and he rose rapidly to prominence, no worse for that. He served as Bishop of Rochester (1881–95), Bishop of Winchester (1896–1902) and Archbishop of Canterbury (1903–1928) throughout the First World War and beyond.

Of a later generation, Cyril Forster Garbett (Bishop of Southwark, 1919–1932; Bishop of Winchester,1932–42; Archbishop of York, 1942–1955) was more typical. After Keble, Oxford, where he read Modern History, he went to theological college at Cuddesdon. It was not his preference, "He had not been particularly desirous to go to a theological college, for his own preference would have been to have spent a year at Oxford House in Bethnal Green, one of three University settlements where graduates of Oxford (Toynbee Hall, east London, and Oxford House, Bethnal Green) and Cambridge (Cambridge House in Camberwell, South London) went to gain experience of social service with a view to ordination. However, he found that Cuddesdon, 'I learned something about the life of devotion, and gained habits of prayer and meditation, which I have never entirely lost.'"[3] The real formational experience was as one of the large group of curates at the largest parish in England, Portsea, serving first (1899–1901) under Cosmo Lang, who left to become Suffragan Bishop of Stepney before translation to York, from whence he followed Randall Davidson at Canterbury in 1928. This was followed by the remarkable Bernard Wilson, from 1901–1909, upon whom Garbett modelled himself (and followed him as Vicar there from 1909–1919). It would be difficult to imagine a more hard-working or zealous parish priest than Wilson, an indefatigable visitor throughout the parish, who expected his curates to act similarly. Formation in this case benefits from a theological college education, but formation really takes place in the placement pattern of those years at Portsea, apprenticed to two Vicars, Lang and Wilson: less effectively from the first, a definite 'high-flyer' who saw Portsea as a step to higher office, but most definitely under Wilson, whose life's work was fulfilled as a parish priest.

The era of established theological education was from the mid-nineteenth century. Up until then the normal education for the Anglican clergy was an Oxford or Cambridge undergraduate degree, followed by a curacy. Specific institutions in which theological education and training took place were limited to the dissenting colleges, established because non-Anglicans could not attend either of the two ancient Universities. When the colleges

---

3. Smyth, *Cyril Forster Garbett*, 56.

at Wells and Chichester were established as High Church places of education, and Cuddesdon was opened in 1854, evangelicals within the Church of England became worried. The call for an evangelical center for training was answered in 1863 with the founding of Peache's College, which became known as St John's College of Divinity, Highbury.[4]

For the majority of those at Oxford or Cambridge, the situation remained very limited.

> The smallest amount of special preparation was considered necessary for graduates. Bishops only required attendance at two courses of lectures by the Divinity professors. There was no examination to show that anything had been assimilated; a certificate of attendance was sufficient. The deficiencies were partially remedied when an honors school of theology was instituted at Oxford in 1870 and a theological tripos as Cambridge in 1871. This enabled the students concerned to read a number of theological books, but it did not mean that they received training in the more definitely spiritual and pastoral aspects of their future work. Indeed, it was difficult to persuade men that they needed any additional training.[5]

Meanwhile, non-evangelicals were opening colleges at Oxford (Keble College and St Stephen's House), Ely, and Leeds. The response from evangelicals was to open Wycliffe Hall in 1877, although it started slowly. In Cambridge, Ridley Hall was opened in 1879 under the principalship of Handley Moule. It became increasingly common for evangelicals to expect to attend a theological college. Indeed, a century later, by the mid-1960s, the evangelical colleges were full (Cranmer Hall, Durham; Oak Hill, London; St John's College, Nottingham; Trinity College, Bristol; and both Ridley Hall and Wycliffe Hall.) Offering University validated degrees in theology, sometimes as a second undergraduate degree, although most commonly as the first higher education experience for those who attended, the pattern of full-time, residential education, focused upon what was needing to be understood. Increasingly however, attention was paid to skills training, especially in pastoral care and homiletics in the 1970s through to the 1990s, to be followed by a more holistic approach of "formation" over the past fifteen years. Similar stories can be told of the broad church approach (for instance at Lincoln) and the High Church Colleges (although these more often had their roots in Anglo-Catholic religious orders: Benedictine at Mirfield, Yorkshire, and the Cowley Fathers at St Stephen's House, Oxford).

4. Hylson-Smith, *Evangelicals in the Church of England, 1734–1984*, 183.
5. Ibid.

This pattern in the established church bears some similarity to the development of theological education in the Free Churches. Some established colleges at Oxford or Cambridge (Presbyterians at Westminster College, Cambridge; Methodists at Wesley Hall, Cambridge; Congregationalists at Mansfield College, Oxford,) while Baptists had, from an earlier instigation, colleges in the north of England (Rawdon in Leeds with its roots in the Northern Educational Society of 1804 and the General Baptists Midland College, Nottingham, founded in 1787); in Bristol, the oldest of them all, established in 1679; and the Stepney College in 1804, later transferred, first to Regent's Park, London in 1865, then in 1922 removed to Oxford. The most distinctive of the colleges was Spurgeon's (originally Pastor's) College, founded in 1856, with the aim to produce preachers, not scholars. The college taught "classic Puritan theology" alongside more general philosophical, scientific and historical knowledge, "with appropriate instruction in biblical language and contemporary church work."[6]

The scope of the Baptist Colleges in training pastors was by no means universal, and as late as 1870 less than half of the ministers in charge of English Baptist churches had been trained in a denominational college, rising to 64 percent in 1901. Even though the length of the training at Spurgeon's College eventually increased to three years in 1880, all too often students left early, as deacons of vacant churches offered invitations to serve.

This pattern of a large proportion of ministers without theological college training reflects a broader debate in the eighteenth century whether "it was exclusively the Spirit's task to prepare men for ministry rather than any educational institution, only some perceiving that the Spirit might prepare such ministers through a disciplined programme of theological education."[7] The older pattern of a form of apprenticeship alongside an older minister gradually came to be replaced by attendance at a theological college as an almost universal mode of formation by the mid-twentieth century, and by then almost wholly residential. There had been concerns along the way, with the North Western Association (separated from the Lancashire and Cheshire Association in 1860) forming in 1866 the new college at Bury, training candidates of strict-communionism persuasion, that was not residential, for that "had some of the disadvantages of the Monkish system," while also eschewing classical, mathematical, and secular studies in favor of biblical exposition.[8]

6. Briggs, *The English Baptists of the Nineteenth Century*, 85.
7. Jones, "Ministerial Formation," 325.
8. Rignal, *Manchester Baptist College*, 80

Apprenticeship to Formation

If the early Free Church model of training ministers was a form of apprenticeship, a form which remained extant amongst Anglicans up to a century ago, and which continues still in the supplementing of a theological course with the practice-based curacy under the guidance of a training incumbent, by the nineteenth century the expectations were that ministers in England would be educated either in the ancient universities with what we might now call a liberal arts emphasis, or in one of the Dissenting academies that sprung up to provide the education unavailable to those who were not members of the Church of England. As the focus became more and more upon providing a preparation specifically for ministry there, the liberal and general arts syllabus became converted increasingly to theological study. So, while Spurgeon required of his students at the Pastors' College that they read literature and history, a century later, the same college was concentrating almost exclusively in its teaching upon theology, in part in preparation for the London BD. The general arts education (unavailable elsewhere in the mid-nineteenth century) was replaced by theological education (liberal arts being commonplace in the mainstream school system by the mid-twentieth), and the course of study became almost exclusively theological in character. The language that predominated was "theological education," and focused upon the developing of a theological mind. In a parallel development, the study of theology at an undergraduate level became increasingly possible. It had been exclusively a postgraduate subject at Oxford and Cambridge until the eighteen-seventies, although in the newly founded King's College in London in 1847 a course in religion leading to the award of Associate of Kings College (AKC) was established. It was not until 1901 that a London BD was possible, but this, and similar awards at Manchester, Durham and those regional colleges that taught the external London degrees (such as Exeter and Nottingham) ensured that theology (and later religious studies) became a widespread feature of the Higher Education landscape by the middle of the twentieth century. That the same landscape is currently shrinking, with fewer and fewer institutions offering theology, reflects different sociological and economic trends, but the fact remains that the majority of ministerial students gain a University validated award, which until 2015 had been from a wide range of institutions, but became more focused upon Durham in the newly configured Common Awards offered to almost all Anglican ordinands from that year.

The ground of formation remains educational and knowledge-based. This is not surprising, given that those who deliver such formation are themselves academics, and combine the role of ministerial formation with a broader role of academic scholarship in their particular theological discipline. A move can be detected, however, by the nineteen-seventies, with language shifting to 'theological training', and a greater emphasis upon acquiring the skills necessary for the practice of ministry: crafting the sermon, conducting the pastoral care of the congregation, administration, and the like. So, Spurgeon's College in the mid-nineteen-eighties, when I was a student there, offered a course to residential students for the first three years that led to an academic theological qualification (a CNNA BA, or Cambridge Diploma in Religious Studies) supplemented by preaching experience, both in and outside college, with a practical placement where ministry was essentially observed. This was followed by a fourth year of pastoral studies, acquiring the knowledge about the skills necessary (so, modules on pastoral counselling, evangelism, music, the occasional offices, and so forth). A move to a new validating body (the University of Wales) provided the opportunity to integrate the two components into an essentially "practice-based" degree, with skills and knowledge running in parallel. A similar award was developed at Regent's Park College, and other Oxford Anglican theological colleges, in the BTh—a "professional" degree, as opposed to the Honors Schools BA/MA.

The new emphasis upon skills acquisition and development paralleled in Baptist contexts a move from college based to what had variously been described as mixed-mode, church-based, or congregation-based, but all of which are essentially a practice-based approach. The student is placed in a church context, either in sole charge of a small congregation, or as an associate in a larger congregation, working alongside a senior practitioner. The current description of such students amongst Baptists would be "minister-in-training," reflecting the status which the church affords its pastor prior to ordination. The latter occasionally is situated in the church from which the student was called and sometimes was already in stipendiary ministry (indeed, this was my own experience at Lewin Road Baptist Church, Streatham). The time spent in the college setting is more limited (typically two days per week) and is sometimes longer in duration than for those training as fully college-based students, extended by a year for those on this track at Bristol Baptist College, for instance. Learning is by doing, and skills are acquired "on the job" through the week-by-week practice of ministry.

Such patterns of training ensure that those completing their course of formal training have gained greater experience of pastoral ministry than others on full-time college courses, and such patterns also make part-time ministry available to churches that otherwise might be bereft of stipendiary ministry (there has been a much lower proportion of part-time or non-stipendiary ministers in Baptist churches than in The Church of England, for instance). There are disadvantages as well: (i) it remains challenging to gain the same level of theological education, when gained alongside the time-consuming business of pastoral ministry four days a week, and at some colleges a degree is not attainable through this route, students leaving with a graduate diploma; (ii) the level of experience on day one of the placement is sometimes too limited for immediately effective pastoral ministry, although this will progressively be deepened, and so the effectiveness relies upon quite intense levels of supervision; and (iii) the very intensity and sheer hard work of this mode of training does not allow for a sense of playfulness and space to think, pray, and experiment that college-based modes of delivery could offer. It could be said to favor the impatient, the arrogant and the impecunious (although that would be generally unfair!)

Alongside these trends, a shift in the pedagogical ideology has been apparent over the past fifteen years. Language of training, supplementing that of education, has increasingly been replaced by language of formation. The idea is that what is required is the shaping of a whole life, not merely the acquisition of knowledge or skills. Note, "not merely", because with this shift there has been no eschewing of theological understanding, or any diminishing of the significance in acquiring the skills to become an effective practitioner, but both have been subsumed within a broader task of shaping the life, relationships, spirituality, and morality of a man or woman, so as to fit them to be a minister. This is variously understood as an intentional pattern of focused discipleship, so that the minister might be an "exemplary disciple" to the congregation they pastor; a growth in wisdom, so that there is maturity to the ministry offered; or the shaping of the character and spirituality of a person so that they might be recognized as a man or woman of God.

Clearly, this is a continuum of what has preceded intentional training and formation for ministry, since the person seeking to be prepared for ministry will be expected to demonstrate certain levels of personal maturity, holiness and experience as they candidate for selection for training. The continuum extends to what lies beyond the formal period of formation, whether understood as simply a college course, or, more helpfully, that and the first period immediately following ordination, which together comprise the period of "Initial Ministerial Formation" (IMF). This period comprises years one to three in college, or alongside college, and years four to six, the three years of probationary ministry (in Baptist terms) or first curacy, post-ordination in Anglican terms. Other denominations will generally have similar terminology and understanding of this significant first whole-time experience of ministry. What lies beyond should be half a life-time or more of continuing growth in wisdom understanding and holiness, with formation never being complete, any more than discipleship is ever perfect. The pivotal experience between the prior ways of being and levels of comprehension, and the ensuing offering of ministry is the issue here. How might that experience so shape a life for good, that the ministry they proceed to offer is wholesome and fruitful, under God's grace?

It is the way in which ministers are formed, then, which is the concern of this book: the way in which what they learn about theology, and themselves; the manner of acquisition of skills and habits necessary for ministry; and the forming of the kind of life that is appropriate to those called to lead God's people and shepherd the flock of Christ, is integrated and shaped. The thesis that I will expound is that the most helpful over-arching framework for such integration is that of virtue ethics within a community of practitioners.

We have seen that the development of seminaries and theological colleges had been a feature predominantly of the nineteenth century (although Dissenting academies for those excluded from the Universities were an earlier development) so that by the second half of the twentieth century the numbers were at their peak. From thereafter the story is one of retrenchment, first in the denominational colleges, then in the non-denominational ones (with some notable exceptions.) Among Baptists this has been limited, although the two northern colleges, Manchester and Rawdon were amalgamated into Northern Baptist College in 1964[9], and was itself joined by Methodists, United Reformed Church and Unitarians in *The Partnership of Theological Education, Manchester* located at Luther King House on the site of the old Manchester College and south of the University quarter. The Methodist Church through its proposals in the document *The Fruitful Field* project,[10] saw its centers of training reduced to two: Cliff College, Calver and Queen's Foundation, Birmingham. The Guy Chester Centre, London; Wesley College, Bristol; Wesley House, Cambridge; and the Wesley Study Centre, Durham all were closed or found a new purpose. The Church of England, meanwhile, had been closing smaller diocesan theological colleges for a longer period. Colleges at Chichester,[11] Salisbury,[12] Wells,[13] and

---

9. See Shepherd, *The Making of Northern Baptist College*, 207–17.

10. Conference Agenda, *The Methodist Church*, 2012, 643–760.

11. Founded in 1838 by Bishop Otter as the first such Diocesan college in England, it closed in 1994.

12. Founded in 1860, it merged with Wells Theological College in 1971 and became Sarum College, an ecumenical institution, in 1995. Its buildings also became the home of The Southern Theological Education and Training Scheme (STETS)

13. Founded in 1840, it merged with Salisbury in 1971, and became essentially a non-denominational college in 1995.

Lincoln[14] were closed, for instance, in the mid nineteen-nineties. Alone among the main English denominations, however, it has also see the development of new theological colleges, most notably the London-based St Milletus College, with its roots in the charismatic and evangelical parish of Holy Trinity Brompton (and its many off-shoots), and now with an outpost in Liverpool; and the similar St Barnabas Theological Centre in Yorkshire, pioneered by St Thomas Crookes Anglican and Baptist Local Ecumenical Partnership, training ordinands for both Anglican and Baptist ministry.[15]

We have seen also how the focus of seminary training was "education" until the nineteen-seventies, most especially where this took place in one of the historic universities in Oxford, Cambridge or Durham. To the academic courses leading to a BA were added some pastoralia, but the emphasis was upon acquiring the academic skills necessary for ministry. A lengthy period of two or three assistant curacies provided the ministry training. From the nineteen-eighties, the model became one of ministerial training (reflected, for instance, in the title of the non-residential course based in the dioceses of Salisbury, Winchester and Portsmouth, STETS: Southern Theological Education and Training Scheme, established in 1997) and the addition of training in ministerial skills to acquisition of knowledge.

Since the nineteen-nineties the language has primarily been "formation." The so-called Hind Report (after its chair, Bishop John Hind) notes that "The term 'formation' has come to mean either the whole process or that part of it which refers to personal, liturgical and spiritual development in preparation for the distinctive role of the ordained."[16] It then proceeds to use the term "theological education" widely to embrace the whole process, or sometimes the short-hand "training."

The change in terminology belies a deeper change in emphasis, one that this book advances: from the cerebral (education) and practical (training) to a renewed emphasis upon the whole person being shaped and formed for ministry. It is at this point that virtue ethics, with its understanding of the way in which persons are formed by the traditions of their communities of practice, acquiring the virtues as they engage in the development of the skills and understanding appropriate to their profession, has much to offer.

---

14. Opened in 1874, it closed in 1995. It was replaced by Lincoln Theological Institute for the Study of Religion and Society.

15. St Barnabas has links to the Yorkshire Ministry Course, itself rooted at Mirfield, a Benedictine Abbey and theological course with Anglo-Catholic traditions, while its DNA is strongly evangelical and charismatic from its congregational roots in Sheffield. This "cross-party" feature is also true for St Milletus in London.

16. Ministry Division of the Archbishops' Council, *Formation for Ministry within a Learning Church*, 2.

It is the shaping of a person rather than a reductionist offering of skills-training or the passing of academic examinations that ministry demands.

The Postmodern Context

Part of the context within which ministerial formation is considered here is the wider cultural landscape, sometimes dubbed "postmodern." Twenty years ago I wrote a book about pastoral care and postmodern culture,[17] and used the postmodern descriptor. I now have some sympathy with those who prefer the term late-modern, since much of modernity that postmodernism threatened to sweep away seems stubbornly resistant to erosion. Trust in technology (a very "modern" response) remains as widespread as ever, with even those otherwise premodern movements like radical Islamism, that has become such a feature of the global context since the late 1990s, utilizing the technology that suits them as assuredly as any Western secularist. While the impact of globalism continues to grow, its impact upon Western culture travels in both directions, with both global cultures affecting the West and Western capitalist consumerism impacting the globe in ever-increasingly powerful ways.

In his revised 2005 Bampton Lectures, Paul Fiddes[18] explores three relationships of the self to the world in the development of modernism post-Enlightenment. First, the Cartesian and Kantian detachment of the self from the world,[19] with its distinction between the *res cognitans* and the *res extensans*. This objectifies the world to the self, and makes it an object to be controlled and mastered. Descartes equated knowledge of the world with mastery over it, "it is possible to attain knowledge which is very useful in life . . . . and thus render ourselves the masters and possessors of nature."[20] In this move, God is the unknowable supreme Reason (Descartes) or law-Giver (Kant) but never an object capable of being known in itself in the world (hence Schleiermacher's understanding of God as the "whence of the self's feeling of absolute dependence"[21])

The second relationship is the Hegelian world as an expression of the self, an attempt to bridge that gulf between the self and the world recognized by Descartes, Kant, and their theological disciple, Schleiermacher. Fiddes

---

17. Goodliff, *Care in a Confused Climate*.
18. Fiddes, *Seeing the World and Knowing God*, chap. 2.
19. See also Taylor, *Sources of the Self*, 143–58.
20. Descartes, *The Philosophical Works of Descartes*, 31.
21. Schleiermacher, *The Christian Faith*, 12–26.

argues that the necessity of the dialectical process nonetheless maintains a gulf between the world and the self.

The third sort of relationship is the existentialist, seeing the world as a threat to the self. This is the form of modernity that comes to birth in the cultural period we call 'modernism', in the first half of the twentieth century. Sartre is its classic exponent, and describes the world around the free subject as a threat in its absurdity, giving rise to anxiety. In this response God becomes restricted to the inner subjectivity of the believer, and has little room to act in the world, and so we return to Kant.

Late-Modernism, or postmodernism, has radically changed the relationship of the self to the world. Fiddes identifies four sets of ideas that together contribute to the fragmentation of the world identified by David Harvey as plural, indeterminate, and distrustful of universalizing and totalizing discourses.[22] The four are: immersion in the world, a hermeneutic of suspicion, openness of meaning, and the impact of the sublime.

Immersion in the world collapses the gulf between the thinking subject and the objective world. There is no gap between the world as apprehended in the consciousness of the thinking self and the "world out there." The origins of this collapse lie in phenomenology and especially Edmund Husserl. As Levinas observes, the world is already and always given to the subject, and perception immerses the self in the world.[23] The danger in this is to then envisage the self as a construct of that world, especially the social or linguistic worlds, so that the self is merely a creation of social forces, or the inner-psychic and hidden forces of the sub-conscious. "The self which exercises 'virtues' has, it seems, often collapsed into a product of social, linguistic and psychological forces."[24]

The hermeneutic of suspicion derives from Nietzsche's observation that all claims to truth are attempts to legitimize self-interest and bids for power. In differing ways, Roland Barthes, Jacques Derrida and, above all, Jean-Francois Lyotard, have inherited this Nietzschean suspicion. This is the oft-repeated rejection of the "big stories," or grand narratives (*les grandes recites*) in favor of local stories in postmodernity. It is represented in a culture "of the disposable image and sound-bite, which is not congenial to stories with universal claims,"[25] and in religion by a pick and mix spirituality. Into this context is set both the Christian story, and that of Islam (to name but two). The challenge for the Christian faith is to represent its story in such a

---

22. Harvey, *The Condition of Postmodernity*.
23. Levinas, *The Theory of Intuition in Husserl's Phenomenology*.
24. Fiddes, *Seeing the World and Knowing God*, 42.
25. Ibid., 46.

way as to avoid any domination of local narratives "or a rhetoric of power projected by the corporate 'self' of the Christian institution."[26]

The third characteristic identified by Fiddes is that of the openness of meaning. Derived from the insights of structuralism, this constantly defers any final meaning to a text (Derrida coins the word *difference* to combine the idea of both differing and deferring: meaning of words comes from their difference from each other, while ultimate meaning is always deferred, never settled.) Meaning is multi-valent, open, and, especially, susceptible to the eruption of insight from the Other, from the margins. This is actually redolent of much biblical interpretation, where a fixed meaning of a text is always open to new insight, or to alternative understanding. Augustine understood the nature of the biblical text to be polysemic, and Medieval theology had a fourfold exegesis of literal, allegorical, moral, and spiritual meanings.

At its most destructive, this can become a nihilistic suspicion that nothing is real, all is a simulacrum (Jean Baudrillard) where nothing can be known beyond signs that signify other signs. Georges Steiner speaks of the breaking of a contract that existed in Western civilization that there was actually some kind of relationship between the word and the world, however slippery words might become. Words could be trusted to refer to something that actually existed beyond the linguistic sign.[27]

The fourth set of ideas in postmodernity is the challenge of the sublime. It is sometimes expressed in terms of the "narratives of the 'unrepresentable'" (Lyotard), whether it be called "difference" (Jacques Derrida), "chaos" (Gilles Deleuze), "being" (Martin Heidegger), or "otherness" (Emmanuel Levinas), and represents a challenge to the representable, "in summary, there is an aspect of the late-modern mood which proposes that what is true, good, and just lies just beyond the surface of things and enters to break up the conventional structures of objects in the world."[28] The experience of the "alterity" in the sublime undermines the totalizing meta-narratives, and affirms difference.

I have explored the character of late-modernity in this way because the formation of ministers does not take place in a cultural vacuum. While some of the mood of late-modernity is antithetical to Christian formation, there is no easy safe-haven of modernity into which to seek refuge from the cultural storms of our day. In many ways, the Enlightenment project (to borrow MacIntyre's phrase) was even more hostile to a form of Christianity

---

26. Ibid., 48.
27. Steiner, *Real Presence*, 90–92.
28. Fiddes, *Seeing the World and Knowing God*, 55.

that was rooted in a lived experience of the immanence of the living God, heard by the Spirit through Scripture, and which reflects "the great tradition" of the church through two thousand years. The suspicion that God could be reduced to a religious experience, or that in some ways God was simply a moral back-cloth to the enterprise of just human living, was almost as important as anything else in the world of ideas, at least, in giving rise to atheism.

Aspects of the late modern mood such as "immersion in the world" which insists that the objective world is apprehended by the self and calls for responsibility towards it and others, and "the openness of meaning," allowing multiple readings of Scripture, while celebrating "the other" and "the Other" equally, both resonate more with the Christian faith than Enlightenment positions.

A combination of compassion and generosity— virtues that together with humility come to define the ministerial disposition— are found in a response to "the other." Levinas's theme of responsibility before the face of the other, and the trace this gives of the face of God, gives us the shape of these virtues in their distinctive collaboration as life lived before the face of God, even of the God who in Job's experience, hunts him down with his relentless gaze ("Will you not look away from me for a while, / let me alone until I swallow my spittle? / If I sin, what do I do to you, you watcher of humanity? / Why have you made me your target? / Why have I become a burden to you?" Job 7:19–20) For Levinas, what Job portrays as the accusations of the Divine Other, the heavenly hunter, is in fact the demand upon us of all others in the world. It is a call to us to substitute ourselves completely for the other.[29]

Generosity for the other requires an ingratitude of the Other, otherwise it is a comfortable give-and-take ('even the Gentiles do that' Matt 5:46-48.) Luce Irigaray criticizes this emotional distance,[30] and Martin Buber emphasizes mutual reciprocity in respect between others, with the space between persons not an exact matching and equal response, yet with genuine mutuality.[31]

So, let Fiddes have the final word:

> In making a wisdom theology for today, I shall be exploring the way that the self participates in the divine Other through immersion into the contingent details of the world, or how *phronesis* becomes *sophia*—in short, how seeing the world is

29. Levinas, *Time and Other*, 75.
30. Irigaray, "Questions to Emmanuel Levinas," 180.
31. Buber, *Between Man and Man*, 19–22, 32–33.

knowing God. In their own way, Levinas and Ricoeur consider this issue through their reflections on two areas in the Book of Job—the theophany of chapters 38–41, and the passages in which Job protests against the God who 'sees' and pursues him. I aim to show that participation in the divine Other, which is inseparable from responsibility for human others, occurs when the self is mediated through the Christian symbol of the Trinity, and through the personal reality it expresses.[32]

---

32. Fiddes *Seeing the World and Knowing God*, 83.

3

Virtue Ethics and Practitioners

Until recently, virtue ethics was confined to the ancient world, but since the nineteen-sixties, there has been something of a renaissance in this ethical theory, both in academic philosophy, and in more practical applications, for instance, in business or health care. While its roots lie in Aristotle, the revival in virtue ethics can be dated from the publication of a paper by the Oxford philosopher Elizabeth Anscombe, "Modern Moral Philosophy."[1] Together with Philippa Foot and Iris Murdoch,[2] she pioneered this movement in contemporary ethics. Its subsequent popularity owes much to Alasdair MacIntyre's *After Virtue,* and theologically to the work of Stanley Hauerwas, while another stream has pursued a Neo-Thomastic exploration of the moral philosophy in Aquinas.[3] This revival in virtue ethics places virtue center stage (as opposed to virtue being simply one part of a moral theory—Kant has a place for virtue, but his is not virtue ethics) and self-standing, rather than derived from some other fundamental moral theory.

Virtue ethicists "regard it as one of their main tasks to say something about how people should act or live, and under this assumption the task of virtue ethics includes giving a distinctive virtue-ethical account of the rightness or wrongness, goodness or badness, of human actions."[4] The particular variant of virtue ethics that I am commending is that primarily derived from Aristotle, and mediated through MacIntyre. Aristotle understands that the virtuous person is perceptive of the rightness or wrongness of any given situation because of the way that they have, by practice, come to inhabit

---

1. Anscombe "Modern Moral Philosophy", *Philosophy* 33.

2. Foot, *Virtues and Vices and Other Essays in Moral Philosophy*; Murdoch, *The Sovereignty of Good*.

3. Porter, *The Recovery of Virtue*.

4 Stone, "Virtue Ethics," 326.

the world. It is not a matter of following pre-existing rules or regulations, and Aristotle thinks that such rules are inadequate to the complexity and subtlety of lived experience. Instead, the virtuous person intuits sensitively what is right or wrong—some have likened it to a form of connoisseurship—through having been formed by virtuous practices. Acts count as right because a virtuous person would choose them.

Rosalind Hursthouse[5] interprets virtue ethics as roughly, "acts are right or wrong depending on whether the virtuous person would choose them; a individual counts as virtuous is s/he has and exercises all the virtues; and virtues are qualities of character that an agent needs in order to attain *eudaimonia,* overall well-being or a good life."[6] This is not the only way to interpret Aristotle. It can be argued that virtuous people are those who are perfect judges of what is right or noble, and reliably see what is pre-existently noble and right, derived from some prior gift. This would accord more closely with a notion of morality as given from a prior divine account, given from outside of human existence. The very existence of what we might define as the virtues (courage, as opposed to betrayal, for instance) presupposes that a culture understands what the good life looks like, and Aristotle characteristically sees the virtues as a way of achieving the good life.

I want to work with something of a blend of these two approaches, as we consider ministerial formation. That there is not a complete set of rules for every pastoral situation is self-evident and ministers need to be capable of some kind of intuition, within a broadly-based set of prior characteristics of 'the good.' Formed as virtuous persons, they need to see what the rightness and wrongness of actions look like, but the prior identification of the good life will, for the Christian virtue ethicist, be constrained by the virtues that flow from the person of Jesus Christ, from his character and life as the incarnate Son. The virtuous person is exactly so according to their conformity to Christ, and here is the ground of the good life, and its *telos*: the attainment of eternal life "which is to know God and the One who he has sent" (John 17.3). Thus, it treats the whole person as the agent, rather than one who simply makes moral choices from a prior set of given rules (either God-derived, or derived from a particular cultural context and historical account of the good life).

As a place to start exploring virtue ethics further, I commend Tom Wright's *Virtue Reborn,*[7] as a popular account of the relationship between

5. Hursthouse, "Virtue Theory and Abortion."
6. Stone, "Virtue Ethics," 327.
7. Wright, *Virtue Reborn.* Cf. other accounts of the relationship between virtue ethics and the New Testament: Kotva, *The Christian Case for Virtue Ethics*; Harrington and Keenan, *Jesus and Virtue Ethics.*

virtue ethics and the New Testament. In it he contends that the New Testament has continuity with the ancient conceptions of virtue, in that it sets forth a vision of being human whereby, through an encounter with Christ by the Spirit, we learn what it is to be authentically human, both in ways that inform our moral judgments, and also forms the character that means that we can live by those judgments. The name he gives for this way of being human is virtue, a concept transformed by Jesus himself.

An important line of theological enquiry uses the work of Alasdair MacIntyre[8] and his scheme of Aristotelian virtue, communities of practice and their supporting institutions to understand the character of a virtue-based ecclesiology. MacIntyre is amongst the most influential of philosophers and ethicists at the beginning of the twenty-first century, arguing that in modernity there has been a fragmentation of morality, with no common shared conception of what it is to be human, nor of the good to which humanity is directed, and that this fragmentation has resulted in moral judgments being little more than arbitrary expressions of the individual, originating in emotional preferences. In response to this, MacIntyre argues that a recovery of Aristotelian virtues, and the practices in which they are formed, offers a hopeful alternative to post-Enlightenment social forces dominated by the market. This has already been applied to other organizational contexts, such as commercial businesses or health care institutions[9], as well as some preliminary investigation of its application to the Christian church[10]. Here, I want to explore first the notion of the community of practice within which virtue is constructed.

Communities of Practice

How learning takes place in 'communities of practice' owes much of its ideological and pedagogical theory to the work of the early twentieth century Russian educationalist and psychologist Lev Vygotsky. Working in the context of the Russian revolution, he created an approach to social science commensurate with the Marxist political order. Appointed to the People's Commissariat for Public Education in 1924, the twenty-eight-year-old

---

8. MacIntyre, *After Virtue*; MacIntyre, *Dependent, Rational Animals*.

9. Moore, "Humanizing Business: A Modern Virtue-Ethics Approach"; Moore, "Reimagining the Morality of Management: A Modern Virtue-Ethics Approach"; Moore and Beadle, "In Search of Organizational Virtue in Business: Agents, Goods, Practices, Institutions and Environments"; Beadle and Moore, "MacIntyre: Neo-Aristotelianism and Organizational Theory."

10. Moore, "Churches as Organizations"; Mannion, *Ecclesiology and Postmodernity*; Stone, *Evangelism after Christendom*.

Vygostsky argued for a profound transformation of the Russian educational system, and guided by a cultural-historical theory of the formation of mind, he created psychological theories that were used as approaches to the pedagogies of all learners, not simply children's learning. Arising from this sociocultural theory of development, the notion of a "community of practice" in which learning takes place, has become an important line of research and understanding in Western educational theory.

In a community of practice participants are brought together and sustained in relation to some common practice, within which a common language and shared understandings are developed.

> In using the term community, we do not imply some primordial culture sharing entity. We assume that members hold different interests, make diverse contributions to activity and hold varied viewpoints. In our view, participation at multiple levels is entailed in membership in a community of practice. Nor does the term community imply necessary co-presence, a well-defined, identifiable group or socially visible boundaries. It does imply participation in an activity system about which participants share understandings concerning whatever they are doing and what that means.[11]

Participation in the activities of a community of practice enable the person to "become", moving from peripheral participation to full membership. A person finds their identity being constructed, and re-constructed, formed and re-formed, over personal lifetimes, and Wenger argues, learning changes who we are. Thus, in the language of ministerial formation, the learning within a community of practice (those who practice ministry) that takes place in the college and congregation contexts creates the identity of the person as a "minister." They not only acquire knowledge and skills appropriate to the practice of ministry, through this acquisition they "become" ministers, moving from the periphery of that community (as one whose call has been recognized and therefore commended for training) to the mainstream (practitioners of ministry) and participants in the tasks of handing on the practice: those who shape the next generation of ministers.

> Participants start out as newcomers on the periphery of the community and gradually, through observation and incremental participation with the established community members, the so-called old-timers, acquire the understandings and values along with the way of speaking that constitutes the community. In this way, they gradually move to the center of the community

---

11. Lave and Wenger, *Situated Learning*, 171.

and newcomers become old-timers equipped with the knowledge, understanding, language and identities of full community members.[12]

The knowledge that is gained through community participation is not so much a series of self-contained units of cognitive capital, but rather the embodied ability to behave as community members. Concepts are tools that enable community members to act, and which can only be understood through use. Here is a powerful case for practice-based learning in ministerial formation. "In our view, learning is not merely situated in practice—as if it were some independently reifiable process that just happened to be located somewhere; learning is an integral part of a generative social practice in the lived-in world."[13]

So, communities of practice are something like the guild where a common set of practices are developed over a long period of time, with a common purpose and a shared repertoire of tools, discourses and actions. Indeed, we might want to engage a notion of scale here, with hierarchies of communities within communities: in ministerial terms, the global community of those who practice ministry, within which there are tradition-based sub-communities (such as Baptist ministry); and within those sub-communities there are smaller-scale communities whose role it is to bring participants from the margins to the center—from junior members, learning the craft, to full members (symbolized by ordination and accreditation). It is important to understanding the ways in which (i) those communities of learning (colleges) and the church communities within which much of the learning takes place (placements) vie for influence upon the person being formed for ministry, and (ii) how certain practices and actions, understandings and goals, are held in tension between them. It is in the interaction between the two that the real learning takes place, negotiating what is communicated didactically in the lecture hall with the pre-existing practices and patterns of activity in the church into which the minister-in-training enters for a while, partly shaping them in that context, as well as being re-shaped, through their presence and participation.

Rogoff proposes that learning and development takes place in three "inseparable, mutually-constituting planes comprising activities that can become the focus of analysis at different times, but with others necessarily remaining in the background of the analysis."[14] Learning takes place either

---

12. Daniels, *Vygotsky and Research*, 97

13. Lave and Wenger, "Legitimate Peripheral Participation," 99.

14. Rogoff, "Observing Sociocultural Activity on Three Planes," 139, cited in Daniels *Vygotsky and Research*, 101.

personally, through participatory observation, or interpersonally where learning is guided, as, also, within an institutional or community engagement: an apprenticeship. Ministers learn by simply observing others, by being guided, perhaps in an ad hoc way, or intentionally by a supervising minister. They can also be apprenticed to a skilled practitioner, with whom they have an intentional and long-term relationship purposed to develop the person joining the community of practice.

Two other aspects of Vygotskian theory that have traction in the understanding of ministry formation are his ideas of the "Zone of Proximal Development" (ZPD) and *perezhivanie*. First, ZPD concerns the relationship between instruction and development. It is the role of supporters of learning (such as the teacher) to enable the child to move ahead of their developmental level. "A process whereby the adult controlled those elements of the task that were originally beyond the learner's capacity, thus allowing the learner to complete those that were within existing capabilities."[15] The presence of a teacher may be actual, or may be distant, so that when a child seeks to solve a problem at home, having first been shown the solution in class, the "solution is accomplished with the teacher's help. This help—this aspect of collaboration—is invisibly present. It is contained in what looks from the outside like the child's independent solution of the problem."[16] The notion of the support offered by the teacher, carried psychologically by the child, can be transposed to the way in which, consciously or subconsciously, the tutor or teacher supports the minister-in-training, even when not physically present. In formation, the tutors, and other significant shapers of ministry are carried, so that their voice is heard "on the shoulder," as it were. Another term used in this context is scaffolding, where the tutor provides a supportive structure to enable the learning of skills to be developed. This scaffolder creates the safe environment in which the ability is developed to the point of self-supporting usage. So, a child learning to ride a bike is provided first with an adult arm, and a set of rear-wheel stabilizers, then just the proximity of the adult's arm, until finally no scaffold is needed at all. The bicycle can be ridden safely alone as balance becomes unconscious. Similarly, in the development of preaching as a key ministerial task, the early attempts can be reviewed before "performance" by a supervising tutor or the apprentice's master craftsman and the performance reflected upon afterwards; later, review can take place after the performance of the sermon alone, until, both preparation and performance, text and delivery, can be accomplished with some proficiency with the tutor being "invisibly"

---

15. Daniels *Vygotsky and Pedagogy*, 107.
16. Vygotsky, *Collected Works*, 1:216, cited in Daniels, *Vygotsky and Research*, 20.

present alone. The development of this skill takes place in the ZPD, where the development of the practitioner is led by the tutor in the learning process, with teaching leading development. A similar situation was discussed by Vygotsky in relation to play in early childhood: in play the child could become temporarily higher than his usual everyday behavior, pushing at the possibilities available. In play, as in instruction, the abilities at the edge of capability, at the limits of development are pushed, nurtured and stretched. Could this be applicable also to the development of ministry, where abilities in pastoral care, for instance, are stretched as the student "plays" within a supported situation? Permission to "play", to explore possibilities and use creative imagination, might be a significant role of the formal college formational process.

The second Vygotskyan idea that may be incorporated into our understanding of the formational process is that of *perezhivanie*, a Russian term that describes the integration of cognitive and affective elements, and which presupposes the presence of emotion. The links between the social situation of development and psychological development pervades the later work of Vygotsky in the crucial final years before his death in 1933. *Perezhivanie is* the emotional experience of the child in the learning process. Vygotsky again:

> The emotional experience [*perezhivanie*] arising from any situation or from any aspect of environment, determines what kind of influence this situation or this environment will have on the child. Therefore, it is not any of the factors themselves (if taken without the reference of the child) which determines how they will influence the future course of his development, but the same factors refracted through the prism of the child's emotional experience.[17]

The emotional dimensions of ministry have perhaps been under-investigated, or inadequately factored into the formational process. Ministry by its very nature deals in the currency of emotions: the deepest grief, the greatest joy, the sharpest anger, the fullness of compassion, all are present within a ministerial life. The combination of personal circumstances, professional encounters within church and society, and the community dimensions of the formational process create the context in which learning and formation is mediated. Social relations work not only from the outside of us, but also from the inside—the internalization of social relations and interactions, both conscious and, more significantly, unconscious (especially

---

17. Vygotsky "The Socialist Alteration of Man," 339, cited in Daniel, *Vygotsky and Research*, 44.

in the processes of transference and counter-transference.) Where Vygotsky argues that we must look at 'the experiences of the child, that is, a study of the environment which is transferred to a significant degree to within the child himself and is not reduced to a study of the external circumstances of his life,'[18] we might transpose minister for child. The internal world of the minister must be recognized as of great significance in the formational process: learning, social relations, and the experience of the work of the Spirit (a rather unique form of social relation perhaps) influence the degree to which a person is shaped for ministry. Where, for instance, the social relations in a placement church are fractured, confrontational, and antagonistic towards the minister-in-training, or indeed towards ministry *per se*, for either actual or transferential reasons, then this emotionally charged and enervating environment will become internalized in the psyche of the minister and inevitably shape to some degree their practice of ministry. They may become cautious or internalize a notion that the church, or a sector of it, is "against them", or is in some way the enemy to be fought, or the community to be dominated and subdued. Vygotsky's pointer towards the *perezhivanie* of the minister-in-training is of great help here.

MacIntyrean Virtue Ethics[19]

MacIntyre critiques modernity for its lack of any coherent moral framework, and the seeming impossibility of competing claims to truth to engage in rational debate. In *After Virtue*, he develops a narrative of late modernity in which Enlightenment liberalism, attempting to construct a philosophy and a society on the basis of non-teleological reason, falls into intellectual and especially moral incoherence.[20] In contrast with antiquity or the medieval period when moral discourse was given coherence through the virtues, supported by reflection on the rules necessary to sustain a moral community, "We have lost the unifying frameworks that are necessary for any coherent moral discourse; what we have instead are fragments from earlier discourses, which no longer make sense now that they have been wrenched out of their contexts, and which can serve only as vehicles for the assertion of power."[21]

18. Ratner, "Prologue," xiv

19. This exploration of MacIntyre's virtue ethics was first developed in a thesis presented for a doctorate and later published as Goodliff, *Ministry, Sacrament and Representation*, 139–44.

20. Porter, "Tradition in the Recent Work of Alasdair MacIntyre" 38.

21. Ibid., 39.

In *After Virtue*, MacIntyre questions whether both socialists and capitalists do not tend towards bureaucratic and managerial power because the only test of their value is instrumental effectiveness. As he puts it in *After Virtue*,

> What if effectiveness were a quality widely imputed to managers and bureaucrats both by themselves and others, but in fact a quality that rarely exists apart from this imputation . . . [S]uch effectiveness does turn out to be one more moral fiction, because the kind of knowledge which would be required to sustain it does not exist . . . Consider the following possibility: what we are oppressed by is not power, but impotence.[22]

And yet, it is precisely such instrumental effectiveness that has become one of the tests of ministerial quality: the ability to lead and manage a local church in pursuit of growth in numbers, and, it must be acknowledged, financial support. Unwittingly, this ethos buys into a philosophy of instrumental reasoning that is concerned with finding the most effective way of delivering the goods (be that health care, motor cars or educational outcomes) without questioning the morality of those goods. This is one of the most characteristic features of modernity, and its significance for virtue ethics is the way in which some forms of ministry have co-opted these values in the name of effectiveness (be that cashed in terms of church growth or an understanding of ministry as leadership). MacIntyre argues that the means do not justify the ends, and that the epistemological self-righteousness of the followers of Enlightenment philosophy, such as Marx or Weber, could be avoided by a return to Aristotelian virtue ethics. This enables ethics to move from a description of "what is," as apprehended by an analysis of the various alternative answers to the question "what is good?" to an apprehension of "what ought to be," as "derived from the pursuit of humankind's *telos*, its end, its purpose." The "good" results from the achievement of the purpose of human endeavor, which, in the concluding chapter of *After Virtue*, MacIntyre argues is what Aristotle calls friendship. While accepting the compelling critique of the Enlightenment's project by Nietzsche, he would not accept Nietzsche's alternative: the will to power of the *Übermensch*, but turned instead to both Trotsky and St Benedict, exemplars of what Aristotle describes as friendship. We might reflect upon this turn to friendship as a way of articulating the New Testament category of *koinonia*, fellowship, both with God through Jesus Christ and with others, and cashed out in the currency of love of the believers and, following Christ, of enemies and strangers. In other words, the habits of hospitality.

22. MacIntyre, *After Virtue*, 75.

The cultivation of these virtues takes place within the school of practices, as practitioners emulate the standards of excellence already established through the practice they wish to embrace. Such practitioners come to realize that they can achieve such excellence and that it not only constitutes goods for themselves, but also for wider society. Thus, the moral structure of a society is promoted as practitioners within it develop justice, courage and truthfulness (for MacIntyre, the three virtues required for the common good of society). These virtues are internal to practitioners and common to them as proper practitioners. There are other goods, certainly, and these include money, power and status, but these are instrumental goods, goods of effectiveness. They are also finite goods (there is only so much power or money to go around), whereas the internal goods are not limited in this way. The amount of courage or truth is infinite. Indeed, the acquisition of these external goods is only likely to impede the development of the internal virtues such as justice or truthfulness. They are the currency of what MacIntyre describes as institutions.

Institutions are necessary for the organization and sustenance of practices, but they constantly threaten to corrupt them. Here, we might argue, the church and its institutional structures are necessary for the flourishing of communities of justice, courage and truthfulness, yet also threatens in its structures and bureaucracy to diminish them in its pursuit of instrumental effectiveness. The church is necessary for the recognition and validation of ministry, but then tends to co-opt ministry to its own ends, unless there is exercised a constant vigilance and self-reflexivity to counter those ends. This might be achieved as the church is not only the proclaimer of gospel, of Scripture, of the truths of the faith to a watching or listening world, but is first itself the object of that gospel: it remains the human community to which Scripture and the Spirit are first addressed, and which must sit under Scripture before it attempts to proclaim it more widely.

In the sequel to *After Virtue*, titled *Whose Justice, Whose Rationality*, MacIntyre establishes Aristotelian philosophy as the tradition that most clearly uses the kind of teleological reasoning that is used by those who, rightly, he argues, "act in pursuit of the goods of excellence internal to social practices."[23] In this argument, it is both Hume and modern liberalism that constitute the alternatives to the Aristotelian teleological tradition. Both Humean and contemporary liberals prioritize the effectiveness of goods over goods of excellence.

> Both Humean and contemporary liberals regard money, power and status as susceptible to rational evaluation but anything

---

23. Knight, *The MacIntyre Reader*, 12.

postulated as a final end to be beyond the scope of reason. Both articulate the presuppositions of a social order that found early institutional embodiment in a legally regulated market and was then increasingly reinforced by bureaucratic organization.[24]

For the later MacIntyre it is not Aristotle *per se*, but the reading of Aristotle through the writing of Thomas Aquinas that achieves the necessary superiority of argument over any of his predecessors or, indeed, his successors. Aquinas combined Christianity, derived from Augustine, with Aristotle, and produced the most coherent account of rationality and justice. This account is fully realist, "conceiving the *telos* of enquiry as perfected understanding, as the adequacy of an intellect to its object."[25] This is understood by almost every practicing scientist, of course, but is denied by both liberal epistemology and Nietzschean perspectivism.

> The failure of the Enlightenment project left open two alternatives: to reconstruct the moral theory and communal practice of Aristotelianism in whatever version would provide the best theory so far, explaining the failure of the Enlightenment as part of the aftermath of the breakdown of a tradition; or, instead, to understand the failure of the Enlightenment as a symptom of the impossibility of discovering any rational justification for morality as hitherto understood, a sign of the truth of Nietzsche's diagnosis . . . Aristotelianism . . . finally emerged in its Thomistic version as a more adequate account of the human good, of virtues, and of rules, than any other I have encountered.[26]

Three aspects of MacIntyre's alternative strategy to the incoherence of modernity concern us here. First, the development of practices as a lens through which to understand the way of being that is ministry; second, the narrative unity of a human life; and third, the tradition-based context in which ministry is exercised.

Practices

MacIntyre understands practices to have rules and histories that aim at standards of excellence gained by submitting to those who have already attained them. MacIntyre writes,

---

24. Ibid., 14.
25. Ibid., 19.
26. MacIntyre in an interview with Giovanna Borradori, "An interview with Giovanna Borradori," 255–66, in Knight, ed., *The MacIntyre Reader*, 263.

> By a "practice" I am going to mean any coherent and complex form of socially established cooperative human activity through which goods internal to that form of activity are realized in the course of trying to achieve those standards of excellence which are appropriate to, and partially derivative of, that form of activity, with the result that human powers to achieve excellence, and human conceptions of the ends and goods involved, are systematically extended.[27]

And,

> Its goods can only be achieved by subordinating ourselves within the practice in our relationship to other practitioners . . . To enter into a practice is to enter into a relationship not only with its contemporary practitioners, but also with those who have preceded us in the practice, particularly those whose achievements extended the reach of the practice to its present point. It is thus the achievement, and *a fortiori* the authority, of a tradition which I then confront and from which I have to learn.[28]

In ministry, therefore, the habits, practices and standards that represent excellence are not subjective, but agreed by the community, or guild, that preserves them. Any conception of ministry that over-emphasizes the individual's sense of call, that individualizes ministry in other words, loses this sense of communal solidarity. What matters is not so much the individual's sense of vocation as its recognition by the church, its transformation by ministerial formation (which is closer to an apprenticeship in a craft than simply the attainment of a theological education) and its continuing practice, sustained by virtues that correspond to its *telos*, its purpose.

> The virtues therefore are to be understood as those dispositions which will not only sustain practices and enable us to achieve the goods internal to practices, but which will sustain us in the relevant kind of quest for the good, by enabling us to overcome the harms, dangers, temptations and distractions which we encounter, and which will furnish us with increasing self-knowledge and increasing knowledge of the good.[29]

The tradition of ministry as word and sacrament fulfilled just such a function until its eclipse in recent years, and its replacement by a functional

---

27. MacIntyre, *After Virtue*, 187.
28. Ibid., 191, 194.
29. Ibid., 219.

approach has proved inadequate to the task of forming ministerial virtues where it has not also been embedded in a sacramental theology.

Narrative Unity

In the fragmentation of the self that modernity produces,[30] MacIntyre understands the lack of any narrative unity to a human life as rendering it incapable of fostering virtue: "the liquidation of the self into a set of demarcated areas of role-playing allows no scope for the exercise of dispositions which could genuinely be accounted virtues in any sense remotely Aristotelian."[31]

Instead, virtues require a conception of human life as a unified whole where actions are embedded in an ongoing narrative giving practices meaning and point. It is in just such a unified whole that ministry, and its practice, will flourish. A conception that emphasizes the whole of life as a way of being will inculcate the virtues that ministry demands with greater effectiveness than one that sees ministry as a set of roles to be played (preacher, manager, leader, and so forth). Here again, an ontological approach perhaps is better able to give that narrative unity to life.

Tradition-based Contexts and Institutions

The virtues and practices MacIntyre promotes are not the product of a universal rationality but are forged in particular traditions. These tradition-based contexts, however, require institutions to support them. This has, however, an ambiguous impact in late-modernity which is fixated on efficiency and profit. The institutional context in which these practices flourish, supported by virtues, is for MacIntyre always undermined by the very institutions that they are predicated upon. So there can be no ministry without a church, the institution that provides its context, yet the same institution demands of its ministers practices that produce greater and greater efficiencies, to the detriment of the virtues themselves.

> For no practices can survive for any length of time unsustained by institutions. Indeed, so intimate is the relationship of practices to institutions—and consequently of the goods external to the goods internal to the practices in question—that institutions and practices characteristically form a single causal order

---

30. Cf. Taylor, *Sources of the Self,* 48–52. Cf. Woodhead, "Theology and the Fragmentation of the Self."

31. MacIntyre, *After Virtue,* 205.

> in which the ideals and the creativity of the practice are always vulnerable to the acquisitiveness of the institution, in which the cooperative care for common goods of the practice is always vulnerable to the competitiveness of the institution. In this context the essential feature of the virtues is clear. Without them, without justice, courage and truthfulness, practices could not resist the corrupting power of institutions.[32]

This places ministry and church in a relationship of potential conflict, where the minister needs to resist the imposition upon their self-understanding and practice of the "characters" that MacIntyre places as typical of modernity: the therapist and manager.

We have seen how virtue ethics has much to offer in its understanding of ministerial formation, its processes and purpose. From Aristotle through Anscombe, Murdoch and MacIntyre, the growth in virtue by means of formation in the practices of ministry, conveyed through the communities of learning and practice, has the potential to form the good minister: virtuous, effective and Christ-like. We turn now to four related models of ministerial formation: a theological one, rooting it in the doctrines of creation and eschatology; the model of ministry as practical wisdom, ministry as a form of focused or exemplary discipleship and ministerial formation as a form of apprenticeship.

---

32. Ibid., 194.

4

Creation, Eschaton, and the Formation and Practice of Ministry

Discussions of ministerial formation are often dominated by evaluation of the differing modes of study, the concentration of study, and benefits of communal living for so-called college-based courses, as opposed to the practical intensity and pastoral reality of mixed-mode delivery, called by Baptists church-based or congregation-based. An honest evaluation will also reflect the financial benefits to student and college of mixed-mode delivery, as well as the suitability of that mode for the older student. While the average age of those beginning ministerial training might be reducing slightly since the middle of the first decade of the twenty-first century, many come to ministry as older adults with family commitments, considerable experience of church life and an already established career in some sphere of work out of which they have been called. There is a tendency in some of these to be impatient with a pedagogy that does not appropriately honor that experience, and a church-based course gives them a taste of real ministry that reflects their maturity. To an extent the discussion concerns issues of educational utility and reflects the fact that this process of ministerial formation takes place in a higher education institution, with courses validated by a secular university.

What is less widely discussed is a theological rationale for formation. Chris Ellis, former Principal of Bristol Baptist College, notes that "'ministerial formation' language implies a culture shift away from seeing 'ministerial training' as primarily the acquisition of knowledge and skills to a more holistic view in which character and calling are important perspectives."[1] The three overlapping spheres of knowing, being and doing are familiar enough,

---

1. Ellis, "Being a Minister: Spirituality and the Pastor," in Lalleman, ed., *Challenge to Change*, 57.

CREATION, ESCHATON, AND THE FORMATION AND PRACTICE OF MINISTRY   57

but it lacks the "central and all-encompassing position of the *person* of the minister. In other words, the being of the minister, their character and spirituality, is not simply a *part* of the whole, however interactive, it is a vital way of *viewing* the whole."[2] This emphasis upon who the minister is rather than upon what they do (or in formational language, what they learn and acquire in terms of knowledge and skills) is vital. "This is what it means to be a Christian minister. Beyond professionalism, beyond ecclesiastical function, beyond competence, there is a calling to be a minister as the way in which this particular person is called to be a Christian."[3] Ellis proceeds to elucidate good practices and gracious disciplines that enable this growth in grace: worship, Sabbath keeping, reading Scripture, prayer, spiritual direction, and so forth. This rule of life becomes the way of being a minister.

While Ellis takes an important step in the right direction, there is room for a deeper theological rationale for such a way of being. This chapter attempts to take some tentative steps in that direction through engagement with a structure of the grand narrative of the Christian faith as creation, salvation and *eschaton,* and attending to two very specific Scriptures: the beginning in Genesis 1 and the end in Revelation 21 and 22.

Introduction

In his argument for "a better theology of the Christian narrative"[4] Francis Watson is suspicious of the way in which narrative theologies can display a "christomonism in their preoccupation with the 'story of Jesus.'"[5] So, for example, one might choose a Marcan model of discipleship where following Jesus is a form of life centered upon the cross. But Jesus Christ's story must be seen as the midpoint between creation and *eschaton*, and where there is insufficient reference to either, the Christian narrative makes little sense. Ballard notes how Christianity has always "been a religion of creation, salvation and eschatological culmination."[6] What might ministry formation look like if it took this wide theological horizon seriously? In this chapter I want to argue that paying attention to both the story of the creation and the eschatological hope illumines the task of ministerial formation in such a way that any tendency to see ministerial formation as either hints and tips for pastoral practice or a pietistic Jesuology (what would Jesus do?) can be

2. Ibid., 59.
3. Ibid., 63.
4. Watson, *Text, Church and World*, 137.
5. Ibid.
6. Ballard, "Theological Reflection and Providence," 286.

resisted in the name of a more robust set of practices and a "way of being" that will meet the call for ministry to be authentic and resistant to the corrosion of managerialism or amateurism.

In his *Text, Church and World*, Watson engages with the postmodern privileging of particularity and its conviction that language is "constitutive of the multiple social worlds we variously inhabit."[7] The fact that God is more than mere language is important. Cupitt might think that God is "a symbol for the continuously upsurging creative movement of language itself, in which we live and move and have our being,"[8] but Watson argues that God is not simply the creature of our human existence and language, but exists outside of our language. He is not to be made subject to a Feuerbachian reversal where he is the creature of language and a human product, but exists independently of human language. Theology must resist any surreptitious conversion of its subject matter, God, into an intratextual enterprise, a language game played by human beings with no independent existence beyond.

This is important for any discussion of ministry, for the same postmodern and secular forces would reduce ministry to a particular form of employment, with its own particular practices and body of knowledge. Those who practice it do so because it is a job, like any other, in this reductionist mood.[9] Resulting from human choices about careers, and derived from its particular socio-religious contexts, ministry can be investigated like any other profession, and any notion of there being a call from God as the most significant factor in determining that choice is interpreted as just another language game played by the community to which the minister belongs, and wholly lacking in any existential reality. With such a reductionist analysis, selection of ministers and their deployment amounts to issues of suitability, academic achievement and the appropriation of competencies that will enable the minister to act with professional integrity.

However, the Church has always insisted that ministry is a response to the call of God, and that this is no mere psychological or linguistic trick, but a fundamental reality in the life of the Church. In the theological reading of Genesis 1 that Watson engages in his overall argument, he acknowledges that the "understanding of the world as divine creation is indeed textually mediated, but to regard its extra-textual truth or falsehood as a matter

7. Watson, *Text, Church and World*, 139.

8. Cupitt, *Creation out of Nothing*, 151, cited in Watson, *Text, Church and World*, 139.

9. Discussion between the British Government's Department of Trade and Industry and faith groups in the early years of the twenty-first century demonstrated how such a view is utilized in the name of employment rights and good practice.

of indifference is to deny precisely the universality that is integral to the narrative."[10] God does speak, and divine speech is involved in the initial production of existence *ex nihilo*, but divine action is by no means confined to speech. In the discussion that follows I will seek to show how the same patterns of speech-act that delineate the Genesis creation story are reflected in the call and formation of ministers. As God calls the world into existence and shapes it, so he calls ministry into being and forms it.

Modes of Creation in Genesis 1

The first way in which creation is expressed in Genesis 1, and the way that the writer of John 1:1 understands it,[11] is *speech-act*. God speaks, and the act of speaking brings the object into existence. So, in Gen.1:3, God says "Let there be light, and there was light." This is repeated in verse 9, "God said: 'Let the waters under the sky be gathered together into one place, and let the dry land appear.' And it was so," and in verse 11, with the creation of vegetation, God commands an as yet uncreated entity into existence.

This is not the form used for the second day, when God creates the "dome in the midst of the waters" (1:6) to separate the waters below from those above. Here God "made the dome and separated the water." Watson argues that unlike the light, "the firmament does not spring immediately into being; it has to be constructed."[12] This is the *fabrication model* of creation: God wills something to be so, but then makes it. This model is used for the creation of humankind also, "Let us make humankind in our image." (1:26)

These two models can be combined, as in the creation of sun and moon. God says "Let there be lights . . . And it was so," but then immediately the writer of Genesis says "God made the two lights." (1:16)

The third model, which Watson calls the *mediation model*, has the earth bring forth what God wills into being. So, "Let the earth bring forth swarms of living creatures" (1:20) and "Let the earth bring forth living creatures of every kind" (1:24.) God here wills into existence ("So God created . . . " 1:21; "And it was so." 1:24.) but the mechanism is that already existing matter, stuff, if you will, mediates that creative process. Mediation is as much the mode of God's creative action, argues Watson, as speech-act.

---

10. Watson *Text, Church and World*, 140.

11. Cf. Westermann, *Genesis 1–11*, 110. "The beginning of the Gospel of John echoes Gen 1:3."

12. Watson *Text, Church and World*, 141.

These three models indicate how God is both transcendent: he speaks and it is so, and intimately involved with shaping and making the creation with his touch. Also, he so indwells this creation that through itself it brings forth new dimensions of existence, notably living matter, the world of living and breathing creatures. It is tempting in this three-fold creative process to see the Father who is transcendent, the Son who shapes by his touch and the Spirit who indwells creation with her powerful life so that it multiplies and reproduces. Watson certainly sees echoes here of a triune God at work, albeit operating under the principle of *opera trinitatis ad extra sunt indivisa*.[13]

The sheer immateriality of light is conjured up by the similarly ethereal "speech," while the very solid earth is laboriously made. Living creatures are created through the indwelling God who breathes life into them. This Trinitarian view of the creation is further affirmed with the remarkable "Let us make" of verse 26. The one creature that images God, humankind, is made by the joint will of the Three-in-One precisely because it is in the relatedness of humankind to itself and to the rest of creation that images the creator God.

This threefold creative process informs the overall continuing creativity of God, and informs the creative and formational processes involved in bringing forth ministry. God creates ministry, first, through a speech-act. He "calls" and the person responds with obedience and recognition. That call may be heard mediated through the recognition of others (and indeed for it to be an authentic call requires the discernment of the whole Church) but its origins are not in the decision of either an individual, attracted, perhaps, by a misguided sense of glamour that lingers about the idea of ministry; or the Church, desirous of engaging in human resource management and recruitment; but in a speech-act event. God calls, and ministry comes into being, albeit pregnant with potential as yet unrealized. The call of the Father, as expressed to Jeremiah "Now the word of the Lord came to me . . . ." (Jer. 1:4) appointing him a prophet, or the call of the Risen Christ to Paul on the Damascus Road (Acts 9:4) calling him to repentance and obedience, is primary.[14]

There follows a process whereby ministry is laboriously "formed" in the person, a process that shapes a life after the image of Christ. This process is one that shapes character and orientates life after the *telos* of service of Christ and his Church; it instils godly virtues and traits that image Christ so that ministry might truly be Christ's ministry; and it develops skills and

---

13. Ibid., 145.

14. The Apostle Paul's sense of call to a specific vocation is more strongly expressed in Galatians 1:13–17, "so that I might proclaim him among the Gentile" (Gal 1:16).

CREATION, ESCHATON, AND THE FORMATION AND PRACTICE OF MINISTRY 61

capabilities so that the minister might do the work of Christ. This process begins before formal theological education starts, and continues long after it has been completed, even if the focus of that process is, for Baptists, as for others also, the three or four years at College and the three or four years immediately post-ordination.

Importantly for Baptists, the third dimension is also present. If creation is mediated in part by the existing world of matter bringing forth fresh life through the indwelling Spirit, so ministry is exercised always in relationship to others. There can be no ministry apart from God's people, who sustain it and support it, even as its focus is their support and shaping. Ministry is there to build up the people of God, and it has no existence separate from them. We give practical expression to this conviction in the insistence that post-ordination, a minister be called to serve in a local church. Indeed, without that call being issued first, there can be no ordination to follow. It is here with the challenges and joys of pastoral ministry to a concrete iteration of the Church that ministry is offered and received.

Secondly, this third dimension of mediated creation also reminds us that ministry is not conceived afresh with each call, or even with each generation. There will always be calls to renew or radically re-envision ministry for a new culture, and for British Baptists in the early twenty-first century this was expressed as ministry in a primarily missional mode, or ministry fitted to so-called emerging church, but for ministry to be authentically Christian ministry, there will always be some orientation to the great traditions of the Church, such as ministry of Word and Sacrament. In other words, ministry formation is mediated through the existing story of the Church and its traditions (even if it is an expression of rebellion against one of those traditions)

The three-fold character of God's creative process, speech-act, fabrication and mediation, is then repeated in this 'new creation' of every disciple (who must hear the call of Christ to "come follow me", be shaped after his likeness in lifestyle and character and live out that discipleship in relation to others, whereby the grace of God is mediated through relationship to them) and given a particular focus in the call, formation and context for Christian ministry.

Eschatological Orientation

If the beginning of all things as narrated in Genesis gives shape to the way in which ministry is formed, the opposite horizon, the *eschaton*, shapes the way in which ministry might be practiced. In the anticipation of the coming

Kingdom, Christ calls forth communities that live out their love of God through love of neighbor that is both the fulfilling of the Law, according to Jesus of Nazareth, and proleptic of that perfect coming Kingdom.

> A theological understanding of the present praxis of love of neighbor must emphasize not only the past in which it is grounded but also the future towards which it looks for the fulfilment of *koinonia*, and thus for the full disclosure of the truth about past and present.[15]

Such an approach has become commonplace amongst those who, rightly I believe, stress the place of virtue ethics in the formation of Christian character.[16] Wright argues that Christian behavior is not an automatic response to baptism or the indwelling Spirit, but "more like what Paul himself calls *dokimh*, 'character' in the sense of 'a well-formed character, a tried and tested personality': a life formed by a long succession of choices that have become habit-forming."[17]

Talk of virtue in Aristotle has a forward looking perspective to the *telos* of human happiness, *eudaimonia*, which means to become our full selves through the virtues, supremely the exercise of reason. The New Testament also looks to the future, but anticipates a different goal, and by a different virtue, not the disembodied immortality of the Platonic vision, but a new heaven and a new earth in which death and decay have been banished, and by the virtue of love. It is in anticipation of the redeemed community in this renewed existence that Christian ethics signals the way to live in obedience to Christ. As T. S. Eliot puts it, "the end is where we start from."[18] This end has already been established in Jesus Christ, and it is his life, the life of God, that will fill the eschaton. Having come to hear his call and followed him we journey towards the future knowing what it looks like already. Wright again,

> We do not simply make ourselves good by learning about virtues and then trying hard to practice them, ending up producing a self-made human being that could, in the end, be presented before God for inspection and approval. Rather we find ourselves caught up in the story of Jesus, by the events of his life, his kingdom announcement, his death and his resurrection, and we find both that he is himself the goal, the fullness of humanity as well

---

15. Watson, *Text, Church and World*, 280.

16. Such as Hauerwas and Pinches, *Christians among the Virtues*; Wells, *Improvisation: The Drama of Christian Ethics*; Colwell, *Living the Christian Story*.

17. N. T. Wright, "Faith, Virtue, Justification and the Journey to Freedom," 474.

18. Eliot, "Little Gidding," 208.

as the fullness of divinity, and that he himself is the way, the journey by which we may ourselves come to that goal.[19]

So, turning from the beginning of all things in Genesis 1 that illumines the formation of ministry, to the end of all things in the beatific vision of Revelation 21 and 22, we find a similar echo in the context of ministry. If ministry is oriented to this vision of the end of all things in a new heaven and a new earth, it will, I believe, be shaped for the important tasks.

What God does in the *eschaton* is absolute. He "will wipe every tear from their eyes" (21:4) and "mourning and crying and pain will be no more." Night is no more (22:5) and "they will reign for ever and ever." (22:5) However, what is absolute then is proleptically present only in part now. The challenge to injustice and oppression reduces the misery of humankind, or at least reduces its otherwise totalitizing presence, but it cannot be eradicated. Sickness might be ameliorated, but death remains inevitable. Holiness of life might be sought, but sin remains an ever-present reality. How might we gain some purchase upon the practice of ministry in eschatological perspective?

The model of Christ as Prophet, Priest and King has been famously applied to ministry by Tom Torrance, of course.[20] Here in Revelation we might discern these elements in eschatological intensity. In Christ, prophetic ministry is given to John on Patmos. "Also he said, 'Write this, for these words are trustworthy and true'" (21:5) and "And he said to me, 'Do not seal up the words of the prophecy of this book.'" (22:10) It is John's task because it is first Christ's work. In the opening scenes of the Revelation the Son of Man has a voice like many waters and from his mouth comes a two-edged sword. The One who creates by speech rules also by his word. It is the task of ministry to proclaim the truth, to form the life of the Church through, first, what is spoken. Ministers are bearers of the Word of God, both the Word preached and the Word enacted in the sacraments.

The priestly task is to mediate the grace of God, to stand in the place of the sinner and plead for mercy and to stand in God's name and proclaim the forgiving and healing absolution. This task of "inclusive representation," to use Nigel Wright's evocative phrase,[21] is to embody those virtues of gracious and generous acceptance, healing, and peacemaking. Their absolute evocation is seen in Revelation: their present anticipation is lived out in faithful *koinonia*. The home of God is with mortals and the result is healing and shalom (21:3–4). The eternal City has the River of the water of life in

19. N. T. Wright, "Faith, Virtue, Justification and the Journey to Freedom," 477.

20. Torrance, *Royal Priesthood*.

21. N. G. Wright, "Inclusive Representation: Towards a Doctrine of Christian Ministry."

its midst, whose leaves are for the healing of the nations (22:1–2). The kings of the earth, who in earlier chapters made war on the lamb and his people, are here reconciled, bringing their glory to the City (21:24–6). The priestly task is to point to this the end of all things and to embody it in pastoral care and ministry. The minister is an agent of healing, of peacemaking, of thirst-quenching (21:6) and of purity. It therefore implies that ministry will not be exercised, if faithful to this vision, as divisive, self-aggrandizing, or abusive of others. The echoes of the beatitudes are obvious.

The third office that Christ fulfils is that of King, and this vision at the close of Revelation places the people of God as both those who reign for ever (22:5) and who worship the One who sits upon the throne (22:3). Indeed, it is as they worship the One on the throne that is in the midst of the city that they themselves share in that rule. Ministry is an expression of the worship of God, and thus must be oriented towards God. In the competing claims that individuals and groups make upon the minister, seeking to co-opt her to this cause or that, or to their bidding in the furtherance of this enterprise or that, the minister must remain true to Christ. The minister is called to be a man or woman of God in the church, and not the chaplain to the congregation, to be bent to its will. The ministerial role of expressing Christ's kingship is never a warrant for dominance or control of others, but equally it should not become an instrument to bring about the personal plans of any group or faction in the church. The twin dangers of ungodly power over others and ungodly submission to the control of others are both a betrayal of kingly ministry exercised after the pattern of Christ. This exercise of ministry that is subject to Christ alone is illustrated in an interesting event after the vision has been given to John, where John falls down to worship the angel who had showed him these things (22:8), but the angel is appalled (22:9) and commands John to "Worship God!" (22:9) Ministry that neither dominates in Christ's name, nor is dominated by others, is fundamentally about worship and lordship.

The typically Johannine images of light and life, glory, water, and the Lamb are all present in these closing chapters, as in the Fourth Gospel. Water is given to the thirsty ("Let anyone who is thirsty come to me," John 7:38), the city is filled with light (Rev 22:5) (Jesus is the light of the world, John 8:12) and the river gives life (Rev 22:1–2) (Jesus is the Life, John 11:25; 14:6; 17:3). The city is full of glory, even as the prologue describes the logos made flesh ("we have seen his glory . . . . Full of grace and truth", John 1:14) and on the throne of that city sits the Lamb (Rev 22:1,3) ("behold the lamb of God", says John the Baptist, John 1:29). Ministry will be oriented to these signs of the character of God expressed through these images: giving water to the thirsty, light to the darkened in mind and spirit, and both graciously exercised and truthfully practiced in all integrity, so that all are drawn to the one who sits upon the throne.

Seeing the Face of God

The culmination in Revelation is to see God's face ("and his servants will worship him, and they will see his face." Rev 22:3–4) and this anticipation is perhaps the most powerful image for the understanding of ministry. It has its echoes in the Genesis narrative also, where the image of God is the defining theological description of humankind. To see the other is to see something of the Other. The metaphor of the face of God has particular utility in terms of a Trinitarian understanding of ministry. One might say that in God the Father we have the unseen face of God, in Christ the Son we have the incarnate face, and in those who minister we have instances of the many faces of those who have in common the indwelling of the one Spirit of God, and reflecting the One face. I do not want to imply that there is not something hidden or mysterious also about the Son and the Spirit, nor that the face of the Son is somehow separated from the Father's face (or the face of God before whom we live,) or the Spirit's own being, as distinct from the creatures whom the Spirit indwells. The principle that *opera trinitatis ad extra indivisa sunt* is to be maintained, because of the essentially relational character of the Godhead. However, there is clearly a human face to the Son in a way which is not true of the Father and is differently true of the Spirit, and taking our clue from the Scriptures, we can see that while the face of God which passes before Moses is hidden from him,[22] clearly the face of Christ is recognizably that of the man Jesus of Nazareth.[23]

In the Old Testament the Spirit is not personalized in human form. He is breath, *ruach,* or wind, a presence which broods over the primordial chaos. In the New Testament, the Spirit is again represented in non-human symbols. He is the dove at Jesus' baptism, and he is encountered through the tongues of fire and rushing might wind at Pentecost. It is not so much that he has a hidden face, it is as if he has no face at all. Yet, his unmistakable presence is seen in human faces, the shining face of Moses coming

---

22. Exod 33:17–23.

23. The resurrection appearances are ambiguous, with the resurrected Jesus sometimes being recognized by sight, but often unrecognizable (Luke 24:16, Cleopas and his companion on the road to Emmaus, or John 20:14, where Mary Magdalene seems to not know that "the gardener" is in fact Jesus, although the Gospel narrative might imply that this was simply a matter of lack of recognition due to the absence of expectation).

down from God's presence,[24] or heard on the lips that speak glossolalia. The face of the Spirit becomes the face of the disciple of Jesus Christ who faces Godwards and is filled with the Spirit. His face is given substance in our faces, in all their many particular and unique differences of physiognomy, color, and gender.

Even in their non-human representation, the dove and the tongue of fire are not independent of Jesus or the disciples. It is the dove descending on Jesus, not the dove just flying around of its own volition. The tongues rest on the disciples at Pentecost. It is the presence of God in relation to the person, and in this sense, acts symbolically like the Old Testament *panim*: it is God in his relationship to humankind, and in particular the Father in relation to his Son through the Spirit.

Thus we have the unseen face, the revealed face and the many faces of God, and our ability to find traces of the Trinity in this way is crucially anchored in the reality that Jesus was not a face-less man, but was one in whose face the glory of God was seen. The search for *vestigia trinitatis* in aspects of nature is, in this sense, a step further removed from what I have argued for here. It might be helpful to think of God as water or light (and indeed Jesus employs metaphors specifically using those creaturely characters, "I am the light of the world",[25] "Let anyone who is thirsty come to me,"[26]) but we do not think of Jesus as being a human one hundred watt bulb, or a man composed of any greater proportion of water than any other human. He did, however, have a face, and has one still in his heavenly reign (albeit one which shines like the sun; perhaps an oblique reference to the shining face of Moses, what is reflected in even that most privileged of humans, is effulgent in the Son of Man[27].) To describe, then, the face of God as a case of a *vestigia*, like any other, is not entirely accurate. It carries some greater significance than that. For that reason, we might move to employ the concept as it is applied to ministry with some confidence.

However, there is a subordination of the Spirit to the Father and the Son in this metaphor of the face, since creaturely faces are not intrinsically the faces of the Spirit beyond a general affirmation of the *imago Dei* in every human being. I argue for degrees of likeness as the process of transformation proceeds: "And all of us, with unveiled faces, seeing the glory of the Lord as though reflected in a mirror, are being transformed into the same image from one degree of glory to another, for this comes from the Lord, the

---

24. Exod 34:29; 2 Cor 3:13.
25. John 8:12.
26. John 7:37.
27. Rev 1:16.

Spirit" (2 Cor 3:18). The derivation of a transformed "face" (in other words, character and personality) as the work of the Spirit is not independent of the creative and redemptive work of Father and Son, but I also argue that this is not to imply a subordinationist understanding of the person of the Spirit.

The affirmation that the minister (like every Christian) bears the face of the Spirit, or to put it differently, through his or her life and character, summed up in the metaphor of the face, the Spirit is encountered by others in their relationship to that minister, raises the methodological question of the primacy of pneumatology. Traditionally in theological enquiry methodological priority is given to Christology. So, the minister is designated as a "minister of Jesus Christ," or as a "minister of word and sacrament," the latter at least being the ordinances of Jesus Christ. The tendency then is to drift towards a "bi-nity" of Father and Son. Yong proposes that,

> a pneumatological approach to theology.... opens up toward a trinitarianism that is so much more robust than that which has emerged to date from a Christological starting point. The latter, especially as developed in the West, has resulted in pneumatology being not much more than an afterthought – an appendix regarding the "shy member of the Trinity," as it were—to Christology and patrology.[28]

He argues that this robust trinitarianism is produced by a mutual interpenetration of Spirit and Word, co-inhering in Community "without losing their distinctness ... The dialectical relationship between Word and Community is played out in the context of Community," and begins with the Spirit.[29] The methodological primacy of pneumatology, then, coincides with the phenomenological primacy of the lived encounter between minister and another human in the process of meeting God. In a postmodern culture it is usually as we meet God in others that we first encounter him, and thus meet the "faceless" God in the many faces of others. This is expressed pastorally in many encounters graced by the Spirit's presence, but liturgically it is expressed most clearly in the Eucharist.

In the Eucharist we are faced by others. In the peace we greet and face the other, in receiving the cup, we are faced by the one who serves us. It shapes a *habitus* of facing. It is here that the Macintyrean understanding of virtue as habit, an understanding that has been so influential upon the virtue school of Christian ethics, has its echo. The reason we do this "in remembrance of him" time and again is not only that we are forgetful (although we are) but because it forms a habit of orientation of life towards the

28. Yong, *Spirit-Word-Community*, 9.
29. Ibid., 18.

Christian story. Above all, it orientates us to the face of Christ. This is symbolized in some Eastern traditions by the great icons of Christ in majesty in the apse above the altar, or in Western traditions by the Crucified One. It might be the icon, before which we encounter Christ, or probably, just the Christ we configure in our mind's eye. But it is in the encounter of offering and receiving, of gift and giving, that we meet the God whose nature is to give himself. Similarly, in Baptismal practices, we face Christ. "Do you turn to Christ?" the candidate is asked in Baptist practice, or "Will you follow Christ?" We face up to our old sinful past, and face Christ.

But in every case, the face of Christ is immediately seen in the faces of others. The "do this" of the Synoptic Gospels is echoed in St John's narrative of the example that Jesus gives of washing the disciple's feet. To face Christ is to go wash feet, die to live, take up a cross, live compassionately and joyfully for others. To see this face of Christ as we share in the Eucharist meal is to see a face alive with the life and glory of God, open to all that is new and alive, but oriented to others who are seen by this face. This face of Jesus Christ is so oriented to others that knowing and loving this face means being called to know and love them, to recognize this face in theirs.

This encounter of God in the face of another, however, is not without its conditions. It is clearly not in every face that we meet God. In the blind hatred of the suicide bomber we do not meet God's face, nor in the cunning obsession of the serial sexual abuser. It is obscured in the angry dominance of the controlling pastor, and seems inauthentic in the shallow bonhomie of the people-pleaser. The conditions of meeting God in the face of the other, in the face of the one offering ministry, revolve around the degree to which the minister herself or himself faces God. It is as she herself lives before the face of God, the Father whose face is unseen, the Son whose face is human, albeit now inevitably imagined, and the Spirit whose face becomes ours. To live before the face of God is a metaphor for a life oriented to worship and prayer. Jesus himself tells us how to worship God, for he is the one whose life is lived radically for God and others. "He embodies the facing of God and the facing of humanity."[30] To worship and live before this face is to be faced by him, and the way in which God faces us, leads us inevitably back to facing others in sacrificial service. However we meet the face of God: in others, or through the imagination fired by Scripture or art, or indeed through the glory of God revealed in "the things that he has made,"[31] we do not encounter an unresponsive face, but rather find ourselves "more radically

30. Ford, *Self and Salvation*, 214.
31. Rom 1:20.

looked at,"[32] and as we meet that gaze, so we are "transformed into the same image from one degree of glory to another."[33]

The encounter with God through ministry becomes an encounter in the Spirit as God graciously chooses to meet us, to face us and to smile upon us. The face of the other is inhabited by the face of the Spirit, who himself points us to Christ, who is the revelation of the unseen face of God. The greater the orientation of the minister's face to face God, the more readily God's facing of us is conveyed through that human agent.

This immediately returns our discussion to that of ministerial formation. Amidst all of the theological understanding to be grasped, ancient languages to be mastered, skills to be acquired and practices by which to be shaped, the degree to which ministerial formation enables the orientation of a human life to be lived before the face of God is of paramount importance. Without this dimension of spiritual formation, we are left with very little more than the reductionist conception caricatured earlier: ministry as mere employment.

So, attention must be paid to the formation of habits of facing Christ in daily prayer, corporate worship and fellowship. These habits might be learnt in the community of a college, or partly in the context of a local church, but be learnt they must. In the training of ministers if there ever was a golden age, when young men (sic) lived in community and gave their minds to intellectual endeavor, it was flawed nonetheless. Spiritual formation as an intentional discipline is still a fairly recent innovation, and the default formational practice is to teach about spirituality, in the hope that something might rub off in terms of practice. The influence of the placement church will not be entirely wholesome, either, with the demands of pastoral practice in a half-time pastorate militating against the leisure required to learn how to pray.

The creative process of Genesis's narrative sheds light upon the process whereby ministry is initiated and formed, while the description of the end of all things in the closing chapters of Revelation, calls for an anticipatory way of life in ministry, orientated towards the future in Jesus Christ, and lived facing the One whose face we shall see in the New Jerusalem.

---

32. Marion, *God without Being*, 22.
33. Second Cor 3:18.

PART TWO

Models of Ministerial Formation

5

Formation and Wisdom

> *"The Lord created me (Wisdom) at the beginning of his work . . . then I was beside him, like a master worker, and I was daily his delight, rejoicing before him always"* Prov. 8:22,30.

"I am so glad my daughter did not decide to study theology at University. I didn't want her to lose her faith." Such comments will not be uncommon to many pastors from an evangelical background. Theology, the study of God, is a dangerous thing, best avoided if a biblical faith is to be maintained, and a simple faith remain unthreatened. The desire is for a lived faith, or wisdom, *sapientia*, we might say, to be kept away from *scientia*, knowledge. This fracturing of the church and the academy, theology and practice, and wisdom from knowledge has a long pedigree, and contributes to the suspicion that many beginning ministerial formation have towards the academic and theological components to their formation. Best stick to the Bible, they assume.

The manifest nonsense of these comments and prejudices are almost immediately obvious, yet they remain commonplace in many churches, and have a considerable foundation in the historic split between wisdom and the "science" of theology, a split that is being challenged widely today. Ministerial formation is one context in which wisdom and knowledge can be reunited, and therefore ministerial formation as growth in wisdom is a helpful model to place alongside the others offered in this analysis.

Virtue and the Voice of God

The way in which theology, practice and wisdom relate as practiced in the early church is described by Daniel Treier as "in hot pursuit of *sapientia* (wisdom), a kind of knowledge with teleology: the formation of virtue in

God's people."[1] The fragmentation of this early coherent endeavor, separating theology and wisdom, is a complex story, but until the rise of the medieval university, theology was not unified into a separate discipline under one disciplinary rubric, but was seen as commentary upon Scripture (as indeed, Calvin conceived of his *Institutes of The Christian Religion*,) and an apologetic tool.

Yves Congar[2] and Edward Farley[3] identify two different moments when this separation emerged. Congar points to Peter Abelard, when *theologia* takes its modern meaning, and in the thirteenth century "its epistemological flavor."[4] Contemplative illumination became subordinated to *scientia*, to knowledge, although, notably, in Thomas Aquinas the link was not broken. Indeed, while Aquinas is often thought of as the archetypal representative of *scientia*, he remains a sapiential theologian, with a strong contemplative streak. Others naturally look to the Age of Enlightenment as the moment, but the loss of wisdom was evident long before the Enlightenment. Farley identifies the loss with the rise of the modern age, with theology as a habit of the human soul, as opposed to a scholarly discipline within the academy lingering long after the Reformation.

In the earlier case, the breaking of the link between wisdom and understanding as knowledge is epitomized by the dispute between Abelard and Bernard, "Theology as speculation would be distinguished from theology as contemplation of Scripture and the church fathers; theology as schooled *speculativa* would be distinguished from theology as cloistered *activa*."[5] Love and knowledge no longer co-inhered.

The Reformers were ambiguous about scholasticism, opposed to its arid speculation, yet adopting its systematic approach, such that Calvin's *Institutes* lent themselves to a seventeenth century Reformed form of Scholasticism. Nonetheless, theology was deemed to be the servant of the task of Christian living, and in Calvin, as indeed in Aquinas before him, knowledge of God and knowledge about God are intimately connected to virtue and wisdom.[6] The Biblical scholasticism that followed was an attempt to move from immediate knowledge of God to one mediated by Scripture, further separating theology from wisdom as the contemplation of God.

---

1. Treier, *Virtue and the Voice of God*, 3.
2. Congar, *A History of Theology*, 32–33.
3. Farley, *Theologia: The Fragmentation and Unity of Theological Education*.
4. Treier, *Virtue and the Voice of God*, 6.
5. Ibid., 7, reliant upon Evans, *Old Arts and New Theology*, 82–83.
6. "For Calvin, theology is a first-order pastoral undertaking, not a second-order academic discipline." Charry, "To What End Knowledge?," 76.

In the contemporary modernist and postmodern context, there have been various attempts to relate the faith of the church to the academy, or to relate prayer and knowledge. The continual erosion of epistemic justification for belief since (at least) Descartes continues to undermine the Biblical foundationalism that starts by stating that the Bible is God's Word, which begs precisely the question asked in the modern academy, on what possible foundation can you say that? One response is to attempt to make those justifications, while another is to retreat into a religious ghetto where the question is never asked.

Another move is to replace "talk about God" with the study of the God-talk of those who confer with it, the Christian community. So, the problem of God disappears to be replaced with theology as a social science, discussing the anthropology and psychology of a peculiar community that continues to believe in God in the face of the onslaught from a materialist and skeptical culture.[7] Where the object of theology, grounded in a post-Enlightenment epistemology, is moved from God to talk about God, then "What should be joined together – God and Word, love and knowledge, *sapientia* and *scientia*, church and school – tends to be put asunder, despite good intentions."[8]

Another attempt, allied to Lindbeck's Experiential-Expressive knowledge, is a move to view theology as a disposition of the soul that has the character of knowledge that shapes the soul. The work of Edward Farley is a prime example here.[9] This approach is not without its problems, notably the readiness with which it turns again to theological anthropology.

A final attempt has been to re-order theology to reflection into the validity of Christian witness. Charles Wood finds in theology a unity of vision and discernment, and attends to the task of theology, rather than its subject *per se*.[10] Theology is concerned with a historical question, "is this truly Christian witness?"; a philosophical question, "is this witness true?"; and a practical question, "is this witness fit for purpose?" This is a turn to

---

7. One attempt was that of Pannenberg's *Wissenschaftstheorie und Theologie*: "allgemeinen Grundlagen der systematischen Theologie wird man daher in der Anthropologie zu suchen haben," 424.

8. Treier, *Virtue and the Voice of God*, 16.

9. Farley, *The Fragility of Knowledge*.

10. Wood, *Vision and Discernment: An Orientation in Theological Study*.

the practical, be it, with Browning, a turn to reflection upon the transformation of individuals and communities[11] or theology as mission, or prayer.[12]

Here also is where MacIntyre's discussion of the practices of a tradition comes into play. If theology is about formation, then MacIntyre's focus upon a recovery of the ancient notion of practices creates the place where virtue is exhibited. In this sense, it is not so much theology itself that is a practice, as the formational task that theology serves. So James McClendon, developing a baptist (sic) theological frame, sees theology as a second order practice located in the church's teaching ministry[13] while David Kelsey has noted how widespread is agreement that the aim of theological education is a kind of wisdom. "This wisdom concerning God embraces contemplation, discursive reasoning, the affections, and the actions that comprise a Christian's life."[14] This agreement about the focus upon wisdom is important, but the content of that wisdom is more variously expressed: is it contemplation of the divine, or reasoning about God? Is it obedience or practice? Reinhard Hütter's answer is a renewed vision of theology as church practice.[15] Theology for him is a first-order practice, and

> The teleological logic of theology's salvific-economic taxis is the immediate consequence of theology as a reflective actualization of the church's soteriological telos. Therefore, the learning of the faith remains the goal of its presentative-communicative aspect, albeit not its criterion for truth . . . . . The initiatory acquisition of faith is joined by a learning of faith, one immanent to faith that begins daily anew and never ends. . . . . perhaps best called *perigrinational* learning, that is, the learning inhering in the Christian *perigrinatio*.[16]

This notion of theology as the learning of the faith on the journey of faith, its pilgrimage, is tied to "a specific and binding horizon (the biblical

---

11. Browning uses the hermeneutical model of Hans Georg Gadamer, Paul Ricoeur, and Jürgen Habermas in developing a "fundamental practical theology as critical reflection on the church's dialogue with Christian sources and other communities with the aim of guiding its action toward social and individual transformation," Browning, *A Fundamental Practical Theology: Descriptive and Strategic Proposals*, 297.

12. Thornton, *The Function of Theology*.

13. McClendon, *Systematic Theology*, 2:46.

14. Kelsey, *To Understand God Truly*, 34.

15. Hütter, *Suffering Divine Things*. This is a particularly dense argument for the church as the location of theological reflection in the light of the erosion of the church as public space. The orientation missing in the modern academy is a first-hand response to God, and this response is the prime one for the church.

16. Ibid., 189–191.

canon and *doctrina,*) and by specific and binding configurations of language and activity (the core practices.)"[17] Here, then theology becomes the discovery of wisdom, and the formation of the Christian a growth in that wisdom.

In his extended consideration of theology and wisdom, Daniel Treier asks whether theology is practical reflection on or for practice, or reflection embedded in another practice, such as education within the academy, or itself a practice? He also asks which wisdom and answers from within a biblical-theological framework. Wisdom might be *techne*, a skill or craft, or it might be *phronesis*, Aristotle's higher-order instrumental virtue of practical reason, whereby the prudent person knows what to do in any given situation. This could be simply sophistry replacing wisdom, and turning all human knowledge to a scientific technical utility without any reference to God. Such, for Old Testament Wisdom, is the way of folly. The heart of this way of life, this way of wisdom is *sapientia*, the knowledge of God, or, in Proverbial language, the fear of the Lord.

In considering the roots of this wisdom Paul Fiddes argues that, whereas the late-modern world has sought them in Aristotelean *phronesis*, there should be a shift to locate them in the Hebrew idea of *hokmah*, which develops into the *sophia* of the New Testament. Fiddes brings this concept of *hokmah* into conversation with "a Christian theology which is aware of its context in a late-modern world."[18] He notes how there has been a suspicion of *scientia* in the new search for wisdom, and a recalling of the Christian tradition of *sapientia*. This has resulted in a stress on practice over theory, and is a mood that Alasdair MacIntyre's discussion of the virtues has influenced, not only in theology. In his argument Fiddes supports Treier's assertion that "a Christian *phronesis*, or ethical discernment in practical situations, is entirely enabled by *sophia*, or by seeing God in Christ through revelation, as normatively found in Scripture . . . the Scripture thus forms the *person* in *phronesis* rather than providing comprehensive material for application to particular judgments. *Phronesis* is a gift from God, and 'is nurtured by the Spirit in response to prayer, who hones it through habits of obedience, and informs it by Scripture . . . '"[19] It is precisely here, says Fiddes, that the Hebrew concept of wisdom has much to offer, with its unique integration of *phronesis* and *sophia*. It also sounds a common note with late-modern culture, and its central concern about the relation of self to the observable world around, and the sense of crisis in the dissolution of older "modern" certainties that the human self controls its own destiny.

17. Ibid., 192.
18. Fiddes, *Seeing the World and Knowing God*, 6.
19. Ibid., 9.

Turning to the New Testament, the fear of Yahweh is fulfilled in Jesus Christ, the Wisdom of God. In 1 Corinthians Christ is both our wisdom (1:30) and he enables us to become wise as we have his mind by the Spirit (2:7–16). In his argument in 1 Corinthians 1, Paul cites Isaiah 29:14, "The wisdom of their wise shall perish, and the discernment of the discerning shall be hidden," rendering it as "I will destroy the wisdom of the wise, and the discernment of the discerning I will thwart" (1 Cor. 1:19). The learned, political counsellors had urged shaking off the Assyrian yoke, but God's plans were different, and the wisdom of actions that seemed to be weak and a failure would ultimately be seen as wise. This is exactly the point Paul wishes to make here about his own ministry, rooted as it is in the gospel of a suffering Christ being the wisdom of God. The Hebrew for "the discerning" (*chakam*) translated as σύνεσις by Paul from the LXX, may mean, to paraphrase, "street-wise," distinguishing a worldly wisdom or political shrewdness from the true wisdom. I note here that in arguing that ministerial formation should be about acquiring wisdom, this is not cashed out as "sanctified common-sense," an ecclesial version of political shrewdness. It is altogether of a different quality, privileging mercy and grace over self-preservation and aggrandizement. Street-wise common sense actually belongs to this world's order, του αιωνος τούτου (of this age, 1.20) and is fatally flawed as part of the old order that will be renewed in Christ, the wisdom of God, and the one that "makes a fool of this world's wisdom."

Where the Proverbial teacher was concerned with contrasting the wisdom of God from human wisdom, which is in fact folly, Paul has in mind a Hellenistic philosophy, perhaps one with an ascetic bent that provides one of the roots for Gnosticism (argued by Bultmann, Schmittals, and Wilckens). Thiselton argues that we should be reticent about attributing a specific Greek philosophy to this wisdom of the world, "in spite of a massive research literature on the subject."[20] While Paul is not attacking reason as such, he recognizes that it "can be flawed by epistemic vices of instrumental manipulation and self-deception"[21] Reason has firm limits, and contributes to a limited wisdom of this age that only sees things from a worldly perspective. Rather, the wisdom that Paul commends is cruciform in structure, "a gift of God to people who have lived foolishly together and would never find it on their own."[22] "God's wisdom" that Paul refers to in 1 Cor 1:21 is definitive, not fallible and temporary as is the wisdom of this world, against

---

20. Thiselton, *The First Epistle to the Corinthians*, 166.
21. Ibid.
22. Theier, *Virtue and the Voice of God*, 48.

which it is contrasted.[23] If Christ fulfils the Torah as wisdom, then the Holy Spirit also fulfils the Torah by enabling wisdom to be found. The particular shape of such wisdom is cruciform (1 Cor. 1:23-25).

> Yet to those, both Jews and Greeks (τε καί . . .), whom God has called, the cross of Christ constitutes precisely the mode of action which conveys God's power and God's wisdom. It does not rest on human calculations about signs of the times, nor upon manipulative devices that entice belief, nor does it rest on self-defeating strategies to master life by techniques of human wisdom. God's manifestation of power and wisdom operates on a different basis, namely, the way of love which accepts the constraints imposed by the human condition or plight and the prior divine act of promise, and becomes effective and operative (has power) in *God's own way*, for it corresponds with God's own nature as revealed in Christ and in the cross. Any version of the gospel which substitutes a message of personal success for the cross is a manipulative counterfeit.[24]

This wisdom, found by the Spirit through prayer, feeds into the Christian tradition through an adaptation of Aristotle's practical reason. He distinguishes "five qualities through which the mind achieves truth in affirmation or denial, namely Art or technical skill [*techne*], Scientific Knowledge [*episteme*], Prudence [*phronesis*], Wisdom [*sophia*], and intelligence [*nous*]."[25] In the Old Testament a number of Hebrew terms are rendered in the LXX by φρόνησις vocabulary, and there is a place for the idea of prudence in, for instance, Proverbs 3:13; 7:4; 8:1; 10:23. Its usage in the New Testament is ambiguous, and can be seen as negative as a mindset separated from Christ, but nonetheless it is used Christianly, albeit reframed through Christ. So, the distinctively Christian virtue of humility and self-lessness is the Christian way of prudence. Paul uses the verb φρονέω in Philippians (2:2, 5; 3:15, 19; 4:2), and elsewhere to redefine what prudence looks like: "only by a radical transformation of meaning can this action be motivated by anything that is recognizably [Greek] *phronesis*."[26]

The New Testament re-ordering of phronesis is nurtured through Scripture, its transmission by those who teach it, and by the Spirit.

---

23. For a discussion of the various interpretations of this, see Thiselton, *The First Epistle to the Corinthians*, 167-69.

24. Ibid.,172.

25. Aristotle, *Nicomachean Ethics* 1139b.16.

26. Gunton, "Christ, the Wisdom of God: A Study in Divine and Human Action," 254.

> This φρόνησις is a type of knowledge and a regulative virtue, standing at the intersection of ethics and epistemology within an ethos of divine creation and command. φρόνησις is nurtured by the Spirit in response to prayer, who hones it through habits of obedience, and informs it by Scripture and Christian teaching. This combination of gift and nurture—indeed grace given by various means of communal nurture—strongly implies that wisdom is not a possession for a privileged few, but a privilege for all who live in God's New Covenant.[27]

The purpose of this is to bear fruit, pre-eminently, love. Furthermore, this possession of prudence is corporate, achievable only in relationship to others. Treier argues for a full integration of *theologia* into Christian practice. In his argument, Treier then proceeds to make steps that need not concern us here: leaning to speak of God (doctrine), the nature of biblical interpretation (the question of hermeneutics) and the relationship between *Phronesis* and *Wissenschaft*. However, he then turns to theological education as the school of the Triune God. He calls for theology to regain its *sapiential* voice, that is, its Biblical voice, within the community of the church and by the Spirit's role in the formation of reception of doctrine.

> An account of the *Regula fidei* in terms of a particular Sophia-phronesis oscillation accomplishes this: (1) providing the substantive account of Christian virtue, and accountability for Christian phronesis . . . .. (2) while avoiding a construal of divine communicative action that makes theology exclusively propositional or biblical interpretation excessively theoretical and methodological; (3) especially by construing the Bible's narrative coherence around the God-man Jesus Christ, not only in terms of the Father's revelation or discourse but in terms of Spirit-led faithful humanity in the formation of reception. This gives wisdom an embodied, active, communicative and fully Trinitarian character that other notions of biblical unity or functional descriptions of the *Regula fidei* can lack.[28]

Here, then, we have an argument for the reconfiguring of theology as wisdom, and the formation of the Christian community as a process of conformity by the Spirit to the way of Christ as determined in Scripture. This has considerable benefits to our concern for models of ministerial formation. It enables the conveying of the faith, the *Regula fidei*, to be less about a series of propositions that theological students must learn and accept,

---

27. Theier, *Virtue and the Voice of God*, 55.
28. Ibid., 205.

as a process whereby people are formed in the Spirit by those doctrines understood as wisdom. It enables theological education, the acquisition of ministerial skills and practical formation of character and spirituality to co-inhere, without collapsing any one into another. They maintain their distinct contributions, but relate to one another as dimension of this training in wisdom: understanding, *epistome*, skill, *techne* and prudence, *phronesis* are woven together to form Christian *Sophia,* which elsewhere we shall call discipleship.

Paul Fiddes wants to take things a step further than wisdom enabling an authentic discipleship. In his Bampton Lectures already referred to[29] in which he engages the late-modern culture with Hebrew Wisdom Literature and its world, he moves from language of God being mediated by, for instance, the incarnate Son, to one of participation in God's movement. "Hebrew wisdom literature does not at all present wisdom as a mediator between different levels or spheres of reality."[30] The early Christian theologians employed the concept of an intermediate Logos, adapting to reflect their conviction that this Christ was not some inferior semi-divine principle, but fully one with God. They lived with the contradiction that this mediator was at one and the same time equal with God (except for Arius, who logically concluded that this paradox was unsustainable, and argued that this mediator was simply a creature, albeit "the highest"). This language of a mediator bridging the gap has left its indelible mark upon the whole of theology subsequently: The Son of God bridges the gap between a world of divine perfection and a fallen creation. "It has resulted in the tension of ascribing to God the philosophical attributes proper to unchanging Being—impassibility, immutability, non-temporality—while at the same time upholding the biblical picture of a God who has a compassionate love for the world."[31]

If, however, we start not with a mediating Logos but divine Wisdom, we find language of participation replacing language of mediation. This is important, since the ecclesial consequences of mediating language is to look for those humans who also mediate God's presence in as singular a fashion as Christ: The Bishop of Rome in the Church, the priest in the parish, the Emperor of Christendom in the secular world. The consequences are often those of political and religious oppression. Fiddes argues instead that,

> when the writer of the Wisdom of Solomon celebrates wisdom as "one and many" (abiding in herself she can do all things) he

---

29. In their published form, Fiddes, *Seeing the World and Knowing God.*
30. Ibid., 211.
31. Ibid., 210.

> is not thinking of a bridge between a transcendent One and the plurality of the finite world, but a wisdom who enables her friends to enjoy the manifold phenomena among which they live. Wisdom is not projected or extrapolated from a remote deity in order to make contact with a world of change and decay. Wisdom does not in any way bridge a gap between transcendence and immanence, between creator and created. Rather, we have seen that the spirit of wisdom which stands over against the world as its observer is also the same spirit which is within the world, holding all things together. We might say that wisdom flows forth from God so that human beings can participate in that same flowing movement. . . . Reading the wisdom literature should encourage a paradigm change in Christian theology, from mediation to participation. Wisdom as spirit in the Wisdom of Solomon hints at a complexity within God's life that is later to flower fully in the Christian doctrine of the Trinity. It is not that either Lady Wisdom or spirit can be simply equated with persons of the Trinity as the Church later articulated them – whether Son or Holy Spirit. . . . The point is that similar insights into movements of personal life within and from God, inviting participation, are later to be expressed in the Christian concept of Trinity. The Son or Logos comes forth from the Father, as does the Spirit, not to link a remote God with the world as in the mediation model, but so that the world can share in the movements of self-giving within God, participating in the flowing movement of love between the Father and the Son in the ever-surprising newness of the Spirit.[32]

Thus, in terms of ministerial formation, the forming of wisdom in a person, so that the acquisition of ministerial skills and practical formation of character and spirituality co-inhere, without collapsing any one into another, is deepened by an understanding that this formation is a means (one amongst many) of participating in the divine live. Christ is being formed in the life of the person, not simply knowledge imparted, skills acquired and character shaped. I have argued elsewhere that this participation is expressed in the human face as being reflected glory.[33] Fiddes puts it thus: "As we relate to others in compassion and empathy, as we become sympathetic readers with God, so we find our true self."[34]

It is this participational model that helps us distance ourselves from an overly-technical version of ministerial formation, where, at its worst, it

32. Ibid., 211–12.
33. Goodliff, *With Unveiled Face*, 109–15.
34. Fiddes, *Seeing the World and Knowing God*, 217.

is a collection of hints and tips for the conduct of ministry, or at a more sophisticated level, an emphasis upon the tools, skills and abilities that give expression to ministerial practice. This emphasis upon "core ministerial competencies," to the diminishment of ministerial virtues and ministerial character, is always a risk in a culture that wants the maximum effectiveness at the minimum cost in time and money. This is a culture to which the church has become too accustomed. The Book of Job might serve as a counter to such a tendency. I do not intend to fully discuss here the nature or theology of Job: others have done so quite adequately.[35] Suffice it to say that Job is a protest at the reduction of the way of wisdom to a simple cause-and-effect linkage (act thus, and you will be rewarded, act wickedly, and you will suffer,) where instead there should have been a continual disposition to live according to the fear of the Lord, with religious humility. This leads to an interpretation of human experience that reads back into it divine action: if Job is suffering (which he most assuredly is) then it must be because he deserves this form of divine retribution: so, his counsellors argue, recognize your sin, God will forgive, and you will be rewarded. Indeed, Job subscribes himself to this transaction, except he knows that he does not deserve it: he has not sinned. "The book bursts through the hardened arteries of dogmatic wisdom to return the flow of wisdom to its original well-spring."[36]

We live in an age of technical explanations for the efficacy of action, and the temptation is to promote a way of ministerial formation that accommodates itself to this spirit of the age. Follow this method of church growth, practice those pastoral exchanges, use these evangelistic tool, and ministry will be successful, we are told. But there is a mystery about this: good and effective ministers come unstuck, their ministry fails—not because of personal moral failure, but because of the exigencies of life in their community. What is needed is a different model, one that starts with a participation in wisdom as virtues are acquired: virtues that are not in themselves another set of tools, but dispositions of the heart, movements of the soul, habits of the spirit. "Where shall wisdom be found?" asks the riddle? (Job 28:12) It can only be found by exercising it, "an experience one comes to through appropriate behavior in religion and ethics."[37] Here we

> live in an open space, through wisdom, in which we can know a God who is hidden but not absent. This is a presence which never imposes, and where we can learn to be present to others

---

35. Ibid., 230–56; Levinas, *Otherwise Than Being: Or Beyond Essence*; Levinas, "Postface." Cf. the various commentaries on Job.

36. Fiddes, *Seeing the World and Knowing God*, 237.

37. Clines, *Job 21–37*, 920.

without forcing ourselves on them. . . . A wisdom theology for today will maintain that at any moment, anywhere, any place can become holy. It can become the "no-place" where wisdom is encountered, opening up a space in which there is room to dwell.[38]

The Book of Proverbs

One of the benefits of taking wisdom as a model for ministerial formation is its integrative approach. While much of this book adopts a systematic approach, for the sake of analysis, the way in which the various elements of formation cohere is essential. Forming the wise minister, or, developing wisdom in the minister's life and practice, cuts through the distinctions between function and being, between character and spirituality.

One might do worse than make a reading of the Book of Proverbs a requirement at the beginning of the testing of a sense of call, and again at the significant stages of formation that ensues. The way in which the themes seem chaotic, or haphazard, reflects the way in which formation is not a steady, planned, progression, despite the best intentions of those who plan college course, but rather a growth and re-growth of a variety of themes that are inter-related. The variations in personal stories, temperament, calling, ability and gifting amongst those being formed for ministry gives a wide range of possibilities for the formational process. Some will come from a steady, loving and Christian background, others converted from backgrounds that are inimical to the development of stability in personality. Some will come with high levels of intellectual functioning, others with lower; some with already developed skills in relationships, others with marked "edges" to them that make relational functioning difficult; some start with a strongly developed pattern of discipleship, others less so; and some will come with a disciplined pattern of spiritual practices, others with next to nothing in that regard. This is the reality of human nature, and wisdom is an ancient way of encompassing much of this, especially in the areas of way of life, relationships and work.

The first way of approaching formation in this model will be to reflect on the origins of this concept, in both ancient Israel, through its Wisdom literature[39] and in the ancient Greek world, through *phronesis*, practical wisdom, where Aristotle features significantly.

38. Fiddes, *Seeing the World and Knowing God*, 265.

39. Ably accomplished by Sadgrove in his series of addresses for those about to be ordained: Sadgrove, *Wisdom and Ministry*.

The second approach in this chapter is to extract some themes from the Book of Proverbs in Scripture, and explore what those biblical writers had to say to the young approaching the beginnings of adult responsibility, and how this might offer some insights to the elements involved in ministerial formation. It is not a book that says much about habits and patterns of prayer or worship (and neither is this true of Ecclesiastes, for instance), nor is it so helpful in describing the areas of knowledge required of the minister beyond the basic orientation towards 'the fear of the Lord' (biblical studies, theology, history, culture, liturgy and so forth), but it does say a great deal about habits of life, dispositions of the spirit or soul and the dangers to be avoided. These are the areas of character development that lie deeply within the formational process. Through the pursuit of intellectual formation, the developing of habits in the spiritual life and the acquisition of those skills in preaching, pastoral care and mission that are among the training elements of formation, there is at the heart of formation the growth in a godly wisdom, a stable and humble character and the work and speech that flows from it that becomes the way of life, or "the way of being" a minister of Jesus Christ.

The young man instructed by the writers of Proverbs is admonished to seek wisdom, to be humble, to resist laziness, to be holy, and calm-tempered. He is instructed in relationships with women, children, parents, and his wife. He is to have an integrity of life that is reflected in business, home, the wider community, and his neighbors. He is to be gracious towards those who oppose him, avoid excess in eating and drinking, and seek advice from the wise. There is much to learn about how to speak wisely, and the need to obtain discernment and a single-minded devotion to God. The young man in the later chapters, at least, appears to be the one who will come to rule over Israel, and so there is advice about conducting state affairs and warfare. We will want to reframe the teaching of Proverbs to reflect the differences between its patriarchal society and our more egalitarian and gender-equal one, but this is not insurmountable.

The minister who lacks understanding of this or that theologian, or is ignorant of a particular period of church history; who lacks proficiency in the biblical languages or a grounding in philosophy will probably survive in ministry if they are wise and compassionate and humble. The minister who is not a very powerful preacher, is rather awkward in some pastoral situations, and is neither a great evangelist nor a visionary leader may struggle at times, but if they are wise, of Godly character, and known for being a prayerful person, then they will survive. Such a person is probably the more typical minister than the great leader, powerful preacher, transformative pastor, saintly guide, and effective evangelist that most would aspire to be.

But if the latter lacks wisdom, then despite their great gifting, disaster always lurks in the background.

Our theme overall is ministerial formation through a lens of developing the practices associated with virtue ethics. These practices do not themselves focus on the virtues, but provide the context in which the virtuous life is formed, and something very similar might be said about wisdom. There are certain habits of life that are self-evidently ethical in nature: eschewing adultery, having honest business practices, and being generous-hearted towards enemies, for instance, but much of what characterizes the wise life has a deeper vein of integrity running through it. Single-minded, it begins with the fear of the Lord, with a relationship to God. It is discerning, hard working, and refrains from saying or speaking too much. Above all it is not proud or arrogant, but willing to be instructed, teachable, and disciplined. The foundational ministerial virtue I think is humility, and in Proverbs, this virtue is similarly foundational.

I would even say that the New Testament descriptions of the ministerial life in, for instance, the Pastoral Epistles, make little sense without the background of the Proverbs. The qualities of a bishop or deacon in 1 Timothy 3 reflect the qualities of the wise person in Proverbs: "temperate" and "not a drunkard" (1 Timothy 3:2–3; Proverbs 23:29–35); "an apt teacher" (1 Timothy 3:2; Proverbs 15:23) and not "puffed up with conceit" (1 Timothy 3:6; Proverbs 11:2; 16:18).

Amongst the many accounts of Wisdom Literature as a genre and tradition in Israel,[40] I have chosen Fiddes', not least because his purpose, like mine, is not to lay a foundation by discussing the literature for its own sake, but rather to put it to the use of a wider discourse. The texts primarily are Proverbs, Job, Koheleth (Ecclesiastes), The Wisdom of Jesus Ben Sira (or Ecclesiasticus), and the Wisdom of Solomon. Where the prophetic literature is a call to hear the word of the Lord, Wisdom literature's call is to look at the world around. Now, the prophets often see visions, and the learners in the school of wisdom should listen to their teachers and parents, but the "characteristic cast of mind which persists from the earliest to the latest period of wisdom is one of observing the details and particularities of the human and natural world."[41]

---

40. For instance, Crenshaw, *Old Testament Wisdom: An Introduction*; McKane, *Prophets and Wise Men*; Murphy, *The Tree of Life: An Exploration of Biblical Wisdom Literature*; Noth and Winton, *Wisdom Literature in Israel and the Ancient Near East*; Weeks, *Early Israelite Wisdom*; Whybray, *Wisdom in Proverbs: The Concept of Wisdom in Proverbs 1–9:45*.

41. Fiddes, *Seeing the World and Knowing God*, 12.

The concept of creation in Wisdom Literature is different to that of Genesis 1–3, bent as that is to the story of redemption. In Proverbs, people are created beings, but not shaped by a story of paradise and fall: the "real you" is simply the quotidian you, and so Wisdom lays stress on the flourishing of the human self in its relationship to others and the creation. The material that has survived to form the extant Wisdom literature probably emerged from several social and cultural contexts, and the search for a profession of the wise to accompany the priest and the prophet is probably misguided. "We might then speak of a 'wisdom movement' or 'wisdom mood' rather than a 'wisdom school' (just as I am suggesting a 'late-modern mood' in our present world.)"[42]

Proverbs undoubtedly is influenced by other cultures,[43] but the mechanism for that influence is uncertain. Equally certain is that the editors of this collection of sayings adapted foreign sayings to its own religious convictions. At its heart is the search for *Hokmah*, translated "wisdom," but broadly meaning "the knowledge of what to do." It incorporates learning and intelligence, skills, such as those of an artisan, and the character that is transformed by the education received at the hands of the wise.

Central are sentences that contrast right behavior with erroneous, righteousness with wickedness and wisdom with folly. Some are presented in the early chapters as instructions from a father to his son, and prominent is a narrative that uses two female figures, Wisdom, present at creation and carrying divine authority, and her contrast, the foreign woman, evoking those foreign women who ruled Israel, and led her astray. In Proverbs 1–9 wisdom is essentially the light that enables her followers to stay on the path to life, and in effect "exhortations to live life according to the Torah."[44] Where the Deuteronomist sees the consequences of following or disobeying the Torah on a national scale, Proverbs takes the individual, micro-scale viewpoint. Both assume that the Torah is normative for Israelite life. At its heart, therefore, *Hokmah* is not so much intelligence or theoretical understanding as "right conduct in obedience to the will of God."[45] Wisdom becomes the mediator of revelation (Proverbs 8:1–21) who summons and invites men (Proverbs 9:1–18) to understand the original divine order in creation, albeit available fully to God alone (Job 28).

---

42. Ibid., 18.

43. The parallels between the Egyptian book of the Wisdom of Amenomope and Proverbs 22:17–23:11, for instance, is striking. Cf. Würthwein, "Egyptian Wisdom and the Old Testament."

44. Weeks, "Wisdom in the Old Testament," 26.

45. Goetzmann, "Wisdom," 1028.

Humility

The one who seeks wisdom requires a basic disposition of humility, for this is the stance of the student before their teacher, the disciple before their master. In a church culture that often privileges success over faithfulness, strength of leadership over godly example, this fundamental disposition is sometimes overlooked. In part this is because ministers in training often come now from an already successful career elsewhere, have half a life of experience to offer and often in church leadership. This sometimes breeds a resistance to learning, to being formed afresh for a new calling and reflects the way in which poor practice can be tolerated.

So, Proverbs' emphasis upon humility is significant. Wisdom comes from being reproved by God, changed by him; "My child, do not despise the Lord's discipline or be wary of his reproof, for the Lord reproves the one he loves" (3:11–12) "Those who hate to be rebuked are stupid" (12:1, see also 15:12) but "the wise listen to advice." (12:15). Pride is dangerous: "Before destruction one's heart is haughty but humility goes before honor" (18:12) and "A person's pride will bring humiliation, but one who is lowly in spirit will obtain honor" (29:23 see also 11:2; 16:18–19). "The fool thinks their own way is right" (12:15) but the wise person seeks out those who will offer them counsel, "Without counsel, plans go wrong, but with many advisors they succeed" (15:22). The reward for humility is "riches and honor and life" (22:4) and with it the esteem of others, "Let another praise you, and not your own mouth—a stranger, and not your own lips" (27:2); "Do not be wise in your own eyes; fear the Lord and turn away from evil" (3:7). This humble self-knowledge, open to the transformative power of the Spirit of God to reprove us and resisting proud self-promotion lies as a foundation for the wise life and the ministerial calling. "The fear of the Lord is instruction in wisdom and humility goes before honor" (15:33).

Single-minded

The writer of Proverbs asks his young disciple to "Keep your heart with all vigilance, for from it flow the springs of life. Put away from you crooked speech, and put devious talk far from you. Let your eyes look directly forwards, and your gaze be straight before you. Keep straight the path of your feet, and all your ways will be sure. Do not swerve to the right or to the left;

turn your foot away from evil" (4:23–27). The character that is developed in the minister needs such single-minded focus and direction, arising from "the fear of the Lord" that "is the beginning of wisdom, and the knowledge of the Holy One" that "is insight." (9:10). This single-minded integrity of life will then issue in avoidance of sexual immorality (such as adultery, Proverbs 5, 6:24–35) and moderation in those ways of life that can so easily bring he ministry into disrepute, such as gluttony or drunkenness (Proverbs 23:29–35; 25:16, 27.)

Right Relationships

Two themes especially emerge from Proverbs in the conduct of relationships: how to avoid quarrelsome behavior, and the sustaining of a stable and supportive marriage.

Where the initiative lies with the minister, then quarrels are to be avoided: "Do not quarrel with anyone without cause, when no harm has been done to you" (3:30) and if a dispute seems to be breaking out, then attempt to restrict it as much as is possible, "The beginning of strife is like letting out water; so stop before the quarrel breaks out" (17:14). There may be disputes between others, but do not meddle unnecessarily: "Like someone who takes a passing dog by the ears is one who meddles in the quarrel of another" (26:17). This is also echoed by the writer of the Pastoral Epistles, who recommends that "the Lord's servant must not be quarrelsome" (2 Timothy 2:24) and warning that anyone who does not agree with the teaching given to Timothy "is conceited, understanding nothing, and has a morbid craving for controversy and for disputes about words" (1 Timothy 6:4). Note the link between quarrelling and ignorance in the Pastorals that echoes the theme in Proverbs.

The wise learn how to handle controversy with patience and gentleness, as "a soft answer turns away wrath" (15:1) and to handle arguments discretely: "Argue your case with your neighbor directly, and do not disclose another's secret; or else someone who hears you will bring shame upon you and your ill repute will have no end." (25:9–10). Opponents are to be handled with grace, neither rejoicing at their downfall (24:17–18), nor seeking retribution, "Do not say 'I will do to others as they have done to me; I will repay them back for what they have done,'" (24:29). Rather, as Paul quotes in Romans 12:20, "if your enemies are hungry, give them bread to eat . . ." (25:21–2). The wise minister understands how to cope with controversy, and where possible, avoid it, and at all times seeking the well being of those who will oppose her, will be reminded of Jesus' teaching in the Sermon on the Mount (Matthew 5:44). There is a certain kind of personality that is very zealous for the truth, as they see it, and enjoy nothing better than defending it with vigor. It seems to them quite the holy thing to do, but the writer of Proverbs would disagree. The wise minister will not be tossed here and there by winds of controversial doctrine (Ephesians 4:14), but neither will they enter into unnecessary quarrels, undermining their ministry by a reputation for harshness and anger. "Those who are hot-tempered stir up strife, but those who are slow to anger calm contention" (15:18. See also 29:22).

Anger

Indeed, those controversies are often conducted with anger and loss of temper. It takes but a moment's loss of control, and a harsh or angry word spoken at a leader's meeting or in a pastoral encounter, and trust can be lost. The writer of Proverbs has much to say here. "One who is quick-tempered acts foolishly" (14:17); and "one who has a hasty temper exalts folly" (14:29) but "whoever is slow to anger has great understanding" (14:29), and "is better than the mighty" (16:32). It is best to avoid the company of such people, "Make no friends with those given to anger, and do not associate with hotheads." (22:24). Growing in wisdom means picking the controversies that really matter, and engaging in debate without losing one's temper.

Discernment

Discriminating the urgent from the necessary, the important from the unnecessary, the fleeting from the lasting are all marks of the wisdom which ministry calls for. Proverbs states that "The wise of heart is called perceptive" (16:21) while "sometimes there is a way that seems to be right, but in the end it is the way to death." (16:25). Similarly, "The clever see danger and hide; but the simple go on, and suffer for it." (22:3). The discernment of the wise means that dangers are avoided, shipwreck of faith and ministry perceived long before the rocks are upon them, and thus corrections to the direction made and disaster averted. They see where a close relationship is heading, or where that inability to adjust is ending up. I think of ministers who refused to adjust the length of their sermon, thinking it a sign of the shallowness of faith in their detractors, while in fact, it was a sign of their ineptitude in the skills required for homiletics. It used to be said of such that, while they preached for as long as the famously expansive Dr. Martin Lloyd Jones, they lacked all of the other qualities which made him such a captivating preacher, able to hold a congregation for an hour or more. Others made a cause of things that were only their own opinion, forgetting that "A fool takes no pleasure in understanding, but only in expressing personal opinion" (18:2) while all too many succumb to their own sexual drives, and the attractions of that which seems like honey, but is in fact "bitter as wormwood" (5:4) and instead of keeping their way "far from her," "avoiding the door of her house" (5:8) they give their "honor to another" and their "years to the merciless" (5:9). No, "drink water from your own cistern" is the forthright advice of the writer of Proverbs (5:15–23).

Marriage

Not that marriage is a trouble-free area, though. The most effective of ministries can be shipwrecked by the indulgence and impatience of a spouse. I have heard too often the comment, "if it weren't for his wife, then he would still be in pastorate"; "if it were not for her husband, then she would be able to accomplish more." The writer of Proverbs in his rather patriarchal way identifies the problems with wives, and gives in the closing chapter the picture of the ideal wife. I am not sure I want to prolong these prejudices, except to note that both wives and husbands can quarrel so continually that it is like "continual dripping rain" (19:13; 27:15). For such, the retreat into the study can be the equivalent of the corner of the housetop for the unfortunate in Proverbs (21:9; 25:24). While the writer of Proverbs assigns the blame to the wife (or, alternatively, husband,) who is the contentious one, the wise minister must find a way to address this, or find their ministry hampered and constrained. This is not accomplished by harshness (and men's tendency to resort to violence) but by affection and love, and a willingness to admit that since ministry is costly to all involved in the close family, at least their first calling is to that family. There is wisdom required also on the part of those selecting for ministry, and admitting that, for all the exceptional gifts in evidence, some are ill-suited to ministry because of the choice of partner they made long before a call was sensed. I am enormously grateful that Gill, my wife, knew I was called to ministry before she agreed to marriage, and I knew that her temperament, her own sense of call and faith were able to cope with the challenges. Not that she has ever been the traditional minister's wife, staying at home to act as an unpaid second pastor, except perhaps when our children were very young: she has had her own career as a further education and then university lecturer, held leadership roles in the church we attend and, as far as I recall, never led the women's meeting nor arranged the flowers. Nevertheless, sharing life with a ministerial spouse is demanding, and calls for a certain kind of person to rise to that challenge. It is better to admit that for this couple, ministry will not really flourish, and avoid the distress to themselves and others.

Work Ethic

At least in part, ministerial marriage stresses arise from the sheer expectations of hard work that arise, the loss of privacy as life is lived in the goldfish bowl of the local church, and the way in which unpredictability and availability combine to frustrate well-made plans. The writer of Proverbs has much to say about the lazy. They are "Like vinegar to the teeth and smoke to the eyes . . . to their employers" (10:26); and their ways become overgrown with thorns (15:19; 24:31) They do not plough in season (20:4) and the walls of their vineyards are broken down (24:31) Much is made of their sleeping in bed, and the woeful effects upon their prosperity. "A little sleep, a little slumber, a little folding of the hands to rest, and poverty will come upon you like a robber, and want, like an armed warrior" (24:33–34), a proverb that repeats its earlier version in chapter 6, where the ant is the example to follow, "Go to the ant, you lazybones . . . when will you rise from slumber" (6:6–11).

I think that overwork is probably a more frequently observed besetting sin of ministry than laziness, but the fact remains that the minister, alone and self-determining for much of the time, can easily succumb to laziness. It is not so much that a prolonged after-lunch snooze becomes too-regular a feature of the working day (and with a very late evening the night before, and another anticipated the forth-coming evening, a siesta is perhaps a sensible thing), but that the difficult and unpleasant things are avoided. The difficult relationship is not confronted, even if the visits to the compliant elderly are assiduously carried out; the attractions of the sermon preparation elbow out the difficult demands of administration (or vice versa); while mission and reaching those who are not part of the community is replaced by a mild chaplaincy to the faithful. Yes, the hours are long still, the right people impressed, the aspirations and expectations of managing trustees satisfied, but the hard edge to the call to go the way of the cross is avoided, the demands of courageous ministry replaced by the familiar and safe. The minister has become lazy. It is all talk and no walk, "In all toil there is a profit, but mere talk leads only to poverty" (14:23).

Speech

The minister's voice and language is their most oft-used tool. Losing your voice with laryngitis for a day or so is one thing, but ask any minister who has had to rest their voice for a prolonged period, and they will tell you how disabling and worrying this is. Who am I if I cannot proclaim the gospel, counsel the needy, or give guidance to the lost?

The writer of Proverbs has much to say about lying speech ("it conceals hatred," 10:18; see also 12:17–19, 22) and the babbling of the fool (10:14), but two things in particular are appropriate for ministers. The first is to learn how to not speak, to restrain the tongue and to keep quiet. "When words are many, transgression is not lacking" (10:19); "the prudent are restrained in speech" (10:19) and "Those who guard their mouths preserve their lives, those who open wide their lips come to ruin" (13:3) and "Even fools who keep silent are considered wise, when they close their lips they are deemed intelligent" (17:28). How much ministers need to heed those wise words!

The second theme is the content of that speech, full of wisdom and understanding. Wisdom herself knows that "All the words of my mouth are righteous; there is nothing twisted or crooked in them" (8:8). So, the "mouth of the righteous brings forth wisdom" (10:31) "the tongue of the wise brings healing" (12:18) and "a truthful witness saves lives" (14:25). Under particular rebuke is "the whisperer", the gossip who spreads rumors and strife (18:8).

Careful reading and application of the wisdom encapsulated in the book of Proverbs is able to play a significant role in that growth in godly virtue necessary for the minister, as the practices of pastoral care and leadership are exercised and developed. Such wisdom might be said to lie at the heart of what it is to live as a disciple of Jesus Christ, and it is to the role of exemplary disciple that we turn next.

6

Focused Discipleship

Athanasius prescribed Lenten practices for lay people that were versions of the usual ascetical practices for "the professional" Christians of his day, priests and monks. He understood the need for continuity between "ordinary" and "professional" Christians, because the "relationship should not be one of quality but of degree."[1] A fourth model of ministerial formation is that of focused discipleship, developing, deepening even, what is expected of any follower of Jesus Christ, any person who self-identifies as a Christian. The formation of ministers clearly begins long before they sense a call, the church recognizes that, and proceeds to intentionally form them for Christian ministry. Are ministers called to be people of prayer? So is every believer. Are ministers called to be people of generous hearts? Only because that is how every follower patterns their own life after that of Jesus of Nazareth. Are ministers formed as witnesses to the Jesus Christ? Yes, because every disciple is so to live. Much of what we describe as ministerial formation might be re-framed as discipleship of particular intensity. Indeed, those who would have no truck with a separated and ordained ministry would see ministry in terms of Christian leadership by those who are exemplary disciples, and this, really, the only qualification.

I would argue that there are certain characteristics of ministerial formation that have to do with the unique identity of the minister: their set-apartness so that the whole of life might be focused upon the calling to minister (but then, we should not forget that there are ministers who serve bi-vocationally, and there are formational programmes that are also intentionally bi-vocational) and their role as ministers of word and sacrament, but much of what we recognize as ministerial formation could also be understood as discipleship formation. The character of the minister, their

---

1. Volpe, *Rethinking Christian Identity*, 3.

spiritual disciplines, their role as witness, servant, pastoral carer and enabler of others, all have their roots and richest expression in discipleship. In this regard, much of the life and functioning of ministry is simply exemplary discipleship. We might also note how some aspects of the identity of Christian discipleship might also be seen in those who are committed practitioners of other faiths: Jews will pray, and care for the needy; Hindus will fast, while Moslems see it as essential that alms are given. Each of these practices has a Christian equivalent, which takes a particular expression, or set of expressions, amongst the followers of Jesus Christ.

Volpe asks in her book, "how do we think about Christian identity so that it is meaningful and specific without tying identity to a set of propositions or behaviors that remain precisely the same from one local and historical context to another?"[2] She answers that question by interaction with Kathryn Tanner, Rowan Williams and John Milbank, as contemporaries, together with Gregory of Nyssa, and I begin the exposition of this model of ministerial formation through an account of that argument. Her concern is with Christian formation in continuity with the tradition, and this will find considerable resonance with the forming of ministers within the tradition of the Church, and the specific expression of that universality.

Volpe identifies five themes that can be identified in all three theological accounts: *fluidity* (faithful Christian practice varies from place to place and time to time,) *continuity* with Christian tradition, the way in which identity is constructed is a function of the *imagination* (the neophyte begins to imagine herself as part of the Christian community, as distinct from the world,) and the recognition of considerable *ambiguity* in the theological accounts, for Christianity is not conferred upon us but lived by us, which is *performance*. For Kathryn Tanner, continuity depends upon our continuing participation in becoming disciples, for Williams it is faithfulness to the sources of the tradition (Scripture, creeds, and their interpretation through the ages,) while for Milbank it is much more explicitly the Holy Spirit that ensures continuity.

The corollary for Volpe of an identification of Christian identity is the question of Christian formation. In Williams particularly she observes that the center of Christian faith is an appropriate desire, one that is fixed on God and attentive to the movements of the Holy Spirit (expounded in *The Wound of Knowledge*), but it is in Gregory of Nyssa that she identifies the account of sin and desire that provides the view point from which to capture the landscape, not least because of the way in which he does not separate what we would now call theology and spirituality,

2. Ibid., 4.

> Because the scope of Gregory's thinking covers the now-divided disciplines of theology and spirituality, the way he considers theological topics is not separated from the spiritual practices he finds appropriate to orthodox Christian belief. That is, for Gregory, thinking Christianly, in a way that we would think of as propositional and creedal, is inseparable from a host of practices that we would not consider connected intrinsically to those specific beliefs.[3]

John Colwell and others have argued that the fragmentations we currently face, including that between the academy and the church, between belief and practice and between prayer and study is precisely at the root of much of the current malaise in shallow discipleship and unredeemed individualism. For Gregory the practices that marked Christians were habits of attention, the kind of habits that are required for the performance of Christian identity in the accounts of Tanner, Williams and Milbank. The social forces that shape our desires and in which we are inscribed run counter to the habits of attention that build the desire for God. It was true in Gregory's day and remains so in ours: the Christian life is lived within the love of Christ, a desire ordered to the self-emptying love of God, and which Jesus knew was foreign to the way of the world (remembering his High Priestly prayer in John 17.)

Volpe takes as her starting point the post-liberal theology of George Lindbeck's *The Nature of Doctrine*.[4] Lindbeck describes two opposing approaches to being religious: the cognitive and the experiential-expressive, and finds neither adequate. The first, where propositions determined the meaning of Christian doctrine, was too rigid, while the second, an expressive approach, lacked the necessary connection between a doctrine and its meaning. He replaced both with a cultural-linguistic approach to Christian doctrine that he likened to learning a language, "to interiorize a set of skills by practice and training."[5] It is not learning about a religion that is the primary knowledge, nor "*that* the religion teaches such and such, but rather *how* to be religious in such and such ways."[6] Thus, to the telling of the gospel story is added the power and meaning "as it is embodied in the total gestalt of community life and action."[7] Learning this language brings with it the ability to discriminate intuitively, rather like the grammatical or rhetorical

---

3. Ibid., 10–11.
4. Lindbeck, *The Nature of Doctrine*.
5. Ibid., 35.
6. Ibid.
7. Ibid., 36.

knowledge of the poet. Thus Christian formation is the learning of the skills and language of a new culture, practicing new modes of behavior, not just the acknowledgement of a new set of propositional realities. This habituation, learning the way to live Christianly in the world, involves the skills of narration and imagination: attention to God and the following of Jesus Christ.

Volpe criticizes Lindbeck precisely at this point. His scheme seems to suggest that the new acquisition of skills and language to become habituated to the way of being Christian fills an empty vacuum, a vacant center, but for the ancient catechists this was not the case. They understood that the soul was already habituated to a different way of life: sinful and defective, the soul was not ordered towards desire for God, but elsewhere. Thus becoming a disciple involves a "restructuring of the soul's desire,"[8] and the recognition that the formation of disciples takes place within a secular culture that continues to socialize and shape the developing believer, even as the story and practices of the faith continue to run counter to it. Volpe argues that attention to the role of desire is vital if Christian formation is to be understood, and criticizes Tanner at this point for her failure to address this question.[9]

For Kathryn Tanner and for Rowan Williams Christian practice is a form of improvisational performance, and for Tanner, faithful practice "does not include all the same beliefs and practices from one generation to the next, and there are no means by which we might ascertain which of those beliefs and/or practices ought to remain the same."[10] Not that every belief will change, but that a new arrangement of practices and beliefs are negotiated in community with each new generation. Thus, the individual disciple, in Tanner's account, listens respectively to the accounts given around the table, where the voices from present and past are heard, then comes to her own conclusion. What is lacking is any notion of a Magisterium, a teaching office that carries authority, and while this is inimical to Tanner's approach, Volpe argues that it is necessary, and turns to MacIntyre to show how an account of tradition helps. Discipleship, as ministry, is not a matter of choosing from a range of practices and beliefs and individually creating something that somehow coheres, but locating oneself in a tradition. It involves not simply discrimination, but also obedience.

Where Tanner sees Christian tradition as something that arises from cultural materials, and free from the authority of the community of practice,

---

8. Volpe, *Rethinking Christian Identity*, 20.
9. Ibid., 38.
10. Ibid., 31.

MacIntyre conceives of tradition as an inheritance that is passed on as its practitioners participate in the practices of that tradition. It is as they share in those practices that desire is formed, expressed in the virtues. Volpe argues that Tanner's failure to give an account of Christian formation fatally injures her account of what it is to live as a Christian.

> It is not merely a matter of learning the story, but learning how to live in the light of that story, coming to understand its significance for us and for the world. . . . Making the kinds of judgments Tanner sees as indispensable for Christian faith depends on knowing one's place in the story and being able to discern the meaning of the narrative for our thinking and action.[11]

Turning to Rowan Williams, Volpe shows how he presents a more effective description of what it is to be formed as a Christian, and central to that vision is the notion of taking time, and that we understand who we are as Christians (our identity) only provisionally: our identity is always under construction as we attempt to make sense of who or what we are. This making sense is offered in a community of common interest, and is about learning to direct oneself towards God. The results are transformed social relationships, and a love that does not seek its own good but the well-being of others. This is precisely and most fully seen in Christ, and thus one follows Christ as one is drawn into God's love.

For Williams, the performance of Christian identity is, first, narration of the story that finds its richest description in the Eucharist.[12] Here we understand that God's grace is gift, and so we seek to transform the world into a community of gift and sharing. The identities of both individual Christians and the community they inhabit come together here. It is secondly, a response to God's initiative, through human participation in God. It is as we take time and make sense that we grow in Christian discipleship, and grow into the image of Christ. The process of growth in likeness to Christ that Williams identifies, and which Volpe approves of, is traced by Williams in *The Wound of Knowledge*.[13] This is the conversion of desire, a process that is also shaped by the reality of sin.

Desiring God involves an opening up to the Other, of taking a risk, of being receptive to the object of desire. We shall say more of this when we come later to discuss the spiritual formation of the minister, but here we

---

11. Ibid., 51.

12. For Williams, the Christian seems more like Michel de Certeau's *raconteur* than Tanner's builder—the *bricoleur* of Pierre Bourdieu. See Certeau, *The Practice of Everyday Life*, 80–82.

13. Williams, *The Wound of Knowledge*.

simply note that this transformation of desire is not something especially ministerial, but rather the character of discipleship for any who seek to follow Jesus.

> The conversion of desire from the inclination to control to the attitude of receptivity that characterizes transformed desire involves the development of the same habits of attention that make conversation fruitful: the willingness to take time and to forego explanation. To talk about the transformation of desire is thus to talk about the transformation of habits that give shape to everyday life . . . transforming desire involves cultivating a vision of the world that orientates desire towards its proper object: God.[14]

Volpe's third conversation partner in her attempt to articulate what it is to be a disciple is John Milbank. His contribution, she argues, is giving greater attention to the God-givenness of Christian identity. Although Milbank does not articulate an account of formation, his complex account of the nature of the Christian life provides some hints. Milbank's thoroughly post-modern theology rejects Kantian epistemology, with its refusal to accept there is any possibility of knowledge about God, and develops a notion of living by participation in God through the indwelling of the Holy Spirit.

Milbank contrasts the ontology of peace with the ontology of violence; the way of God and the way of the world. The ontological priority we presume, be it peace or violence, will inform our imagination and our practice. As we narrate the story of peace, instantiated by forgiveness, we re-imagine our place in the universe and develop responses appropriate to that place.[15] "*Poesis* is the work of (re)narrating and constructing the counter-history and in so doing performing the counter-ethics and thereby instantiating the counter-ontology."[16] Volpe finds once again, as with Tanner and with Williams, that Milbank pays insufficient attention to the question of the formation of the Christian. In order to rectify this lack, she turns to Gregory of Nyssa.

Simply put, Gregory describes the soul as linking memory and imagination to the body. The soul requires shaping and purification, and for Gregory ascetic practice trains humans for participation in God. This

---

14. Volpe, *Rethinking Christian Identity*, 70.

15. "For if forgiveness alone, a gratuitous self-offering beyond the demands of the law, reflects virtue then this is because virtue itself as charity is originally the gratuitous, creative positing of difference, and the offering to others of a space of freedom, which is existence." Milbank, *Theology and Social Theory*, 416.

16. Ibid., 114.

endless movement into the divine is situated on a broader horizon than initial catechesis, as formation continues throughout the life of the individual. The soul is intended to reflect the divine brightness, to reflect God, and so, empowered by the indwelling Spirit, we tend the soul so that it performs this function.

Without asceticism, the constant discipline of resisting the passions, and the grace of God, we are subject to sinful passivity. Gregory pays attention to the quality of those activities that enable us to properly receive the grace of God (whereas Milbank focuses on the active receptivity to the gift of God.) Sin affects the ability of the soul to reflect God's activity, so ascetic practice is required to clear the soul to function as a mirror to God's glory, while it is the work of the Holy Spirit to re-orientate the soul towards God. It is likened to a mirror: the Spirit orientates the mirror towards its object, God, and the practices shine the surface, so that it properly reflects the light.[17]

The process of attention to the things of God–to beauty–increases perception and draws the soul to participate in that beauty, and thus increases the desire to attend to God. The practices (for Gregory, ascetical practices, such as abstaining from sexual activity, or fasting,) increase the desire, and thus, to use other spiritual language, the soul ascends. "Imitation, learning Scripture, and participating in the practices of the community are essential to the display of divine life commensurate with being in the image of God."[18] This process of deification is an infinite one, the desire that is rightly orientated towards God is never satisfied, as each insight into God's beauty incites the desire for more. In Gregory's thought, ascetical practices, attention to Scripture and, thirdly, the formation of a Christian imagination that contemplates God through understanding the doctrine of God.[19]

I have used Volpe's *Rethinking Christian Identity* as a way into this model of ministerial formation as discipleship because she engages with both contemporary theologians, working in our contemporary culturally post-modern context, but also returns to the fathers in the person of Gregory of Nyssa. Discipleship, from this reading, is both a work of God's grace, through the Holy Spirit's empowering presence (in other words, gift,) as celebrated by both Milbank and Williams, and also it is a process whereby we actively seek to deepen our attentiveness to God, through participating in the practices of the faith, such as reading Scripture, prayer, fasting and so forth, so that our desires are transformed or re-orientated towards their

---

17. Gregory of Nyssa, "On Virginity."
18. Volpe, *Rethinking Christian Identity*, 160.
19. In Gregory's "Catechetical Oration"; *Homilies on the Song of Songs*.

true goal, which is God. In this way discipleship is a recovery of the image of God within us, becoming more like the supreme Image of God, that is, Jesus Christ. This happens within the community of those who are also seeking to be disciples in the church. We have seen how that community learns the narrative of the faith and re-imagines its place within that continuing narrative through the Eucharist, where we learn the *habitus* of receiving, ever anew, the gift of Christ. I have argued elsewhere that this orientation towards the Other, through facing Christ, is a means of renewing the person afflicted by toxic shame.[20] Here I want to suggest that orienting the life of the believer towards God is a process of re-orientation of desires, accomplished within the community of the faithful. This should be primarily the local congregation, but the shallowness of much that passes for the church means that such discipleship formation probably will take place in other, or smaller, more intentional groups, such as some developed by neo-monastic movements or new religious orders.[21]

Such formation must have begun long before a call to ministry is sensed, and intentional ministerial formation commenced, and will continue long after any sense of intentional ministerial formation has ceased. It is the journey of the soul, the shaping of a Christian life after the renewal of the image of its creator, a deep following of Jesus Christ and his way through the practices of the Christian faith and church, that enables the minister not just to be formed as a particular professional, but rather as the man or woman of God that might offer authentic ministry to the church and world. It lies at the heart of what is termed character, and is closely allied to the area of formation that is spiritual. The practices of ministry, its functions or tasks, flow from here alone, or they become mere religiously colored exercises in social work or community development, public entertainment or personal individual self-realization. The minister is first and foremost an authentic disciple of Jesus Christ, growing in the likeness of Christ and reflecting in increasing beauty and grace, the *Imago Dei*.

The *Telos* of Ministry

Finally, in this exploration of ministry as focused discipleship, we turn again to the question of the purpose of ministry, its aim and vocation, and its relation to the whole people of God. We shall do so in conversation particularly with John Calvin.

---

20. Goodliff, *With Unveiled Face*, 99–100.

21. For instance, the work of cell groups in *The Order for Baptist Ministry* function with such a process in mind, if not always in reality.

Sooner or later any reflection upon ministry will need to grapple with the question of its status in regard to the whole people of God. At the one extreme is ministry as an elite, separated order, set apart for a role that incorporates a priestly function unavailable to the laity. Into such a camp would fall Orthodoxy, The Roman Catholic Church and, to a lesser extent, Anglicanism (as a form of reformed Catholicism). For this expression of church, presidency at the central act of worship, the Eucharist, is reserved for those ordained to the priesthood (and with anxiety about apostolic succession, no extension of such recognition between Catholicism, Orthodoxy and Anglican Orders.) Certain other sacramental acts are likewise unavailable to those who have not been ordained.

At the other end of that spectrum are churches that so emphasize an understanding of "the priesthood of all believers" (which is often misconstrued as the priesthood of *every* believer) that there is little depth to any distinction between those who lead and those who are led. In some cases, there is a thoroughgoing rejection of ordination, while elsewhere, ordination is a form of "passing out parade" to mark the end of initial training at theological college, with little ontological or sacramental significance. At its worst, this leads to an "anybody can" approach to ministry, that diminishes the significance of call, vocation, formation and office.

Baptist churches tend to gravitate to this latter end of the spectrum, although my own research into the understanding of ordination held by those who actually practice it, suggests that the extreme expression of ministry, as having no sacramental or ontological significance, is waning.[22] It has been replaced by a widespread conviction that ministry is a form of inclusive representation of the whole people of God, but allied to a strong form of vocational separation expressed in ordination as a sacramental act that conveys what it represents: empowerment for ministry.

Here, the priesthood of all believers is understood as what it actually expresses: that the whole people of God are a priesthood, with uninhibited access to God's grace in prayer and Eucharist, but that does not mean that everybody is a presbyter ("priest" in Anglican terms–itself a contraction of the Medieval English prester, from presbyter, or "minister" in Baptist and Free Church understanding.) There remains a separated (or called out) ministry of pastoral leadership, requiring formation and recognition by the church (local or wider), and which normally undertakes certain roles, without accruing to itself exclusive rights. So, while usually a Baptist service of Communion, or The Lord's Supper (the Eucharist) will be presided over by the minister in the church, it is not exclusively the preserve of the

---

22. Goodliff, *Ministry, Sacrament and Representation*, 86, 151–52.

minister. Other, non-ordained and appointed people can preside on occasions. Indeed, some Baptist ministers, and their churches would ensure that at least once a year the president at the Table would be a lay person, simply to signify that ordination does not convey a power in terms of transformation of the elements (variously understood), such that without ordination of the president, the Lord's Supper is invalid. This is far from the "anybody can" approach of others, as the appointed person would have some recognized office in the church (as deacon, Church Secretary, or the like), but the point being is that it is not the minister who delegates the responsibility, but Church Meeting—the whole church gathered—from which the minister themselves derives their appointment. Similarly, presidency at the occasional offices of baptism, funerals, infant dedications and weddings would normally be the responsibility of the minister, or ministers if the church calls more than one, as would be the preaching office, but not necessarily so. Others can take such services, and on occasion, will do so.

In neither Lutheranism, where the doctrine of the priesthood of all believers originated, nor in Calvinism or Presbyterianism, were the roles associated with the office of pastor or the ministry of word and sacrament available to simply anybody, as in today's radical anti-clericalism. All the main historic traditions have a recognized and set-apart ministry. To argue, for instance, that Calvin's opposition to the elitism of the Late-Medieval monasticism resulted in a rejection of ministry is mistaken. What was opposed was the restricted vision of the holy life confined to the monastery. In its place was a vision of the holy life for all God's people and a recovery of the formed discipleship for every believer.

Matthew Boulton has argued that the basis of Calvin's quarrel with monasticism in *The Institutes of the Christian Religion* is an endorsement of an ancient form of monastic life, understood as an "immersive path of practical formation."

> For Calvin, monastics are mistaken only insofar as they make elite, difficult, and rare what should be ordinary, accessible, and common in Christian communities: namely, whole human lives formed in and through the church's distinctive répertoire of disciplines, from singing psalms to daily prayer to communing with Christ at the sacred supper.[23]

Calvin views the ancient monastic life as one of disciplined formation. It is not as an end in itself, but rather formative preliminaries by which the monks "prepared themselves for greater tasks," namely the leadership

---

23. Boulton, *Life in God: John Calvin, Practical Formation and the Future of Protestant Theology*, 13.

of the church. Calvin writes, "pious men customarily prepared themselves by monastic discipline to govern the church, that thus they might be fitter and better trained to undertake so great an office."[24] His criticism is reserved for his present-day monasticism's separation from the whole body of the church. "Our monks are not content with that piety to which Christ enjoins his followers to attend with unremitting zeal. Instead they dream up some new sort of piety to meditate upon in order to become more perfect than all other people."[25]

The purpose of the monastic life, therefore, was consistent with the "duties of piety" that apply to every disciple, bar none.

> a shepherd's practical piety should never surpass the capacities of his flock. "Augustine requires a kind of monasticism," he writes, "which is but an exercise and aid to those duties of piety enjoined upon all Christians" (*Institutes* 4.13.10). Far from a special, independent class of Christian virtuosos, these monks were taught to serve so that "by their example they may shed a light" for other Christians in their own education and development, the better to help "preserve the unity of the church" (*Institutes* 4.13.10). Accordingly an ancient monk's piety was typical and accessible, not extraordinary.[26]

Calvin rejects a "double Christianity" that creates a two-tiered ladder of Christian perfection. While he commends the ancient monastic life (as he sees it: the historical accuracy of his understanding is besides the point here) he does not want a return to it. Instead he believes that the same piety and discipline exercised in everyday life is more in keeping with Christian humility and responsibility. In fact, the ancient monastic life did not go far enough, for Calvin. It did not exhibit its exemplary model widely enough. "Calvin is no son of monasticism, but he is close kin, and the family resemblance is striking."[27]

> Is this an attack on monasticism in its ancient form? It is, and it strikes at the very root of the idea that in order to pursue Christian perfection, an individual or group of disciples should set themselves alone, and therefore apart from common human life . . . But at the same time, Calvin grounds the attack in a profound affirmation of the basic formative project undertaken by the ancient cenobitic (i.e., communal) monks: to live lives of

---

24. Calvin, *Institutes*, 4.13.8.
25. Ibid., 4.13.10.
26. Boulton, *Life in God*, 14–15.
27. Ibid., 24.

comprehensive religious discipline, immersed in 'prayers, readings, and discussions' such that even the most mundane, everyday activity—"diet, speech, clothing, countenance"—is formed by love (*Institutes* 4.13.9). Far from condemning this kind of life, Calvin commends it, not only for am elite class of spiritual savants, but even for every Christian man and woman without exception, since all properly live under God's single "rule of life" revealed in Scripture.[28]

At its heart is an argument over formation, Christian *paideia*. Monasticism was a disciplined programme of *paideia*, which Calvin wants to apply to everyday life. He and the ancient monastic fathers agree, largely, upon the proper paideutic répertoire: scriptural study, daily prayer and worship, psalm singing, moral accountability, the Lord's Supper, and so on. Whereas the ancient vision was a retreat to the desert, so that it might become a city of God, Calvin wants to make the city of Geneva a "desert" where spiritual formation and intimacy with God, and ultimately union with Christ, is forged in the midst of life. His vision is of the whole city a kind of monastery, its citizens enrolled in a city-wide programme of Christian *paideia* of practical formation. It is the whole city gathered at the Lord's Table, and sitting under the word, that is to constitute the cloistered life.

Applying this to the purpose of ministry, then, I argue that while the initial formation of ministry needs to take some concentrated form within a community, albeit one set in the midst of the world, not apart from it, the goal, the *telos* of this ministry is not to create a spiritual elite, a clerical class that is somehow set apart for a holier form of life. Rather, it is to be the exemplification of the way of life that all are called to, and to which every Christian disciple should aspire. Daily prayer and Scripture reading is not to be the privilege of ministers only, but the expectation of all followers of Christ. So far, so good. Protestantism tends to reject the daily attendance at mass that is offered to Roman Catholics, even if in Anglicanism there remains in some places the mid-week Communion on a Thursday morning, and on Feast days. However, more could be offered. For a period of years at the Baptist church where I first served as minister in the 1980s, we held a mid-week Communion Service, attended faithfully by a few. More could be made of accountability groups to deepen faithful discipleship (indeed, even amongst those expected to exemplify this, ministers themselves, this is rare) and an integration of daily work into a holistic understanding of calling and discipleship.

---

28. Ibid., 19.

Those who criticize this democratization of the spiritual life will point out how far short of the idealized rule of life many, if not most, of Geneva's citizens fell. The Genevan consistory records tell of the many ingenious reasons why this or that citizen did not attend church on this or that occasion. Even in the heady, apocalyptic atmosphere of Calvin's Geneva, discipleship was lax. Indeed, it is this reality, applied to sixteenth century England that inspired the early Baptists and other Congregationalists to find a middle way between a clerical and heroic elitism on the one hand (the monastic model removed from the cloister), and an unachievable level of piety of everyone set as the Reformed model, by preferring a gathered church of the disciplined believer, set apart from, and called out of, a more mundane Christendom. In today's more secular (or post-secular, perhaps) world, the context in which the gathered church congregates may not be a bastardized Christianity, but a pagan and anti-Christian world, more akin to the culture that predated the Constantinian settlement in its antipathy to the church. However, the ideal remains, if itself considerably watered down, that in the believer's church —gathered out of the world, but set in its midst as a witness to Christ—every member is to fully live the pious and disciplined life. The minister, then, is formed to lead this community, but formed in a life of discipleship that is no different to that of every other believer, apart from the expectation that she or he will exemplify it in a focused way. Steve Holmes has argued that the Baptist way of being church, far from abolishing a distinctive priesthood for the people of God comprising only those who have been ordained to a life set apart for ministry, abolishes instead the laity, "if we have to work with the religious-secular distinction, I think a Baptist vision of the church abolishes the secular life."[29] In its idealized form, Baptist life is much more a commitment to a community that echoes a "religious" life, with solemn vows made in baptism than a parochial model (either Catholic or Anglican) allows. The calling out and setting apart of the Christian from her community echoes the setting apart and calling out of a man or woman to the priesthood in more parochial or Christendom ecclesiologies. This essentially re-shapes how we think of ministry as Baptists, for if the whole community is set apart through baptism, how can there be any absolute ontological distinction between the ordained and others, other than focus of life and distinctive way of being as one whose focus is the church's well-being? Baptists believe in ordination and the setting apart of its ministers in this way: as those called from amongst the gathered community to set before it the Word, administer the sacraments, offer leader-

---

29. Steve Holmes, post "Abolishing the Secular Life," http://steverholmes.org.uk/blog/?p=7413 (accessed November 29, 2016).

ship where welcomed and express in their own way of life, character and discipleship, what is expected of every other baptized believer.

The need for exemplars is clear, for there are attendant dangers in the life of discipleship, excesses that distort the life of following Christ and Boulton explores three of these distortions particularly associated with Calvin, although there are more than these. Calvin's doctrine of providence, the perception that in the events of everyday life we discern God's hand, can lead to a quietism that accepts the human condition without attempting to alleviate suffering or hardship. After all, what is given by God's providential hand can seem to be negated if we kick against the traces. At its worst (and Calvin was a creature of his time in this) the poor can be encouraged to simply accept their lot, and thus harden social inequality. Discernment is required to understand when to accept a situation, and when to challenge it, and the work of theological and spiritual guidance explored elsewhere in this book is vital in this regard.

A second danger is masochism, a search for suffering in an attempt to identify with Christ's sufferings. Certainly much of mediaeval monastic mysticism colluded with this in its attempts to mortify the flesh, and one only has to think of, for instance, of Calvin's near-contemporary, Ignatius Loyola (1491?–1556) after whose conversion in 1521, his first instinct was to imitate as closely as possible the austerities described in the lives of the saints, until his health was dangerously compromised. With a growing maturity, especially in discerning the source of the spiritual consolation and despair (desolation in Ignatian terms) that visited him, he found his vocation. In the eleven months at Manresa, following his leaving of sword and dagger on the altar at the nearby monastery at Montserrat in 1522, he moved from joy to acute suffering, until illumination came and he was imbued with the confidence and serenity that never left him, culminating in "the final transfiguring moment" on the bank of the river Cardoner when "the eyes of his mind were opened and he received an understanding of many things, spiritual as well as matters concerning faith and theology, with such enlightenment that these things seemed altogether new."[30]

In many ways Ignatius' life followed a pattern similar to Calvin. After his period of spiritual awakening he studied theology (at Alcala, 1526–27; Salamanca, 1527–28; and Paris, 1528–35) before embarking on his life's work through forming *The Society of Jesus*. Similarly, Calvin studied theology and law at Paris, Orleans and Bourges, although this was before his conversion to the Reformation cause in 1533–34. His first *Institutes* were published shortly afterwards, in 1536, but it was the 1539 edition, designed

---

30. Ivens, "The Catholic Reformation 1. Spain I. Ignatius Loyola," 358.

as a kind of catechism for the faithful, that we know as the Genevan work, *Institutio Christianae Religionis*. The English translation, *The Institutes of the Christian Religion* is unfortunate. It sounds like the work of theology that it is often assumed to be, but *Religionis* might better be rendered "innate piety", or more elegantly, something akin to spirituality. It is this sense that we still use when we talk about "the Religious Life", meaning those who live as monks, nuns, or friars. In other words, rather than Benedictine Religious, or Franciscan Religious, Calvin is universalising this way of life and applying it to all Christians, as we have seen above. Since elsewhere in Calvin's sermons, he translates the Greek *paideia* into Latin for his commentary, and uses the word *institutionem*, we might actually translate the title of the *Institutio* as "Training in Christian Piety," or Christian Discipleship. Read in this way, the *Institutes* seem somewhat closer to The Spiritual Exercises (and not least in the debt both works owe to Scripture, especially the Gospels.)

At the same time, Ignatius was writing the notes for those who guide retreatants, a work that we now know as *The Spiritual Exercises*, with a similar aim: the formation of a holy life. On opposite sides of the Reformation divide, they nevertheless had similar aims, both were inspired administrators and leaders, and both gave rise to movements that have endured and works of Christian theology and guidance that continue to be very influential.

Neither work attributes growth in spiritual depth and vitality to severe physical mortification or an especially ascetic life. Masochism has no place in these versions of the Christian life, and "taking up the cross" is an experience that is common to humanity in its suffering and death.

A third danger identified by Boulton is misanthropy, an unwarranted despair at the level and ubiquity of human depravity. This is often seen as a characteristic of Calvin's theology, with its emphasis upon the utter depravity of the human soul. However, it is not a doctrine of despair but of hope, since human nature has all the potential to be something glorious and good, created as it is by God, and while Calvin has a serious view of the extent of sin, so that there is no room for any self-effort to be saved (perhaps countering the idea of gaining merit by works of penance familiar in popular Catholic religion), he also has a profound expectation of the thoroughness of sanctification, and our restoration to the divine communion. All is grounded in Calvin's Christology, since the true human being is Jesus Christ, and it is after his likeness that are being refashioned through the Spirit as we participate in Christian *paideia*: 'a disciple is a ruined masterpiece, but a masterpiece nonetheless, and one currently in the process of being restored by the master himself.'[31]

---

31. Boulton, *Life in God*, 205.

Once again we see how the modern divide between theology and practice, between theology and spirituality, is unthinkable for Calvin. Doctrine is always already practical, its purpose to form Christian disciples in a practical *paideia*. Its location is the Christian community, rather than the academy, and we again note that ministerial formation is primarily a function of the church not the university. At least, the problem with the university is that it undertakes its work separate to the church, and theology can be an independent field of human enquiry, with little relationship to the God who is the object of its enquiry. Ministerial formation in the life of the church (both in its communal and intensive location at a seminary or theological college, and in its extensive location in the body of the church and the wider world) has as its aim not the creation of a spiritual elite, those formed to run the church, but rather, through (at least in part) those it forms as ministers, the formation of the whole people of God as disciples and witnesses to Christ. Never an end in itself, ministerial formation prepares those for whom amongst their primary tasks (perhaps, the prime task) is Christian *paideai*. As Paul puts it, those gifts of ministry–some apostles, some prophets, some evangelists, some pastor-teachers–are purposed to equip the saints for the work of ministry, "until all of us come to the unity of the faith and of the knowledge of the Son of God, to maturity, to the measure of the full stature of Christ" (Eph 4:13) and "must grow up in every way into him who is the head, into Christ . . ." (Eph 4:15).

Here is the repost to those who wish to remove all intense formation, all set-apart ministry, in favor of a supposed-egalitarianism. If there is any spiritual elite, it is the whole church, but achieving this is the work of ministry under the hand of the Spirit. In part, this is a moral growth, as Paul suggests when he says that licentiousness, greed and so forth is not "the way you learned Christ" (Eph 4:20) but much more it is to "clothe yourselves with the new self, created according to the likeness of God in true righteousness and holiness" (Eph 4:24).

7

Ministerial Formation as Apprenticeship

So prevalent has the collegiate and residential model of ministerial formation become that we forget that much ministerial formation in the past and currently elsewhere in the world adopted a model that emphasizes apprenticeship as its foundational concept. Ministers-in-training learn their trade by working closely with an experienced minister, seeing what they do and how they do it. This has been an important means of formation for Anglican priests for over a century, at least, where much of the skills and habits of ministry—many of the practices, we would say— are learned with a training incumbent who shapes their work in the first three or four years after theological college and ordination as a deacon. The value of this model over the more "distant" concept of mentoring for Newly Accredited Ministers among British Baptists lies in the close proximity between the training incumbent and their assistant curate: they are co-located in the same benefice, even if there are multiple congregations within a group of parishes which that united benefice comprises. There is room for both some independence to develop as well as close supervision of ministry when necessary. By contrast, for Baptists, the mentor, by definition in another church, albeit one normally not too far distant from the newly-ordained minister, can only really see and hear of their mentee's progress second-hand, and mostly through the medium of what that minister chooses to reveal.

The exception for Baptists is found in those, admittedly few, churches where there are sufficient funds to call more than one minister, and where there is a vision to appoint an inexperienced minister with, at least partly, the purpose of contributing to their continuing formation, and to forego the more immediate value of either an experienced second minister, or, more likely, a specialist in form of a youth minister, evangelist or children and community worker. The traditional training church, which would call a succession of men and women from college to a three year "curacy" under an experienced and gifted senior minister are now almost extinct. Almost universal, therefore, for a newly ordained Baptist minister is some form of sole charge in a church that probably aspires to a more experienced minister, but lacks the resources or kudos to attract such a one. More often than not, this leads to an unsatisfactory initial experience of continuing formation for the minister concerned, the context lacking the breadth of opportunity to give a wide experience of ministry; or the lay leadership of the church so controlling as to be suspicious of an experienced minister "muscling-in" on their areas of power and control, with unhappy struggles ensuing; or the church lacking the will to embrace change, with the consequence that the minister becomes frustrated at their inability to bring about any meaningful transformation of the life and mission of the congregation.

Even where there has been a deliberate apprenticeship model adopted, the lack of any meaningful training in team work or how to manage trainee relationships has sometimes rendered the opportunity ineffectual, with Regional Ministers or Superintendents called in to resolve tensions between senior and junior colleagues. Unrealistic expectations of equivalence in responsibility on the part of the trainee, and an over-bearing dominance by the trainer out of concern that, since they will continue to lead this church long after their trainee has moved to another church, things need to be done their way, combine to make the value of being in a training context almost overwhelmed by the relational struggles that ensue.

However, even if for Baptists the model is fraught with difficulty (as for the Anglicans also, if truth be told), the value of an apprenticeship model should not too readily be ignored. A week-by-week support in the shaping and delivery of sermons (where the trainee is allowed such frequency of opportunity); reflection upon pastoral cases and missional opportunities; and the freedom to experiment and, perhaps, fail in the attempt, all are of significant value in the shaping and formation of an inexperienced minister in their first pastorate.

The most prevalent context for apprenticeship schemes in ministry lie in gap year models for those exploring full time ministry of some kind. The large evangelical Anglican church in central London, All Souls, Langham Place, offers The All Souls Apprentice Scheme "to provide a more intensive training in gospel ministry for those showing leadership potential."[1] This combination of hands on experience and Biblical and theological training runs for one or two years, September to July and is self-funding. The large independent evangelical church in central Cardiff, Highfields Church, also

1. All Souls, www.allsouls.org (accessed June 2015).

runs a small apprenticeship scheme. Its pastor, Dave Gobbett, served as an apprentice at Christchurch Mayfair, while completing the Cornhill Training Course prior to working with UCCF and followed this with ministerial training at Oak Hill Theological College. At Christ Church, Mayfair, London (an evangelical Anglican church planted in 2001, with its roots in the St Helen's Bishopsgate stream of conservative evangelical Anglicanism) the apprenticeship scheme lasts for two years and seeks to develop godliness of character, skills in ministry and knowledge of Scripture. It is part of the 9:38 scheme associated with Cornhill Training Course, The Proclamation Trust and Oak Hill Anglican theological college: all of which are conservative in their evangelicalism. Other large churches within this stream that have run similar apprenticeship schemes include Chessington Evangelical Church; Duke Street Baptist Church, Richmond (a church, despite its name, that is actually rather Presbyterian in character); Dundonald, Wimbledon (another Anglican Evangelical church plant from 1990 that works outside the parish system); International Presbyterian Church (IPC), Ealing; St James Muswell Hill and St Nicholas Sevenoaks. It does not take too much research to discover that the location of these large evangelical congregations have a similarly wealthy catchment, and some would hold to an understanding of the faith with which I would not wish to be too closely associated. For instance, it is hard to find women on their staff fulfilling roles other than "Women's ministry facilitator" or PA to the lead pastor (none of these churches seem to have teaching or leading women ministers: IPC Ealing has no women elders, for instance, and all of St James' Muswell Hill's vicars are male, while women administrate, run under-fives' work or work as PAs; and a similar distribution of roles is present at St Nicholas, Sevenoaks—four clergy, all male, and women serving as pastoral or parish assistants). A very full description of the apprenticeship scheme (called Associates) run by the conservative evangelical Anglican church, Lyonsdown, New Barnet,[2] in North London gives a flavor of the work, the training and the theology of the typical context of these apprenticeships.[3] Both Hebrew and Greek are taught, the devotional structure requires the use of the M'Cheyne daily Bible reading course, "all staff and associates are encouraged to set aside a fixed daily period for serious reading of a 'heavy' theological book (for example by writers such as Jonathan Edwards or John Owen)" and the close proximity of Oak Hill and St Helen's Bishopsgate colors the theological

---

2. As Holy Trinity, New Barnet it controversially refused to pay any of its Parish Share to the Diocese of St. Albans in 2004 in protest at the appointment of Dr. Jeffrey John as Dean of St. Albans, simultaneously not expecting the Church Commissioners to pay for the Vicar's stipend.

3. Lyonsdown, www.lyonsdown.org (accessed November 29, 2016).

perspective. The website in 2015 indicated that all five of this church's current staff team were former Associates. This clearly indicates the success of bringing younger people through a system that shapes them for ministry of a certain character, but also perhaps a narrowness of theology and paranoia about the wider Church of England that is characteristic of this strand of Anglicanism.

There is also a cultural familiarity with the concept of this kind of apprenticeship. Many of the members of these churches who work in professional contexts would be very familiar with internships, with which these apprenticeships have a good deal in common.

Aware, then, that this apprenticeship model is widely adopted by large, conservative evangelical churches in affluent areas of the South East of England, with a church polity that I believe devalues the ministry of women, and a theology that would no doubt reject some of my beliefs as unbiblical, it might seem an unpropitious model to advocate. However, the fact that this stream of churches has enthusiastically adopted the model should not prevent the wider church from also exploring it, without adopting wholesale the theology of these churches.

Furthermore, it is sympathetic to a rediscovery of the value in apprenticeships after decades of relentless widening of access to universities, with the result that some who have pursued a less-than rewarding undergraduate degree, because there was little else to choose from, might have been better suited to a skilled apprenticeship that fitted them with skills and work-experience. Gaining a skill that is in high demand, while earning an income (albeit a low one as befits a trainee) and finding work as a result, looks altogether better than studying for a degree whilst incurring high levels of debt with only unskilled work in the service sector of the economy as a prospect after graduation. Other European economies, and Germany in particular, have valued highly-skilled workers who have been apprenticed in a way that in Britain has been rare. The resulting imbalance in skills and the shortage of, for instance, skilled engineers or IT specialists in the British economy has now been recognized and a fresh drive to establish and recruit to apprenticeships has been evident in recent years.

The kind of apprenticeship model suited to ministry needs to encompass an equally high level of understanding and cognition: a simple apprenticeship model where essentially a set of skills is acquired is unsuited to the intellectual challenge of ministry that this book argues is essential. The tasks of pastoral care, apologetics and exposition of Scripture and faith all require high levels of understanding, but much of the skills element of ministry formation—skills in listening and accompanying, in administration and organization, in leadership and both self-awareness and the understanding of human dynamic—all might be aided when learnt not only in the classroom but also through observing the skilled ministry of a more experienced practitioner.

Let us explore this strand of formation through three of the lenses that have run through this book: Scripture, personal story and art.

It needs to be said that my own sense of being formed for ministry has a strong apprenticeship element to it. Leaving a happy four years as a schoolmaster with a renewed sense of God's call to serve him in pastoral ministry (a call that was first sensed as a teenager in the Anglican parish where I grew up), I did not go straightway to theological college, but was called to the staff of Streatham Baptist Church (everyone referred to it as Lewin Road after the location of its buildings) as a "full-time elder." This was a church in the throes of charismatic renewal, where an eldership had been established in the late-1970s, and to which I was elected in 1980 aged twenty-four years old (which seems to me now, inordinately young— except that we also have ordained ministers at that age elsewhere). With two years watching its minister, Douglas McBain, from the perspective of being on that eldership while working full-time as a schoolmaster, I was thrust into the hurly-burly of full-time ministry as he left the pastorate for a wider "apostolic" ministry: one that evolved into the Baptist Union's Metropolitan Superintendent covering the London Baptist Association a few years later.

Douglas kept a watchful eye on this raw young pastor and living still in the vicinity he often offered good advice, and when it came to my first funeral, took it with me to show me the ropes. Nine months later, the church called Douglas's replacement, and Mike Wood became the senior minister. Once again, the formational process was largely in an apprenticeship model, Mike giving me both close oversight when I needed it, and plenty of space to do and be my own person when not. Thus, when I started at Spurgeon's College after two years as an unaccredited pastor, initially simply to engage with theological education as an independent student, I already had some experience of pastoral leadership and ministry. The following year I became a Baptist Union ministerial student, having succeeded in candidating for accredited ministry through the London Baptist Association, completed the Cambridge Diploma in Religious Studies (the only alternative Spurgeon's College offered to the BA in Theology) and started pastoral studies (such was the structure of training at Spurgeon's in the mid-1980s.) As one of the first couple of church-based students, with my placement at Lewin Road, of course, I continued to learn apprentice-wise under Mike Wood while studying at college.

Such a pattern is far more common today than it was thirty years ago, and the apprenticeship element more common, although by no means ubiquitous. As we saw earlier, my experience of training as a junior member of a team has become increasingly rare, although there are still churches that will call a young man or woman from its membership, and essentially form them from within its own life. The dangers that such formation will be imbalanced or eccentric are profound, with the character of ministry constrained by the emphases of that church and its practices. At Lewin Road I pretty quickly discovered the necessity for engaging in deliverance ministry following a visit from John Wimber and his team at the end of August 1982. Almost as quickly I discovered that most of my older, more experienced, and trained Baptist minister colleagues from surrounding churches seemed to know even less than I, and were sending their cases to me! Only later did I find out that Douglas McBain had been quietly engaging in this ministry for some years while in pastorate, and so his oversight and experience in the background created the safe space for me to learn by experience and some reading. In other regards, Lewin Road was no different to many other churches: there was routine pastoral visiting to do, committees to chair, sermons to write, evangelism, pastoral counselling and management to fulfil. Much was learned at college in all of these areas, but I was essentially already a practitioner (albeit very unskilled) by the time I arrived at college, and so had experience to draw upon and reflect upon.

I do not suggest that this story should become normative for all. I arrived on staff at Lewin Road with two assets that are not available to every ministerial candidate: transferable experience in both Christian leadership (I had led the Youth Fellowship at my Anglican parish church while a sixth-former, and the Christian Union at school also, followed by leadership, including presidency, at the Christian Union at King's College London as an undergraduate) and in my previous career as a teacher; and I had an enquiring mind. To be formed in this way does require a certain innate ability, I think, and perhaps the most successful of people who train in this way will probably do well in a fully college-based mode also. Mixed-mode formation (part college, part participant-church context) is not for the faint-hearted, for it makes huge demands upon the minister-in-training, and there are two groups who will probably benefit from a college-based course: those who are less able pastorally, and those who are very academically able: the mixed-mode formation does not lend itself easily to an academically outstanding outcome. Those who deliberately have set their sights on an academic strand to their ministerial career would be well-advised to be full-time at college.

One great advantage of the apprenticeship model is its dominical precedent. Jesus of Nazareth seems to adopt this model almost exclusively in forming the Twelve, and Mark's Gospel might be described as the story of the apprenticeship of the first disciples as much as it is a passion narrative with an extended introduction. Similarly, Paul seems to have taken younger colleagues under his wing, and in Timothy we have advice to a younger pastor (or is that bishop?) from his mentor, Paul. Certainly, the Twelve seem not to have had prior experience of rabbinical study (unlike Paul, under Gamaliel, before his conversion) nor any kind of "professional education » as religious leaders. Their education and formation was through being with Jesus, seeing what he did, how he did it and then trying this for themselves. In Mark 3:13-19 Jesus chooses the Twelve "to be with him" (3:14) and to be sent out, and following ministry and healings in Galilee, he sends them out two by two (Mark 6:6-13), reporting back to Jesus in Mark 6:30. In the ensuing chapters there is continuing ministry by Jesus, and we suppose, by the disciples, as well as personal formation. For instance, nearing the end of Jesus' ministry, Mark recalls the embarrassing argument over who is the greatest (Mark 10:35-45) and Jesus instructions about servanthood and humility, "whoever wishes to be first among you must be slave of all. For the Son of Man did not come to be served but to serve and to give his life as a ransom for many." (Mark 10:44-45)

Timothy is a protégée of Paul who joins him at Lystra (Acts 16:1-3) and is the son of a Jewish woman who was already a believer and a Greek father. He accompanies Paul through Phrygia and Galatia until they reach the western coast of Asia Minor where they cross into Macedonia and Philippi. There Paul and Silas are imprisoned (Acts 16:16-40) while Timothy seems to have remained free. Further uproar in Thessalonica and a calmer welcome in Beroea until the troublemakers from Thessalonica turned up, led the church to send Paul on his way alone, while Timothy and Silas remained, joining him later in Corinth, recorded in Acts 18:5. Paul stayed in Corinth for eighteen months, and, we assume, Timothy stayed too. We do not hear of Timothy's movements, but we may well assume he travelled with Paul to Jerusalem (Acts 18:22) and then through Galatia to Ephesus. Here, again, Paul stayed for two years (Acts 19:10) and Timothy is mentioned as one of the two helpers who he sends to Macedonia ahead of his anticipated journey to Rome (Acts 19:21-22) while he remains in Ephesus alone. The remainder of Luke's account focuses upon Paul and his last, troubled journey, and we hear no more from Luke in Acts about Timothy.

However, whenever Romans was written, Timothy's greetings are included, he being described as "my co-worker" (Romans 16:21). The context for the writing of Romans is disputed, but the consensus, such as it is, locates the place at Corinth during the period recorded by Luke in Acts 18, "immediately before departing on the final trip to Jerusalem to deliver the offering from the Gentile churches."⁴ He is also mentioned as a coauthor of Paul's earliest two letters, 1 and 2 Thessalonians (I Thess 1:1 and 2 Thess 1:1); of Second Corinthians (2 Cor. 1:1) and the three prison epistles to the Philippians and Colossians (Phil 1:1 and Col 1:1) and to Philemon.

The first two Pastoral Epistles are written to this junior partner in the team, but the authorship is widely contested. Assuming it was Paul who wrote to Timothy, by now acting as bishop in Ephesus, then they are very personal late writings of Paul from Rome shortly before his death (2 Tim 4:6–18), continuing the mentoring role at some distance. If they are pseudonymous writings, then they are not written to Timothy, but are intended for some later context for which "Timothy" stands as a cipher for a later church. For many the work of Harrison is decisive,⁵ concluding that Paul was not the author of the Pastoral Epistles, and a small cottage industry has arisen from this scholarly question, the details of which need not concern us here. However, I. Howard Marshall, setting out the options, concludes that the question cannot be definitively settled at present.⁶ That Timothy was an "apprentice" of Paul is not in question, whether or not he emerges to leadership without Paul's proximity later, and if we allow that perhaps Paul did write to him, the close affection and concern Paul has for this man, one of his closest companions, and his continuing role as guide and mentor, can be discerned.

Turning from personal story—a form of narrative theology—and Scripture, with its emphasis upon apprenticeship of necessity as the model of leadership formation in the earliest years of the church, we move to another work of art. We will look at John Everett Millais' *The Return of the Dove to the Ark* elsewhere, but now we turn to his *Christ in the House of His Parents*, or *The Carpenter's Shop*. It was signed and dated 1850, and exhibited at the Royal Academy that year and bought by the Tate gallery in 1921.⁷ It was controversial at the time of its exhibition⁸ and remains so today, as witness Waldemar Januszczak reviewing the 2007 Tate Britain retrospective in *The Sunday Times*, describing it as "a lurid, wild-eyed and ludicrous religious hallucination made up of heightened states", with the observation that

---

4. Jewett, *Romans*, 18.

5. Harrison, *The Problem of the Pastoral Epistles*.

6. Marshall, *The Pastoral Epistles*, 57–66.

7. Its title at the RA was a quotation from Zech 13:6, "And one shall say unto him, 'What are these wounds in thine hands?' Then, he shall answer, 'Those with which I was wounded in the house of my friends.'"

8. "This was probably the most notorious image produced by a member of the Brotherhood. The picture aroused such widespread comment that it was removed from the exhibition and brought to Queen Victoria for a special viewing." Smith, *Millais*, 46.

"John the Baptist looks as if he is about to be sick." Janusszczak's conclusion is that Millais cannot turn off the sentimentality. I disagree.

The picture depicts a scene in Joseph's workshop, dominated by a long work-bench that fills the central foreground like some monumental altar. Around it are gathered six figures: to the left an unnamed assistant; while central and behind the bench, St Anne proffers some pincers towards the nail that is, we assume, the offending item that has wounded the young Jesus. She looks directly at Jesus and her daughter, her hands swollen with age. To the right of the bench stands Joseph, reaching across it to touch Jesus on his shoulder with is right hand, and hold the fingers of the wounded hand with his left. An anxious-looking John the Baptist, visibly a little older than Jesus, and already sporting a camel hair loin-cloth that covers his thighs, carefully carries a bowl of water to wash the wound. Central and in front of the bench are the figures of Mary (in her customary blue robe) and Jesus: she kneeling and facing to the right of the picture tilts her head so that the standing figure of Jesus might kiss her cheek, and Jesus standing at an angle shows us his wounded hand (the one Joseph holds) while supporting its arm with the other that together make a gesture redolent of benediction. Stacks of wood stand in the background of the house, while the floor is covered in wood shavings and on a ladder (tall enough to reach the top of a cross, no doubt) a dove rests, looking at the unfolding drama. Outside, beyond the fenced garden and to the left of the background a flock of sheep look in at the scene, on the horizon a wooden structure that is a well pump, that might double for some form of gibbet.

Millais used a mixture of exacting realism (Millais slept in a carpenters' shop in Oxford Street in order to paint there in December 1849 and January 1850[9]) with a genuine Hebrew cloak around the waist of the assistant reflecting historical accuracy, and contemporary elements: Joseph appears to be wearing a modern jumper and over-shirt. The mixture of realism and its subject constituted one dimension of its offending nature. A similarly imagined scene by Millais' contemporary John Rogers Herbert, *Our Savior Subject to his Parents at Nazareth*, was altogether less radical: Mary, cloaked in blue looks untouched by age or circumstance, Joseph is typically bearded while Jesus himself is beautiful and immaculate. By contrast every toe in Millais' picture, including Jesus', has ingrained dirt under its nails, while Jesus as depicted by Millais has red hair, to suggest ancestry among Ashkenazi Jews.[10] This also offended mid-Nineteenth Century English taste, for whom Jesus' obvious and biblical Jewishness was largely downplayed (he should

---

9. Rosenfeld, *John Everett Millais*, 45–46.
10. Smith, *Millais*, 46.

instead have been drawn from the playing fields of Rugby or Eton, perhaps). One anti-Semitic reviewer noted the "studied vulgarity of portraying the youthful Savior as a red-headed Jew-boy."[11]

Charles Dickens took great exception to the picture, and attacked the picture in his essay *Old Lamps for New Ones* in the 15 June 1850 issue of *Household Words*. His comments only serve to undermine his reputation as Victorian England's greatest polemical novelist, for they are rank with anti-Semitism and condemnations of realism, threatening as it did the humanity of Christ. This is the work of a closet Docetist (if Dickens understood that at all, which I doubt). It reflects a kind of religious sentimentalism that Millais and the other members of the Pre-Raphaelite Brotherhood were themselves exposing, and remains the predictable response of the secular press to this day when it encounters any dimension of Christianity that cannot be domesticated and mythologized. The furore indicates something other than simply the actual work, or the offence of its realism: it implies the threat of Roman Catholicism to an Anglican hegemony that was supposed to lie behind this work and movement (although the actual painting is very far from expressing Catholic sentiments) and in particular the depiction of the Virgin Mary is far from the Mariolotry of popular Catholic art in her haggard expression. It comes as no surprise then to remember that the picture, sold to the dealer Henry Farrer prior to its exhibition, was subsequently sold to the prominent Nonconformist collector in Leeds, Thomas Plint.

The picture, however, has a background in the High Church Tractarianism that was itself so controversial at the time. Millais probably heard Pusey preach a sermon in Oxford in the summer of 1849 for he lived in Oxford then. Pusey linked the text from Zechariah, which was its original title, with the passion of Christ, echoing the resulting painting in the imagery with which it prefigures the passion, following the interpretation of the medieval mystic Rupert of Deutz's commentary. The wooden tools and the ladder prefigure the making of the cross, the sheep the sacrificial lamb; the water carried by John the Baptist and the well-head pump echoes the water of baptism, the work-bench the altar of Communion, and both the nail that has cut Jesus' hand and the hammer that Joseph grips whilst at the same time gently touching Jesus shoulder in comfort, the tools of crucifixion. Mary, care-worn and rather plain (it is untrue to say she is ugly, as Dickens did) kneels like a supplicant at the Mass, or the figure at the foot of the cross, while John, the older boy, comes to serve Jesus, the younger. All is quietly observed by the dove, symbol of the Spirit, which perches where the cross

---

11. *The Builder* 7, no. 382 (1 June 1850), 256, cited in Rosenfeld, *John Everett Millais*, 46n46.

will be made. Above all, the central figure of Jesus, at this stage an apprentice carpenter, stares past Mary and out of the canvas, and seems to be caught up in some sudden presentient moment of realization that the wound in his palm, dripping blood onto his foot, foretold the manner of his death. The expected kiss by Jesus on Mary's proffered cheek (had she already offered her kiss, and was waiting for its reciprocation) is stalled by this awareness, and the resulting gesture looks like a benediction. Indeed, the passion, of which this a prescient moment, is God's most profound blessing upon a work-a-day world in all of its sweaty and grubby reality.

What does this have to say about apprenticeship? Jesus is the apprentice here, learning his trade the hard way in his father's workshop. He is not at Nazareth College of Further Education learning his trade from books and carefully organized lessons, but in the reality of the family business. Apprenticeship applied to ministry is similarly lived out in real world pastoral and missional situations, learning the craft of ministry by working alongside those who know the trade. It is accompanied by the generations of Christians, those both older and younger, amongst whom ministry is exercised, and watched from outside (by those "sheep that are lost.") Ministry can be wounding, and this is best learned early on, in the apprenticeship, lest for too long false hopes of glamour and success grow until, when shattered, much else is lost. What happens in ministerial apprenticeship echoes what will take place routinely and unguarded in the future, but for the time being with the close support of those whose love protects and comforts, and gives meaning to the wounds. Is it too fanciful to see in this picture a vision of ministerial apprenticeship? The senior colleagues with whom one works (Joseph and the assistant carpenter) and who get on with real, local congregation ministry while the apprentice observes and helps; the wisdom of an older generation, not necessarily in ministry (St Anne), who lean in to offer support and encouragement; and fellow apprentices (John the Baptist): all are present, while those closest to us, be they spouse or parents, are ready to give and receive the kiss of benediction. All is overshadowed by the cross and the Spirit, and worked out through sacrament and Word.

Millais worked hard to represent real, laboring life. The body of St Joseph was based upon a Holborn grocer, in his search for a genuine working-class musculature, and so this is no idealized depiction of human anatomy, but real muscles, veins and sun-burnt flesh. "The picture is replete with a Pre-Raphaelite approach to observed reality."[12] Apprenticeship as a model of ministerial formation is replete with attention to lived reality, to the actual ministry itself.

12. Rosenfeld, *Millais*, 45.

Like the infamous exhibition of *Olympia* by Manet in 1865, itself a source of scandal for very different reasons, Millais is exploding the sentimental conventions of art that served to distance the observer from the harsher realities of life. Manet's nude is no classically inflected source of hypocritical fantasy, but modeled by an infamous courtesan (probably familiar to many of the bourgeois habitués of the Salon) and without a doubt a prostitute, from her name to her slippers—she wears nothing else besides. Manet is saying, if you want to see a nude, here is a real one, not a fantasy figure from supposed antiquity. Millais is saying, if you want to depict Christ, then see it for the reality it is, not a saccharine version devoid of pain. If apprenticeships in ministry can do the same for the fantasies about serving Christ with which some approach formation, and, dangerously, then seek to perpetuate in their characterization of ministry, then it will have served a good purpose beyond an effective means of learning skills. It will have contributed to the formation in practices, which themselves, when properly ordered to the *telos* of Christ-conformity, shape both character and ministry in the virtues.

We now turn from those perspectives upon formation in ministry to the first of two parts that explore specific areas of formation viewed through the lens of virtue ethics. The first, which follows, takes a broad view of intellectual formation, spiritual formation, and the formation of character and practice. The second part explores in greater detail the practices summarized in the final chapter of this next section: the formation of the liturgist, the pastor, the spiritual guide, the missioner or evangelist, preacher and leader.

PART THREE

Forming the Person

8

Intellectual Formation

Such has been the growing emphasis in recent years upon the formation of appropriate spiritualities for ministry, the development of skills and competence in the practice of ministry and the shaping of character, it could seem as if the preoccupation of an earlier generation of theological educators with the grounding of the ministerial student in an adequate intellectual formation has been almost lost. This is to over-emphasize the point, of course, but it remains true, I believe, that the range of areas of concern for today's theological educators would seem extraordinary to the generation of ministers who, trained in the years after the Second World War, are now drawing to the close of their lives. Until comparatively recently, theological education (that is, the development of a theologically competent mind) dominated ministerial formation to the point where the two were almost synonymous.

Going back even further in time, the education that Spurgeon himself offered to his students embraced a breadth of subject matter that would astound today. His students read widely in the classical English literature, studied history (and not just church history) and philosophy because The Pastor's College was their university education. By no means confined to intellectual formation, it was, nonetheless, a vital element in the formation of those ministers.

Chris Ellis notes that it has long been the expectation that ministers will combine "learning and spiritual zeal," and quotes Caleb Evans, son of Principal Hugh Evans (and who succeeded him as Principal of the Bristol Academy.) The intentions of his father were, "as not merely to form substantial scholars but as far as in him lay he was desirous of being made an instrument in God's hand of forming them, able, evangelical, lively, zealous ministers of the Gospel."[1]

1. Evans, *"Elisha's Exclamation: A Sermon Occasioned by the Death of Rev. Hugh*

While the suspicion articulated was that "book-learning" was detrimental to the spiritual well-being of the minister—a suspicion that has lasted to this day—it is cited here to note that, at least, the counter-foil to all of the formational emphases encouraged then as now (zeal for the gospel, character, spirituality and so forth) was the formation of "substantial scholars." In his essay on the spiritual formation of ministers, Ellis notes how knowing, being and doing interact, but says little in that paper about the "knowing."[2]

By no means wishing to decry the increasing emphasis upon spiritual and moral formation for ministry (far from it: it has been the most urgent and necessary of changes to the tenor of theological education and ministerial formation) there remains, however, the need for a rounded and focused intellectual training for those called to ministry and who seek to acquire an adequate formation for the demands that ministry will make upon them.

There is virtue in maintaining a sufficient breadth to that intellectual formation in order to develop a 'rounded' education. I attended my interview for admission to Spurgeon's College as a ministerial candidate during my first year of study as an independent student. I had spent that year studying for the Cambridge Diploma, while continuing as a full-time pastoral member of staff at the large and busy Streatham Baptist Church (and raising a young family to boot.) Determined to do well, I regularly studied into the early hours, putting the final touches to the weekly essay at 3.00 a.m., and enjoyed immensely the intellectual challenge of a new sphere of enquiry. However, it did not leave much time for wider reading for pleasure, as the list of books cited in my Baptist Union Application for Ministry form revealed (a long litany of sound academic theological works.) The lack of anything remotely literary caused one member of the interviewing Council to suggest that I find some time to read a novel or two, a suggestion that I wisely did not respond to at the time! I think I might have embarrassed myself with a rather intemperate response. Now, thirty years later, I see the wisdom in the suggestion, and am ashamed of my rather dismissive approach to that counsel.

The areas of concern in this chapter are epistemology (theory of knowledge) and the ways in which adults acquire knowledge (adult learning) in order to frame the formation of an adequate intellect for ministry. I do not want to argue that ministry can only be exercised where practitioners are academically able, although that is no bar to effective ministry. Rather,

---

Evans, preached at Broadmead, Bristol, April 8, 1781," cited in Ellis, "Being a Minister. Spirituality and the Pastor," in (ed.) Lalleman, *Challenging to Change*, 57.

2. Ellis, "Being a Minister. Spirituality and the Pastor."

that engaging with today's world (indeed any culture at any time) requires the exercise of intellect and the acquisition of some knowledge, and that this dimension of formation remains essential to the proper equipping of ministers, even if it does not have quite the same exclusive and privileged status as it did fifty years ago.

Epistemology

This reflexive study of knowledge, the study not so much of spheres of human enquiry but of the nature of human enquiry itself, asks what is knowledge, what are its limits and how do we acquire it? A book about formation is not the place for a full-blown exploration of epistemology (even if this author could provide such a thing) but if we are to say anything about intellectual formation, then we must say something about epistemology.

From Plato's denial that the senses can be trusted in seeking knowledge, to David Hume's denial that anything beyond the senses can be trusted, the answers given to the questions of epistemology are various and contradictory. In the first half of the last century questions of the nature of sensation and perception dominated the discussion. Empiricists thought that science could deliver incontrovertible truth, accessed through the data we capture through our senses. Certainly, they claimed, it offered greater assurance of veracity than either metaphysics or religion could, and if we could only ally logic to accurate sensory perception, then knowledge could be assured. Further reflection pointed out that knowledge is always captured by minds that are already laden with theory and pre-conceptions. I recognize this table upon which my computer sits because I already have some experience of "table," and the neurologists and developmental psychologists have worked away at the processes by which the infant begins to make sense of what it sees, tastes, hears and feels.

While the means by which we acquire knowledge was debated, until 1963 most epistemologists agreed that what we mean by knowledge is justified true belief. That consensus was overturned by Edmund Gettier's "famous three-pager."[3] Gettier's paper[4] pulled the thread that set the whole 2,000 years of the definition of knowledge unravelling. Since then (apart from a host of attempts to patch up the damage) various options have been offered. Roberts and Wood annunciate the following: some have argued the whole endeavor should be handed over to cognitive scientists (W.V.O. Quine); others that we should look to other areas of human knowing, such

---

3. Roberts and Wood, *Intellectual Virtue*, 5.
4. Gettier, "Is Justified True Belief Knowledge?"

as poetry; and still others, that the endeavor is doomed to failure. Charles Taylor writes, "it seems to be rapidly becoming a new orthodoxy that the whole enterprise from Descartes, through Locke and Kant, and pursued by various nineteenth and twentieth century succession movements, was a mistake."[5]

Roberts and Wood argue that a promising move in this disarray is the turn to human virtues. Linda Zagzebski [6] has focused upon virtues as character traits, rather than faculties, and thus brought epistemology much closer to the concerns of contemporary ordinary language, and humanizes the debate. Virtues are human character attributes that are admirable and excellent, and intellectual or epistemic virtues are "bases of excellent epistemic functioning."[7] Alvin Plantinga has applied this concept to the deep questions of knowing God, and has followed the eighteenth century theologian, Jonathan Edwards in giving the emotions an important role to play in that kind of knowing. "The life of virtue is composed of appetitive dispositions, and emotions are the consequences of caring about things, of taking some things to be important, of having steady, long-term desires for things of value."[8]

Much of the sophistry of epistemological enquiry has focused upon what Nicholas Wolterstorff has called "analytical epistemology," theories of knowledge, warrant, justification, and so forth. By contrast "regulative epistemology" aims to produce guidance for epistemic practice, and states how we should conduct enquiry. Wolterstorff chooses the kind of habit-forming regulative epistemology that was exemplified by Locke (rather than the rule-oriented kind of Descartes) and it is this shaping of the habits of mind that are crucial to the formation of the intellectual virtues. "We need not rule books, but a *training* that nurtures *people* in the right intellectual *dispositions*."[9]

Roberts and Wood advocate a return to this seventeenth century tradition, to a regulative epistemology that focuses upon forming the practitioner's character and is strongly education-oriented, and happily accompanies a virtue ethics approach to personal formation and discipleship that lies at the heart of the formation of people for ministry.

---

5. Taylor, "Overcoming Epistemology," 6.

6. Zagzebski, *Virtues of the Mind: An Enquiry into the Nature and the Ethical Foundations of Knowledge.*)

7. Roberts and Wood, *Intellectual Virtue*, 7.

8. Ibid., 8.

9. Ibid., 22.

The virtues that Roberts and Wood advocate are love of knowledge, firmness, courage and caution, humility, autonomy, generosity, and practical wisdom. Before we can investigate these in a little more detail, we follow Roberts and Wood as they describe virtues and practices.

Virtue

Much has been made of the rebirth of virtue ethics, and this resurgence, as we have seen, owes a great deal to Alasdair MacIntyre,[10] and most recently has been popularized by Tom Wright.[11] When we come to discuss the ethical formation of the minister we shall return to virtue ethics as the controlling ethical paradigm, and the notion of virtues are also significant in the way we develop skills and habits of practice, but here we should concentrate on intellectual virtues.

Thomas Aquinas defines a virtue as a "maximum of a power (*potentia*)," that is a maximum development of a human faculty (*Summa Theologiae*, Ia2ae 55,I) and, following Aristotle, places centrally the power of human reason as the defining maxima to be developed. It is by the mind that the virtues are developed, as Wright powerfully argues in chapter 5 of *Virtue Reborn*. Thus, through training and education and formation, the potential to be an excellent human being is realized and matured. No wonder then, that in the aftermath of the August 2011 riots in England's conurbations (London especially) the debate about causes pointed to failures in the two most significant social endeavors that shape a person's life, build citizenship and character and build a hopeful and positive attitude to the future: the family and school. The very lack of "virtue" in those who looted, burnt, rioted, and killed was traced to too little parental restraint and an education system that failed so many by lack of discipline and a failure of expectation of success. We might argue that where ministerial "looting and arson'" occurs (by which I mean the abuses of power that leads to ministers using churches and their members for personal gain and prestige, and the wreckage that occurs when ministers fail morally in spectacular form) it might, in part at least, be attributed to a failure in formation and education.

Virtues fit us for living the good life, functioning as an excellent human being, and, only secondly, as a minister. This is important, as the intellectual virtues of, say, firmness and humility, are not specific to just ministers, but to all human beings. In this regard, while I want to view the minister as

---

10. MacIntyre *After Virtue: A Study in Moral Theory*; MacIntyre, *Whose Justice, Which Rationality?*
11. Wright, *Virtue Reborn*.

many things (a leader, a pastor, a teacher) at the heart of what makes a good minister is the way in which they exemplify the best of redeemed humanity: they are a virtuous or "good" person. No amount of skill in people management nor ability in Greek can compensate for the reality that a particular minister is not a good woman or man. So, Zagzebski's definition of a virtue is "a deep and enduring acquired excellence of a person, involving a characteristic motivation to produce a certain desired end and reliable success in bringing about that end."[12] Therefore, taking the basic intellectual virtue as the *love of knowledge*, it is clear that as well as the tools to acquire knowledge—which in most cultures includes the ability to read and communicate, and to store and recall that knowledge—that ability does not become a virtue without the will to do so. I may be able to gain knowledge, but unless I exercise that faculty, and actually read, understand, and pass that knowledge on, I will not develop the love of knowledge. I will argue, following Roberts and Wood, that there are intellectual virtues that shape a person, and not just develop an intellect. The value in a virtue-oriented approach to intellectual formation lies precisely in the way this connects the shaping of a Christian mind with the shaping of a Christian character to form the exemplary person who models what it is to be a disciple of Jesus Christ.

In his analysis of the late-modern world MacIntyre places emphasis upon the way in which skills and virtues are acquired through certain practices. The metaphor of the apprentice is central to this conception of what the development of morality looks like, as we demonstrated previously. We develop by learning habits of action or thought, practicing those skills and honing those habits until they become second-nature. I now drive without consciously thinking of depressing the clutch pedal when changing gear. I do it almost automatically, so that I can concentrate on what is happening elsewhere on the road, or elsewhere in the car, at the same time. It is the equivalent of walking and chewing gum at the same time. But it was not always so, and at the start of learning to drive, a conscious decision to depress the pedal was required before the gear was engaged, or the grinding of gears and the stalling of the engine would ensue (as it did on occasion.) However, by practice, I learnt the habit of depressing the pedal, and so now drive without constantly destroying the gear box on my car. The development of that habit, of that practice, has enabled me to be a competent driver. What habits, or practices are required for the development of the intellectual virtues?

The intellectual practices that I want to identify are all aimed at prizing the "internal" goods intrinsic to the intellectual life. MacIntyre distinguishes

---

12. Zagzebski, *Virtues of the Mind*, 137, cited in Roberts and Wood, *Intellectual Virtue*, 69.

between "internal" goods and "external," where internal goods are those that must be aimed at in the development of a practice, in order to become excellent, whereas external goods are those that accrue to those practitioners who demonstrate excellence in their particular skill or practice. Those goods that are internal to cricket, for instance, include the ability to bowl a good line, defend the crease and as a batsman place a ball to where sufficient time might elapse before the opponent retrieves it, so that with some speed, a run or two may be scored. I possess none of those goods, which explains in small part why I shall never benefit from the external goods that accrue to the best cricketers: financial reward, employment, fame and, if you are Tendulkar, the ability to bring the second largest nation on earth to a virtual standstill when you occupied the crease.

The goods internal to the intellectual virtues include understanding of "what is" (of history, of nature, of texts, of human functioning), of confirming the veracity of that understanding, and the concomitant rejection of what is false, and the conveying of that knowledge and understanding through speech and writing. These goods are acquired through study, self-discipline, and perseverance. The practices that I believe develop these intellectual virtues are reading, critical enquiry, debate, and argument and, secondarily, the passing on of that understanding in teaching and writing. Part of the proper functioning of ministerial formation will be to inculcate those practices until they become second-nature, until they become normative and part of the daily round of what it means to be a minister. Just as it would be pretty hard work for me to develop the practices to make me a competent cricketer, I know that for some called to ministry, developing study skills, reading habits and a love of knowledge is hard work. But where cricket is an optional skill for a minister, growth in knowledge and understanding of the world and of the faith is not. The intellectual virtues are indispensable to the practice and being of ministry.

Let me illustrate this. As I wrote the first draft of this chapter, the August 2011 English riots occurred days earlier. On the Sunday following those riots I was scheduled to preach at Bunyan Meeting, Bedford, a Baptist-Congregational Church where John Bunyan himself had been pastor. It was inconceivable that in the sermon I should not refer to the tumultuous events of earlier in the week, and the church expected me to choose the readings from the Revised Common Lectionary as specified. In order to fulfil both expectations, it required me to read as much as possible about reactions to those riots, to critically understand what was being said and to reflect theologically upon them. It also called for those skills that enable me to interpret and expound a text, read commentaries and so forth. This called for the intellectual virtues of love of knowledge, courage and humility, and the practices of reading, researching and critically evaluating different points of view, all encompassed by prayerful attention to God. None of this would have been possible without the intellectual virtues and their associated habits being formed in me. It does not constitute the summation of ministry, but it is not an optional extra for those so inclined. Rather, it is an indispensable dimension of what it is to be a minister of the gospel, a teacher of the faith, a pastor to God's people.

The Intellectual Virtues

The Love of Knowledge

Scripture enjoins us to think about whatever is honorable, just, pure, lovely, gracious, excellent, or worthy of praise (Phil. 4:8), and the love of knowledge requires a similar discrimination. Not all knowledge is worth possessing, for some is unworthy, compromising the purity of the soul, while other knowledge is simply insignificant. While an extreme form of postmodernism fails to make such distinctions, so that the knowledge of the great tradition of classical music is of no greater value than knowledge of which songs the talent show *The X Factor*'s contestants choose to perform (and here I expose my own prejudices), a true love of knowledge will discriminate and prioritize what is worthy of pursuit. It had long been thought that in ministerial formation, the learning of the ancient languages of Greek and Hebrew had a privileged place, but recent usurpers such as psychology, sociology, missiology and the study of religion as a human phenomenon have displaced the priorities of an earlier generation. Within a limited time scale the luxury of learning two ancient languages has been replaced by the development of a deeper understanding of the context in which ministry is exercised. Discrimination is being exercised (although some would argue precisely the opposite.) What Roberts and Wood call "more load-bearing beliefs, acquaintances and understandings," and "worthiness" assist in that discrimination.[13] This is not to argue that practical knowledge should be prioritized over that which has no practical application. This is to run the risk of being tyrannized by the contemporary, and some forms of ministerial education sail rather too close to that particular reef, but rather to call for the ability to exercise discrimination. One way in which this is developed is through individual research, where the ability to distinguish between sources and their relative worth or weight is essential. The undergraduate essay that quotes Wikipedia alone is hardly likely to succeed in conveying a discrimi-

---

13. Roberts and Wood, *Intellectual Virtue*, 159.

nating mind able to access a suitable range of authorities. The ability to discriminate must be accompanied by the avoidance of prejudice. This too is an ability learnt in the context of ministerial education: to read only those commentaries published by certain "sound evangelical" publishers, such as IVP, smacks of prejudice (and the obverse, where only SCM Press is to be trusted, is equally invidious) and this avoidance of prejudice relates to another virtue, that of generosity.

The intellectual vices that correspond with this virtue are best discussed by illustration. Returning to my preparation for preaching on the Sunday after the riots, a failure would have been to be indifferent to the understanding of what had happened on the streets of English cities the Monday previously, and to purvey mere anecdote or tabloid deadline. Another failure would have been to attempt to understand and then convey what would meet with the warmest approval from what I perceived to be the prevailing mood of the congregation. In other words, knowledge obtained for personal gain, an unvirtuous concern to know. There is a vice in this regard that fails to see all truth as God's truth, and so avoids listening to, reading about, or understanding anything that contradicts a particular theological or religious presupposition.

Humility

The astonishing way in which the first generation of Christians applauded as a virtue what their prevailing Graeco-Roman culture understood to be a vice— humility—demonstrates how powerfully the faith was grounded in the person of Jesus Christ. The self-understanding of Jesus of Nazareth, the way of life he followed and the death he died, all reverse that prevailing human characteristic of pride. We might imagine St Paul berating some of our contemporary forms of Christianity, with all their dominance, vanity and arrogance with "That is not the way you learned Christ!" (Eph. 4.20)

Humility is also a foundational intellectual virtue, and its corresponding vices are arrogance, vanity, conceit, domination, selfish ambition, and pretentiousness. The dispositions that humility opposes include the holding of an unwarrantedly high opinion of oneself (a lack of self-criticism;) a disinclination to acknowledge reliance upon others (ultimately, plagiarism); grandiosity, snobbishness; and presumption, which lacks proper respect for the boundaries of one's abilities. Of a different ilk is dominance, the exercise and enjoyment of excessive control over others; and selfish ambition, that advances one's own interests over the interests of others (a prevailing academic sin, if ever there was one).[14]

Humility, on the other hand, avoids undue attention to the self, is not concerned to focus upon that egotistical self, but, in this context, rather to be concerned about the pursuit of knowledge for its own sake. This combination of low attention to status with concern for the epistemic good of understanding is what makes humility such a powerful intellectual virtue. It neutralizes the arrogance that dismisses other's viewpoints, or looks down upon other disciplines. As a pastoral theologian, I have occasionally encountered those who dismiss this sphere of enquiry as standing on a par with a degree in knitting or golf management (and here, I demonstrate my own arrogance, perhaps with some justification!) There is a tendency for systematic theologians or biblical specialists to see themselves as the true intellectual elite of the theological world (and again I speak as a systematic theologian) and this too betrays a lack of proper intellectual humility.

Humility is essential for the collegiality that is not only a characteristic of much of the best learning and enquiry, but specifically of a Baptist way of doing theology, or, for that matter, of being a disciple. Forming all ministers intellectually should take particular notice of the growth of this intellectual virtue.

Generosity

The final example of intellectual virtues is generosity, or liberality. It gives valuable things to others and bestows upon them goods that they have not purchased. It is the virtue associated with gift (about which I have written elsewhere[15]) and grace. A lack of generosity results in the kind of academic abuse that saw two male researchers at Cambridge, Crick and Watson, eradicate the essential contribution of a (female) researcher at King's College, London, Rosalind Franklin, from recognition as they discovered the structure of DNA, and win the "external good" of the Nobel Prize. It is clear from the story of their research that the prize of winning the Nobel was a stronger motivation than the discovery itself, and restricting it to their own contribution (which would have been impossible without the crystallographic study of DNA being achieved by Franklin at King's) demonstrated a distinct lack of generosity, to the point of overweening competitiveness. The gloss of reputation that the Nobel gave them has become considerably tarnished by their lack of generosity, to the point where they are almost

14. See Roberts and Wood, *Intellectual Virtue*, 236–37.
15. Goodliff, *Care in a Confused Climate*, 123–28.

infamous rather than being appropriately famous. One might remark that the same lack of concern for others, recklessness and gross self-interest are precisely the characteristics of both bankers who brought about the 2008 financial crisis, and the rioters who trashed the English city centers in 2011, both groups being composed of young men in their early twenties to thirties, an age and gender group that is not under-represented amongst ministerial candidates either.

Generosity expresses itself in the giving of attention and time to the other, especially of the teacher to the student (and its obverse, the research supervisor "stealing" the research of their benighted student or colleague) but more generally, is exhibited in an approach to the viewpoints of others that believes the best, rather than is suspicious of the worst. The rather fierce and ungenerous squabbles between various American evangelical groupings, most recently heard in the rather overwrought pronouncements of some of the neo-Calvinists, would seem to illustrate precisely the tenor shaped by a lack of generosity. Another way of presenting this virtue is to talk of open-mindedness, the willingness to listen beyond one's immediate sphere of ease ("outside the comfort-zone" would be a rather crass but familiar way of expressing that) to other voices. We should note how deeply such a disposition is rooted in Baptist ways of doing theology and being church.

It is significant to note the Christian commitment of Roberts and Wood in the volume, *Intellectual Virtues* that has been such a seminal work in the development of the ideas behind virtue as the schemata for intellectual formation. Robert Roberts is Distinguished Professor of Philosophy at Baylor, a predominantly Baptist college, and Jay Wood, Professor of Philosophy at Wheaton College, an evangelical school in Illinois. Their choice of both a virtue approach to epistemology and the choices of virtues that such an approach encompasses are deeply shaped by their Christian faith.

Adult Learning

The literature in adult learning is broad in its scope, and much has been written about the ways in which this might be applied to theological education and ministerial formation. Much theological learning, however, takes little note of much of this literature. Traditional forms of learning, such as the delivery of a lecture may well have their place, but when they predominate, we should not be surprised when education may occur, but formation remains limited.

David Heywood argues that those who hold to a propositional model of truth, be they Protestant evangelicals locating such revelation in Scripture, or Catholics who place revelation in the magisterium of the Church, justify the emphasis upon preaching and traditional content-based teaching methods on the nature of their conception of revelation. Liberals, on the other hand, espousing a method where the experience of the individual takes precedence, seek to provide the reflexive tools to enable the Christian learner to create their own metanarrative. Both have insights to assist us in determining where formation takes place: there are truths to be passed on, but the process involves the natural processes of human learning, and in very few cases is "straightforward authoritative transmission an effective strategy for teaching and learning."[16] Effective learning involves every stage of the learning cycle: experience, reflection, conceptualization, and action. Religious learners need to take part in the wrestling, rather than be passive recipients of a hand-me-down faith.

However, Heywood argues that because revelation is given as tacit knowledge, it must be taught as tacit knowledge. Christian learning takes place where our identity in Jesus Christ is applied in experience. A man or woman may become extremely knowledgeable in the facts and values of Christian faith but fail to live them out. He or she may even be a pillar of the church on Sundays or in mid-week activities but fail to make any impact on his family or working environment or may even bring the name of Christ into disrepute by his failure to live out the truths he proclaims. Christian growth does not consist of learning to look *at* the truths of Christian faith so as to reproduce them in sermons, Bible-studies, and conversations with Christian friends, but in learning to look at the world *through the perspective* of those truths so that they become a part of the way we think about the world and respond to it. Christian faith thus becomes a *habitus* or wisdom for living, consisting of tacit rather than explicit knowledge.[17]

Heywood continues, "In ministerial training, as in every context of Christian education, what is required is the skill to enable Christian disciples to interpret their lives and experiences through the spectacles of their faith; in other words, the skills of good teaching."[18] There will be, on the part of the teacher, an eye for the learner's preferred learning style, a need that Croft and Walton acknowledge in their primer for Anglican theological students embarking upon training.[19] The Honey and Mumford learning

---

16. Heywood, *Divine Revelation and Human Learning*, 172.
17. Ibid., 173.
18. Ibid., 174.
19. Croft and Walton, *Learning for Ministry*, 17.

styles schemata identifies four broad groups: activists, reflectors, theorists and pragmatists. Closely allied are the Myers-Briggs Type Indicator, and the idea of Helen Gardner of multiple intelligences. Awareness of this will aid the learning of the broad range of personality types who are called to ministry.

However, if Christian learning, as a foundational concept in ministerial formation, is to be effective, the twin goals of the effective acquisition of knowledge and the development of a life that reflects what has been understood and accepted by that acquisition must be kept in focus. A rounded approach that moves beyond theological education to discipleship/ministerial formation is the vital movement called for here. The conceptual bond that links this intellectual growth and personal conformity to Christ is that of virtue. Intellectual virtue allied to ethical virtue and expressed in radical and deep Christian formation, or conformity to Christ, must be the goal of ministerial formation, and acknowledged as the work of a life-time, and not merely the task of three or four years of college experience (or IMF1–3, in the ecclesial jargon.)

9

Spiritual Formation

A generation ago, those training for ministry in the 1980s (the language of "formation" was not yet widely used), as I did, had little provided by way of formal spiritual formation. I cannot recall attending any lectures on it, nor was it suggested that I read any books about it. There appeared to be no disciplines explicitly expected of me, although I guess I was expected to pray and read my Bible. I presume it was assumed that I would, but it was presumed, nonetheless, and not obviously a particular concern of the college to ask if I did or did not. There was one occasion, however, at the so-called college retreat day (a euphemism for a day's conference with addresses, normally,) when Tim Marks, formerly a Baptist minister, but by then an Anglican priest, used the retreat to attend to the questions of spiritual discipline. It was memorable because it was so unusual, and because of the arrogant response of one student towards the end of the day demanding to know where was the gospel in all of this. These were the days when spirituality was still a rather suspect area for those zealous for evangelical truth, after all.

Was this just my unfortunate experience? Talking to my former colleague Jonathan Edwards, who served as General Secretary of the Baptist Union when I was Head of Ministry there, about his experience at another Baptist College at a similar time, confirmed that, no, it was not just me. This avoidance of any attention to spiritual formation was normal and widespread. It was everywhere assumed that those training for ministry would take responsibility for their own spiritual life, that they came to college with a well-developed set of spiritual habits that would sustain them in ministry, and that the priority was the development of the intellectual and practical dimensions of pastoral ministry.

Times have changed, and spirituality is no longer a suspect category for evangelicals. Of course, it was never suspect for others, but even in theological education delivered in very different cultural and theological milieus, an over-dependence upon what could be measured prevailed. During the last thirty years, in Baptist Colleges, at least, this significant lacuna, this absence of any conscious attempt to develop a person spiritually, has been recognized and addressed in various ways. Most frequently, the response has been to run a course on spirituality, so that students can learn about desert spirituality (interestingly the theme of my sermon delivered at sermon class as a ministerial student), Thomas Merton, Ignatian, Benedictine, evangelical, or Celtic spirituality.

A recent Regent's Study Guide published in 2008 is *Under the Rule of Christ*,[1] and consists of a collection of papers on Baptist spirituality written by the then principals of the six British Baptist colleges at the behest of the Baptist Union Retreat Group. One College principal engaged with a thirty-day silent retreat, and most colleges, when they run a college retreat, genuinely attempt to deliver something that resembles that kind of event, rather than simply another set of addresses by a visiting lecturer. I have delivered college retreats at both Northern and Bristol colleges in the past ten years, and while both asked for some input, they also requested that I provide plenty of time for reflection and silence. All the colleges deliver courses on spirituality, and it was the enquiry by a group of Spurgeon's College students in 2005 to their tutor in doctrine and ethics, Dr John Colwell, that provided the seed bed for the formation of a Baptist *Order for Ministry*. While they thought of something akin to a Baptist Order of Preachers, modelled on a Dominican third order model, the Order that I had a role in establishing, and which is emerging, looks rather different. The significant thing for this purpose was the origins of the idea in a college context. The very college that in the mid-1980s gave space for a student to question where was the gospel in anything that looked like spirituality, now provided the seed bed for a vision of a Baptist religious order. Things had certainly changed.

However, where the default means of delivering the spiritual formation of student ministers is to deliver a course, a lecture series, or similar, and perhaps examine their understanding using similar means of assessment that examines the student's understanding of church history, ethics or New Testament Theology, this somehow misses the point. It is not what I know about the spiritual masters and their guidance on prayer that really matters. It is whether I pray, and how I pray, and what impact that has on me as a person, let alone a minister. Certainly, a broad understanding of the various spiritualities that have developed throughout the church's history, and especially a working knowledge of those particularly found amongst

1. Fiddes, ed., *Under the Rule of Christ*.

Baptists throughout their story, is a welcome development. It provides an intellectual framework within which ministerial students can examine the relationship between personality and practice, and at the very least demonstrates that the default evangelical quiet time is by no means the only structure of spiritual discipline available or acceptable to Baptists. I suspect the very lack of any attention given to spiritual formation as I trained was because it was assumed that this was the practice for all of us, and it need not be questioned.

However, my experience of caring for fellow ministers, first as a Superintendent, and subsequently as a denominational leader with responsibility for its ministers (where hands-on pastoral care tends to be limited to crisis care for those crashing out of ministry under grim circumstances of personal moral failure or breakdown) led me to suspect that for many, this lack of spiritual formation, either prior to training or during the whole experience of formation, is a significant factor in their weakness and the ensuing ineffectiveness of ministry. Those now training for ministry cannot be assumed to have a formed rule of life, habits of prayer or Scripture reading or engage in regular retreat that will sustain them for the long-haul. Courses on spirituality can never substitute for personal formation within a spiritual tradition.

Fiddes and his fellow principals note that for Baptists, spirituality is marked by living "under the rule of Christ," derived from their ecclesiology. The congregation stands directly under the rule of Christ without intermediate authorities, and this has been translated personally into an expectation that Baptists will live under Christ's rule, with a personal commitment to discipleship. This is not unique to Baptists, but shared with the broader evangelical movement that Baptists have contributed to with such significance. At its least helpful, it is reduced to a form of personal piety that is intensely individualistic and disconnected from community (I am reminded, in one of Stanley Hauerwas's books, of a Catholic, Ken Woodward, commentating on the phrase "finding Christ as your personal Savior" and remarking how strange this is for Catholics.[2]) Baptists have always understood that the growth in faith that is expressed in discipleship is also discovered and nurtured within the community of the gathered church.

At its heart, then, spiritual formation is closely allied to authentic discipleship and membership of the church. However, in its more typical use, spirituality is also closely associated with prayer, especially in its more contemplative forms; an awareness of the transcendent, or mysterious, and ultimately, of God's presence; and a move towards those expressions of

---

2. Hauerwas, *Sanctify The in the Truth*, 235.

spirituality that have taken a particular and regulated form in Christian history, especially those associated with monasticism. Recently, the similarities between Baptist spirituality and St Benedict's Monastic Rule has been noted, for instance, and Fiddes remarks that where the Benedictines looked to the Abbot as the father of the community, Baptists from the beginning allowed for "spiritual oversight (*episkope*) both by the *whole* congregation gathered together in church meeting, and by the minister(s) called to lead the congregation. Oversight flows to and fro between the individual and the community, and there is no legalistic definition of the balance between them, everything depending on mutual trust."[3] The covenantal language of walking together and watching over one another so that the members of the church are "all to walk by one and the same Rule, and by all meanes convenient to have the counsel and help of one another in all needful affaires of the Church, as members of one body in the common faith under Christ their onely head,"[4] echoes the monastic rules found in more Catholic traditions.

Quite apart from ministerial formation, Nigel Wright argues that membership in a Baptist church should entail a corporate rule of life,[5] which if it were applied widely would require ministry to exemplify what such a common rule might consist in. I will argue here that spiritual formation takes place most effectively within an agreed rule of life, and that while such rules may change from place to place, and from time to time (without losing entirely their common elements of, say, prayer and common worship) there is benefit to be had by a more comprehensive Rule of life to be expected of those who are part of a college community, both tutorial staff and ministerial students, echoing something of the insights of Bonhoeffer in the establishment of the community of pastoral formation given written shape in *Life Together*.[6] Similarly, Nigel Wright interprets in the community of disciples so characteristic of Anabaptism, a form of "laicized monasticism" (Fiddes's phrase) and he argues that through the lay movements of the *Devotio Moderna*, the most widely known product of which is Thomas a Kempis's *The Imitation of Christ*, there is a mediation of the older monastic concern to "will what God wills"[7] in a synthesis that is neither Protestant nor Catholic, "in that it neither imagines that justification is the end product

3. Fiddes, ed., *Under the Rule of Christ*, 9.

4. The London Confession (1644), Art. XLVII, in Lumpkin, *Baptist Confessions*, 168–69.

5. N. G. Wright, "Spirituality as Discipleship: The Anabaptist Heritage," 95.

6. Bonhoeffer, *Life Together*.

7. N. G. Wright, "Spirituality as Discipleship," citing Arnold Snyder, *Following in the Footsteps of Christ: The Anabaptist Tradition*.

of a process of sanctification nor that faith alone without inner transformation is an adequate understanding of the divine remedy for sin."[8]

This drawing upon appropriate Baptist and Anabaptist traditions would provide a model of spiritual formation that other traditions have explored in earlier generations. The origins of St Stephen's House, the Anglican theological college in the Anglo-Catholic tradition in Oxford, owed a great deal to the Tractarian tradition, and currently occupies the site of the Cowley Fathers, while The College of the Resurrection, Mirfield, is closely allied to the monastic community there. I do not want to suggest that a similar ethos, or culture would be imitated, but simply to argue that the training of ministers in a strongly community-focused environment has ecumenical traction, and that there are considerable benefits to be had in spiritual formation where such patterns are adapted.

The mere fact of those elements of shared worship and a common rule, in and of themselves, do not ensure that formation is adequate. The November 2008 Quality in Formation Inspection Report on St Stephen's House noted that while the House stressed the Catholic tradition of the "importance of learning virtuous habits of ordered prayer, thoughtful study and charitable relations as the necessary underpinning of *koinonia* and mission," in reality, "too much is left to chance. It is too often assumed that simply living together, ideas and attitudes rubbing up against one another will assist relationships . . ." and that the various elements "need more structured attention."[9] At Mirfield, however, the 2011 Report of the Inspectors noted, "The College . . . provides students with a model of traditional religious life to enable them to grow in Christian discipleship . . . the intensity of life in such a small community offers many opportunities for growth in holiness as people move from tolerance to love of those with whom they differ."[10] Mirfield uses spiritual directors widely to achieve this, "All students are encouraged to have a spiritual director . . . This provides a further opportunity for students to integrate their learning and their personal experience and development. It also helps to consolidate the Mirfield tradition of spirituality."[11] Furthermore, at Mirfield, "Students are required to spend at least twenty

---

8. N. G. Wright, "Spirituality as Discipleship: The Anabaptist Heritage," citing Walter Klaasen, *Anabaptism: Neither Catholic nor Protestant*.

9. Quality in Formation Panel, *Inspector's Report, November 2008, St Stephen's House Oxford*, para. G.1, G.2

10. Quality in Formation Panel, *Inspector's Report, March 2011, The College of the Resurrection, Mirfield*, para. 56.

11. Quality in Formation Panel, *Inspector's Report, March 2011, The College of the Resurrection, Mirfield*, para.59

minutes a day in private prayer."[12] While it would be highly inappropriate for any Baptist College to embrace the particular stream of churchmanship embraced by St Stephen's House or The College of the Resurrection, the sense of deliberate and regularized development of spiritual disciplines has something to offer.

In traditions closer to Baptist, there have historically been guides to living that constitute, in effect, a Rule. Jeremy Taylor (1613–1667) wrote an "agenda," and many Puritans compiled extensive guides to godliness, of which Richard Baxter's *A Christian Directory* (1674) is an example.[13] A common rule, such as the Rule of the Third Order of St Francis, can be adapted for personal use, or for a renewed common use within a community. It goes a long way to challenging what Bloesch says characterizes more than anything else modern Protestantism, "the absence of spiritual discipline, or spiritual exercises."[14]

Chris Ellis views the "way of being" a minister as a rule of life, that is, a cluster of practices embraced with the intention of seeking faithful Christian living.[15] Philip Sheldrake argues that these rules are not so much legislative as examples of wisdom writing, the adoption of proven wisdom by the ensuing generations.[16] Ellis goes on to suggest that a Rule is more than just a description of devotional practices, but embraces practical concerns too. He suggests that "a rule of life for ministers should be a combination of spiritual disciplines with practical examples of good ministerial practice and behavior, good practices that might relate to the other two spheres of 'doing' and 'knowing.'"[17] The 2011 *Guide to Good Pastoral Practice* issued by the BUGB Ministry Department goes some way to providing part of that rule, while there is room for the development of a list of core comprehensions to accompany the agreed core competences that are already embedded in BUGB practice.

There have been religious orders acting as a superstructure around which a rule of life can be built, or spiritual disciplines attached, for as long as there has been deliberate ministerial education, and have been a familiar way to enable spiritual formation in non-evangelical contexts. We have already seen the link between The Cowley Fathers and theological

---

12. Quality in Formation Panel, *Inspector's Report, March 2011, The College of the Resurrection, Mirfield*, para.62

13. Chan, *Spiritual Theology*, 191.

14. Bloesch, *The Crisis of Piety*, 49.

15. Ellis, "Being a Minister. Spirituality and the Pastor," 69.

16. Sheldrake, "Religious Rules," 549.

17. Ellis, "Being a Minister. Spirituality and the Pastor," 70.

education among Tractarians in Oxford, or the link that exists to this day between Charles Gore's Community of the Resurrection at Mirfield, and the theological college there. James Lawson argues that "The disciplines and practices of formation that shape us, by the power and grace of the Holy Spirit, into the knowledge and likeness of Jesus Christ, and that sustain our ministries, draw upon the earlier monastic repertoire of the 'Deep Church.'"[18] He notes with approval how Sarah Coakley[19] "believes that the loss of disciplined clerical prayer is quietly but corrosively devastating," and so she sustains a weekly hour of contemplative prayer for ordinands at Westcott House, Cambridge. Similarly, in this regard, James K. A. Smith offers an Augustinian account of the significance of liturgy, formation and desire in theological education that proposes a new monasticism for the university. He contends that desire forms knowledge, and following Charles Taylor's notion of "social imaginaries" and Heidegger's notion of understanding (*Verstehen*) to argue that we love before we know, he finds that this epistemology vindicates a patristic emphasis on the importance of purifying desire in order to know. This can happen through acquiring the virtues, which Smith describes as precognitive dispositions of desire.[20]

What has been surprising has been the much more recent adoption of such practices amongst evangelicals. Perhaps best seen as a phenomenon of the emerging church movement, "new monastic movements" have sprung up in a range of contexts. For Baptists, for instance, *The Northumbria Community* has for a couple of decades been the community of choice, although it is by no means the first. An attempt was made by Rev'd Margaret Jarman in the 1980s to establish a community, although it never really became much beyond the vehicle for her to inhabit an enclosed life. Earlier, others, such as Sr. Mary Magdalene of the Anglican Benedictine community in Wantage, or Br. Ramon,[21] a Franciscan, had begun life as Baptists (Sr. Mary Magdalene had been a BMS missionary, and Br. Ramon, as Raymond Lloyd, had trained at Spurgeon's College.) They explored their call to the religious life through other denominations, most typically Anglican. For them there was no alternative. This continues to this day, with one former Baptist minister now a fully professed Franciscan, who, having lived in a small community

---

18. Lawson, "Theological Formation in the Church of 'the Last Men and Women,'" 335

19. Sarah Coakley, unpublished address at Westcot House, Cambridge, 16–18 September 2009.

20. Coakley, "Deepening Practices: Perspectives from Ascetical and Mystical Theology," 88.

21. His obituary can be found at http://www.franciscanarchive.org.uk/rip-ramonssf.html (accessed August 2013). He died aged sixty-four in 2000.

in inner-city Leeds, now lives in a Franciscan house in the north of England, and another a professed Benedictine oblate. The latter, where membership of the Benedictine order involves living out the rule of life in the midst of ordinary life (Br. Stephen is a Baptist pastor) is where most will find their calling to "the religious life" ("religious," here, meaning commitment to the life of a religious order, such as The Benedictines, Franciscans or Augustinians). This kind of commitment is called, typically, a third order, to distinguish it from those who are members of monastic communities living out vows of chastity, poverty and obedience in a community house.

The Northumbria Community has a small core of those who live in or near its mother house in Northumbria, including its "bishop" or leader, Rev'd. Roy Searle, a Baptist minister, but a larger group of some two to three hundred are companions, or professed members of the community, scattered across the world. A larger group of "friends of the community" support its work and use its resources of liturgy and retreat. The spiritual ethos of the *Northumbria Community* is strongly Celtic in origin, and the saints it honors in particular are those of the early British church in Northumbria.

More recently, the Anglican-Baptist ecumenical church in Sheffield, St Thomas Crooke's, has developed through its Philadelphia congregation of mainly people in their twenties, *The Order of Mission*. Again, this has a scattered community worldwide of those who are attracted to emerging church and want a structure within which to engage in mission.

All of these developments are attractive to those who have neither desire nor call to an enclosed monastic life, but who want to engage with the spirituality of the monastic life, and shape their spirituality within the shared rules of a third order community.[22] Within the new monasticism there are also those who create their own community living, but unrelated to one of the historic orders. Often living within the most demanding urban areas, these small communities are small outposts of mission to deprived localities.

Others will want to adopt something of the spirituality of the monastic way of life, without membership of an order or group. Ian Adams describes how monastic practice, wisdom and spirituality can be brought into everyday life, through, for instance, a rhythm of life, the practice of hospitality, and living a way of simplicity, devotion, humility, and rootedness.[23]

The antecedents of this new monasticism are to be found in the middle years of the previous century. Dietrich Bonhoeffer's seminary community at Finkenwalde, described in *Life Together*, is one of its roots. This community

---

22. Grimley and Wooding, *Living the Hours*, 24.
23. Adams, *Cave, Refectory, Road*.

sought to train pastors for the confessing church that stood opposed to Hitler and Nazism, and lived a communal life in the face of persecution. The students sang the Psalms daily, engaged in periods of reflective spiritual reading (with echoes of *lectio divina*) as they studied theology and the Scriptures. Bonhoeffer clearly had a vision of a kind of monastic community, without being in a monastery. Writing to Erwin Sutz on Reformation Day, Oct 31, 1943, he says, "the entire training of budding theologians today belongs in church, monastery-like schools in which the pure doctrine, the sermon on the Mount, and worship can be taken seriously—which is not the case with all three things at the university and, in present-day circumstances is impossible."[24] In Glasgow, facing the grinding poverty of post-depression urban life, *The Iona Community* was formed with a strong political agenda, as well as an imaginative ministry in creative liturgy. It's founder, George MacCleod, a Church of Scotland minister, stopped short of creating a traditional monastic community, although it has its spiritual home in the Abbey on Iona, and its members, like those of the *Northumbria Community*, live out their life in a "secular" way of living (here, "secular" means not enclosed in a religious house, but living "in the world.") *The Iona Community* is perhaps best known for its songs and hymns, with John Bell and Kathy Galloway, both members of the community, being the most widely sung writers. In a similar way, a community that straddled the Protestant/Catholic divide in Europe, Taize, founded after the Second World War by Br. Roger Schutze, is best known for its Taize chants, sung by a far greater number of people than have ever been to the Taize Community.

Looking to these antecedents from an age, eighty years ago, when the church in the West was far stronger than it is today in its post-Christendom, postmodern context, a new crop of new-monastic groups has sprung up. For them, building a community that seeks to inculcate the virtues within its members is vital as an antidote to the corrosive effects of secular, materialist consumerism. The work of Alasdair MacIntyre that we consider elsewhere in this book, is seminal in this regard.

Returning to our theme of spiritual formation, membership of a new monastic community, giving a structure to a rule of life, providing accountability and shared identity in fellowship, could be describing loosely the characteristics of theological education when it was populated mainly by single young men, living on site, and was full-time. It was the closest any of them got to a quasi-monastic existence. Now that much theological education is not residential, is not full-time, comprises in the main those who are

---

24. Cited in Lawson, "Theological Formation in the Church of 'the Last Men and Women,'" 342.

married, and is much more fragmented in the challenges posed by combining practical pastoral responsibilities for much of the week, academic study and family life in the remainder, the value of membership of a new monastic group seems obvious.

In this regard, for Baptists, the emerging Baptist Order that took shape in 2010–12, and provides a shared daily office, cell groups and an annual convocation within the framework of a third order community rooted in Baptist values and polity, offers an opportunity to shape such an order with formational ideas at its heart.

Whether or not lived out within the context of an organized and recognized order, the disciplines and practices embodied in the monastic life remain the cornerstone of the disciplined spiritual life, and in some way must be captured and valued by those we are forming for ministry. Prayer, reading the Scriptures and singing the Psalms, *lectio divina*, silence, hospitality, work, and play, all have their part to play in the spiritual formation process. We now turn to a particular expression of spiritual formation, expressed by Bernard of Clairvaux.

St Bernard of Clairvaux's Sermons on the Song of Songs and Spiritual Formation in Ministerial Development

When so much contemporary worship luxuriates in an affective turn—an emphasis upon the emotions and the direct encounter with the Divine through intimacy—it is surprising that St Bernard of Clairvaux has not risen to a more prominent position, for he is the quintessential theologian uniting the Bible and experience. Born in 1090, he was well-educated and from a noble background, and aged twenty-one entered the protomonastery of the Cistercian Order at Citeaux. Still in its reforming vigor, the Cistercians had sought to return to the strictest possible interpretation of the Rule of St Benedict, and Bernard proved himself such an exemplary monk that he was appointed abbot of the newly founded house at Clairvaux a mere four years after entering Citeaux. Clairvaux became a model of strict Cistercian observance, and he attracted thousands to the cloistered life of contemplation and work.

Such was his ability that he became active in wider Church politics, mediating between the two Orders of the Cluniacs and the Cistercians in their conflict, and in the schism that had started in 1130 when Anacletus claimed that he, not Innocent II, was the legitimate pope. He led the attack on Abelard at the Council of Sens in 1140, and preached the Second Crusade in 1146–7. By force of personality, rather than intellect, he was the dominant figure in Western Christianity in the twelfth century. As much a man of action and mission as one of contemplation, he combined what we might today call active missional leadership and contemplative prayer, although Bernard described himself as the "chimera" of his day, a strange beast, neither secular nor monastic. As such he has something to offer to the minister seeking a balance between personal devotion and love of God, and the activities and duties of the pastoral and missional office.

Indeed, his lasting contribution to the life of the Church lies not in his active life but in the fruit of his contemplative life: the many sermons, hymns, and other writings that expound the ascent of the soul to God through mystical experience. Profoundly Christo-centric, he verges upon the kind of Jesuology that infects much of today's plebeian theology, but avoids it in the end through his being steeped in the Scriptures and the Fathers. He "remembers" the life, death and resurrection of Jesus Christ in order to imitate him, praying the story so that "the affections for our Lord Jesus should be both tender and intimate, to oppose the sweet enticements of the sensual life."[25] He was thought the author of "O sacred head sore wounded" and "Jesus, the very thought of thee/ with sweetness fills the breast/ But sweeter far thy face to see/ And in thy presence rest" (although scholarship now doubts that attribution.) The fourth verse of that hymn is a poetic summary of his thought (in Edward Caswell's 1858 translation,)

> But what to those who find? Ah! This
>
> Nor tongue nor pen can show
>
> The love of Jesus, what it is
>
> None but his loved ones know.

Even if Bernard did not write these lyrics, they certainly owe their thought-world to him.

His writings are profoundly biblical, after the tradition of the pre-modern age. He follows the Fathers by starting with the plain, historical sense of Scripture, but this is only a prelude to the spiritual sense that is the work and gift of the Spirit. His close identification of the Scripture and the Holy Spirit prefigure in many ways the doctrine of Word and Spirit espoused by John Calvin. This spiritual reading is closely allied to his personal experience, such that Leclerque has argued "the verses of the Song of Songs are little more than a pretext for the expression of a personal experience."[26] These sermons are not expositions of the text as we might expect: by Sermon 43 we have only reached verse 13 of chapter 1 of the Songs. *The Sermons*

---

25. Sermon 20.4, *Three Qualities of Love*.

26. St Bernard, *Selected Works*, cited in Tamburello, *Bernard of Clairvaux*, 190.

on The Song of Songs function as an exposition of the mystical union with Christ that is the goal of the contemplative life. "He achieved the first great synthesis in the West between all of Scripture and patristic theology on the one hand, and the totality of human experience on the other."[27]

1. Spiritual Formation and Ministerial Development

The context for considering St Bernard's *Sermons on the Song of Songs* is the wider horizon of re-formulating ministerial formation through a virtue ethics framework. Training or the formation of those preparing for the ministry in the churches has begun to pay greater attention to the spiritual life of the ordinand, within a broad psychological, spiritual, and moral matrix. Our development as spiritually capable men and women is not simply a matter of learning how to establish a pattern of personal devotional disciplines, be it the evangelical Quiet Time, the quasi-monastic office or time speaking in tongues. It embraces our development as autonomous adults, aware of our deeper drives, hopes and fears; our sexuality and search for meaning, companionship and intimacy; and of our need for interior change.

Traditionally, such spiritual development has been centered upon a common liturgical life of shared worship within the community of the theological college. It was believed that by insisting upon attendance at the daily act or acts of prayer and worship, those being formed communally for three or four years would develop the patterns that would serve them for a lifetime. Such acts of worship, however, all too-easily become pedagogical tools to develop skills in leading worship, preaching and praying in public, and their developmental character in establishing a deepening spiritual life minimized. Indeed, the ubiquity of the mixed-mode form of ministerial training, with the majority of the time being spent in a placement rather than communally in college, ensures that for the majority of ministers-in-training, any regular, collegiate pattern of worship is weekly, rather than daily, and that if there ever was a golden age of collegial spiritual formation through shared daily worship, such an age is long departed. I am not sure that if the intended fruit of such a pattern was stability in the personal, spiritual and moral lives of those undergoing training, that the evidence of the rates of ensuing ministerial failure and collapse would demonstrate much effectiveness in the model, even at its best.

While I would advocate, where possible, a return to patterns of shared daily worship (both morning and evening, actually), and while my personal preference now would be for at least one of those to follow an ordered

27. Ibid., 14.

pattern of prayer, rather than the essentially extempore pattern that predominates at other times, by itself liturgical discipline is inadequate to the task of spiritual formation. A vital element, no doubt, but shared daily worship must be supplemented by the specific development of a personal life of prayer, attentiveness to Scripture and to the integration of the inner life. If ministers are to be first and foremost examples for others to follow, then in formation, those preparing for such a life must submit to the challenges and disciplines of such a life. Our contemporary fetishism with individual freedoms counters such a pattern, which is perhaps why it is both neglected, and of vital significance.

It was the particular gift of the greatest masters of such a spiritual life—masters such as Bernard of Clairvaux, or Ignatius of Loyola, Catherine of Sienna or Theresa of Avila, or, from a stable perhaps more familiar to evangelicals, The Christian and Missionary Alliance pastor, A.W.Tozer [28] or the Quaker, Thomas Kelly[29] —to understand both the working of the human psyche and the deep things of the spiritual life. Growth in spiritual vitality connects the work of the Spirit and the life of the individual. Thus spiritual development consists not just in learning the techniques, disciplines or patterns of prayer, but rather, in seeing the goal of such disciplines as growth in conformity to Christ, union with God, and awareness of the holy.

Turning from this over-view of spiritual formation, we focus upon Bernard's *Sermons on the Song of Songs* as an example of how such growth might be sought within the contemplative component of a life otherwise given to action and ministry.

2. The Song of Songs

The use of the *Song of Songs* by the Church has had a chequered history. Today it is largely ignored, because the Church finds a place for either explicitly erotic poetry about the love between a man and a woman, or an allegory of the love between Christ and the believer, frankly, problematic. The one seems inappropriate, the other faintly weird. It is either simply erotic love poetry or allegorical. Or perhaps it is both, starting life as simply celebrating the erotic love between two people (and there is nothing strange in that,) but finding in that such echoes of the relationship of God and the soul,

---

28. Primarily a pastoral preacher, A. W. Tozer (1897–1963) was influenced by Bernard of Clairvaux, and Fenelon, amongst others, in his emphasis upon the experience of God by his Spirit. His most well-known book is *The Knowledge of the Holy*. Cf. Mitchell, "Tozer, A. W."

29. Kelly, *A Testament of Devotion*.

that it has taken on a new level of meaning, and affording an expression of spiritual love that is rooted clearly in the biblical tradition.

Critical scholarship emphasizes the human eroticism of the book, while Protestant evangelicalism, as well as Catholicism, has held on to the older, allegorical tradition. A third dimension of the book's utility has been to link the spiritual life with the erotic: sensuality plays a significant role in a healthy spirituality. The deep psychological roots of a profound spiritual response to the Other, God or Christ are found in the same place that a healthy erotic response is made to a lover or spouse. If the roots of spiritual development in early childhood are in the growth of wonder, love, and affirmation or trust, then somewhere in that same mix are the responses that, beyond puberty, will flower in the love for another human being expressed in sexual passion. These are two branches of the one tree.

But, from Origen onwards, this book has found a significant place in Christian mystical spirituality. He was the first to see it as an allegory of the individual soul and Christ, thus making it intimate and personal but it was Bernard of Clairvaux who, in a series of sermons, popularized the imagery, and was immensely influential upon a host of other mystical writers, such as Richard of St Victor, Teresa of Avila and John of the Cross.

While the preferred hermeneutical approach for Scripture has been the literal approach, the opposite is true of this book, especially in Bernard's account. The passion between the lovers in the book has been generally interpreted as the even more passionate love between God and the individual soul invited to mystical union.

This Book begins with a kiss. "Let him kiss me with the kisses of his mouth." (1:2) In the Ancient world, an approach to a lord or king might be expressed in kissing their ring (this still happens for Roman Catholics and their bishop), their feet or even the ground on which they walked, but never kissing their lips. This is reserved for the closest of relationships, that relationship where status is subsumed in mutual love. The woman in this poem is not simply greeting her king, but welcoming her lover. This kiss of tender love distinguishes their relationship from that of mere submission or reverence.

It is this extraordinary image that has been taken up in the allegorical tradition of interpretation. God remains God, and is never anything but our Lord, but it seems that he does not invite us to keep him distant, otherworldly, or remote, but to draw close, to intimacy and to love. Jesus says to the disciple, "I no longer call you servants, but friends." (John 15:15.) Now, this is not at all the same as the kind of faux intimacy of "Jesus is my buddy." Friend, yes; pal, no. In the friendship there is always an imbalance in status. It is possible to be the King's friend, but the King always remains the King, and power and lordship are his. Here again, worship must never lose reverence, even if it plumbs the depths of intimate love and affection.

This is exactly what St Bernard says:

> For her it is no mean or contemptible thing to be kissed by the kiss, because it is nothing less than the gift of the Holy Spirit. If, as is properly understood, the Father is he who kisses, the Son he who is kissed, then it cannot be wrong to see in the kiss the Holy Spirit, for he is the imperturbable peace of the Father and the Son, their unshakable bond, their undivided love, their indivisible unity.[30]

We could expound allegorically at length on the anointing oil (the Holy Spirit) and the name of the lover (the name of God is his whole character and being), but suffice it to say again, that the development of character and love of God is the work of the Spirit as we discover increasingly who Christ is, his love and his character. For Bernard, what we are invited to participate in is the inner-trinitarian life, where the Father and Son kiss one another, and then reach out to the created world with the redeeming kiss of love. This participation in the life of the Trinity is the domain of the Spirit, and the ability to share in it, a gift of the Spirit.

This may sound quite pious to our ears, quaint even, used as we are to arguing for the meaning of this or that Hebrew word, this or that Greek source, and so forth. But we are not reflecting in this aspect of formation on the academic tools of the ministerial trade, but rather on something that is more needful, more important, more significant for the formation of ministry. Few ministries failed because of lack of Greek or the ability to understand Barth; more fail because of significant shortcomings in this or that ministerial skill; many because of weaknesses in character or personality, or a lack of those people-skills so essential for pastoral ministry. Yet, I am convinced that most fail because we pay too little attention to our souls, to our love of Christ, to our walking close with him, to spiritual formation. People will forgive ministers much if they sense they are, fundamentally, men and women of prayer and men and women of God. Here, the Song of Songs is our fountain source.

Here is St Bernard himself,

> Today the text we are to study is the book of our own experience. You must therefore turn your attention inwards, each one must take note of his own particular awareness of the things I am about to discuss. I am attempting to discover if any of you

---

30. Bernard, *Sermons on the Song of Songs* 8.2

has been privileged to say from his heart: "Let him kiss me with the kiss of his mouth." Those to whom it is given to utter these words sincerely are comparatively few, but anyone who has received this mystical kiss from the mouth of Christ at least once, seeks again that intimate experience, and eagerly looks for its frequent renewal. I think that nobody can grasp what it is except the one who receives it. For it is "a hidden manna," and only he who eats it still hungers for more. It is "a sealed fountain" to which no stranger has access; only he who drinks still thirsts for more. Listen to one who has had the experience, how urgently he demands: "Be my savior again, renew my joy." But a soul like mine, burdened with sins, still subject to carnal passions, devoid of any knowledge of spiritual delights, may not presume to make such a request, almost totally unacquainted as it is with the joys of the supernatural life.[31]

Bernard is aware that the progress of the soul is not an immediate one. In our culture of immediate gratification, we may assume that the spiritual life is equally susceptible to a swift conclusion. Much of our contemporary worship promises an easy intimacy with Christ, an emotional experience of love and devotion enabled by a few words sung in the worship set. Actually, what is delivered is the equivalent of plastic fruit placed in a fruit bowl: it looks OK, but the taste is artificial and the nutritional value pitiful. However, the real thing takes some time to be sampled, and is costly in its pursuit. St Bernard again: He has spoken of two kisses that precede the kiss of the lips: the first is the kiss of the feet in repentance, the second is the kiss of the Lord's hand in acknowledgement of his glory and his grace: "you must kiss his hand, that is, you must give glory to his name, not to yourself. First of all you must glorify him because he has forgiven your sins, secondly because he has adorned you with virtues."

> Once you have had this twofold experience of God's benevolence in these two kisses, you need no longer feel abashed in aspiring to a holier intimacy. Growth in grace brings expansion of confidence You will love with greater ardor, and knock on the door with greater assurance, in order to gain what you perceive to be still wanting to you. "The one who knocks will always have the door opened to him." It is my belief that to a person so disposed, God will not refuse that most intimate kiss of all, a mystery of supreme generosity and ineffable sweetness. You have seen the way that we must follow, the order of procedure: first, we cast ourselves at his feet, we weep before the Lord who made

---

31. Bernard, *Sermons on the Song of Songs* 3.1.

us, deploring the evil we have done. Then we reach out for the hand that will lift us up, that will steady our trembling knees. And finally, when we shall have obtained these favors through many prayers and tears, we humbly dare to raise our eyes to his mouth, so divinely beautiful, not merely to gaze upon it, but I say it with fear and trembling—to receive its kiss. "Christ the Lord is a Spirit before our face," and he who is joined to him in a holy kiss becomes through his good pleasure, one spirit with him.[32]

There follows the kiss of the mouth. This, Bernard begins, is the kiss of the Word of God, the incarnation. "The kiss of his mouth signifies the complete embrace by which the Son of God has assumed our humanity. In the incarnation, the mouth which kisses is the eternal Word."[33] In our experience, following the kiss of the feet in repentance and the kiss of the hands of God in gratitude and honor for his forgiveness, comes the "kiss of the mouth." Here Bernard draws upon Augustine's dual procession of the Spirit from the Father and the Son, and the nature of the Spirit as the eternal gift of love.[34] The reciprocity of gift exchange, between the Father and the Son, is the Holy Spirit, "a certain unutterable communion of the Father and the Son,"[35] and this unutterable communion can best be described as love. Thus, the kiss of God is his gift of the Holy Spirit. "The kiss of the Father is incarnate in the Son, but is mediated to us in the power of the Holy Spirit. Sent by both the Father and the Son, the Spirit conveys to us 'the light of knowledge' and 'the fire of love.'"[36] Bernard employs the combination of imaginative biblical interpretation, scholastic theology and his own spiritual experience, reflecting that of countless other believers, to expound what it is to receive the Spirit and enter into spiritual communion with God, or, rather, to be given the grace to enter into the communion between the Father and the Son, the inner life of the Trinity through the Spirit. This is in contrast to much contemporary spiritual formation, which lacks both the theological grasp of doctrine, and a biblically-formed imagination, while offering a shallow emotionalism in an effort to induce intimacy in worship. The reality is that most of the contemporary songs are written by theological illiterates, and when older hymns are appropriated by this "worship culture," they often come from either an early Pentecostal or a holiness stable, neither

32. Bernard, *Sermons on the Song of Songs* 3.5.

33. Ngien, *Gifted Response: The Triune God as the Causative Agency of Our Responsive Worship*, 66.

34. Augustine, *De Trinitate* 5.16.

35. Ibid., 5.2.

36. Ngien, *Gifted Response: The Triune God as the Causative Agency of Our Responsive Worship*, 78.

of which, at the time of their composing, engaged with the older, catholic tradition of spiritual writing. The result is an impoverished kind of worship cut loose from the great traditions of the church. Thus, even where some attention to spiritual formation is attempted, it often focuses upon developing dimensions of worship that themselves lack depth.

I turn now to a section of The Song of Songs that Bernard does not consider in his Sermons: 5:2–8, and question of spiritual stability. If the three steps to an encounter with the divine are first the kiss of the feet in repentance, the second is the kiss of the Lord's hand in acknowledgement of his glory and his grace, and the third the kiss of the lips in reception of the love of God, then what is the pattern of this process? It is not a single episode, but one that is repeated time and again. Bernard speaks in Sermon 74 of the experience of Christ coming to him, perceived by "the movement of my heart."

> He is life and power, and as soon as he enters in, he awakens my slumbering soul; he stirs and soothes and pierces my heart, for before it was as hard as stone, and diseased . . . . . . But when the Word has left me, all these spiritual powers become weak and faint and begin to grow cold, as though you had removed the fire from beneath the boiling pot, and this is the sign of his going. Then my soul must needs be sorrowful until he returns, and my heart again kindles within me – the sign of his returning.[37]

The language here echoes the language of others' experience in the mystical tradition. Richard Rolle (d.1349) writes "the mind is kindled by the fire of the Holy Spirit . . . . Made sweet in the torrent of God's love, for it is always looking at him, and not considering earthly things at all, until that day when it is glorified with the perfect vision of its Beloved."[38] Rolles' contemporary, Walter Hilton, writes:

> Seek then what you have lost, so that you may find it . . . . And if, when you feel this desire for God, for Jesus—for it is all one— you are helped and strengthened by a supernatural might so strong that it is changed into love and affection, spiritual savor and sweetness and the knowledge of truth, so that for the time your mind is set on no created thing . . . so that you are enclosed in Jesus alone, resting in him with the warmth of tender love, then you have found something of Jesus. Not Jesus as he is, but

---

37. Bernard, *Sermons on the Song of Songs* 74.2.6–7.
38. Rolle, *The Fire of God*, 131.

an inward sight of him; and the more fully you find him, the more you will desire him.[39]

The similar experience of encounters with Christ can be multiplied in the mystics, and echoed in the experience of many a searcher after Christ. In Richard Fosters' *Streams of Living Water*, articulating the *Renovare* movement's embracing of six spiritual traditions,[40] he writes of the contemplative tradition as a life of loving attention to God, "Every one of us is called to be a contemplative—not in the sense of a particular vocation we call 'the contemplative life,' but in the sense of a holy habit of contemplative love that leads us forth in partnership with God into creative and redeeming work."[41] While the depths of encounter described by Bernard, Rolle or Hilton might be rare, the hunger and search for God that they describe somehow needs to be the characteristic of every Christian, and certainly those who seek to lead God's people. This is the well-spring from which those other virtues spring: the intellectual, the moral, the practical.

This life of prayerful attention to God is far from a constant, glorious, upward journey. For all, including the greatest of those exponents of the prayerful or contemplative life, the hunger for God ebbs and flows. To this reality we turn.

3. Spiritual Stability: Song of Songs 5:2–8

This section of the Song is frankly erotic (5:4–5 has been expounded upon in the most intimate of terms) and forms a part of the Ancient Near East love poem that is beautifully phrased. But, within the allegorical exegetical tradition it has another meaning, and that is, the experience of the soul that love of God is far from constant. God makes his advances towards us, yet, we sleep, we are put out by those approaches. We've gone to bed and it's a hassle to get up. The nineteenth century American Presbyterian, George Burrowes, comments upon this passage:

> Our religious life consists of a series of revivals and withdrawals by Jesus, for calling into exercise and putting to the test our graces. When under the influence of first love, we determine never to forget the Savior, and think the thing most impossible.

39. Hilton, *The Ladder of Perfection*, 57.

40. Foster, *Streams of Living Water*. The six traditions are (i) contemplative—the prayer-filled life; (ii) holiness—the virtuous life; (iii) charismatic—the Spirit-empowered life; (iv) social justice—the compassionate life; (v) evangelical—the word-centered life; (vi) incarnational—the sacramental life.

41. Foster, *Streams of Living Water*, 58.

SPIRITUAL FORMATION

> After some experience of the deceitfulness of the heart, when at some subsequent period, we have had our souls restored and made to lie down in green pastures, beside the still waters, we resolve again to be faithful in close adherence to our Lord, under the impression, that with our present knowledge of the workings of sin, and the glorious displays of made to us of the loveliness of Christ, and of his love towards us personally, we shall now at length persevere; but we soon find to our sorrow, that, left to ourselves, we are as unsteady and unfaithful as ever. It is surprising how swiftly coldness will succeed great religious fervor.
>
> Even with grace in the soul, with the heart awake, we find ourselves falling asleep, borne down by the business of life, the charms of the world, or the infirmities of the flesh.[42]

Spiritual formation in ministerial development must come to terms with this reality of the inconstancy of our affections and desires. If one of the purposes of theological education is to evaluate those simple and childish views of God and Scripture that we may carry into the College, and discover which stand the fire of enquiry, so that our faith might be all the stronger for it, then I believe a vital dimension of spiritual formation for ministry is to deepen our experience of the journey of our own soul, in order to be the better equipped to serve the flock of Christ as pastors and guides. Our own spiritual journey becomes intentionally the laboratory in which we explore prayer and our own wretched weaknesses.

If we do not recognize this experience for ourselves, how shall we assist others as spiritual guides and directors? One of the most significant absences in much contemporary pastoral care is the work of spiritual direction. We know how to assist in a person's bereavement, or in guiding them towards this or that sphere of service, but deepening their spiritual life, guiding their prayers, that's another matter! Ministers must be men and women who walk the ways of spiritual guides, soul friends, and as such must be on that journey themselves. Spiritual formation is more than knowing about spirituality: it is to know the One who kisses us with the kisses of his mouth.

4. Patterns of Prayer

How, then, might prayerful attentiveness to God become embedded in ministerial formation? The over-arching framework of this understanding of ministerial formation is virtue-ethics: the understanding that the

---

42. Burrowes, *The Song of Songs*, 405, 410.

characteristics of effective ministry are captured by practices, both taught and caught, and developed under the oversight of both tutors and existing practitioners who serve as apprentice-masters. This all takes place within communities of practice, both the local church and the college. These contexts of intentional formational practice collaborate to shape the life of the minister, embed in them those habits that will enrich their ministry and give to them the tools of their trade for the changing contexts in which ministry will be practiced.

What practices might be developed to shape the minister as a woman or man of prayer? We noted above how this was traditionally the shared daily act of worship in a collegiate setting, but how the changing pattern of formation to a predominantly mixed-mode delivery has made such a tool difficult to use with the regularity required for the inculcation of habits of daily devotion within the college context. Certainly, those preparing for ministry should share together in worship as they gather, weekly probably in term-time, or for others, on more extended forms of preparation, as they meet for weekends and residential schools, but the limits of time, and the necessity that such acts of worship also bear the pedagogical burden of developing the skills of leading worship and preaching, means that any focus upon their developing patterns of personal prayer will be very limited.

Instead I want to suggest a range of practices that seem practicable. Given limitless resources, a year spent in some form of monastic community, learning how to pray, might be a profound formative experience, but this is simply impractical and ill-suited to the temperament of most. Better to leave something of that life to be discovered later (such as a forty day Ignatian Retreat) than inoculate the unwilling and resistant to its virtues by imposing it!

If the bread-and-butter of the ministerial life of prayer is the daily reading of Scripture and praying, then requiring all those in formation to practice this, at least, seems essential. Those traditions where a daily public act of prayer is routine clearly have an advantage. Anglican ordinands, whether in college or in the parish have a pattern of shared prayer in the Daily Office of Morning and Evening Prayer that provides the disciplinary framework. Indeed, this is establishing a habit of prayer that becomes part of the daily duties of the priest, praying in the Parish Church, with or without others, throughout the year. In Free Church traditions, there is generally no expectation in Britain of such a practice. Instead, the pattern of prayer is private, and therein lies its weakness as a formational practice. Who knows, checks or even bothers if the minister-in-training does not pray or read the Scriptures for themselves. More likely is the development of a pattern of 'professional reading and praying', where all is directed towards the pastoral duties and sermon preparation.

One remedy might be to require those preparing for ministry to be in mutual accountability groups, where the avoidance of prayer might be less easily accomplished. A common feature of the dispersed religious communities often associated with the new-monasticism is the requirement of their members to be in some form of cell group, be it the 'huddle' of *The Order of Mission,* or the cell group of *The Order for Baptist Ministry.* Undergirding such a cell is the expectation of a shared form of prayer, but in formational terms this is not necessarily the case (although I could make a case for its benefits) since the key element is the practice of examen. Here, the small group of four or five ministers-in-training would devote their time (say, two hours) to mutual accountability: perhaps in years one and two of formation with their peers and led by an older student, but in the final year, in leading a cell of those embarking upon training, giving the cell some consistency of practice. Meeting twice a term, the focus would be upon the development of practices and habits of prayer, whether of a shared character, or across a range of options, from the traditional Quiet Time, a Daily Office or a more contemplative practice.

For some ministers-in-training, where their placement is as part of a team, then the presence of such a trainee might stimulate the development of a shared practice of daily prayer across the team. This happens at Philadelphia in Sheffield, the home of *The Order of Mission,* and where a large staff group can gather for daily prayers. However, even where a minister-in-training is in sole charge, there might be possibilities of sharing in daily prayer with others in the congregation at an agreed time.

Where there are denominational or ecumenical religious orders, such as *The Order for Baptist Ministry,* or the *Northumbria Community,* then ministers-in-training could be encouraged to join as ordinands, and develop the practices of daily prayer within such a discipline. For some this might mean a life-long commitment, while for others it might serve simply as the framework for the developing of habits of prayer. Others may wish to join a *Renovare* group, or form a prayer triplet within their local church or network of churches. The key element is not so much the nature of the group, but rather the expectation that these habits will be formed in some communal way, within accountable relationships.

One radical (but probably impossible) move would be to re-conceive the college or seminary as itself a neo-monastic community. Impossible? It has been a powerful shaper of the formational context in two instances, both mentioned above: amongst the Church of England in its mid-nineteenth century Tractarian stream, where both Mirfield and St Stephen's House,

Oxford continue to offer ministerial formation rooted in a religious context (St Stephen's House occupies the original mother house of the Cowley Fathers,) and, famously, at Finkenwald, where Bonhoeffer presided over the seminary for the pastors of the Confessing Church, organized along neo-monastic lines. This is not the context to explore what this might look like within a Baptist context, or indeed, if it would be at all possible, yet it is not without significance that where the church has felt a powerful missional imperative (as the Anglo-Catholics did in the face of rapidly urbanizing Britain in the nineteenth century) or known itself to be facing hugely challenging socio-political forces inimical to the Gospel, as in 1930s Germany, it has been to the monastic template that some in the Church have looked. Are our times so very different, I wonder?

Some form of intentional attentiveness to the spiritual life of the minister-in-training would be constructive, be it working with a spiritual director, or simply a termly conversation, one-on-one with another mature and wise guide (preferably one who has no direct reporting to the college itself, to ensure some frankness and reality on the part of the trainee). This could also be within the context of a guided retreat, perhaps.

Within the three or four years of formation (or longer if in a more extended mode of delivery) experimentation with different styles of prayer is invaluable. Part of the purpose of college is to give permission to play. There might be ways of integrating learning about spirituality with its practice, while avoiding any notion that the practice carries academic weight. Similarly, an encouragement to experiment with others in the placement setting could be explored: holding a church retreat, or finding new ways to engage in shared prayer, from half-nights of intercession to a week of short prayer meetings every morning or evening.

The development of a person's spiritual and prayer life could be a feature of the period between testing a call to ministry and embarking upon formal training. This period is sometimes regrettably short, and so it would be dependent upon extending the duration to become a first phase of intentional ministerial formation prior to entrance upon a college course. This might add value to the whole process of ministerial formation, offer a purpose to the months that precede the changes required as a course is commenced and enable the candidate to focus upon this aspect of ministerial formation for a few months, unencumbered by essay deadlines, college and placement commitments or the challenges of accommodating to a new environment for spouse and children. Those who know the candidate well are best equipped to assist them in this focused development, and so this would be primarily located in the congregation from which they are being sent into formation. To commence training with habits of daily prayer well-embedded, especially if in mixed-mode delivery, enhances the overall formational process, I believe. Some will need no encouragement to do so, for this will already be their practice and habit, and the focus can then be upon deepening the experience, but in an individualistic age, where duty, habit and submission to a discipline are challenged at every turn, it cannot be assumed that those who seek formation for ministry pray much. As is discussed elsewhere, humility and obedience, as central ministerial virtues, counter this zeitgeist, and the sooner they are practiced, the better.

An American Evangelical Perspective: Robert Webber

If this all sounds far too exotic to Baptist or evangelical tastes, a similar set of concerns are raised by Robert Webber, writing from the perspective of North American evangelical culture. He argues that in the ancient church, theology and spirituality were not separated. He uses the image of God's saving embrace (paralleling Bernard's kiss) to summarize the economy of salvation, and describes how spirituality has become separated from the story of that embrace.

When we allow ourselves to be read and to be described by this embrace, we have come onto the path of Christian spirituality; we have started the Christian journey. Christian spirituality is not a journey into self, as if spirituality is found in the deep recesses of our nature, hidden inside us, waiting for release. No, true spirituality is the embrace of Jesus, who, united to God, restores our union with God that we lost because of sin. This is how the ancient church understood God's embrace.[43]

In summary, his argument is that this original spirituality, inextricably linked to theology and the narrative of Scripture, became detached through Platonic dualism, replacing theosis with a monastic withdrawal from the world in order to contemplate God though listening prayer, and mysticism, which replaces the journey of God into our self with the journey of the self into God. He disapproves of both moves. "The focus on my inner life rather than the mysteries of the Triune God at work in history to redeem the world becomes narcissistic and even expresses itself in bizarre, direct encounters with God that are viewed as more important than the divine embrace of God, which took place on the hard wood of the cross."[44] I am not sure that Bernard's carefully theological spirituality is identifiable in those terms, but Webber argues that the medieval church had lost its contact with biblical spirituality.

43. Webber, *The Divine Embrace*, 127.
44. Ibid., 53.

This was recovered by Reformation spirituality, with both Luther and Calvin focusing upon union with Christ. Luther's understanding that Christ became one of us so that we might be united with God corresponds to theosis, while Calvin and the Anabaptists similarly emphasized participation in the divine nature. However, as the inheritors of scholasticism, the Reformers also made the separation of a lived theology from a forensic justification with its turn towards intellectual knowledge. So, evangelicals have inherited an understanding of Christian beginnings that is overly intellectual, while equating spirituality with experience.

This produced two kinds of spirituality amongst Protestants: the spirituality of intellectualism and the spirituality of experientialism. The latter includes the rise of Pietism, a response to the perceived deadness of intellectual Lutheranism, and the Evangelical Revival of the Wesleys and Jonathan Edwards. The same trends continue into the twentieth century, Webber argues, with a twist towards individualism. So, the preoccupation with knowing the date of the conversion experience (when were you born again?) or the focus on a highly personalized and individualized devotional pattern— the quiet time— comprising bible study and prayer. The result of both is an emphasis upon feeling forgiven, feeling spiritual, and with the Pentecostal and charismatic expression of this spirituality, feeling "baptized in the Spirit."

Webber describes the current trends arising from this individualized spirituality: an antinomian reaction to evangelical legalism, a mistrust of intellectualism, the language of romance applied to Jesus and the narcissism of much contemporary worship.[45] There are voices that counter these trends, Eugene Peterson, Dallas Willard and Richard Foster amongst them, but Webber's caricature of the parlous state of evangelical spirituality is essentially, and regrettably, accurate. It is this spirituality with which those beginning the formal stages of ministerial formation often come encumbered, and for which something more radical than a course of spirituality is required if a depth of spirituality necessary for the challenges of ministry is to be generated.

Having described the crisis, Webber expounds the cure. The pattern that he develops follows the sequence recovering God's story; finding my place within that story through baptism, where I embrace the new life by the Spirit; living into that baptized life by dying to all that is sin and death, and rising to the new life; the practices that are steadfastly followed; and the all within the community of the church.

---

45. Ibid., 87–99.

In his discussion of the practices of the spiritual life (with an evangelical tenor, to be sure,) he describes it as "a long obedience in the same direction," and frames it around the Rule of St Benedict, translated from its context in an enclosed Order to the life of the common Christian. The three essentials are stability, steadfastness and endurance to the end. "Like the ancient monk who took a vow to live in the stability of his baptism into Christ through the embodied life of the monastic community, so we who have been baptized into the death and resurrection of Jesus should vow to remain stable in our living into the pattern of death and resurrection."[46] Obedient submission to this way of life builds not only the spirituality of the minister, but also the character.

Perhaps the weakness of this translation of the monastic vow to the more individualized "vow to remain stable in our living into the pattern of death and resurrection" lies in its context: the monastic vow was lived out within a community, while this becomes much more tenuous when "secular" living is concerned. The ability to live in such stability envisages strong church communities that actually care about the spiritual and moral welfare of their members, and which will provide the shared community that can assist in keeping such a vow.

The vow to live according to the rule, be it St Benedict's or another's, is kept by discipline, and the Benedictine Rule divides them into prayer, study and work. The disciplines are not the *source* of spirituality, Webber argues, so that if we were more faithful in our practices of prayer, Bible study or contemplation we would be more spiritual, but rather the means of living out of the gift of the Spirit that has been granted us by God's mercy and grace. "Our goal is never to *become spiritual* but to *live out* the spirituality we have in Jesus through the choices that spring forth from continually living in God's embrace affirmed in baptism."[47]

In the challenge of a contemporary church culture that is obsessed with relevance, effectiveness, success and size, the call to an authentic life that shuns these as neither virtuous nor spiritual will seem like a recipe for disaster. However, I profoundly believe that if the church in the West is to survive the coming exile it is not the size of its membership that will count, but rather the depth of discipleship of its members, and ministers must be amongst the exemplars of that. Shallow, consumer-oriented religion will not cut the ice: faithful obedience and endurance to the end, "the long obedience in the same direction," might.

---

46. Ibid., 202.
47. Ibid., 207.

Perhaps we should make candidating for ministry much harder from the earliest stages (and make membership similarly, troublingly, challenging.) Instead of allowing a person to think that within six months of sensing a call to ministry they might expect to be in training, we should delay, test, slow down, and allow the Spirit to deepen the call. Formation should require much greater adherence to obedience, instead of the reluctance to put anything too demanding upon the shoulders of our ordinands. A recent conversation with a newly ordained minister bewailing how the demands of continuing formation were not flexible enough, self-directing enough, or immediately relevant enough, demonstrated to me how entirely we have missed the point. It is in disciplines of study, prayer, and obedient submission that the real virtues are inculcated. Freedom to do exactly as we please, however well-meaning, is but one more accommodation to the age of self-determination and individualism.

10

Character Formation

The role of the college in ministerial formation can all too easily be over-estimated. Obviously, its role in intellectual formation is well established, as is its role in the formation of a set of practices that equip the minister-in-training for their role within the congregation, mission agency or youth work setting. I have argued that spiritual formation is a dimension of overall formation that could more intentionally be nurtured within a college community, and related to that is character formation, or moral formation. This, however, is the dimension of ministerial formation that is least tractable within the three or four years of a minister's college course. This is not to say that the college has no role in this, for the way in which "rough edges" are knocked off the minister-in-training through interaction with a mixture of those with whom they get on well and others who they find more difficult, has traditionally been a feature of community or collegial living. This is much harder to achieve with mixed-mode delivery in church or congregation-based courses. Over the course of two days a week in term time alone, probably no more than sixty days a year, often less, it is possible to avoid the awkward fellow student in a way that living together for three or four years makes much harder. However, to lay all the weight of expectation for character development and formation on the shoulders of the college course is both unrealistic and narrow, even if there is a small role that the college can play.

Character formation begins long before a call to ministry is discerned, or even a conscious and lived faith owned. It will also continue long after initial ministerial formation has been concluded. It is the work of a life-time. A certain core of a moral life will already be expected of the person whose call to ministry will be tested by the church. They will exhibit the kind of lifestyle that would be expected of any faithful Christian disciple, and such a lifestyle, to a degree, becomes regulated by church authorities once ministry is authorized or accredited. So, to take the obvious example of sexual ethics, the candidate for ministry will need to demonstrate that they are living in accordance with the sexual moral code the church proclaims, with certain sexual practices deemed unacceptable in the minister, even if tolerated, perhaps, within the wider church community, and certainly taken for granted as normative within a wider secular and Western society. Fornication, adultery and homosexual genital sexual practice will normally be considered conduct unbecoming of a minister, and thus the minister-in-training will be expected to live accordingly: faithful to one partner if married, celibate if unmarried and in all cases careful to live with all propriety. For both sexes, but perhaps more obviously for women ministers within a culture that continues to pay greater attention to what women wear than men (whether we disapprove of such sexism—as I do—or not), careful decisions about dress are necessary. In a culture where casual dress is ubiquitous and almost *de rigoeur*, the distinction between work and play is often signified through dress. But what of the young female minister-in-training who dresses at college as if she is going clubbing on Friday night? Is this acceptable? If much "undress" is sometimes viewed as an unspoken invitation to sexual allure, is this ever acceptable in a minister-in-training? Or are these outdated standards that play to the lack of restraint in men and to be resisted in the name of Gospel freedom and justice for women? There seems little virtue in deliberately dressing drably if something of the connection with today's culture is to be encouraged. But where are the boundaries here? Dress is but one of the minefields that beset the minister-in-training as much as the minister after ordination, connecting as it does biblical calls for modesty in dress with missional calls for the minister to seem normal. These standards of behavior will be expected of the minister throughout their life, living as a witness to the truth in Jesus Christ by living by the ethical code advocated by the biblical record.

However, simply living by a code that avoids censure is only the minimum expected of a minister. Something more profound is demanded of the minister if they are to become the man or woman of God that congregation and minister alike aspire to. Something like "the good minister" incorporates more than simply "the competent minister": it has something to do with exemplary discipleship and godly character.

While the notion of the moral life involves the full range of virtues, and is summed up in the fruit of the Spirit that Paul describes in Galatians 5:22–23 (and which, *in nuce*, is descriptive of the character of Jesus Christ, and thus descriptive of God's character or nature: to this we shall return later,) a way of approaching the formation of character in ministry is to begin with the besetting sins of ministry, and to analyze their corresponding virtues.

These besetting sins arise out of the peculiar demands of pastoral leadership, and while they are common amongst all manner of disciples, these vices are particularly destructive of the minister's character. Pride, anger, envy, lust and sloth are amongst those ministerial sins that are most destructive. Their counterparts, the ministerial virtues, are humility, patience, generosity, self-control and zeal. Overarching these virtues is the great virtue, the one St Paul says that we should put on above all else, "above all, clothe yourselves with love, which binds everything together in perfect harmony." (Col. 3:14)

The Virtues

We have seen in the second chapter how virtue ethics has been undergoing something of a renaissance, since the Oxford philosopher Elizabeth Anscombe first published her paper, and others, such as Iris Murdoch, joined her in arguing for this rather neglected ethical theory. Virtue is not concerned with a list of what is right or wrong (and how often the Christian religion has been characterized as being precisely that, even if that is utterly mistaken) so much as the development of a rounded and virtuous person. We saw how one expression of that starts with the virtuous person, and determines what is right or wrong by what that person would do (begging the questions, how do they become virtuous in the first place, and by what criteria do we say they are indeed virtuous people.) Those difficulties notwithstanding, there is indeed something of the correct emphasis here: the virtuous person is not so much the person who knows what the rules are and how to keep them, as someone who intuitively, even we might say, instinctively, knows how to behave, because the habits of making the right choices over a lifetime have shaped their lives accordingly. Tom Wright in *Virtue Reborn* tells the story of the crash of Flight 1549 into the freezing Hudson river in New York after a flock of geese put out of action both engines on the Airbus A320. The instinctive actions of the pilot, Chesley Sullenburger III saved every life on board as he made manoeuvres that he had previously practiced so many times that they came as second-nature, putting the plane into the river in such a way as to prevent it breaking up. What was needed in those two minutes to save the plane was character, and specifically, courage, restraint, cool judgment and determination. Indeed, just those components of virtue that Aristotle identified as the keys to human well-being.

Since ministerial formation shares something of the landscape of pedagogy with the education of children (even if there are very real differences, of course) it is significant to note that virtue ethics has become an important resource for the cultivation of moral character and virtue in schools through virtue education. It remains controversial, however: the Final Report of the Riots Communities and Victims' Panel, published in the wake of the August 2011,[1] which recommended "new school initiatives to help children build character,"[2] notwithstanding. Kristiansson argues for interdisciplinary research into virtue education, since we do not know clearly enough how previous virtue educational initiatives have fared.

> In the present context, we need as a matter of urgency to acknowledge that there cannot be a serviceable social scientific theory of virtue or its constitutive elements without significant input from philosophical virtue ethics, any more than there can be a reasonably developed philosophical theory of virtue without grounding in the empirical knowledge of how people actually think about virtues and the way virtues actually inform their character.[3]

He is similarly concerned that there is little in the way of empirical testing of the virtues in education, but argues, nonetheless, that virtue education and the building of character is a legitimate and necessary purpose of schooling. While rejecting the myth that character and virtue are essentially religious notions, he does not dismiss the fact that religion-based divine-command ethics might be an alternative to the much more widely adopted alternative offered by Elizabeth Anscombe in her famous 1958 paper—an Aristotelian teleology of virtue as *eudaimonia* grounded in contemporary moral psychology.

> Virtue ethics in our day and age has been, more than anything else, an attempt to flesh out a plausible and feasible account of moral virtue in post-religious terms . . . In this regard, while psychology may not yet have provided us with the empirical ammunition we need to underpin a satisfactory form of virtue ethics, . . . the alternative of giving up on that project altogether and opting for the other prong of Anscombe's fork is, in our

---

1. Riots Communities and Victims Panel, "After the Riots: The Final Report of the Riots Communities and Victims Panel," 2012, http:/riotspanel.independent.gov.uk/wp-content/uploads/2012/03/Riots-Panel-Final-Report1.pdf (accessed November 30, 2016).

2. Kristjansson, "Ten Myths About Character, Virtue and Virtue Education," 269.

3. Ibid., 283.

present-day multicultural contexts, one that seems hardly to have occurred to any contemporary virtue ethicists—irrespective of their own personal religious commitments.[4]

Within the specifically Christian context of ministerial formation no such reluctance need prevail. The virtues formed by habit and practice derive their authenticity not from a psychological account of what makes for human flourishing *per se*, but from the life and character of Jesus Christ. What might be inadmissible in a secular educational polity that must not privilege any one religious account of *eudaimonia* (or indeed, any at all), can become absolutely normative in the fashioning of men and women after the life of Jesus Christ.

The Christian life calls for habits of heart and life that create the character of Christ in us, and the creation of that character involves bridging the gap between conversion and resurrection, in knowing how it is that our lives are conformed to Christ, or, to use another theological term, sanctified. Particularly in those forms of evangelicalism that emphasize grace and eschew works, all of the focus is upon the initial conversion process, coming to faith, forgiveness of sins and so forth. It seems salvation is nothing to do with our efforts, to be sure, but what next? Is the sanctified life the result of other spiritual crises, such as the perfection that Wesleyan holiness proclaimed, or that Keswick popularized in the twentieth century? Or is it a process of daily re-ordering of life, heart and priorities until new habits are formed? If it is just an unpredictable, sovereign act of God, then ministerial formation will not be concerned with developing it, so much as hoping and praying some divine intervention might happen before ordination. But if this transformation of character is something in which the believer must co-operate with the Spirit who empowers its possibility, if it a process of a thousand daily choices, then ministerial formation, as all forms of discipleship more generally, must pay some attention to it.

I have been involved in reflecting upon a particular ethical and theological question for the past decade, ever since being invited to chair the Baptist Union of Great Britain's working group on human sexuality: is homosexual practice ever acceptable in the life of the church, or indeed, acceptable to God? In the many times that I have led congregations in reflecting upon these questions, two answers to those questions (which, in some senses, is the same question) seem to predominate. The first points to particular Scriptures that seem to straightforwardly denounce homosexual sexual practice, both in the New Testament, and the Old. So, the answer that one group will give is "never" are such practices acceptable. However much

4. Ibid., 275.

society's views have changed, the Word of God does not change, and the rules are the rules: Scripture forbids it, so we must too. We might describe this as a "concordance" approach to such questions: locate the texts and apply them without too much contextualizing or hermeneutical analysis.

The second response starts elsewhere, with a whole range of questions that avoid the precise scriptural objections as a starting point. Is it partly nature to be homosexual by orientation, they say, and is not the starting point a question of relationships, not rules? Hermeneutical questions are raised about the real meaning of Scripture (does it actually say what the objectors want it to say, or are there textual, interpretive and cognitive questions to be asked first) but really what is going on is not primarily a question of which scriptural hermeneutic, but rather what is the response most in keeping with the perceived person of Christ or character of God? If the first approach, the concordance one, is a question that privileges certain rules and precepts (the ethical theory is a version of deontology: divine command theory), the second, a contextual approach, looks closer to virtue theory. Put starkly, is our response to homosexual practice to condemn it as contrary to Scripture and divine command, or to more or less accept it, as either a form of "what would Jesus do?" question, or a response to the privileging of faithful, covenant-keeping love over specific culturally-conditioned rules. Is it a matter of following the rules, or following a deeper sense of what is right, born of the virtuous life? Wright puts it like this:

> Character—the transforming, shaping, and marking of a life and its habits—will generate the sort of behavior that rules might have pointed toward but which "rule keeping" mentality can never achieve. And it will produce the sort of life which will in fact be true to itself—though the "self" to which it will at last be true is the redeemed self, the transformed self, not merely the "discovered" self of popular thought . . . In the last analysis, what matters after you believe is neither rules nor spontaneous self-discovery, but character. And the development of character is what we call virtue. Not just any kind of virtue, either, but the specifically Christian kind: virtue reborn.[5]

In almost every area of life in the wider public space, firstly corruption, from journalistic phone-hacking to political expense-fiddling, abuse of trust by powerful people towards the vulnerable, and, secondly, the financial crises in the banking sector, and its continuing fall-out in fixed bank rates (LIBOR) and mis-selling of unnecessary insurance and useless investments, it could be said that a root cause is a loss of character. Perhaps this loss has

---

5. N. T. Wright *Virtue Reborn*, 19.

arisen from a more general withdrawal from religious faith, or the letting-go of a wider Christian ethic, but the response of a technocratic and bureaucratic culture is to regulate, to write new rules and strengthen the existing ones. But it is not really the answer: rule writing is perhaps necessary in a culture that does not know what virtue is any more, but what is needed are people who would not think of acting corruptly, whether there were rules there to prohibit it, or not, but would rather act rightly because they are virtuous. And because ministers-in-training come from exactly the same culture as the rest of society, the answer here is not to regulate with detailed rules, although some guidance might be helpful, but to develop Christian character.

The male minister, who, visiting mid-evening, finds the door opened by an attractive woman already attired for bed should not need a rule that says "do not visit if the occupant is ready for bed," for virtue would suggest that a polite apology for disturbing her, and a parting assurance that a visit at a more convenient time is altogether possible, is obvious (is second-nature if you will). However, at the same time, the virtuous, while knowing that general guidance instinctively, but recognizing that the call to visit has come suddenly, that the woman's husband has just suffered a heart attack, that she is deeply distressed, and that the ambulance are working to resuscitate him as the door is opened, will know that the rule in this context is over-ridden by a more profound need. What is needed are "good" ministers: neither rule-keeping pedants, nor opportunistic abusers, for sure; but rather ministers who have been formed to recognize that what is necessary is the virtuous response.

The rule-keeping pedant simply watches their own back, and is driven by fear, while the ungodly opportunist is driven by their own needs, and meets them whatever the cost to others. The virtuous, however, know that, like Christ calling Zacchaeus down from his sycamore tree, doing the "wrong thing" is sometimes the "good thing," even at a cost to one's own reputation. This is the fruit of knowing what the good looks like, knowing how to live by it, then taking those steps so many times previously that it has become habitual, and instinctive. Or, to put it another way, to have developed a Christian conscience that is so responsive to the Holy Spirit, that it becomes second nature to do as he prompts, and to recognize when the prompting is not his. This is the fruit of a character quietly formed over many small moral choices, so that when the crisis comes, it can respond appropriately. Big moral crises are rare, but the ability to act rightly at such a time comes from the many small choices made previously. It is rather like building up core body strength through regular exercise, so that when the stamina is needed, it is there.

This latter metaphor is one that Aristotle himself uses. The way to attain *eudaimonia* (meaning not so much "happiness," as "flourishing or well-being") for him was to practice the *arete*, the strengths of character, or *virtus* in Latin, from which virtue arises. Aristotle's core virtues were courage, justice, prudence and temperance, the so-called cardinal virtues (*cardo* being the hinge upon which the door swings, the cardinal virtues are those that allow the door of *eudaimonia* to open.)

Aristotle's virtues formed the cultural milieu in which the early church existed, and so it is not surprising that something of the Aristotelian model is absorbed by that church, even if it is modified by the presence of a different goal, a different *telos*. If the Aristotelian goal is human happiness, then the goal of the Christian is conformity to Christ's coming Kingdom, and thus absorbing the vision of the kind of God revealed in both the Old Testament and in the life of Christ. Aristotle did not rate forgiveness very highly, but it is central to the Christian conception of the virtuous, and at least one virtue—humility, as argued here, a core ministerial virtue—was dismissed altogether in the pagan world.

The Aristotelian method of habituating the virtues is also transformed by the Gospel: no longer is it simply the individual practicing the virtues until they become second nature, although there is a strong thread of such practice running through the New Testament. Speaking of the necessity to move from infant's food to adult's, the writer of Hebrews says, "But solid food is for the mature, for those whose faculties have been trained by practice to distinguish good from evil," [6](Heb 5:14) while Paul admonished Timothy to train himself to be godly, [7](1 Tim 4:7). We enter a process whereby we come into a new way of being through faith and baptism, with the gift of the Spirit enabling us to live for the coming Kingdom here and now. We anticipate this new Kingdom—coming in all its fullness in the New Heaven and the New Earth—by a Spirit-empowered living-out of our identity in Christ and through the inhabiting of the story of the Gospel as revealed in Scripture in the life, death and resurrection of Jesus Christ. This means forming habits that reflect that new identity; habits of love, faith, and hope; compassion, courageous witness, and humble service.

6. Westcott writes, "The mature Christian has already gained the power which he can at once apply as the occasion arises. This power comes through the discipline of use which shapes a stable character" (Westcott, *The Epistle to the Hebrews*, 136). The mature, τελειοσ, is a term used of those who had followed a course of education and qualified to be teachers (cf. Philo, *On the Special Laws* 4.140, cited in O'Brien, *The Letter to the Hebrews*, 207); the term γεγυμνασμένα, "having been exercised," refers to the constant exercise of this moral discrimination, the exercise of virtue.

7. γύμναζε δὲ σεαυτὸν πρὸς εὐσέβειαν, applying the same root word of the gymnasium. The picture is of the moral athlete training in the virtues.

The idea of such "hard work" runs contrary to the culture of the age, with its reliance upon Romanticism, existentialism or emotivism as spurs for morality. It runs contrary to much contemporary Christian teaching too, which resorts either to a rule-based deontology, or to a sub-Christian reliance upon feelings. The genuine Spirit-led, habit-forming development of virtue is closer to the New Testament than either.

If this is the way of living the transformed life as a disciple, is there anything particular we might say about ministry? Certainly its ability to live this transformed life will be no less demanding, and in some ways more so. Ministry carries with it a representative function, or, I would argue, a sacramental way of being. Ministry is about leadership, in part, and leadership that is effective embodies in the leader the virtues of the whole community: ministers are expected to be exemplary disciples, those who others trust to exemplify the way of life that is appropriate for that community. So, "putting on Christ," forming the habits that will shape a virtuous life—above all love—are not pretensions for the holier than average minister, but obligations for the whole community. These habits are what it means to minister in Christ's name. The character thus being formed is central to who the minister is, and therefore central to a formational understanding of what precisely it is we are doing when we prepare men and women for ministry.

The Shape of the Virtuous Life as Ministry

Ministry embodies that subtle wedding of service and leadership, so often combined in that common-place phrase servant leadership. It became popularized through Robert Greenleaf's work of 1988.[8] The Aristotelian cardinal virtues of courage, justice, prudence and temperance are transfigured in Christian living to the Pauline triad of faith, hope and love (love being the greatest), with the fruits of the Spirit in Galatians 5:22–23 acting as a secondary set of virtues.

The Context

The church can be an unforgiving and demanding context in which to work. It rightly demands high standards, but does not always offer much by way of grace or compassion towards those who do not maintain the good life in their practice of ministry and tenure of pastoral office. Rick Lewis has

---

8. Greenleaf, *The Power of Servant Leadership*. Cf. Ellis, "The Leadership of Some . . . ' Baptist Ministers as Leaders?," 71–86.

looked at the difficult circumstances that ministry sometimes gives rise to, and developed a typology of hazards and their associated outcomes in the light of ministers' vulnerabilities.[9] He argues that the ministerial context is demanding, disempowering, dangerous, isolating and unforgiving. These are systemic hazards of the environment within which ministry is exercised. The resulting corresponding likely outcomes are burnout, depression, termination, disconnection and moral failure. These outcomes are likely for those who have various vulnerabilities: so, the burnout that arises from the demanding context of ministry is the result of those whose vulnerability is too close an identification of the work with the person of the minister. The minister who is performance driven, compulsive and lacks the ability to adequately care for self and for family, is likely to be prone to burnout. The vice here is pride, the virtue that helps to prevent burnout, humility.

The expectations upon ministers are high, but the "tools for the job" are poor, and this results in a disempowerment of the minister. One description of church life is "building with bananas": the task force to achieve the maintenance of a vibrant church life, its growth even, are volunteers, church members or parishioners, only some of whom (perhaps a minority) are reliable, committed, and competent to play their role. This can leave the minister feeling they alone have to deliver what the church expects, and the ensuing sense of disempowerment, exacerbated by the loss of any social status or much authority that generically ministry might once have had, results in depression amongst those who are addicted to success. The addiction is then deflected to compensations over which the minister seems to have greater control: alcohol or food, perhaps, and the development of a passive-aggressive approach to ministry that disempowers the ministry further as people withdraw their support. Depression is a likely outcome.

Pastoral care is a dangerous endeavor, calling for a combination of compassion and intimacy without the ensuing emotional or sexual outcomes that biological drives would normally allow. Ministry must cook in an intimate kind of kitchen, without tasting any of the food! Where a minister lacks self-awareness or accountability, and especially where he or she lacks both in combination, boundaries of behavior are easily breached. The emotional support becomes too easily infatuation and sexual attraction, resulting, most likely, in misconduct. Or, the sense of control that becomes an abuse of power, and a domineering approach to church policy, easily slips into a combative and defensive state. Much failure of ministry, leading to a termination of the post, results from either sexual misconduct (always an abuse of power,) or complaints of bullying, harassment, and dominance.

---

9. Lewis, *Mentoring Matters*.

The vices behind this are pride (again,) anger, and lust. These are especially magnified in those who have a narcissistic personality disorder. Often superficially charming, and, quite often, clever (two qualities almost guaranteed to seduce the ministerial selection panel,) the narcissist uses extreme means in an attempt to keep control of external factors mistaken for the inner disintegration of self worth. They are sometimes sexual predators and have over-confidence in their own abilities, almost amounting to megalomania. Phil Mollon claims,

> A narcissistically vulnerable person is prone to show strong reactions to the narcissistic injuries of feeling slighted, ignored or treated without respect or empathy. The most prominent reaction is of narcissistic rage . . .—with secondary reactions of depressive withdrawal or of a retreat to an arrogant, grandiose and somewhat paranoid state of mind. These overt reactions seem to be protective responses to a more fundamental injury of break-up of the sense of self . . . a ruminatory preoccupation with feelings of grudge and fantasies of revenge and triumph.[10]

I have written elsewhere that,

> Shame is closely related to narcissistic disturbance, where that empathic response is absent or limited, and the individual becomes self-absorbed, interpreting the world only through the lens of their own needs. It is as if they have fallen in love with themselves. A common criticism of the narcissistic is "they only love themselves." Shame is related to this because the person who is suffering from chronic shame becomes painfully aware of their own lack of worth and shortcomings, and compensates by either withdrawal from others (the drive to hide) or by using others to meet their needs (narcissism.)[11]

Amongst the most dangerous of ministers fall into this category, in my experience, even if some are revealed in selection and formation and, one hopes, not allowed to continue to ordination.

Ministry is also isolating, with a common admonition to ministerial students being "do not have friends in the church." The minister must be equitable in their dealings with the congregation and avoid any sense that they have favorites, or that some receive a different level of care to others by virtue of personal relationship (excluding the minister's family, of course, although some compensate by seemingly being harsher upon their family

---

10. Mollon, *The Fragile Self,* 65–66
11. Goodliff, *With Unveiled Face,* 92–93

members than they would upon anyone else). Leadership is always isolating, to a degree: while much can be shared, there will always be some aspects that the minister holds alone—pastoral confidences, burdens of concern, and the unavoidable sense of responsibility, the burden of responsibility to care, that the minister alone carries. Too busy to have friends, or with friends that are part of their leadership group (and thus, their overseers, in some ways) these leaders, should they be strong individualists, become isolated, prone to paranoia, and make bad judgments. Often there is some sexual misconduct, although sometimes "just below the radar." Lonely, suspicious of challenge, and disapproval, they can become paranoid, and eventually, so disconnected from both congregation and self, that disaster ensues.

Churches can be unforgiving organizations to work in. When church heroes fall from grace, they often fall without trace. In an unforgiving context, the leader becomes vulnerable to hiding their weakness, maintaining a veneer of piety to cover their shame. Image becomes very important, and challenges will be met with lies and/or pathological rebuttal and reversed violence. Where there are borderline narcissistic personality traits, the results can be moral failure.

Such are the hazards of not addressing matters of character and of making assumptions that character will somehow just emerge. The benefit of a virtue ethics approach to ministerial formation lies not just in a renewed focus upon what the virtuous minister looks like, but in the way in which such virtues are formed through the deliberate and conscious development of the practices of ministry. So, those approaches to formation that emphasize a growth in skills and practices do not have to be entirely replaced. The development of a high degree of skill in, say, pastoral care or homiletics, or the development of the intellectual virtues, itself allows the broader set of virtues to be formed at the same time. What is perhaps needed is the giving of greater deliberate attention to the virtues, and the attempt at some assessment of how far that process has been effective. This will inevitably require closer relationships between those being formed and those forming them, and relationships that understand that while friendship may well develop between tutor and student, essentially, the relationship does have a power-imbalance.

PART FOUR

Forming the Practices of Ministry

11

Formation of the Practitioner

We have already noted how the language of theological education was replaced by the notion of ministerial training, before morphing into ministerial formation: what do you need to know being replaced by "what do you need to be able to do," before becoming "who do you need to be." This chapter addresses that middle question, focusing upon identifying the skills that ministers require and how to train the minister-in-formation in them. Each will be explored in some greater depth in the next section (the minister as preacher, as pastor, as evangelist, and so forth) but here we will think about the way in which these skills are formed generally.

Traditionally, these skills were learnt in a module or course called 'Pastoral Studies' or ministerial development. The focus was often upon what is learnt in the classroom about, say, pastoral visiting or the preparation and delivery of public worship. Yes, there would be some experiential dimension, especially in the practice of preaching (linking as it does with the preceding emphasis upon theological education) and ministers-in-training would have practical placements in a local church or chaplaincy setting, or engage in a mission in long summer vacation. But the emphasis would be upon learning in the classroom what are, for instance, the stages of grief, rather than pastorally accompanying someone who is recently bereaved. This is understandable, since the potential for damage when an unwitting and ignorant minister-in-training engages clumsily with a church member or parishioner is very real. It is a pattern traditionally replicated in the training of medical doctors: two or three years pre-clinical learning about bio-chemistry, anatomy and human growth and development, for instance, followed by letting the students onto the ward under close supervision. Only upon graduation as a doctor would the person actually treat patients (and then under quite close supervision still) and the rule still applies that it is rather unwise in Britain to go into hospital in August, just as the rooky Junior Housemen are let loose for the first time.

Such a pattern still applies in many places of ministerial education and training, but with an increasing dependence upon mixed-mode training, where ministers-in-training hold pastoral responsibility for a small congregation, the ability to distinguish theological knowledge from practice, and delivered sequentially, is hugely diminished. So, practice-based training requires the training in the practices from the outset; with no obvious priority if the varied circumstances are to be adequately acknowledged. Minister-in-training Jim might need understanding and training in the skills of pastoral care of the dying in week one of his course, as a member of his congregation falls terminally ill; while his fellow first-year student, Jane, in another church, finds a safeguarding crisis concerning a young person is on her agenda long before anyone dies. All will probably need some training in preaching and the leadership of worship, for this is likely to be expected of their ministry from the very first week, and basic or general pastoral skills will do no harm if delivered very early on, but the realities of the life of the church or congregation will not slot neatly into a college curriculum, with no one dying until week five of year two, or being arrested until week three of the final year.

While this form of training exposes the minister-in-training to the real world of pastoral ministry and the hurly-burly of church life, it does so in an unpredictable way, often too-poorly supervised and unprepared. This form of ministry training relies heavily upon theological reflection upon practice, with tutor groups or reflection groups providing the context for the development of practice as case studies, drawn from the experience of the ministers-in-training, are discussed. However, inevitably much will go un-reflected or considered, and the danger is that this way of training too-easily transforms poor practice into normal practice, with the attendant risk that habits of practice, far from being developed into patterns of excellence, remain fixed in mediocrity or worse. This is particularly true where the mixed-mode format is offered to the more mature student (often for very obvious financial reasons) who might have had considerable previous experience of lay leadership in their local church prior to training. All too-easily the assumption is made that the habits and practices they observed in others is normative, or even exemplary, when in fact it was indicative of poor practice. Pre-existing experience and habits then really do become baptized into the practice of ministry, with a perpetuating of such practice for subsequent generations. Where, in their previous church life as a deacon or elder or home group leader (in Baptist terms,) they understood pastoral visitation to be uncommon, or the dominance of a worship leader to go unchecked, it might be assumed that this is normative for pastoral practice, and therefore reproduced, until challenged perhaps in this new pastoral placement. Where teachability is weak in the minister-in-training, lip service might be paid to the guidance of the tutor in the reflection group, and established patterns remain largely untouched. The experience and wisdom of the tutor is also a key element, and the fact that the tutor is a gifted biblical academic might not necessarily result in an experienced pastoral practitioner.

At its heart is the notion that, in some way, every perspective, every conviction, every way of acting has equal validity. With older students, the realization that a younger tutor might know best, that their guidance has greater worth than the student's own experience, is often resisted by that student—more mature in years, perhaps, but not necessarily in either faith or practice. The loss of deference to ministers or experts only exacerbates this response. Stanley Hauerwas, in typically trenchant style, says of his students that they should not be allowed to make up their own minds:

> We think our task is to be free to be what we want even if what we want to be is Christian. As a result, we fail to see that nothing is more destructive, nothing makes us less free, than to have to do what we want to do. Indeed, I can think of no better description of hell than the condition of always having to do what I want to do.
>
> As a way of challenging such a view of freedom, I start my classes by telling my students that I do not teach in a manner that is meant to help them make up their own minds. Instead, I tell them that I do not believe that they have minds worth making up until they have been trained by me. I realize such a statement is deeply offensive to students since it exhibits a complete lack of pedagogical sensitivities. Yet I cannot image any teacher who is serious would allow students to make up their own minds . . . would you trust a physics instructor who thought she or he could teach physics in a manner that students could make up their own minds about whether atoms do or do not exist?[1]

I do not think it helpful in the formation of good practitioners of ministry to allow such latitude in perspective, so that some might consider the absence of pastoral visitation, or leadership and responsibility for public worship, a valid option for able ministry. It is not acceptable for a minister-in-training to believe that ensuring that pastoral work is safe and life-style honoring to God are optional in practice, or that dressing in ways that are indifferent to their calling and others' sensibilities is justified on spurious

---

1. Hauerwas, *Sanctify Them in the Truth*, 220.

cultural grounds. No, there are aspects of ministry, and probably far more than commonly accepted currently, where part of the discipline of being a minister is to submit to the standards and practices of something like "the guild" of ministers and where personal preference should be replaced by adherence to the commonly-held standards of practice. This too is what formation seeks to develop. After all, it is thus in many other professions, where profound human goods are at stake (like health and liberty), so why this anxiety about norms when matters eternal are the concern?

The reality is that with this pattern of mixed-mode training, for all of its practitioner-base and lived experiential training, the shaping of the minister-in-training into a reflective and skilled pastoral practitioner is unpredictable and relatively haphazard unless supplemented strongly with either a structured course that argues what excellence looks like, or is supervised closely by a skilled practitioner who can see not only what is brought to the tutor group, but also what takes place the following day in the church or community as the minister-in-training exercises pastoral charge of that congregation. I salute the risk these small churches take, and admire their courage,[2] but in reality they probably offer more to some students by way of practice than the students offer in terms of robust and skilled ministry. There will always be exceptions: perhaps, thank God, more common than not, where a "natural" pastor or gifted preacher is placed there, and both they and the congregation flourish together. Is there perhaps a better way?

One option that might supplement both (i) the structured learning of the theological education, and (ii) the training in skills that takes place in the mixture of placement church and college theological reflection group, is much greater reliance upon—and use of—the experienced and skilled advanced practitioner as supervisor and mentor in an apprentice/master craftsman relationship. Most ministers-in-training will have appointed to oversee them some form of placement supervisor, but I believe both the degree of interaction is too little, and the authority and power on the part of the "master" challenged too often. An older style of Anglican formation of curates under training incumbents, for all of its faults, had much to commend it. In often large, urban, parishes, with more than one curate in post at any one time, the incumbent priest would shape not only the practice of his curates, but also their spirituality and their character. A classic example is the Parish of Portsea, Hampshire, at the turn of the nineteenth century. While exceptional in both its size (it was the largest urban Parish in England) and in the caliber of its incumbents, it nonetheless exemplified a

---

2. Although recognizing that many such churches opt for a minister-in-training primarily out of financial constraints rather than any vision of selflessly aiding in the formational process.

model of training clergy that was effective both pedagogically and missionally. Edgar Jacob (Vicar of Portsea, 1878–1896, and who was later Bishop of Newcastle and then St Albans) was followed for five years by the great Cosmo Lang (Vicar of Portsea 1896–1901, who left to become Bishop of Stepney, before elevation to York in 1909 and on to Canterbury in 1928), and then by Bernard Wilson (Vicar of Portsea, 1901–1909, dying in office of a stroke aged fifty-two) who included Cyril Forster Garbett amongst his team of over a dozen curates. These were among the skilled training incumbents there.[3] Garbett succeeded him and stayed until he too became a Bishop, of Southwark, in 1919, and then Winchester and York. Garbett, like his great mentor and hero, Wilson, was loved and admired in equal measure (it is said that Lang was respected, but not loved: his heart was not so much in the Parish as in his career.)

Using the resources of those young curates (single to a man, and living in community in the clergy house that had evolved from the Vicarage), Wilson ensured that every home in the Parish was visited regularly, missions undertaken, and lives transformed. They were given considerable responsibility and expected to use their initiative, but also their work was supervised and their lives shaped. Garbett in later life observed that there were matters that Parish clergy in the Archdiocese of York would take to their Bishop, which those curates would not think worthy of taking to their Vicar! 'Thus we learnt self-reliance and gained initiative. Many of the problems which the clergy send to me today as Bishop, we should have hesitated at even asking the Vicar about.'[4]

Clearly, nothing of this order is capable of development today, especially in Baptist settings. Far from the luxury of a number of years under the tutelage of an effective senior minister, today's minister-in-training is likely to be effectively in sole charge with a minimum of supervision from the very start of their formal training. Associate minister roles are increasingly rare, especially of the kind once familiar in, say Hertford Baptist Church or Dagnall Street Baptist Church, St Albans, where a younger college-leaver would serve for three years, completing their probationary period there, before going on the take charge of a church in their own right elsewhere. Men like David Ronco at Hertford or Paul Beasley-Murray at Central Baptist Church, Chelmsford, saw it as their role to tutor and shape the ministry of the succession of college-leavers whose first post was in that wise setting. As Superintendent, one occasionally came across such young associate ministers who kicked against the relative lack of freedom such regimes brought,

---

3. Smyth, *Cyril Forster Garbett,* chap. 3.
4. Ibid., 63, quoting from Garbett himself (*The Church of England Today*, 1953).

but judging by their subsequent success, it seems to have done them nothing but good, on the whole.

Some other means of approaching the same ends must be sought in the straightened circumstances that churches now find themselves in (although, one suspects, the financial lot of a curate in a training parish was meagre, and being unmarried, on the whole, this was borne with understanding.) Might it be possible to use recently retired ministers for the closer supervision of ministers-in-training that is necessary? The cry is that they would be out of touch, but perhaps in the forming of the character and habits of ministry, age and wisdom have a premium over the tyranny of the relevant. If churches were more widely connected in networks, then it might be easier for the experienced ministers in the network to offer the level of regular supervision for both ministers-in-training and newly ordained alike.

A further benefit from this apprenticing and supervising model would be the possibility of greater connectivity and inter-penetration of the various practices than is commonplace. Often, in the course of a structured course in pastoral practice formation, the separate skills remain somewhat isolated. Pastoral care is viewed as distinct from preaching, spiritual guidance as somewhat remote from mission, or pastoral guidance from liturgical structure. However, it is in the inter-connections between the disparate ministerial practices that the most rounded or holistic of ministries develops. This has been explored by the Australian pastoral theologian, Neil Pembroke, in relation to pastoral care and worship, and between divine healing and the art of preaching.[5] In *Pastoral Care in Worship*, Pembroke argues that the whole faith community has a role to play in offering pastoral care, an important counter-balance to the emphasis upon the individual provider of pastoral care through pastoral counselling that has come to dominate discussions about the role. The prime context in which the gathered community corporately provides resources for care lies in the context of Sunday worship: "the community operates as an expression of care as it gathers for Sunday worship."[6] While he is quick to point out that the primary purpose of worship is not healing, but rather praise and worship of God that puts the divine at the center, nonetheless, properly theocentric worship creates "a unique space for the operation of divine grace and mercy."[7] Setting to one side those occasional offices, such as the funeral, where pastoral care might have a greater role by rights, Pembroke argues that the weekly congregational worship has great potency to address themes of reconciliation,

---

5. Pembroke, *Pastoral Care in Worship*; Pembroke, *Divine Therapeia and the Sermon*.
6. Pembroke, *Pastoral Care in Worship*, 1.
7. Ibid., 3.

lament, hope, and communion. Worship can only achieve that capacity for pastoral intervention as it is properly ordered, comprises the full range of human responses to the divine (including lament, self-diminishment, and the more sorrowful dimensions of life, and not just adoration and praise,) and is led by those who are aware of the potential for worship to both heal the wounded soul, and create human community after the pattern of Christ's body. "Baptism and the Eucharist have the power to 're-Christianize' those of us who have unwittingly fallen into the unhealthy habits and patterns set up by the individualization process."[8] He is convinced, as I am, that the liturgy has power to shape the moral life of worshippers, and to provide the first, and normative, context for therapeutic intervention, to which only subsequently is added the individual pastoral encounter.

Pembroke further develops this integrated approach in viewing the sermon as having also a therapeutic purpose. This is not at all the same as converting the sermon into an experience of communal therapy, with God quietly shuffled off into the wings while psychotherapy takes center-stage. The sermon must remain the proclamation of the good news of Christ, with a proper theocentrism, if it is to be a part of the liturgy. But, aware of the insights of counselling and therapy, "psychological theory sheds its own unique and penetrating light. It offers valuable insights and perspectives that are not otherwise available."[9] Using this correlative model, counselling psychology can offer analogues of God's therapeutic action that not only illuminate the Scripture passage at hand, but also "stimulate openness to that therapeutic action. . . . the analogical theology that takes place in the sermon is not simply didactic; it is also catalytic of increased receptivity to divine *therapeia*."[10] The theological basis for such an assertion lies in the various understandings of analogous God-talk, such as the *analogia fidei* associated with Karl Barth and Eberhard Jüngel. Thus, we have integrated pastoral care, preaching and theology, together, necessarily, with biblical hermeneutics. The ability to make the connections between various dimensions of the formational process, in order to encourage holistic practice as normative, is important if rounded practitioners of ministry are to be formed from the outset. A working knowledge of all of the practices, together with an integrative imagination, may be setting a high bar for ministers to reach, but aiming for anything less will only encourage mediocre practitioners.

8. Ibid., 4–5.
9. Pembroke, *Divine Therapeia and the Sermon*, viii–ix.
10. Ibid., ix

So, bearing in mind the necessity for competency in all the practices of ministry, and the ability to make the connections between them, we begin by turning to forming the liturgist.

12

Forming the Liturgist

The claim that ministers only work one day a week arises perhaps from the fact that they are at their most visible on the Lord's Day, leading worship at the church service. Those traditions that expect their ministers to engage in public worship twice daily throughout the week in the church building (I am thinking of the Church of England and its commitment to its priests saying the office publically in the parish church, available for others to join him or her there, for instance,) might argue that this constant reminder that the minister is about his or her work counters that slur, but I suspect that few if any join the Vicar at her prayers, so it remains true that the most obvious time of work is on a Sunday.

Forming those who will exercise leadership of worship, presiding at the Eucharist, leading the church at prayer is itself subject to the changes in the role of liturgist, or, more commonly expressed, "worship leader." In many settings the minister does little of this ministry. Instead, the worship band leads the music, and often their leader chooses the songs. Other members of the congregation will read Scripture, lead intercessory prayers, and sometimes preach, so that for many more recently trained ministers, the burden of leadership of worship is considerably curtailed. Generally, this broadening of participation in leading worship is to be welcomed with some enthusiasm, reflecting a reduction in the threat of sacerdotalism and a recognition that it is the people of God who worship, not just the clergy. So, for many ministers the role on any given Sunday may be restricted to the presiding over the service, like a religious master of ceremonies, or preaching the sermon, or presiding at the Lord's Supper. It comes as something of a shock, then, to those formed in churches where this sharing of roles is commonplace to take services elsewhere, and be expected to choose the songs and hymns, lead the service, read the Scripture(s) and preach the sermon. Yet this was exactly the case in the Evangelical Anglican Parish where I grew up, and where 1662 Morning and Evening Prayer was the almost ubiquitous diet (apart from the occasional 'Youth Service.') The Vicar, or the Assistant Curate would lead it all, until changes were introduced where others read the lessons. The clergy still led the prayers of intercession, though. Something similar pertained widely in Free Church settings too, until, similar to their Anglican counterparts, liturgical change by way of increasing congregational participation was introduced. Something of this change arose from the Parish Communion movement in the Church of England, and was accelerated by the "body ministry" emphasis of the early charismatic movement (that is, before the hegemony of the elite was restored, albeit differently, in the form of the "worship leader").

There remains a role for the minister, however, in this multi-voiced liturgy (which I broadly welcome). It is likely that they will be engaged in almost every aspect of delivery of the liturgy at some point, so ministers need to be trained to speak in public with clarity, formed in the practices of public prayer and reading Scripture, and able to preside over the Eucharist and lead the occasional offices (funerals, weddings, baptisms, infant dedications, and so forth) which widely remain their almost exclusive domain. Not every minister will be a musician, but they must be the guardian of what is required in public worship: liturgically, theologically, and psychologically. Music should serve the congregation and aid its worship, and the temptation for the congregation to serve the musicians' egos should be resisted. The minister should be that resistant.

However, something deeper than simply the ability to organize a "good service" is required in the formation of the minister. Certainly knowledge of the history of the liturgy is involved, so that the reasons for the presence of the various elements are well-understood, and, where freedom is allowed, the sequencing of those elements created to best advantage. For instance, should confession of sin come at the beginning of the service (if present at all, and sadly, it is all-to-often absent altogether), enabling the congregation to proceed with conscience clear, "with clean hands and a pure heart," or might it best be placed after the liturgy of the Word (Scripture and homily,) so that a response to that Word might be made with appropriate repentance? Or should there be room for both? The case for the Eucharist to be celebrated after the Word is widely made, and forms the normal pattern in Catholic and Anglican forms of worship, but in Free Churches, the service often concludes with the sermon. Does this betray the relative significance of Word and Eucharist in those respective traditions? Which sequence has which rhythm of worship is important to understand.

As well as a knowledge of the development of liturgy, and its variations in time, place, and tradition, an understanding of the purpose of the liturgy is also necessary. The insights of Stanley Hauerwas, Sam Wells, and others that it is the liturgy that forms the Christian, especially the Christian's habits and practices, is important. Hauerwas argues that,

> The habits necessary for the formation of the virtues must be those acquired by agents for whom what they do is no different than who they are. When liturgy becomes a motivation for action that does not require the liturgy for the intelligibility of the description of what we have done, then we lose the means as Christians to make our lives our own.[1]

and,

> A focus on the virtues and the narrative necessary for the virtues to be individuated as well as related to one another begs for the kind of enactment the liturgy names. Moreover, just as the liturgy is the work of the whole community, so the virtues reflect the practices of a community, making possible the virtuous formation of the lives that are constituted by that work. It is from the essential practices of a community, practices that name the ongoing habits that make it possible for the community to sustain a history, that liturgy forms and reforms our lives.[2]

Forming the liturgist is also the place to consider whether some dimension of appreciation of beauty is also required. We began the book with an exploration of three works of art, one musical (J.S. Bach's *The Art of Fugue*, with its austere beauty) and two paintings: Piero della Francesca's *The Baptism of Christ*, and Caravaggio's *The Crucifixion of St Peter*, the former with a limpid majesty, the latter with an arresting proletarian power. In the opinion of many, these are works of sublime beauty—an opinion I share. Is there a place for beauty in our acts of public worship, and should ministers be formed to appreciate and cultivate that?

There is certainly a theological thread that attributes beauty to God, and so it might be agreed that if we are worshipping the God of beauty, then something beautiful is required. Not that this has to be limited to Bach cantatas or to old master art works. There is beauty in the well prepared worship band, and the purity of modernist architecture that gives priority to space and light, as much as in a well-tuned organ and traditional church interiors, be that the glory of a gothic parish church, or the serenity of an eighteenth century Meeting House. However, much of the context of public worship places no regard at all for the spatial beauty of the surroundings

---

1. Hauerwas, *Performing the Faith*, 153.
2. Ibid., 156.

(the Baptist church where I live meets in a school drama studio, and while I love my fellow church members, I find the physical context for worship does nothing to bring me closer to God) nor pays any attention to the phrasing of public prayers, when extempore, or the beauty of the music, which is functional, at best.

Yet we claim to worship almighty and loving God, who has cast the night sky with such extraordinary beauty, and whose very character is the prime source of beauty. Perhaps it is because in contemporary Christian theology, especially that of a charismatic and evangelical bent, the notion of God's beauty is largely absent as is any notion of "sacred space."[3]

A Christian account of beauty proved problematic for Barth. He was aware of the danger that beauty would become an *a priori* category, defined by some philosophical or aesthetic concept, then applied to God: an intrusive *a priori* that limits God's freedom, or a transcendental to which God submits. His absolute insistence that God defines himself in Christ Jesus was at odds with any *a priori* statements about divinity, which are then applied to this God. He remains radically free to define himself as the wholly Other, yet fully revealed in the Son. So for Barth, beauty is defined by how God reveals himself in the Son, and that is as the God of self-giving love. Jeremy Begbie puts it like this, "Divine beauty is discovered not in the first instance by reference to a doctrine . . . but by strict attention to a movement in history enacted for us—supremely the story of Jesus Christ, the incarnate Son, living in the Father's presence in the power of the Spirit. Trinitarian beauty has, so to speak, been performed for us."[4] It is in the trinitarian life that God is fundamentally beautiful, and so the beauty in Christian worship will first and foremost be something about the love of God revealed, and the love of humankind expressed. One might say it is relational and ethical beauty, an expression of the ecstatic love of God for the other.

Now, the way in which created beauty, the work of human imagination and skill, is expressed will inevitably be different to God's beauty, as it is finite and not infinite; marred by sin and never entirely pure. Certainly we cannot straightforwardly read off God's beauty in the wonder of creation, although we might see echoes of it. So, for instance, it is in a particular genre of painting, Realism, seeking to replicate and imitate a particular scene perceived as beautiful, that some would identify a "proper" form of Christian art, faithfully depicting what God has created. A scene such as William Holman Hunt's *Our English Coasts 1852 (Strayed Sheep,)* with its hints at Gospel

---

3. See Watts's cautious affirmation that, even for Baptists, there can be a concept of sacred space. Watts, "Can a Baptist Believe in Sacred Space?"

4. Begbie, "Created Beauty," 86.

parables, illustrates this absolute veracity to nature, as does John William Inchbold in his realist, almost photographic, *In Early Spring* (ca.1855), now hanging in the Ashmolean Museum, Oxford, with its vivid blue sky exactly the color of a Spring day. It would be easy to identify this kind of painterly realism as the most appropriate "Christian" art. But this would be mistaken.

A theological account of beauty will be founded in the person and particular beauty of Jesus Christ (a beauty that contradicts the human and worldly expectations, for this Suffering Servant "had no form or majesty that we should look at him, nothing in his appearance that we should desire him." (Isaiah 53:2b). This broken beauty of creation has been recreated in the resurrection, and brought into the midst of time by the Holy Spirit, anticipating what will be the beauty of the new creation in the eschaton. It will also be diverse, never closed to a particular genre, or some attempt at poise and symmetry (although this is not excluded). There will be room for the extravagant, the vivid explosion of color, and excess. Here there will be as much room for abstract, for instance, as realism, in the visual arts: room for an Anthony Caro painted steel sculpture as much as for Michelangelo's *Pieta*; for a late Turner sunset or a Howard Hodgkins abstract, as much as explicitly "Christian" paintings such as Millais' *Christ in the House of his Parents*, or Holman Hunt's *The Scapegoat*.

I have explored the visual arts first, because in much contemporary worship they are the least expressed. Where the strict avoidance of images or color in the Northern Reformation was born of a suspicion of Romish excess, and was seen in the cool white walls of the freshly white-washed Gothic buildings, in contemporary worship spaces it is largely born in utter indifference. The flickering image of the digital projector screen is the one source of visual imagery, so often. However, in terms of language and music, the same proletarian indifference is too often tolerated. The language of worship, especially of prayer, is devoid of poetry, and the music of consisting of one genre and dimension.

The beauty of a well-crafted prayer, rich in imagery and cadence, so that those being led are caught up in its life and together offer this back to God with the voice of the one praying, needs to be taught, and developed in the minister.[5] Similarly, a place for music that is simply other than the predominant gentle rock "worship song" (not replacing it, but complementing it) can arrest a congregation with its beauty: a Bach *Two Part Invention*, or a Debussy *Prelude* (if the pianist is up to it). The ability of jazz to speak of the way that the Spirit "riffs" on the themes of the gospel, ever rooted in the theme, but always with fresh improvisatory intelligence, or the way that

---

5. See Wells, *Crafting Prayers for Public Worship*.

a tune by Thomas Tallis in its sheer simplicity can enable a congregation to concentrate on the words.

There is a tendency, I observe, to struggle in theological colleges with the balance between the two purposes of collective community worship. Clearly, one function of the college at worship is to provide an opportunity for students, as ministers-in-training, to practice their arts, and to experiment. If you cannot experiment at college, where can you? Mistakes can be made and critiqued in such a way as to become opportunities to learn, rather than causes for alarm and calls for resignation. However, if every service is student-led, and a cause for experimentation, something of the routine, the predictable is lost. Much of the power of liturgy to form those engaged in it is the steady repetition of words, prayers, and patterns that have stood the test of time. This is liturgy doing its work, or rather, the Spirit doing its work through the liturgy. This is the forming of the minister in broader ways that simply learning how to prepare liturgy. I suppose ideally I would ensure a mixture of (short) services that allow for no individual variation, taste or experimentation other than the lectionary reading and cycle of prayers: a kind of college office, or indeed, denominational office, if available, and then, supplementing it, the opportunities for radical experimentation that enable other liturgical skills to be formed: those of imagination, ecumenical breadth, and so forth. The purpose of shared worship in a formational setting is much broader than simply training people to lead public worship. It lies somewhere near the heart of what it is to be formed as a minister.

Which is why the lack of a shared worship life, a shared liturgy, is so problematic in those contexts where church-based, or mixed-mode, training predominates. Instead of a call to a community to gather each morning to pray and worship together, instilling habits and patterns, the college service becomes a once-weekly event, and so, special. It has to function as all things. No doubt compromises have to be made in order to capture all the benefits of mixed-mode formation, but this is one compromise that is dearly bought. It might be obviated if all those committed to a formational pattern, committed to becoming ministers, were required to say a common office each morning. This could be one specially devised for that community, or one adapted from elsewhere, such as the *Northumbria Community*, the *Order of Baptist Ministers*, or the Franciscans' Daily Office. The Baptist college in Oxford, Regent's Park, recently endeavored to practice this, using *The Order for Baptist Ministry* office for its dispersed body of ministers-in-training, expecting all to use this each morning for a term. The expectation would be that when dispersed, the office would be said alone, or perhaps, better, with others willing to share in it at the church, or in the home, with the minister-in-training. When the community gathers in college, then the office would be said and sung together. There would still be room for a weekly college Eucharist, for instance, or other service, at some other point in the week when the whole community had gathered.

If the cry is that this takes up too much time in a crowded curriculum and programme, then extend the period of formation. This one thing cannot be hurried, short-changed, made optional for the spiritual few, or translated into an exclusively pedagogical event. Forming creative liturgists who inhabit the practices of daily prayer is a vital part of the formational process.

13

The Formation of Pastoral Integrity

Forming the pastor could be seen to stand as a heading for ministry itself, so much is it a summary of what ministry consists in. However, here I want to restrict its formation to those dimensions of ministry that are concerned with the care of the people of God. In a much earlier work[1] I argued that pastoral care is exercised by representative persons,[2] and so is more narrowly defined than a general neighborliness undertaken by every Christian believer, yet it is at the same time broader than the focus of pastoral counselling, with its therapeutic concern for "troubled persons"[3] and includes formational and reconciling work, alongside the therapeutic work of healing and sustaining Christian life and witness.

I argued in *Care in a Confused Climate* that there were four urgent tasks of pastoral care: the building of Christian community, creating relational health, healing the wounded soul, and nurturing and sustaining faith. I stand by those priorities as a summary of the pastoral ministry in a postmodern culture. They need to be read alongside the prophetic and evangelistic ministry that looks outwards, and so can never be wholly what ministry is about, but they remain broad enough to give some shape to the work of pastoral care, and to give an understanding of what it must be about.

Pastoral ministry calls for the formation of men and women who understand something of human life, relationships (both their formation and disintegration) and the challenges of growth and ageing. It requires a working knowledge of psychology as it relates to "the journey of life," and of the life of the soul, or the spiritual life. The pastor, in this narrow sense, is part therapist, part spiritual director and part mediator.

---

1. Goodliff, *Care in a Confused Climate*.
2. Ibid., 10
3. Clebsch and Jaeckle, *Pastoral Care in Historical Perspective*, gives the classic definition.

In this exposition of the role and its tasks I want to shape it by way of the Pauline triad of faith, hope, and love[4] and approach pastoral care through the lens of this trio of virtues. There will be some biblical analysis first, and in the ensuing exploration of each virtue I will take a sideways look through a painting, bringing all three together in the depiction of the annunciation as it figures in St. Luke's Gospel. In this way I hope to shed fresh light on the formational dimension of pastoral care as a way of forming faith, hope and love.

The Biblical Context: Paul's Trio of Virtues

We saw above that the trio of faith, hope, and love are widespread in Paul's letters. The classic formulation is found in 1 Corinthians 13, where the focus is upon "the greatest" of the three: love. "And now faith, hope and love abide, these three; and the greatest of these is love." (1 Cor.13:13) They provide a canvas against which commentators and others can project their own concerns. So, for instance, Ciampa and Rosner quote Hafemann, who sees these virtues as the antidote to the "suffocating self-love of our modern and postmodern culture." [5] The craving for security is fulfilled in faith, our purpose for living is hope, and the love of which Paul speaks sets us free from the love of self. Horsley[6] and O'Donovan[7] see the link to eschatology, with these virtues standing under the shadow of the last things. All three will remain into eternity, not just love (contra Spicq, *Agape in the New Testament*[8]). The greatness of love is not its eternal duration, but because it is the nature of God himself. Faith, as a description of the life of absolute trust in the divine salvation, continues, as Barrett affirms, "the life of the age to come will rest on faith as completely as does the Christian life now."[9] Hope, similarly, remains, albeit transformed by the perfection of the age to come. The difference with love is it alone abides untransformed from the form in which Christ and the cross has revealed it.

---

4. Not only in its classic formulation in 1 Cor 13:13, but also Rom 5:1–5; Gal 5:5–6; Eph 4:2–5; Col 1:4–5; 1 Thess 1:3; 5:8; Tit 2:2; Heb 6:10–12;10:22–24; 1 Pet 1:3–8.

5. Hafeman, *The God of Promise and the Life of Faith*, 17, cited by Ciampa and Rosner, *The First Letter to the Corinthians*, 660.

6. Horsley, "Gnosis in Corinth: 1 Corinthians 8:1–6," 27, 37–39; and Horsley, *1 Corinthians*, 179.

7. O'Donovan, *Resurrection and the Moral Order*, 246–47.

8. Spicq, *Agape in the New Testament*.

9. Barrett, *A Commentary on the First Epistle to the Corinthians*, 308–9.

learning to love, to have respect and concern for the Other above the self, is grounded in the nature of God as revealed in Christ, and this will never become redundant, obsolete, or irrelevant. The future thus provides the model for the present in working out priorities at Corinth and in the church at large. Agape is much more than a "moral virtue."[10]

In pastoral ministry, then, the task is to support people who are certainly living in the present, but also in the light of eternity, and organizing priorities according to faith, hope and above all love. Growing in faith—an active trust in God and obedience to the will of Christ—this develops the Christian life as one that is oriented to the way of Christ. Growth in hope is a natural response to the growth in faith, for it sees that the promises of God can be trusted, and so that which God orders for eternity will not be altered. But above all, pastoral ministry shapes people by love, for love, and in order that they may love the better, both God and their fellows.

Faith

Piero della Francesca, *The Resurrection*

In 1459 a gothic building known as the Residenza in Sansepulcro was returned to its citizens as a place for the local council to hold its meetings. Placed high on the wall that divides the building into two chambers is a fresco of the resurrection of Christ by della Francesca. There it remains to this day (its most dangerous moment occurred in the Second World War, when, as the Germans were bombarding the town, the officer in charge, knowing the fresco was there, spared the building that housed it.) In the eighteenth century the wall was whitewashed, and the fresco covered, and with the removal of the lime-based covering much detail and color has been washed out. The picture remains, however, astounding, "the great psychological power of the image remains almost miraculously undiminished."[11]

It is a picture of singular power. At the bottom, sleeping in front of a rectangular tomb, are four figures, attired in Florentine military dress. Above them, with his right foot raised to the tomb's lip, and covered in a pink shroud, stands the risen Christ, staring straight out of the wall at us, the viewer. His right hand grasps the pink robe, displaying the still bloody nail print, while the left arm is partially extended and its hand (also nail pierced) holds a standard: a red cross on a white background. This is the

---

10. Thiselton, *The First Epistle to the Corinthians*, 1074.
11. Lavin, *Piero della Francesca*, 245.

labarum, the red-cross banner of his triumph over death. His torso is naked, and the wound in its side seems to bleed still. It is as if with one powerful leap, Jesus will step from the tomb altogether. In the background is a landscape with trees, reminiscent of that in his earlier Baptism with which we opened this book.

This is clearly not intended to be biblically literal. The scheme was an invention of the late tenth or early eleventh century, and Andrea Mantegna portrays the sepulcher in the mouth of the cave,[12] while Giovanni Bellini has Christ floating in the air above the cave.[13] All three depictions include the red cross flag of triumph. Della Francesca's depiction follows closely the composition of an earlier alter piece painted by Niccolo di Segna in ca. 1346-8 housed in Sansepulcro's Cathedral. In this earlier depiction, the sleeping guards are horizontal, but della Francesca composes them in kind of fan shape, concentrating our gaze (if it needed to concentrate) upon Christ.

It is the face that grips the viewer. It is a hypnotic expression, far removed from the sorrowful faces of the Devotio Moderna, and half way towards the stern faces of Byzantine and early Medieval depictions of Christ. This is not a beautiful face, but one of a working man, the eyes still, perhaps, a little tormented by death and hell.

As always in della Francesca, the landscape is no mere decoration. It is certainly Tuscan in character, but the trees behind Christ are strange. To the right are three trees in leaf, leading down to the lush valley, while the two trees to the left, behind the triumphant standard, are bare, and lead up to the treeless hill in the far background. The landscape offers two choices: an easy route, echoed by the guard's spear that points in this direction, of a sleepy indifference to the way of resurrection and the godly life, or a difficult route of virtue, that leads arduously uphill to life.

Faith in the resurrected Christ is demanded of the viewer, as opposed to the sleep of the guards. Pastoral formation demands of the minister, first, the same response: an active faith, with a foot on the edge of the tomb, on the edge of life, ready to propel us to new life. Yet the pursuit of that life also demands of us those choices, daily, between ease and upwards struggle. The road to destruction is broad and easy, says Jesus in Matthew 7:13–14, while the road to life is hard, entered by a narrow gate. The growth in the virtues is a fruit of such upward struggle and godly choice.

12. Andrea Mantegna, *Resurrection of Christ*, 1456–1459, tempera on panel. Now in Musee des Beaux-Arts, Tours.

13. Giovanni Bellini, *Resurrection of Christ*, 1475–1479, oil on panel. Now in Gemaldegalerie, Berlin.

If the pastoral task is to first exemplify this way of living, then the second is to encourage and form it in others. Living in the power of resurrection life—in the life of the age to come—is the call to every disciple. Faith in the risen Christ, translated into purposeful and sacrificial living, rather than sleeping through this life, is the challenge to all, and pastoral ministry challenges the disciple to that way of life. How different to the false gospels of ease and wealth promised by some, as if faith in the risen Christ can be cashed out in terms of riches or decadence.

Hope

Sir John Everett Millais, *The Return of the Dove to the Ark*

In his heyday, Sir John Everett Millais (1829–96) was regarded as the greatest of British painters, the presiding artistic genius of his age. In his youth he was one of the Pre-Raphaelite Brotherhood, and the picture we shall explore, *The Return of the Dove to the Ark*, of 1851, belongs to that period. In his latter years he was the painter of celebrity portraits (our images of Benjamin Disraeli and William Gladstone owe much to his portraits of them,) children in coy poses (*Cherry Ripe* of 1879), and historical, biblical, and romantic pictures, such as the ubiquitous *Bubbles* of 1886, painted at the height of his popularity, and used as an advertisement for Pears Soap. These later commissions brought him wealth and popularity, and perhaps have given rise to the way in which his reputation sank so quickly after his death. In his obituary of Millais, Arthur Symons condemned the later output as sacrificing integrity for the commodity culture of the day, "he painted whatever would bring him ready money and immediate fame; and he deliberately abandoned a career which, with labor, might easily have made him the greatest painter of his age, in order to become with ease, the richest and most popular."[14]

In his youth it was his association with the avant-garde Pre-Raphaelites that cast him as the rebel, and against which his later wealth and fame was contrasted. His outstanding works belong largely to that period: *Isabella* (1848–9); *Christ in the House of His Parents*[15] (1849–50); *Ophelia*(1851–2)

---

14. Symons, "The Lesson of Millais," *Savoy*, 6, 57–58, cited by Smith, "'The Poetic Image': The Art of John Everett Millais," in Rosenfield and Smith, *Millais*, 14.

15. Controversial still: Waldemar Januszczak reviewing the 2007 Tate Britain retrospective in *The Sunday Times* describes it as "a lurid, wild-eyed and ludicrous religious hallucination made up of heightened states," with the observation that "John the Baptist looks as if he is about to be sick." Januszczak's conclusion is that Millais cannot turn off the sentimentality.

and *The Return of the Dove to the Ark*. These paintings are signature announcements of the Pre-Raphaelite style, probing human psychology instead of the prevailing operatic style of the day, with dramatic composition and energy. There is a quietness, a meditative probing about these Pre-Raphaelite paintings, and a respect for the context (the "background" to the painting) as much as for the subject. At the same time, there is huge psychological depth in, for instance, the faces in *Isabella*, a painting based upon Keats's poem about doomed lovers, and narrative power in the bleeding hand of the child Jesus, his hand wounded from a nail in his father's carpenter's shop in the eponymous painting of 1849–50.

Quite apart from the psychological depth of *The Return of the Dove to the Ark*, its simple two figures representing the wives of the sons of Noah tending the returned and exhausted dove bearing the olive branch, it says something about the integrity of the painter himself that is significant. Paintings such as this bore the brunt of the criticism of this avant-garde movement, yet Millais continued his association with the movement and its style for some time. Pastoral ministry conducted with integrity will not always be popular, and sometimes will draw the severest of criticism. As Symons noted, what greatness might Millais have achieved had he not succumbed to the lure to wealth and popularity in later life. The challenge of the formation of pastoral depth and integrity includes maintaining this throughout ministry, especially when the siren voices call to an easier life, perhaps reflected in a "successful" ministry as represented by a large congregation or a place on the conference circuit.

The painting depicts the story in Genesis 8:8–11 when the receding flood waters had prompted the release of a dove in search of land. Its return with an olive branch (actually no more than a twig, really,) was the assurance that land would be found and the occupants of the Ark saved from a lingering death from dehydration and starvation. Millais had intended to include the figure of Noah in the painting, but had insufficient time to complete the work for submission to the Royal Academy exhibition in April by the time of its commencement in February 1851. The finished work consists of just two young women: to the left, holding the dove to her breast with her right hand and the olive twig in her left, is the upright figure dressed in a long blue/green robe. To her right is a stooping figure, her left hand on the other's right arm, kissing the dove, her eyes betraying a weariness born of despair that barely dares to hope that an end to the trials of ark-living might be near. This girl wears what looks like a Catholic chasuble over her purple robe, and we know that Millais was intrigued by Catholicism and the Tractarians at the time. Is he portraying the hope that the church might return to its pre-Protestant roots, as it embraces the Spirit after its long sojourn on the flood waters of Protestant exile? It was certainly a contemporary accusation that the Movement's purpose was Tractarian.

Pastoral ministry is called to embody hope, directing the attention of the people of God to the promises of God, and the future hope that is already present in some measure in the life of the age to come—eternal life. This dimension of hope is one that assists pastoral ministry from being reduced to a form of humanism, devoid of spiritual power. In postmodernism's suspicion about the past and its interpretations, and its inability to see into the future, as culture and globalized life is in such constant flux, the present becomes the focus. While there has been an unhealthy avoidance of present-day elements of salvation in some forms of Christianity—especially in its economic and political dimensions for the poor—and too much of an emphasis upon the life to come beyond the grave, the message of the Christian faith remains one of eternal hope and eschatological promise. Pastoral ministry requires a recovery of such a dimension if it is to be authentic, and as such, attend more closely to the death of women and men, as well as their life.

Love

Titian, *Noli me tangere*

Painted in about 1514, when he was in his twenties, Titian depicts the moment Mary Magdalen reaches out to touch the resurrected Christ, whom she has mistaken for the gardener (Titian adds a hoe to excuse her mistake). This reaching out is instinctive, only to be rebuffed with "Don't touch me" (*Noli me tangere*). Her desire threatens to overwhelm her and is an extraordinary depiction of love: of the Magdalen for her Savior, and of Jesus for his friend. Of course modern psychology cannot but assume they were lovers, and that this was not the first touch that they had experienced, but Scripture does not allow for such a story. It is the stuff of fantasy. Nonetheless, this is a painting of love and desire, most especially of Mary. John Drury comments "landscape and love are in harmony. For whatever is going on between the two people here, it is something to do with love. Their posture speaks it."[16]

The setting is pastoral, and notably, the tomb is absent. A castle and hamlet to the right, and a vale blued with distance fills a strip above the fields and trees of the middle distance, populated by sheep. Cutting the landscape in two is a monumental tree, its trunk springing from the ground compositionally just above Mary's head, and continuing the line of eye

---

16. Drury, *Painting the Word*, 117.

contact between Jesus and Mary. The compositional structure of the painting is two curves: the first, beginning at Jesus' nail-pierced feet, rises steeply, but flattens off as it passes through his head and on to the right hand side of the painting, symbolizing the earthly. The second begins with Mary's robe, rises through her body and soars up to the heavens through the tree. The earthly love soars to heaven through the tree (the Tree of Life transformed by the tree of execution), while the divine love transmitted through Jesus' sacrificial death protects the earthly.

Behind Jesus the sun is rising, indicating that new life has come. Mary wears a sumptuous red robe over a white shift (the Venetian Titian had access to the new rich pigments available from the East and the Americas, in this case Vermillion and Carmine) and kneeling, clutches the jar of burial spices with which she had come prepared to anoint the body that she now sees almost naked before her. In the art of the Renaissance, Mary is always identifiable by her loose hair and the jar she carries. The burial shroud protects Jesus' modesty as he stands, the nail print in his right foot visible, although no other signs of his passion are visible (notably, no wound in his very naked side.) Mary's hair is let down, and her hand reaches out to touch—well, the line of movement suggests Jesus groin—and this gives the painting its erotic charge. But at the moment of rebuke, the gesture of eager touch expressed in her outstretched arm is turned to wonder and praise, as the hand opens in a gesture of wonder. The whole painting turns on this hand and its gesture.

Jesus bends away from this touch, gathering what little of the shroud is available to him, and presumably says, gently (for there is no look of alarm on his face) "don't touch me." Mary uses the physicality of touch to express her love, but the time for this is now past. Sensual touch may well have been her stock in trade, if the rumors of her background as a prostitute are to be believed, but Jesus withdraws from this now (even as he had welcomed an expression of this, without embarrassment, as the woman, unnamed in Luke 7:36–50, but widely assumed in Titian's day to be have been Mary, let down her hair and anointed his feet with her tears at the house of Simon the Pharisee.) Yet at the same time leans in towards her, in an almost balletic move, to express a means of intimacy in the spirit whose time has not yet fully come.

The picture is close to another painting of the same period, *Sacred and Profane Love*, with the same ambiguous atmosphere, landscape and combination of almost naked and fully clothed figures: except here the two figures are both women, one draped in vivid red, revealing her naked figure, while the other, clothed, has an almost white grey dress over a red sleeved undergarment. They sit at a well. The naked figure is probably Venus, while the clothed figure a woman attired for her wedding.

This mixing of sacred and profane love, in both paintings, points to the close relationship between sexual and religious desire, human and divine love. Formation in pastoral care must come to terms with the sexuality of the minister, and others. The existence of the sub-conscious processes called transference means that some members of a congregation will "fall in love" with their pastor. Indeed, for some it will not be unconscious at all, but a very powerful sexual connection. It always remains the responsibility of the minister to keep the boundaries secure, to resist any attempt to exploit that attraction and to find the resources to hold in check their own sexual attraction to others. Their response must be "do not touch me." Titian's painting vividly portrays the restraint that must be present in every encounter, most especially where sexuality is powerfully present.

There is a proper place for love within the church: it is a costly love for one another that bears each other's burdens and maintains with propriety a deep affection one for the other. I am reminded of the story of the aged St. John, too frail to preach, being carried into the congregation gathered in Ephesus: his only words to them were "Little children, love one another." The constant reminder by the pastor of the necessity to love one another, and then to exemplify that in their own life, is amongst the most challenging of the pastoral tasks.

But love for one another within the body of Christ is not the only call to love. Above all we are to love God with heart, soul and mind, and our neighbor as one's self. The love of God is a reaching out in desire to the beloved savior and sustainer, expressed in prayer and wonder, adoration and humility. But desire is contested in the contemporary world. David Runcorn suggests that, "our desires are an expression of the deepest truths about ourselves. Discerning our desires will actually draw us closer to the mystery of who we are and our place within all that makes up the world."[17] But he goes on to explain that much modern living is a need to avoid meeting our desires. He cites the psychotherapist Adam Phillips who argues that we use our desires to avoid facing our desires. We are a culture,

> in flight from confusion and uncertainty about our desires and what we really want . . . . we even hide from ourselves the fact that we are escaping. It is as though, if we can keep ourselves sufficiently busy escaping, we can forget that that is what we are doing.[18]

17. Runcorn, *Choice, Desire and the Will of God*, 76.
18. Phillips, *Houdini's Box*, 51.

To become aware of our real desires is uncomfortable and disturbing, but effective pastoral ministry must at some point encounter this disturbance. Without such awareness of our real selves, pastors are prey to dangerous forces and unpredictable encounters. But since the prime person desiring is God himself, if we are available to his disturbing desire for us, we can begin to discover how to desire him in response.

A similar theme is developed at greater length by Philip Sheldrake in *Befriending our Desires*.[19] Drawing upon the mystical tradition especially, he argues for a spirituality of desire, intimately associated with our capacity to love. From Catherine of Sienna's observation that our desires are one of the few ways in which we are able to touch God's presence, to her contemporary, the Dominican, Meister Eckhart's, suggestion that the reason we find God remote is the weakness of our desire, the mystics understood the power of our desires, for good or ill. Thomas Cranmer phrases it in the Book of Common Prayer as the difference between following "the devises and desires of our own hearts," and "the holy desires," "good counsels," and "just works" that proceed from God.

Because desire can seem such a risky and wayward aspect of our person, to see its key role in the pursuit of God on the spiritual journey comes with some initial reservation, resistance even. In addition, too often we have a notion of God as disengaged, passionless—owing too much to the Aristotelian philosophical god—and so see desire as something to do with our sinful nature that must be rejected as inimical to the rational God of cold detachment. "If we are created in the image of that God, we can easily associate desire and passion with lack of balance, with confusion, loss of control, and dangerous subjectivity. Desire is also closely linked to sexuality, which seems to have little to do with common (traditional male?) perceptions of the spiritual."[20] Sheldrake argues that spirituality is intimately associated with desire—our own and God's—precisely because it is at the heart of what makes both God and humankind love, and describing God as the God of love is central to the Christian tradition. From Gregory of Nyssa to the medieval mystics, from John of the Cross to Thomas Traherne and the Wesleys, the Christian faith has been described in terms of desires. The current focus upon emotional intimacy in worship in some charismatic traditions is but one contemporary expression of a major theme of Western spirituality. Forming women and men as ministers has to come to terms with desires, both in terms of the formation of character, so that "the desires and devises of our hearts" might not disturb the pursuit of holy living, and

---

19. Sheldrake, *Befriending our Desires*.
20. Ibid., 9–10.

the formation of the minister's spirituality. A fundamental element in the effectiveness of ministerial formation, one might almost say, is in the capacity of the minister-in-formation to see their desires bent to the pursuit of God, rather than those devises of the heart that seek after power, or the manipulation of others, or heed the siren voices that make shipwreck of their ministry.

And Now Faith, Hope and Love Abide, These Three

In exploring these three pastoral virtues, I have separated them, but this, according to Paul, is artificial. They co-inhere, belong together and should not be separated. To see them in combination we turn to another artistic theme of the Renaissance: the annunciation. We will focus on the paintings of Fra Angelico, but will situate his work in the longer tradition.

What can seem to a contemporary commentator on the artistic legacy of the annunciation as "the imaginative powers" of Luke, and "a flight of fancy which here shows the angel Gabriel entering the house in Nazareth,"[21] was to the artists of the Renaissance a historical fact (and remains so to many today.) However, it was one that required imaginative powers of considerable depth. This is the moment that the divine takes human form, takes flesh, even if it is a single cell, and painters have to freeze that moment in a set of relationships and symbols.

Duccio, the Sienese painter of the fourteenth century, painted his annunciation, now in the London National Gallery, in 1311. The angel, entering from the left, greets Mary, who pulls her veil close in sign of her being troubled. Her face is serious and her movement suggests a recoil away from the angel. She holds a book, on the page of which is written in Hebrew "Behold, a virgin shall conceive and bear a son, and shall call his name Emmanuel" (*Ecce virgo concipiet et pariet filium et vocabitur*) reminding her, and us, that this has been foreseen. All that remains is her obedience. She indicates this by pointing her finger to the right, where in its original was a depiction of her with the new-born Jesus. Yes, it came to pass, she motions.

In the eves of the open porch that is her house there is a silver bird, the Holy Spirit which was coming upon her in shafts of light emanating from heaven above. In Filippo Lippi's annunciation 150 years later,[22] the heavens are parted by a hand that dispenses the fertilizing grace of the Spirit that

---

21. Drury, *Painting the Word*, 31.

22. Filippo Lippi, late-1450s, *The Annunciation*. Now in the National Gallery, London. Lippi had already painted annunciations a number of times but none as moving as this.

hovers much closer to Mary. No longer in the eves of the house, it flutters in front of her belly, the angel's gaze fixed upon the vision, hers upon the dove in front of her. Careful and delicate brushwork reveals a spray of golden light issuing from the dove's beak, while an answering spray sparkles from Mary through a tiny slit in her tunic. Light from her womb meets light from the Spirit/dove's beak, and the word becomes flesh.

Fra Carnevale's version in the same mid-fifteenth century is altogether more elaborate.[23] The virgin is kneeling in prayer, reading in a wealthy Florentine house (such as the one belonging to the wealthy merchant Jacques Coeur of Bourges, who commissioned it) while the angel genuflects before her. This is an annunciation to declare the wealth of the man who paid for it, and loses the mystery altogether in the process. More restrained is his annunciation, now in the Samuel H. Kress Collection at the National Gallery of Art, Washington. Here Carnevale's interest in architecture and skill with perspective aligns him with Piero della Francesca. The poses of the two figures is similar to the Coeur painting, but the courtyard space in which the event takes place really takes pride of place.

Two hundred years later, Poussin depicts the moment in less reserved mood. Ten years earlier Bernini had completed his extraordinary sculpture of St Teresa in ecstasy (1644–47) for S. Maria della Vittoria, Rome. Depicting the experience recorded by St Teresa in chapter 29 of her autobiography, an angel appears and plunges a fiery iron-tipped spear into her heart "several times so that it penetrated to my entrails. The pain was so severe that it made me utter several moans. The sweetness caused by this intense pain is so extreme that one cannot possibly wish it to cease, nor is one's soul then content with anything but God." The classicist Poussin depicts his Mary in similar pose, if with less Baroque feeling, her arms open in welcome of God's embrace, her eyes closed, her lips parted, and her legs apart. Where Bernini's St Teresa is all convulsive ecstasy, Poussin's Mary is tranquil acceptance. Above her descends a large and realistic dove, while the angel raises one hand in benediction towards the dove, and the other points to the virgin's womb.

All of these paintings follow a similar compositional form: the angel is on the left facing the Virgin on the right, the house behind her at the right hand side of the painting, the entrance to the left hand side. Mary is cloaked in blue, the angel in white, with multi-colored wings. Fra Angelico, the Florentine painter working in the middle of the fifteenth century, painted the scene alone three or four times, and twice more collaboratively.

---

23. Fra Carnevale, ca. 1450, *The Annunciation*. Now in Alte Pinakothek, Munich. Depicted in Christianson, *From Filippo Lippi to Piero della Francesca*, 182–85.

The first, ca.1425–27, in tempera and gold on a wooden panel, is now in the Museo del Prado, Madrid. The second, ca.1432, again in tempera and gold on wood, is now in the Museo Diocesano, Cortona, and the third, a fresco, on the wall of the North Corridor, Museo di san Marco, Florence. A fourth, simpler still, is in cell 3 of the Museo di san Marco, while a fifth painted in the closing years of his life with assistants, ca. 1451–52, is part of a wider collection of scenes.

The first depiction is divided into three horizontal sections, the left hand one portraying the expulsion from the garden, from above which shines the golden light that conveys the Spirit/dove towards the Virgin. Angel and Virgin mimic one another's gestures of humble greeting, crossed arms, and share golden blonde hair. Originally an altarpiece in San Domenico di Fiesole, near Florence, his monastic house, this painting reveals the Dominican Fra Angelico (known then as Fra Giovanni da Fiesole: the 'Angelic Friar' being a later acknowledgement of his greatness) already steeped in Dominican spirituality, with its special devotion to Mary.

Another Dominican convent, in Cortona, was the commissioning place of the second annunciation. Mary's pose remains one of humble response, her arms crossed, but the angel is all energy and speech. His words are written in the space between them, 'The Holy Spirit shall come upon thee, and the power of the Highest shall overshadow thee' (SPS S SUP.. VEIET I TE VIRT ALTISI OBUBRABIT TIBI), with Mary's words upside down ("Here I am the Servant of the Lord . . . ", ECCE ACILLA DOMINI . . . VBV TUUM) "The urgency of the archangel's mission is emphasized by his forceful gesture, the thrust of his head and his tensely poised wings, as he kneels before Mary."[24] This is the moment when the word became flesh, formed by the Spirit of God, the dove that hovers above Mary's head. In painting this annunciation, Fra Angelico was "at present" a friar at the Convent of San Domenico of Cortona, according to his witness statement to a will at the time of its painting, although he was also described as a master painter and of the Florentine Community.

In 1436 Pope Eugenius IV ceded the church and monastery of San Marco in the heart of Florence to San Domenico in Fiesole, Fra Angelico's monastery. Fra Angelico set about painting frescos in the renovated convent, and amongst them is the third great annunciation, found in the North Corridor. The fresco stands at the point of demarcation between the more public space for the lay brothers, and those using the library, and the private dormitory of the friars. This marked "the threshold to the liminal, private

---

24. Ahl, *Fra Angelico*, 104.

space."25 From here, the friars journeyed through the Passion and Resurrection, and the joys and sorrows of the Virgin in murals on the walls of this private space. Everywhere Dominican saints meditate in these frescos, reminding the friars that contemplation was a surer way to God than scholarship.

This version excludes the expulsion of Adam and Eve from Eden (a feature of the two previous works) and is altogether simpler. The arms are once again crossed by both participants in the exchange, Mary's above her womb, the angel's in reciprocity; the setting is a loggia within a garden enclosed by a fence; and the angel's multi-colored wings depicts the polychromaticism of Paradise.

Cell three of San Marco depicts the simplest annunciation. The angel is simply clad in a red robe, while Mary is in pink, devoid of her familiar blue cloak. She kneels on a prayer stool, while the angel stands; the pair are within a simple arched room, while a Dominican friar, St Peter Martyr, looks on in prayerfulness. There is no dove, nor words. The setting reflects the architecture of the convent itself, "heightening the sense of the Virgin's actual presence within the convent itself."26 Here everything is stripped to the basic elements, allowing the friars to contemplate the incarnation with the minimum of disturbance.

Pastoral ministry combines spiritual formation with the bringing of the Christian hope, always in the context of the love of God. The Virgin is greeted as one who has received grace, and for her there is the hope of a child, mixed with all the pain of misunderstanding to come, and the "sword that shall pierce her heart" also: the early death in his thirties of this, as yet unborn, child. Her response is one of obedience to the heavenly call—an expression of love of God. The formation of the pastoral minister will embrace all this: first in their own life, and then in bringing this to others. I do not believe this requires any special reverence for the Virgin, although some will find that helpful. What counts is the one being formed in her womb and in her heart as she submits to the will of God, come what may. This calls for faith in God, even when the call is to painful and costly obedience; hope that in the end God works all things together for good, and an ability to seek out the purpose in the costly discipleship, embrace it and use it (a form of personal Eucharistic taking, blessing and breaking, before giving in service, as it were); and always (the hardest thing by far) the love of God, the church and neighbor (and even enemy). Mary is an example of all this, as befits the one who carries the incarnate Son of God. Carrying images of this

25. Ibid., 137.
26. Ibid., 140.

exemplary disciple, through pictures such as the ones discussed above, for instance, give extra weight to the way in which pastoral ministry requires faith, hope and love.

And how is all this to be achieved? Careful study of texts about pastoral ministry and developmental psychology are a starting point, no doubt. However, this area of formation, more than most, requires face-to-face tuition, personal apprenticeship and above all experience. Wisdom will bring insight into the hearts of men and women, careful attention to people will notice the incongruence between spoken and body languages (for instance, the dry rehearsal of a story, while the skin of the upper chest and neck flushes; or the insistence that "everything is OK" while the whole body is tense with anger) and listening, listening and listening again. This cannot simply be learned from books, but needs reflection and some form of supervision. It calls for prayerful attentiveness to the Spirit and to the person before one: pastoral ministry cannot be reduced to formulae or constrained by regulation if it is to be responsive to the Spirit. All too often, of course, it is so restrained, and pastoral care becomes a form of professionalized (in the worst sense of this term) religiosity, governed by fear and self-protection. The resulting ministry is a form of religious human resource management, and pastors become religious HR professionals. This is not the nuanced, Spirit-led pastoral ministry that the tradition of ministry requires, but it is what it becomes when overly regularized, and anxiety is the predominant motivating spirit.

Forming the minister in pastoral care, then, is a complex blend of gaining intellectual understanding and practical experience, together with a habituation to careful and empathic listening. These skills can be learned, especially listening skills, in the classroom, and knowledge gained there too, but without some opportunities for supervised and apprenticed development of practice, the formation will always be impoverished. In mixed-mode delivery such pastoral practice is unavoidable, although the degree to which the skills are developed in a closely supervised way is variable. In medical training, close supervision of the medical student or junior doctor fresh out of medical school is ubiquitous, and so skills and bed-side manner can be observed and corrected where necessary. Normally, such close apprenticing of pastoral encounters is supervised, if at all, to a much lower degree, and so poor practice, and impatient listening can become normalized and never really challenged. Here formational processes must change, and the development of practices fit-for-purpose become obligatory for all ministers in formation, not just those for whom this is a pre-existing skill transferred from some other context, or where the minister in training is predisposed to such habits. Indeed, not a few ministerial casualties arise from the absence of the ability to listen, and even if such ministers "survive", the effectiveness of their ministry will be diminished for the lack of pastoral skills. The formation of virtues of humility, compassion and courage, for instance, will accompany the development of pastoral skills, and those skills will provide the opportunity for those virtues to be exercised over a life-time of service.

14

Ministry as Guidance

The work of spiritual guidance and theological guidance are often treated as two separate sets of practices: one, spiritual direction, being the task of assisting the spiritual development of people, and often associated closely with Catholic practices, and delivered by Religious (monks, nuns, friars and so forth); while the other, theological shaping of a community or catechesis, more often conducted by the minister. Sometimes this latter role has been described as viewing the minister as the "resident theologian" in a church, although this is to diminish greatly the way in which theologies are being shaped by many people, mostly untrained in the disciplines required. For instance, where the ordained (and presumably theologically trained) minister relinquishes the role of worship leader, and no longer presides with effective leadership over the conduct of public worship, the role of shaping the worship is left to those who may be musically more proficient than he or she, but who will, perhaps, lack the understanding to devise the whole into the rhythm of worship that, embracing the various dimensions of prayer, listening, and response, is holistic. The resulting diet of song and sermon is often impoverished, and the choice of material sung (or perhaps simply heard, if the musical medium is not conducive to congregational participation) will inevitably reflect someone's theology, albeit one that might be deficient or distorted.

Such a separation would be considered strange until recently. Theologians conducted their work within the context of the Church, and would be spiritual guides as well as theologians. True, there may have been an emphasis one way or another—some essentially spiritual directors, but theologically competent, and others, first theologians, who also engaged in the pastoral office of spiritual director—but the way in which the academy and the church have become separated (discussed elsewhere in this book) has led to an unhelpful distinction between prayer and study, faith and learning.

In this chapter I want to overcome such a separation, and argue that the two tasks are really expressions of one larger role: that of guidance to the church. The formation of ministers as spiritual and theological guides can and should be held together.

The necessity to ensure that "those who God hath joined together let no man put asunder"[1] has become a commonly held conviction. Writing of the purpose of his book on spirituality and theology, Philip Sheldrake writes,

> The main purpose of this book is to suggest not only the possibility but the necessity of bridging the historic division between love and knowledge in the human approach to God. To affirm that spirituality and theology are related implies two things. First, and most importantly, our attempts to talk about the Christian doctrine of God cannot be separated from personal faith and spiritual experience. Second, there are signs of a contemporary convergence between theology and the new scholarly field of "spirituality" which has replaced the older disciplines of ascetical and mystical theology.[2]

That the separation of the two spheres has had hugely damaging effects upon spirituality is clear to see. The resulting spirituality is often little more than a form of "practical Unitarianism," with an undifferentiated God, and Jesus as a human teacher and spirit guide. The Holy Spirit is seen not as a person but as some form of pantheistic "spirit of creation." Certainly, any sense of a developed doctrine of the Trinity, which must be the bedrock of any Christian talk about God, is absent in much contemporary talk about spirituality. Sheldrake argues that this decline in a widespread Christian understanding about the nature of God is contemporaneous with an increasing hunger for 'spirituality'—for a way of approaching the world that is not defiantly materialistic and pragmatic. The question "Who is God?" is replaced by the question "Who am I?" and any number of strange answers are given to the latter when the former remains unacknowledged. Of course, the two are linked, as Calvin famously asserts in the introduction to *The Institutes of the Christian Religion*: "Nearly all the wisdom we possess, that is to say, true and sound wisdom, consists in two parts: the knowledge of God and of ourselves. But, while joined by many bonds, which one precedes and brings forth the other is not easy to discern."[3] Julian of Norwich expresses the same sentiment differently when she writes,

1. "The Form of Solemnization of Matrimony," in *The Book of Common Prayer*, 305.
2. Sheldrake, *Spirituality and Theology*, xi.
3. Calvin, *Institutes of the Christian Religion*, 35.

> For our soul is so deeply grounded in God and so endlessly treasured that we cannot come to knowledge of it until we first have knowledge of God, who is the Creator to whom it is united.... And I saw very certainly that we must necessarily be in longing and in penance until the time when we are led so deeply into God that we verily and truly know our own soul.[4]

However, in postmodern spirituality, the answer to the question, "Who is God?" is likely to be answered by some variation on the belief that "God" is the word we use to describe the deepest part of our human nature, or values. And even where the existence of God external to the human psyche is admitted, the resulting spirituality is likely to be perilously individualistic, with little notion of the communal character of human existence and prayer, and disengaged from the world that is the object of God's redeeming purposes. This is "spirituality-lite," devoid of commitment to the salvation of the world and the kingdom purposes of God, and with little connection to others in deep abiding love.

Contrast this with the vision of God and the life of faith in, for instance, the readings for the Feast of Christ the King in Year A of the Common Lectionary: Ephesians 1, Matthew 25 and Ezekiel 34, texts that combine a deep spirituality with a profound commitment to engagement with the poor and hungry, the lost and oppressed. The trio of virtues that we have explored in the chapter on forming the pastoral practitioner are present here in the Epistle to the Ephesians—faith, hope and love. "I have heard of your faith in the Lord Jesus and your love toward the saints . . . I pray that . . . With the eyes of your heart enlightened you may know the hope to which he has called you." (Eph 1:15-18.) True Christian spirituality will see as its aim the drawing of the person-in-relationship-with-others into the very life of the Trinity, the community of Father, Son and Holy Spirit.

Or contrast this with the era of theology in the West from Gregory the Great in the sixth century to Bernard of Clairvaux in the twelfth, when the unity of knowledge and contemplation, theology and prayer, was grounded in the monastic communities in which theology was practiced. The beginning of the separation was apparent in the development of scholasticism in the twelfth century, although its greatest practitioners, such as Thomas Aquinas, continued to integrate prayer and mystical experience with rigorous theological enquiry. Von Balthasar considers that it was not until after Albert the Great, Thomas Aquinas and Bonaventure that we see "the disappearance of the 'complete' theologian . . . . The theologian who is also a

---

4. Julian of Norwich, *The Showings* 56.

saint."[5] The move of theology from the cloister to the university was the seal upon a separation that took four hundred years or more to become evident and widespread,[6] but in ministerial formation, such a separation can no longer be welcomed.

So, in this chapter, because of a desire to see theological and spiritual guidance re-integrated, I shall address both roles under the one head, The Practice of Guidance. The practice of spiritual direction cannot be disengaged from the role of resident theologian, at least so far as the minister is concerned, and it is closely linked to another task, that of pastoral care. We have seen already how spiritual virtues are developed and the place of the intellectual virtues (chapter 8) in the formation and practice of ministry: here we combine these two in the twin role of guidance in faith and its outworking in the spiritual life, or the life of prayer and its associated disciplines.

1. Spiritual Guidance

The work of spiritual guidance has often been focused upon times of crisis in a person's life. At times of bereavement, or redundancy, relationship break-down or serious ill health, the pastor is called upon to offer both support and guidance. The experience of many is that these are the only times when pastoral care is personalized, or that guidance is sought from the minister, apart from that formalized into a course, either upon finding faith or preparing for marriage. However, there is a parallel ministry offered in an increasingly wide range of spiritualities: spiritual direction. Once the preserve of Catholic churchmanship (both Roman and Anglican), this is now embraced by evangelical and charismatic alike, together with all of those disciplines that were once viewed as "popish" by evangelicals—confession, retreats and so forth. Let me explore this move from personal experience.

Growing up in a very "low church" Anglican parish in Sussex, where even candles at Christmas were suspect, let alone a candle lit on the altar (and we did not call it the altar, either: this was "the Lord's Table") anything that had its origins in the Anglo-Catholic tradition was resisted utterly. This avoidance of anything Roman, or, indeed anything even "middle-of-the-road" may have been especially stringent given the strongly High Church character of the Diocese of Chichester, and that much of the Church of England life elsewhere in the greater Brighton area was Anglo-Catholic,

---

5. Balthasar, "Theology and Sanctity," 57.

6. For a fuller description of this journey, see Sheldrake, *Spirituality and Theology*, chap. 2.

including the neighboring parish congregation of south Patcham. We at All Saints, however, were a solidly 1662 Prayer Book tradition Parish, with the Vicar only ever wearing choir dress (cassock, surplice, preaching stole and academic hood), and the congregation, including former Pentecostals and Brethren who felt at home in its strongly low church ethos, avoiding anything that looked Catholic, such as the practice of making the sign of the cross. Indeed, the Reader[7] was ex-Brethren, and the choir master a former Pentecostal. No one crossed themselves, or bowed to the Lord's Table, there was no reserved sacrament, and the Sunday diet of solidly biblical preaching was supplemented by the mid-week Prayer and Bible Study, where a thirty-minute exposition of Scripture was the norm. It did not seem so very different, then, when I found myself attending a charismatic Baptist church in South London as a nineteen-year-old undergraduate. Here was the same solidly evangelical and biblical preaching, and an orderly worship, even if there was a short time for "open worship," where contributions from the congregation were enabled—something entirely absent from public worship at my Anglican church, although expected in the form of prayer at the mid-week meeting. There was the same absence and ignorance of all things Catholic, even if not the more obviously voiced suspicion of my upbringing. Neither context, the Church of England nor the Baptist, looked to the broader traditions of the universal church with any expectation that something from there might contribute to its practices. While I am forever indebted to this tradition for a firm grounding in the faith, and a knowledge of the Scriptures, and recognize that it continues to shape my journey of faith in ways that I am only partly aware of, it nevertheless left me with a sense that there was something more to be explored.

Forty years later, things look very different. I remain in many ways an evangelical—my preaching is normally expositional, I am in many ways still conversionist, and cruci-centric, for instance—but would largely eschew the label. The same elements are found in the wider tradition, and are not the sole preserve of evangelicalism. It has been the experience of a wider ecumenical, and especially moderate Catholicism, that has reshaped my evangelical roots. I am now thoroughly sacramental in my understanding of divine action, find sustenance in Catholic elements of spirituality, and am a founder-member of a Baptist religious order. None of this could have been foreseen from the ferociously anti-Catholic tradition in which I was raised, but none of it seems particularly strange in today's post-evangelical world. From the superficial (I would much prefer to light a candle at every act of

---

7. In "Free Church" parlance, that would be a lay preacher, or non-ordained lay worker.

worship, rather than reserve this for a romanticized Christmas glow), to the more profound, such as the embracing of the daily office as the grounding of personal devotion, and the disciplines of the *Order for Baptist Ministry*, a much broader tree has sprung from those evangelical roots.

This is not unusual, however. This has been the journey taken by many evangelicals, such that evangelicalism as a movement is increasingly divided between those who hold to a thoroughly and narrowly conservative evangelical faith (especially strong amongst those Anglicans for whom the ordination of women to the priesthood is anathema, and even more so, to the episcopacy, and for whom there can be no accommodation to an affirming culture in respect of homosexual relationships) and those embracing a much broader expression that includes ecumenically both Pentecostal and Catholic traditions. The former looks increasingly like a sect, while the latter is no longer clearly and exclusively evangelical. It is this "contested tradition"[8] that threatens to further fragment the church, as evangelicals fight over the declining market share of this expression of Christianity in Britain. In such a struggle certain elements become totemic (the issue of same-sex relationships particularly) and amongst them is the nature of spiritual guidance. The ministry of spiritual direction, most often offered by Catholic Religious, is increasingly welcomed by the broader evangelical stream (Open or Liberal are two epithets used to denominate it) but still viewed with suspicion by the 'conservative' stream, for whom a daily devotional pattern of Scripture study and extempore prayer remains central.

Whether or not spiritual direction as a "Catholic practice" is welcomed, the ministry of spiritual guidance in some form or other is an essential part of the ministry for which formation is necessary. At its broadest, this is the role of spiritual guide in the midst of ordinary life, not restricted to those crises when help might more usually be sought.

It is in this area of spiritual guidance and wisdom that the formational process comes into sharpest focus. Despite the proliferation of courses to train spiritual directors, it is in this area of ministry that the longest apprenticeship is required. The insights of pastoral counselling and the practice of listening may assist in the gathering of the story from the directee, but knowing what response to make is born of personal experience and the accruing of wisdom from the great tradition of spiritual guidance that covers now centuries of experience. Martyn Percy describes formation as a "progressive and subtle journey" where institutions "will speak quite naturally of 'the discipline of prayer' as foundational. But it will invariably

---

8. Warner, "The Widening Gyre," 108.

be something that is instilled rather than imposed."[9] This requires "making haste slowly" and a willingness to be immersed in the formational process. Here tacit knowledge is the result of a prolonged experience of the practices involved, of the virtues acquired. Spiritual guidance is not so much a task that requires prolonged systematic calculation as an improvisation upon a theme, a response under conditions of immediacy and, perhaps, stress, that is more a knack than a theory-based analysis learned from books or lectures. Writing of leading a church, Percy says, "the management of a congregation within the context of the challenges of contemporary culture is much more like a 'knack' than a skill; organizing or shaping the church is about learned habits of wisdom more than it is about rules and theories."[10] I would say that this is exactly what spiritual guidance is about too: learned habits of wisdom and prayer applied with discernment to others' journeys of faith.

2. Theological Guidance

A rather quaint phrase was used in evangelical circles until quite recently: the minister's role was to "guard the pulpit." Images of a stout defense against all-comers, armed with a very large (and probably black) Bible, springs to mind, lest anybody else dare to preach in his (yes, it would be a man) church. In fact, precisely because others would preach, the role of the minister was to ensure doctrinal conformity, and presumably, to correct false teaching if it ever occurred. It was "the gospel" that was to be guarded, a phrase taken from 2 Timothy 1:14, and used by that consummate expositor, John Stott, as the title of his Bible Speaks Today commentary, *Guard the Gospel*.[11] The verb (*phylasso*) means to guard something "so that it is not lost or damaged". It is used of guarding a palace against marauders and possessions against thieves. Howard Marshall notes how God would himself guard the deposit of faith, and Timothy is to "act as his agent and is therefore told to do what is needed so that God's purpose will be accomplished."[12] This is accomplished through the empowering of the Spirit, which here ensures that the truth of the good news is protected, even when threatened by heresy (2 Timothy 3:13).

Perhaps it was reasonably clear to Paul and to Timothy what this gospel proclaimed: summarized as the lordship of Christ, his life, death and resurrection attesting to his status as messiah and his divine origin; the

---

9. Percy, *Anglicanism. Confidence, Commitment and Communion*, 35.
10. Ibid., 36.
11. Stott, *Guard the Gospel*, 43–47.
12. Marshall, *The Pastoral Epistles*, 714–15.

fulfilment of the Old Testament in Jesus of Nazareth; and the new ground of faith being in his sacrificial death for both Jew and gentile, and the absence of any necessity for gentiles to become circumcised Jews if they were to follow "the Way." What it has become two thousand years hence is far more complicated. Which theory of the atonement is at the heart of the gospel, or is there room for a number of metaphors? Is ministry to be exercised by women, in contradiction to some specific prohibitions in the Pauline corpus? Can loving, faithful, monogamous, same-sex partnerships be affirmed by the church? In what manner did creation occur (literal six-day creation, or closer to a time-scale commensurate with scientific understanding), and so forth. These have become the signs of "gospel" truth to some more conservative Christians, but would Paul and Timothy have included them in "the deposit of faith"? I very much doubt it. The church has a habit of making secondary matters definitive of whether one belongs to this or that party, and ignoring by comparison the essential truths.

An essential part of the role of theological guide is to discern the essentials from that which might be negotiated, the ground of faith from its cultural superstructure. At its heart is the person and work of Jesus Christ, or as Paul puts it in 2 Timothy 2:8–9, "Remember Jesus Christ, raised from the dead, a descendent of David—that is my gospel, for which I suffer hardship, even to the point of being chained like a criminal." Paul goes on to admonish Timothy to avoid "stupid and senseless controversies; you know they breed quarrels" (2 Tim 2:23) for "the Lord's servant must not be quarrelsome" (2 Tim 2:24) but "rightly explaining the word of truth." (2 Tim 2:15) The word translated "explaining" in the NRSV is difficult to grasp: ὀρθοτομοῦτνα (*orthotomoutna*) is found previously only in the Septuagint of Proverbs 3:6 and 11:5, where it means "to cut a path in a straight direction." The concept of a straight path is typical of Hebrew Wisdom literature, and the implication is here that Timothy should "rightly handle" the word of truth, in the sense of make it straight for the hearers to travel on. This also implies he applies it first to his own life, so that this is in accord with the teaching of the gospel. Here the insight of virtue ethics come to the fore: it is by constant practice at grappling with the Word of God, and applying it to living, and thus developing the virtues in a rounded sense, that the word is rightly "cut" so that both the expositor and her hearers can travel along the straight paths of the good news. The danger in failing to discern rightly the essential truths from the peripheral ones is precisely to cut a winding path, full of unnecessary diversions and deviations.

This concern for the truth easily slips into a partisan purveying of a particular tradition's truth, no more so than amongst conservative evangelicals. While Peter Jenson's aspiration to "hold tensions in the text without rushing to relieve them"[13] is commendable, the danger is that an overarching theological structure comes to adjudicate between those tensions. He continues to commend doctrine for its capacity to enable discrimination in the Christian, an aspect we shall discuss next. However, the modulating role of doctrine begs the question whose doctrine, and whether that is capable of change. He is right to argue that,

> Doctrine guards the purity of the faith and keeps us in the way of truth. It enables the pastor to drive away falsehood and error. Doctrinal principles firmly adhered to will also protect us from such pragmatic activities as beguile us with their alleged fruitfulness. Doctrinal soundness will protect Christians from the seductions of the latest purveyors of experiential Christianity, thereby enabling them to rejoice in the true experiences of God.[14]

This is all well and good, when tempered with some humility about the theological constructs that come to our aid in creating the whole metanarrative. What so often happens is that Scripture is not allowed to speak for itself, but is managed by the dominant theological party by the superimposition of their metanarrative.

A second essential quality in being a theological guide is to be able to understand how this never-changing gospel is always being forwarded to a new address, as, I believe, Helmut Thielecke said. The cultural context cannot be avoided if the faith is to be meaningfully applied to the life of the church. The minister as theological guide, therefore, needs not only to understand what the deposit of faith is (and importantly, is not) but also the nature of the culture and society to which it is offered. An example would be the debates in the first fifteen years of the twenty-first century about human sexuality. These are at their heart debates about two things: hermeneutics and culture. Is the traditional view of same-sex relationships a simple application of Scripture, or is it itself a culturally conditioned set of beliefs that carries with it a specific hermeneutic, and which has changed in the West as its culture has become more tolerant of difference? The minister handling this issue as the resident theologian needs to know the tradition and the culture equally, and be able to appropriately categorize the debate in terms of its significance for communion and fellowship. The pity of the debate is how too many have elevated it to a first-order theological matter, where the breaking of communion is at stake between those who disagree. Failing to read their own culture, and thus distinguish opinion from truth, for Rowan

---

13. Jenson, "Teaching Doctrine as Part of the Pastor's Role," 87.
14. Ibid., 87–88.

Williams this is a costly "category error," misjudging the secondary to be primary.

> the conservative religious establishment, Protestant and Catholic, has tended to react to the simultaneous trivializing and overloading of sex by a rather panic-stricken moralism, for which dissent about styles of sexual behavior become the main, sometimes the only, touchstone of "orthodoxy" or fidelity to tradition—which is simply to reproduce within the religious sphere the exact distortion and disproportion from which the secular environment suffers.[15]

On the other hand, an approach more accommodating to the cultural zeitgeist can all too easily dispense with tradition merely because it contradicts the spirit of the age. This treats same-sex attraction as an aspect of ordinary sexual variance, and views with disdain any qualification of this approach: a qualification that might be necessary where procreation is concerned. While I am generally sympathetic to the church finding a new way of affirming same-sex relationships, to challenge any questions that raises about the status of such attraction by reverting to ridicule or legal measures is not conducive to dialogue and mutual understanding. The resulting reaction from conservative elements in the churches is understandable: the attribution of a totemic status to the matter. The minister as resident theologian must avoid the raising of these culturally sensitive matters to primary dogmatic significance. There are more important battles to be fought.

In the West, the gospel is addressed to a culture fascinated by celebrity, governed by greed, and a tendency to scapegoat behaviors as a way of avoiding its own failings. Scandals in banking, politics, and the care of young people have become ways in which we distance the large majority of citizens from guilt. After all, "the state we're in is the fault of the bankers, Members of Parliament and pedophiles," or so the message tells us. It means we all avoid looking at the way we borrowed heavily to fund lifestyles we could not afford, have become a culture of suspicion and cynicism that is destroying trust, and have asked our children to bare a responsibility for adult questions at far too early an age.

Let us take the latter as an example to consider how doctrine and culture interact. "Children Matter" is a political statement, not simply in the sense that it allegedly describes United Kingdom government policy,[16] but

---

15. Williams, *Lost Icons*, 171.

16. H. M. Government, *Every Child Matters*, 2004. Presented to Parliament by the Chief Secretary to the Treasury, Paul Boetang MP. http://www.education.gov.uk/publications/eOrderingDownload/DfES10812004.pdf.

in the broader sense that wherever the Christian faith is taken seriously, or its influence is felt in the broader culture, then children will matter. It was not the case, really, in Jesus' day. In the Palestine of Jesus' day children did not matter: they were the least significant members of society, if members at all. Children were adults in waiting. I am not suggesting that parents did not love their children or that the all-too-familiar death of a child was not met with raw grief and deep loss. I am sure it was. Yet that oft repeated saying by parents today who suffer the loss of a child 'parents are not meant to outlive their children' was not the case in Jesus' day. Before clean water was available, before anti-biotics, before modern medicine, parents did indeed outlive most of their children. The most dangerous time of life was naught to five years old, the first year of life most dangerous of all, and the most likely outcome for a live birth was an early death. That this is not so today is wonderful and a tribute to the patient work of generations of scientists inspired by the Christian understanding that not only every child matters to God, but every human does.

In Jesus' day children were at the bottom of the pile. Then, as now, adults vied for power, elbowed their way to influence, "climbed the greasy pole": and children do not yet compete in that struggle. They can be ignored, or worse, abused. I am not talking about the forms of abuse that we as a society are most obsessed about: the sexual abuse of children, or their physical abuse or neglect, although, heaven knows, that is appalling in every instance. I mean the routine abuse by using them as pawns in a marriage break-up, or as little consumers playing their part in the global advance of big business—yes, Disney included—or any attempt to replace childhood playfulness with responsibilities that are premature, especially in the realm of sexualized pre-sexual relationships. Rowan Williams describes this as profound impatience, not least because the acquisition of language is a prolonged matter, and requires years of utterances that we don't have to be held responsible for. He observes,

> The perception of the child as *consumer* is clearly more dominant than it was a few decades ago. The child is the (usually vicarious) purchaser of any number of graded and variegated packages—that is, of goods designed to stimulate further consumer desires. A relatively innocuous example is the familiar 'tie-in', the association of comics, toys and so on with a major new film or television serial; the Disney empire has developed this to an unprecedented pitch of professionalism. . . . Anything but innocuous is the conscription of children into the fetishistic hysteria of style wars . . . what can we say about a marketing

culture that so openly feeds and colludes with obsession? . . . the child as consumer is always a *pseudo*-adult.[17]

But Jesus re-writes the social order in the most profound of ways in the incident recorded in Mark 10, which is why it is such a shocking political act. The least important matter most: indeed, Jesus goes on to say, they exemplify how the order of things in the Kingdom of God is organized. They are powerless, have no influence, do not count in the polling station, contribute nothing to the economic productivity of the nation. Indeed, they are a burden upon the state and the family. Which is why they matter. In the Kingdom of God that's how things shape up: the least important in terms of power are the most important in the Council chamber of Heaven.

I rarely, if ever, walk out of meetings, but I did in Hong Kong a few years ago. The pastor of the largest and richest Pentecostal church in the city was asked about the children's programme in his church. He replied that they don't bother with children at his church, after all "they don't contribute to the offerings do they." I was so enraged I walked out. I thought, why should I stay and listen to such a travesty of the gospel?

The United Kingdom's current educational policies for the Early Years emphasizes school-readiness, so that they are prepared for Primary School, which prepares children for Secondary School, which prepares people for the work-place or further education, which prepares people to be economically productive in a global market place. Once again children matter, but not because of their intrinsic worth, but because they are the work-force of the future. Truly capitalism and the markets are Lord.

But when we confess Jesus is Lord, that's turned upside down. If the first calling upon the church is that it should be the church, then how we treat children will be a significant test. If they are ignored, frowned upon if they make a noise, distracting to the adults and the preacher especially, then we are not church and Jesus is not Lord. In common with our obsession with church growth and mission, the particular brand of Christianity—Evangelical Protestantism in its varieties of expression—has become all-too-often prey to a religious version of consumer-driven Capitalism. It's the powerful and the effective we celebrate, the glamorous worship leader or the preacher beloved of the conference and Bible Week circuit that we admire. These are the people we view on You Tube, and whose churches we emulate, or indeed, join. Because we have become prey to this insidious culture that is so toxic to the church being truly the church, we find it hard to recognize how erosive this is for children. "Children need to be free of the pressure to make adult choices if they are ever to learn how to

17. Williams, *Lost Icons*, 22–23.

make adult choices."[18] Pressurize them too early, and the result, when they grow, is a generation of adults who act like children, passing on in turn to their children, as it were, the virus. "A society that is generally disabled in its choice-making will produce childish adults, bad at the nurture of children because they are not secure in their adult freedoms."[19]

Jesus takes a child, sets it amongst the disciples and identifies with it: "Whoever welcomes one such child in my name welcomes me, and whoever welcomes me welcomes not me but the one who sent me." (Mark 9:37), and later says the Kingdom of God belongs to little children, and "Truly I tell you, whoever does not receive the kingdom of God as a little child will never enter it" (Mark 10:15). When the least are the ones he points to in order to say what the Kingdom of God is like; when it is a toddler who is the living parable of God's values, and when it is the babe in arms, utterly dependent upon its parents for its very survival, and who contribute to the church the very fact that they contribute nothing measurable, then we handling radically alternative ways to the world's bid for power.

Children enter the world with nothing, and everything is gift. So with us, we enter the Kingdom with nothing to contribute: absolutely everything is a gift of grace, and thinking otherwise is a dangerous admission of our pride. So, in church, who is the most important? The pastor or the other leaders? Those who work with children, perhaps? The answer we read from Jesus is that the most important sign of the Kingdom of God in any church is its tiniest child, and it is children who matter most: not because of some romantic notion of how lovely little babies are, but precisely because that is how we all are viewed through the lens of the values of Heaven. So when the child cries in the service that is possibly the most important contribution to the worship of God on that particular day.

I do not mean that as children grow they should not be taught how to moderate their intrinsic propensity for chaos . . . and that there is a time for them to learn to be quiet, to be prayerful, to be aware of God's presence. But they do so as children, not as mini-adults, and their spirituality must not be squeezed into an adult mould before their time, any more than their capacity to participate as consumers or their sexualized identities must not be invoked prematurely.

And, yes churches as elsewhere in society must be safe places, free from the abuse we are so aware of these days. I am in no way minimizing the need for proper safeguarding: the evidence from nearly all the Churches is that this has been a grievous failing over the past half century, at least.

18. Ibid., 27.
19. Ibid., 29.

However, to focus upon that, and demonize the perpetrators of that wickedness alone, misses the point. If we then go on as a society to routinely rob children of their childhood by imposing upon them the demands of adult choices, or sexualize them too soon by the clothes we dress them in, or distort the boyfriend/girlfriend relationships they naturally develop into sexualized ones, or ignore the TV and internet images we expose them to, then we have only scapegoated the few in order to avoid the guilt of what we all should feel at the damage we do to children blessed, or is it cursed, by the great gods of the market and the profit line.

Jesus blesses children precisely because they are children. He does more, though. He turns the values of his culture, and ours, upside down in setting a child in our midst when we argue over power and who is the greatest (Mark 9:36–37), proclaims that welcoming the child, the least and the last in his society, is exactly the same as welcoming him, and to welcome Jesus is to welcome God. God comes to us as a child, and we come to God when we recognize what that really means.[20]

Here is a way of engaging Scripture, theology and culture. But it is more: it is a profound sign that ministry must also embody these values, and be formed around virtues of humility, obedience, trust and courage. The first of the two references to little children in Mark noted above (Mark 9) is set as Jesus' response to an argument between the disciples about who is greatest. This very masculine bid for power is completely turned on its head, and all discipleship, but especially ministry, needs to take note.

Before taking leave of this theme, let me turn to two pictures. The first, a rather second rate painting by a member of the St John's Wood Clique, the second by Mattias Stom.

The poet Blake Morrison wrote an account of his boyhood with a somewhat irascible and eccentric father, *And When Did You Last See Your Father?* It was made into a film starring Colin Firth as the adult poet, and Jim Broadbent as his father. The book spawned a whole genre of confessional memoirs, mostly of dubious literary or biographical merit. Morrison's, however, has the poet's eye for phrasing and language. Its title was taken from a famous picture by W. F. Yeames exhibited in 1878, that now hangs in The Walker Art Gallery, Liverpool. Set in the English Civil War, it depicts a young boy dressed in Royalist clothes being interrogated by a Parliamentarian officer. It is typical of the genre of history paintings beloved of the Victorians, and the scene includes, from left to right, two women, the one hiding behind the other possibly a maidservant, the figure staring directly at the boy his mother. A sergeant in Cromwell's Army holds a halberd and stands

---

20. Cf. Goodliff, *"To Such as These": The Child in Baptist Thought*, 7–19.

with his arm around a young girl, who is hiding her face, and possibly crying. She is the boy's sister, fearful of what the boy in blue silk attire might reveal of their father's whereabouts. In the center background, sprawled on a bench, is a Parliamentarian cavalry officer looking at the boy with disdain, and in the center foreground, illuminated by light from a window, is the boy himself. He stands on a low stool to bring his eyeline close to that of the seated interrogator, across a table spread with a rust red carpet. Around the table are four other Parliamentarian figures: a seated secretary writes down an account of the proceedings, and behind him stands a man holding a bundle of books, possibly those proscribed by Parliament; to the immediate right of the interrogator sits a man dressed in Puritan clothing, black with a white collar, staring impassively at the boy, while the man in the extreme right hand side of the painting seems to be an observer, perhaps another officer hoping to gain some intelligence from the boy's unwitting revelation. The interrogator crosses his hands in front of his chin, and with a seemingly sympathetic demeanor gently questions the boy, his relative gentleness perhaps an interrogative ploy, or maybe a weariness with persecuting children and women. Everything hangs on the answer the boy in blue will give to that question: his father's life depends upon it, perhaps.

Here is the child set in their midst, not as an example as in Jesus' case, but as a tool of power exercised by others, motivated by a severe and violent form of oppressive religion. The tension in the moment is palpable: what will the boy say? Will he lie to save his father, or tell the truth and damn him? Precisely the dilemma faced by Blake Morrison as he wrote the account of his father (who was proud of his deception and lies when facing bureaucracy or petty power.)

Yeames was influenced by the Pre-Raphaelites' work, especially their historical scenes, but together with his fellow St John's Wood Clique artists, the genre had become debased to middle-brow sentimentalism, even if this painting rises above the norm for that group. The inspiration for the figure of the boy goes back a full century to Thomas Gainsborough's *The Blue Boy*, a full-length forward facing portrait of a boy somewhat older than Yeame's figure. The Victorians were the first to really idealize children, seeing in them natural innocence and truthfulness, hence the dilemma the boy faces. In Jesus' placing of a child in the midst of the disciples, it is not its innocence he celebrates, but powerlessness. In some ways the boy in blue is powerless too (he has no weapon with which to fight, unlike the sergeant behind him) but he does have the power to reveal or withhold truth, to save or damn his father.

The second picture is of another trial of a powerfully powerless man: the trial of Jesus. In common with a number of early seventeenth century

Northern European painters, Matthias Stom was influenced by Caravaggio. Born in The Netherlands in about 1600, Stom worked briefly in Rome from his thirties, and then in Naples, where he no doubt encountered Caravaggio's work, and created dramatically lit night time scenes that became his specialty, like his *Christ Before the High Priest* of ca. 1633. By the light of a single candle in the very center of the scene, Ciaphas, on the left, gestures with his left hand's index finger, lifted vertically in parallel with the candle flame, while on the opposite side stands Jesus, depicted three-quarter length to bring the viewer close in to the encounter. Like the work of Caravaggio, we are brought close into the scene, and as observers are forced to participate in the trial. Jesus is refusing to deny that he is the Son of God, and the High Priest is enraged by this, while the false witnesses behind Jesus gloat over their triumph. This is a painting about truth and lies, accusation and innocence, power and powerlessness. Both High Priest and Jesus lean in slightly toward the central candle flame, but Ciaphas is all energy and accusation as he addresses Jesus, while Jesus, his face impassive and looking at the flame, is serene. His hands are loosely crossed in front of him, and bound, the rope just visible around his right wrist, while Ciaphas's hands are all tight with anger and tension. Jesus, the Light of the World, and the Truth itself, stands accused by liars of a distortion of the very truth about him, his divine identity—truth that will condemn the one who said he was the way, the truth and the life to a journey that will end in his death.

All but forgotten after his death sometime after 1652, Matthias Stom deserves the recognition he now receives as amongst the most accomplished of the Dutch *Caravaggisti* (followers of Caravaggio) and his painting of the trial of Jesus is a powerful depiction of this scene, reduced to its essential elements, and dramatically developed.[21] In the way that Ignation exercises invite the the person on retreat to enter into the gospel story, Stom's painting invites us to put our feet in the shoes of Ciaphas, the false witnesses, and Jesus. The little child of Jesus' illustration about welcoming him, helpless and utterly dependent upon God, is now the Son of God before his accusers. Whoever welcomes this Jesus Christ, in all his kenotic self-empting, welcomes God himself, the one who sent him. Theological guidance and spiritual guidance combine here: the one speaking truthfully about the nature of God, in contradiction to all our pretensions to power that we project upon the heavens, the other, spiritual guidance, calling us to step into his shoes in prayer and humility.

21. His recovery of interest largely attributed to the work of Benedict Nicolson, influential editor of *The Burlington* magazine, and colleague of Kenneth Clark. See Nicolson, *The International Caravaggesque Movement: Lists of Pictures by Caravaggio and his Followers throughout Europe from 1590–1650.*

We have explored two areas where theological guidance raises particularly delicate and important questions in the contemporary church, human sexuality and the place of children. We might have explored the role of women, the prevalence of racism or inter-faith relationships, if space allowed. Those two must serve as examples of the ways in which the minister needs to be formed to offer theologically-literate guidance to the churches and Christian communities they serve. But how is such guidance formed?

It has been widely assumed that the primary context in which the minister-in-training finds a broader range of views than those with which they have grown up is the seminary or theological college. Here she or he begins to develop the skills in discerning the significance of various theological matters (for instance, when convictions about the morality of same-sex relationships are raised to the level of significance as beliefs about the Trinity or the full humanity and full divinity of Christ, this is a category error—matters of human sexuality are second-order beliefs, at most, and of third-order significance probably) and thus, those convictions that are negotiable, or where we can "agree to disagree" with others without breaking fellowship. Secondly, the minister-in-training begins to grasp a wider range of theological views, and to distinguish legitimate orthodoxy from the heretical. Those standpoints may include options that were previously discounted in the theological context in which they were initially formed, and yet can be now held as legitimate, even if an option from the theological culture-of-origin continues to be primary. An example would be the student arriving in college convinced that the only way to understand the meaning of the death of Christ is by means of substitutionary atonement in its penal variant, but who, through careful biblical study and theological reflection, comes to admit to the range of options the alternative metaphors of redemption from slavery to sin; the victory of Christ over the powers in the metaphor often described, after Gustav Aulen, as *Christus Victor*; and the idea of Christ's exemplary death. The student may still view as primary the idea of penal substitution, but other ideas are now considered valid, and, indeed, helpful lenses through which greater light is shone upon the atoning work of Christ. It is often this broadening of understanding that is viewed as suspicious and harmful by the student's sending congregation, where such breadth is resisted. However, this is really the significance of such breadth of theological formation, for it enables the unhelpfully narrow to be challenged.

Such theological formation should not be confined to the college phase of ministerial formation, however. The continuing ministerial experience in changing contexts and evolving cultures will require a subtle handling of theological convictions that hold fast to basic orthodoxy, while allowing for a reviewing of their interpretation, and perhaps a change of mind on some matters of secondary or tertiary significance. Thus, a student, coming from a context where women's ordained ministry is deemed unacceptable, will have their viewpoint challenged at theological college, but it might not be until the experience of serving in ministry alongside women that the real change of heart takes place, and resistance to the idea is replaced by advocacy.

While Head of Ministry for the Baptist Union I had responsibility for organizing an annual ministerial refresher conference, to which a fifth of the entire cohort of serving accredited ministers was invited each year on a rolling five-year cycle (and on average half accepted that invitation.) One of the purposes was to enable ministers, some long out of theological college, to be kept abreast of some developments in theology, ministerial practice or biblical studies. This was an organizational way of encouraging continuing growth in understanding and practice, to enable ministers to maintain that ministry of theological guidance. Not least because congregations shape ministers as much as ministers shape congregations, it was an opportunity to offer ministers the broader perspective.

The same growth in understanding of the spiritual life is possible. I have already described something of that journey for my own spiritual pilgrimage, and in formation at seminary or theological college, one of the most important tasks of the formational process is to enlarge the spiritual landscape for the student, introducing them to patterns and aspects of prayer, for instance, previously unknown, or viewed with such suspicion in their home church context as to be avoided at all costs. This broadened understanding should also be accompanied by a deepening of whatever are the core elements to the student minister's own practice (say, a pattern of Scripture reading and extempore prayer) so that they enter into their first pastoral charge of a congregation with both a broad awareness of the spiritual traditions of the Christian faith, and a deeply embedded set of practices to sustain their own current ministry. It is to be hoped that with changing phases of life, those core practices might be subtly changed, or, indeed, perhaps radically altered, when they no longer are fit for purpose, or previously discarded patterns once again taken up with new depth. The minister's own spiritual journey may be amongst the main resources for the gradual development of the skills in spiritual direction (recalling Martyn Percy's advocacy of a slow acquisition of the "knack" of leading a congregation,) but by itself is inadequate to the task of forming spiritual directors of both breadth of interest and depth of insight. Some intentional development of gifts in spiritual guidance is required.

This might be acquired through a course in spiritual direction, although this would be difficult to integrate into a course at college or seminary, and is probably a post-ordination aspect of formation if pursued in this way. Such a course benefits from the luxury of time to be still, to be silent, to pray more extensively than would be possible in the midst of the already over-crowded curriculum of initial formation courses. This is best seen as a development in the formation of the minister that, while it might be signposted in college for later pursuit, is followed as the need for it begins to press itself upon the minister, aware that formation is a life-long process. This might be one of the later areas of formation in that process.

A more readily-available way of growing intentionally in the skills of spiritual and theological direction and guidance—of deepening those practices of listening to others and offering guidance and accompaniment on their journey of faith—would be simply to read. Might it be possible to ensure that a book on the spiritual life, be that from the mystics and masters of that life from of old, or a contemporary exploration, is part of the minister's regular reading? Or that a particular focus upon some area of spiritual life is woven into the expectations for sabbatical leave. I have spent the two sabbaticals that I have been privileged to take, one in 1998 and the other in 2008, largely in writing or research, and I regret that I did not spend more time during those months on attending to my own soul. I hope that I might do things differently now.

Writing at a time when spiritual direction was by no means as widespread in its practice as it is today (and perhaps playing a significant part in the broadcasting of its virtues), Kenneth Leech observed in the introduction to his book *Soul Friend*,

> the guidance of individuals in the life of the spirit is at the heart of the Christian religion. It is not the preserve of a small number of experts based on religious orders or therapy groups. Union with God is not a peripheral area of interest for the Christian, and it is union with God that is the central concern of spiritual direction. The church at the present time is in desperate need of spiritual guides, men and women who are steeped in prayer and in the spirit, and who can therefore be the bearers of the spirit to our age. For, according to the great tradition, the spiritual director is first and foremost a *pneumatophoros*, a carrier, or vehicle, of the spirit.[22]

Leech's book would be a great place to start for a minister wanting to develop a deeper practice of spiritual guidance, integrating as it does a

---

22. Leech, *Soul Friend*, 2

history of the practice of spiritual direction with more contemporary ideas in therapy and psychoanalysis, and offering a succinct guide to the life of prayer. However, there are plenty of alternatives, some much more contemporary than Leech's classic text of 1977. From practical guides, such as Anita Woodwell's *On Holy Ground*, to books that focus upon a specific area of the spiritual life, such as Philip Sheldrake's *Befriending our Desires*, or Brother Ramon's exploration of retreat, *Deeper into God*, as well as the contemporary classics such as Vanstone's *Love's Endeavour, Love's Expense*, the range of texts is now both wide enough and accessible enough to provide a regular diet of reading to stimulate the refining of this practice of spiritual guidance.[23]

What seems clear to me is that Leech's plea for an increase in the number of those who will enable others' spiritual journeys, and be themselves bearers of the Spirit, is no less urgent than it was forty years ago. If the church is to not just survive, but rather, thrive in the coming decades in the West, under pressure from both growing Islamic influence and relentless secularization, it will only be as Christians find ways of holding deeply to the faith, living it joyfully and confessing or witnessing to it confidently. That requires a deeper faith and a richer spiritual experience than has been often thought satisfactory—and that will call for skilful spiritual guides from its ministers, as well as others, to assist in taking nominal Christian faith to deep discipleship. Perhaps more than in most areas of ministry, the development of these practices of spiritual and theological guidance integrates the intellectual, moral, and spiritual virtues into something that is at the heart of forming others as disciples of Christ. One dare not view it as a rather exotic domain of a few catholic-minded individuals who are cloistered away in retreat houses. It must become a mainstream and normal role of the working parish or congregational minister, and thus growth in its skills a developmental aim for all who are called to ministry and who exercise care for Christ's church and God's people.

---

23. Woodwell, *On Holy Ground*; Runcorn, *Choice, Desire and the Will of God*; Sheldrake, *Befriending our Desires*; Ramon, *Deeper into God*; Vanstone, *Love's Endeavour, Love's Expense*.

15

Ministry as Mission

It almost goes without saying that the church has become obsessed with its effectiveness in mission in the twenty-first century in Britain. It tells itself that this is for good gospel reasons of a passion for the lost and a desire to follow Jesus Christ in participating in the *missio Dei*. I suspect that it has actually a great deal more to do with Late-capitalism and secularization, and a deep seated anxiety about the uncertain future of the church, issuing in a frenzy of activity. If the church collapses in Britain (as it has seemed to do in the Middle East in the face of a more aggressive form of persecution from radical Islamism) then it will not be for lack of effort, the church seems to believe. For Baptists this means everything is read through a lens of mission, and in its very ubiquity, mission is evacuated of meaning. For the Church of England, it results in the ascendency of a form of leadership and management that is utterly pragmatic. For both of these traditions (and Methodism and the United Reformed Church have their own versions currently) it results in a way of engaging in mission which is technological (using the latest evangelistic tools exported out of context) and obsessed by numbers. In other words, it is religious mission conducted with the spirit of Late-capitalism, using the very tools that the culture invented, and which that culture deployed in eroding the church. The resulting shallowness of the church is hardly surprising given its *modus operandi* is precisely the same shallowness that Late-capitalism exploits without shame to increase desire for the consumer goods that enable its continuance.

Indeed, the very same tools are used in a capitalist way in the evangelical sub-culture: the selling of music and its superstars, the replacement of intellectual rigor with emotional engagement, and the fetishization of the new and the now over the old and the traditional. Certainly this is not the whole story, as we shall see, for there is a reaction that wants to embrace the polar opposite, and movements such as "Deep Church" and the "New Monasticism" could be seen as attempts to recover authentic church from the wreck of the contemporary "mission-shaped" version.

However, the current obsession with mission as an activity, as opposed to a way of life, is widespread. Writing about evangelistic events as the means by which the gospel is proclaimed, David Jackman observes how church members are put under pressure to "corral their friends in to such occasions", and concludes this strategy is wrong-footed. Pointing to 1 Peter 2:12, "Live such good lives among the pagans," he writes,

> Clearly verbal proclamation is demanded, but it is the quality of life that opens the door of opportunity. . . . Our contemporary danger may well be that the nurture of godliness in character is relegated down the list of church priorities, in favor of "skilling" a workforce of salesmen, whose task is to saturate the market with their product. It has been well observed, however, that what is needed is not more gospel salesmen, equipped with the latest techniques, but more free samples.[1]

In forming missionary ministers, therefore, I am skeptical about programmes that seek to equip people with the kinds of tools and schemes that predominate in the market-place. Instead, I want to emphasize the forming of disciples who naturally replicate because that is what healthy communities do. Martyn Percy remarks that,

> Quality may need to be valued more than quantity, pace, solidarity and connectedness more than haste, energy and apparent achievement. It may be important to encourage ordinands to see the worth of affirming the resonance of the past may have a higher spiritual value than the apparent obviousness of the need for relevance and progress. Presence and deep relational engagement may have a greater missiological impact than overt evangelistic schema and initiatives.[2]

We will begin this exploration using the Baptists as our first case-study. The we shall ask what might missional ministry look like, and how is this formed by practices in those training for ministry.

---

1. Jackman, "Paul's Pastoral Method," 77.
2. Percy, "Sacred Sagacity," 32.

Baptists and Mission

Baptists are, or should be, at least, missional to their core. Born out of a conviction that the Elizabethan Protestant settlement went nowhere near far enough in its adherence to Scripture, their early growth by church-planting officers in Cromwell's New Model Army was not always continued, but its seeds bore fruit throughout the four centuries of Baptist existence. From the pioneering of overseas mission by William Carey and the Baptist Missionary Society, to Spurgeon's church planting throughout London's Metropolis in the second half of the nineteenth century, Baptists have always been associated with proclamation of the gospel with a view to conversion and its sacramental expression, baptism.

In the second half of the twentieth century, and the first decade of the twenty-first, Baptists may not have experienced the numerical decline of most of their ecumenical partners in Britain (Pentecostals are the exception to this pattern) but they are nonetheless an aging union of churches in slow decline, more dependent than most upon current income rather than historical capital resources, and thus anxious about that decline in its impacts upon the viability of local churches and the wider bodies of association and Union.

The value of a virtue ecclesiology lies in its focus upon "what sort of community"[3] the church should be. This is in contrast to much contemporary Baptist ecclesiology that places the emphasis upon what the church is for, its purpose (generally articulated as "the church is for mission," albeit with a nod towards the purpose of worship of God). This is not to dismiss the importance of the *telos* of the church, not least since this will inform its character, but rather to challenge the over-instrumentalization of the church. Stone suggests, "any evangelism for which the church is irrelevant, an afterthought, or instrumental cannot be Christian evangelism . . . the practices of the church that embody . . . social holiness are the witness that becomes evangelism in the hands of the Spirit."[4] Where the mission of the church is considered as separate from the being of the church, the focus will be misplaced.

The over-instrumentalization of the church in regard to evangelism is derived from the individualization of society in post-Enlightenment culture, so that the church becomes the terminus of those individuals who are converts, an "aggregate of autonomous believers,"[5] in a social imagi-

---

3. Mannion, *Ecclesiology and Postmodernity*, 197.
4. Stone, *Evangelism After Christendom*, 16.
5. Ibid.

nation where the person is an autonomous, free individual in competition with other free individuals. In such a culture, the personal self-interest of the individual (including "getting saved") might be joined to others for a mutual and contractual benefit, but church is much more than a self-help group for those who have "a personal relationship with Jesus." Such a culture generates relationships that are, at best, contractual; at worst, violently confrontational. In such an environment the concepts of covenant loyalty, of true *koinonia*, of "a long obedience in the same direction" is judged impossible, or at least unlikely. Yet this is precisely what the gospel calls for. And precisely why it is so difficult in a culture that is individualistic and market-oriented. Stone again:

> reconstructing evangelism will not be an easy task. For the gospel to which evangelism invites people is, by the standards of the Enlightenment, incredible; according to the logic of the market, it is cost-ineffective; measured by modern liberal notions of the social, it is uncivil; by the standards of an aesthetics formed by the capitalist discipline of desire, it is repulsive; and by the chaplaincy standards of Christendom, it may prove to be neither useful nor helpful.[6]

Derived perhaps from a managerial approach to the church's life, and too simple an identification of the nature of the church with its purpose, this teleological approach fails to bridge the gap between an idealized purpose and the reality of the humanity of those agents who are called to fulfil that purpose: church members. At once both saints and sinners, church members who are barely discipled generate the actual character of the local church as inward-looking and missionally weak. So, to use the strap-line for the Baptist Union's strategy from 2009–2012, "encouraging missionary disciples," the essential quality of the church member, here called disciple, is their missionary purpose. While it is true that every disciple is called to witness to their faith and share in the task of evangelization, the transformational process whereby church members become missionary disciples is less clearly understood. Here, the insights of a virtue ethics approach will assist this process.

In recent Baptist thinking the *telos* of the church as the establishment of the new community of Christ, of embodying Christ, or the new humanity, has been largely lost to the emphasis upon the mission of the church. It could be argued that practitioners (disciples, or Baptist Church members) have been understood as advocates and transmitters of the faith before they have been adequate practitioners of it. In other words, there has

6. Ibid., 20.

been insufficient attention paid to the formation of disciples, learners of the practice of discipleship and the various sub-practices that give discipleship its shape (worship, *lectio divina*, caring for neighbor, prayer and so forth), by giving too much attention in theory to the missional purpose. That this has been disappointingly ineffective might be because there has been too little focus upon the missional sub-practice, and so this must be emphasized even more. Or it could be, rather, that there has been too little attention paid to the other dimensions to the practice of discipleship. Using an analogy of potting, there has been too much attention given to the marketing of the pot by those who are rather inept at potting in the first place. The marketing techniques associated with being a successful potter have taken precedence over the skills of throwing and glazing and firing good pots. We have been ineffective at forming missionary disciples not simply because we have not formed a missionary zeal in them, but because the whole pattern of discipleship has been deficient. MacIntyre, we remember, is keen to distinguish between activities and practices: practices are large-order disciplines, such as architecture, medicine or, I would argue, discipleship. Activities are those actions by which the practices are outworked, so for an architect, site appraisal, drawing, and the choice of materials; for the disciple, worship, prayer, evangelism, and care for neighbor and stranger. Some recent discussion about "church practices" confuses these two scales of identity, so that the individual activities become the practices (so, the practice of worship, the practice of evangelism).[7] While in other terms it is legitimate to describe worship or evangelism as practices of the church, or practices of discipleship, this is not how MacIntyre understand the terms. I find the larger-scale use of 'practice' as applied to discipleship alone helpful, since it suggests that all the activities definitive of discipleship are necessary, rather than a more individualistic choice of (sub) practices that avoid the necessity of the more demanding ones. To be a disciple is not possible if, for instance, love for others becomes optional, or witness to Christ an exotic trait for the particularly muscular. To use Bonhoeffer's concept, this would cheap grace, or, to use other language, "discipleship-lite."

The church's overriding purpose is not simply mission *per se*, but the flourishing of the community of Christ. That flourishing is not self-indulgence, however, because the purpose of the flourishing church has as its focus participation in the *missio Dei* as it follows Christ. The order is important. Mission is a vital dimension, of course, for without the mission of the church there would be no community of the church, and the particular

---

7. Healy, "Practices and the New Ecclesiology," 289; Kelsey, *To Understand God Truly*, 118; Volf and Bass, eds., *Practicing Theology*, 3; Tanner, *Theories of Culture*.

character of that community is to participate in the mission of God. However, the emphasis upon mission alone does not create the community, nor the character and virtues of those who become members of that community. The virtues of courage, truthfulness, justice, and compassion are acquired as the members of the community, disciples of Jesus Christ, participate in the life of the community and engage in its mission.

Indeed, if, in a distorted understanding of the missional purpose of the church, the overriding purpose of the church is simply to grow, then it is hard to argue against those means of evangelization that, while effective in increasing church attendance, are inimical to discipleship formation. The gospel that is portrayed by this form of evangelism will be as inoffensive as possible, and challenge the sensibilities of its target market as little as Disneyland or McDonalds. The church that proclaims such a gospel will be understood as "the self-interest of a social order concerned with its own success and effectiveness in the contest with liberal modernity."[8] Stone challenges the prevailing wisdom of this school as it asserts that evangelism must not challenge, but rather reassure the modern world that it has nothing to fear: "It . . . cannot begin with demands. The strangeness of the church and its worship and the offensive nature of its gospel must be mitigated or abolished if evangelism is to be reconstructed and made effective in a post-Christendom world. 'Tolerance,' as R. R. Reno has suggested, 'is the executive virtue of our time.'"[9] By contrast Stone says that "our greatest challenge is that in reaching secular people we will fail to offer them anything specifically Christian . . . the gospel with which we reach them will have become a version of 'Christendom lite.'"[10]

The nature of the practices of the church have been described by, for instance, Nancey Murphy and James McClendon.[11] These activities include, worship of God, witness to Christ, compassionate care, discipleship formation, and corporate discernment, which together make up the practice of Christian discipleship within the institution of the church. As we noted earlier, there is debate whether these are practices in their own right, or sub-practices, or the activities that together comprise the practice of Christian discipleship, but, I argue, there is a central practice that is the church's *telos*: the establishing and maintaining of Christian community. The purpose of God throughout history has been to have a people, a new

---

8. Hamill, "Beyond Ecclesiocentricity," 283.

9. Stone, *Evangelism after Christendom*, 14.

10. Ibid., 15.

11. McClendon, "The Practice of Community Formation"; Murphy, "Using MacIntyre's Method in Christian Ethics"; Wells, *God's Companions*.

humanity, a community of sons and daughters who are renewed after the pattern of his Son, Jesus Christ.

Those called to be disciples of Christ are formed in the character of disciples through the (sub-) practices or activities of the church: worship of God and fellowship with his people, attention to God through prayer and the reading of Scripture, witness to Christ, serving the world, as well as church and discernment. The pedagogical character of discipleship formation, and the sacramental sustaining of that discipleship, together form the means by which the practice of discipleship is established and continued.

If this overriding purpose is admitted, then, at least, any over-emphasis upon the mission of the church within Baptist ecclesiology must be modified to include discipleship formation and community establishment if the missional character of the church is to be developed. The naive appeal that "all we do must be missional" will ultimately prove fruitless because those called to become practitioners participating in this core activity/practice and core characteristic of the church will not have been formed as disciples with the necessary virtues of courage, faithfulness, and compassion. These virtues are developed through all of the practices of the church, not just through missional activity, and there needs to be the establishment of a broader vision of what a healthy church looks like beyond its evangelistic effectiveness. Recent attempts to articulate a spirituality of mission go some way to address this deficiency.

So, Baptist Churches, and the networks of relationships to which they belong, must be as much pedagogical in character and purpose as missional, paying attention to the formation of the community, and the relationships that sustain it, as much as to growing that community through evangelism. The false dichotomy between maintenance and mission is as unhelpful as that between ministry and mission. A healthy church is one in which mission is enabled because it is maintained as a healthy community, and where ministry is not in contradiction to mission, but cares for and leads the people of God in their mission (which is, of course, God's mission first and last). Stone comments, "the *missio Dei* is neither the individual, private, or interior salvation of individuals, nor the Christianization of entire cultures or social orders. It is rather the creation of a people who in every culture are both 'pulpit and paradigm' of a new humanity."[12]

Indeed, in a reductionist understanding of church as merely a body that seeks to be effective in evangelism, might be seen an unwelcome effect of Late-capitalism upon the church. This culture, where all manner of social goods are measured solely by financial criteria, by "the bottom line," can

---

12. Stone, *Evangelism after Christendom*, 15.

have a malign influence upon the church: the ecclesial equivalent can all too easily be measured by the growth or decline of church membership. One of the central claims of *After Virtue* is that in the culture of Modernity, what MacIntyre calls the Enlightenment project, the mutually antagonistic and indeterminate moral stances that have been bequeathed to Western society by rationality, in fact have the status of emotional choices (what he calls emotivism). The central purpose of the Enlightenment was to establish a set of moral rules equally compelling to every rational person, but this enterprise failed, and the result is a set of rival standpoints: utilitarian, contractualist, and so forth. This has deprived Late-modern culture of any shared rational morality or world view. The pragmatist cohabits with the contractualist and the utilitarian in mutual incomprehension. This has released into the culture a set of moral concepts that appear to be based upon reason, but which in fact do not possess any such firm foundation. Key amongst these fictions is the concept of universal human rights and welfare. The means of evaluating choices based upon these unfounded first principles adopts another fiction, that of managerial objectivity and effectiveness. So, in the "culture of the managers," everything is evaluated according to so-called social science laws (when no such laws exist) and then managed or manipulated to the advantage of one of the competing groups in society (generally one which has power and wealth.) MacIntyre understands that it was Nietzsche who unmasked the will to power in post-Enlightenment culture, and so elevated the bid for such power as a worthy aim for humanity (rejecting in the process the weakness of the meek, who, after Christ, have elevated humility rather than denigrating it.) In its milder form, consumerism has produced an affiliation to whichever Church meets the individual's needs best, exploited by a will to power on the part of the competing church bodies or leaders in developing the most attractive congregation. In this culture, it matters not if the small and the weak church is competed out of existence.

This echoes an example of the fiction that by managerial effectiveness it is possible to manipulate church members and congregations to greater efficiency in growth in numbers and commitment. So arises the cult of the church growth expert, and the focus upon a technocratic solution to the problems of ineffective evangelism (tools such as Alpha, Evangelism Explosion, and other highly marketed and controlled programmes that become almost indistinguishable from other self-help and self-improvement programmes in the ubiquitous commercial and market-oriented culture of Late-capitalism). It also gives rise to the view that mission is an activity of the church: something the church ought "to do", rather than a characteristic of what the church actually is. John Colwell comments,

> The mission of the Church, therefore, like the mission of the Son, and the mission of the Holy Spirit, consists in its "being-sentness": it is passive rather than active, it is that which is done to the Church rather than that which the Church does in coherence with that which is done to it; it is ontological rather than functional; it defines the being of the Church.[13]

Certainly there should be action resulting from the church being sent into the world to bear witness to Christ, but those actions do not constitute the church. The church is sent, and so does not 'do mission': rather, because it is sent, it bears witness. To speak of the church "doing mission" is ungrammatical. The church's mission is a matter of being in the world before doing evangelism or caring for the poor. We are a missionary people before we are churches that do mission.

> It is not that the Church is called to "do mission," it is rather that the Church is constituted as the Church by virtue of its mission, by virtue of its being sent into the world. It is a matter of identity. The mere existence of the Church as this "being-sent" community is a sign and a sacrament, a witness and a means of grace.[14]

If the adoption of activism, programmes, and tools have become the default response to the call to bear witness to Christ, it is because the church has failed to separate itself from the very culture that privatized religion in the first place. Little surprise then if the enormous legacy of the Christian faith that Hume, Kant and Descartes baptized into their moral and philosophical systems has, after two hundred years, been largely squandered. The results are the current rapid and colossal decline in the numbers adhering to a committed Christian faith in some sectors of the church in the West, the widespread incomprehension about certain Christian moral stances and the almost complete removal of Christian faith from the public square. Using the tools of that culture to reverse that trajectory is, I think, doomed to failure.[15] MacIntyre comments in an interview for *Cogito*, "the moral presuppositions of liberal modernity, whether in its theory or its social institutions, are inescapably hostile to Christianity and all attempts to adapt Christianity to liberal modernity are bound to fail."[16] Something must be found in its place, something rooted more deeply in the Christian tradition,

---

13. Colwell, "Mission as Ontology," 9.

14. Ibid., 11.

15. "Our greatest challenge is to find ways of practicing evangelism in our post-Christendom culture without at the same time playing by the rules of that culture." Stone, *Evangelism after Christendom*. 13.

16. MacIntyre, interview for *Cogito* in Knight, ed., *The MacIntyre Reader*, 267.

with the capability for a more robust resistance to the corrosive effects of late-modernity in its secular form: as MacIntyre puts it, to "unfit" us for the contemporary world. In other words, shouting more loudly that the answer is "a missional movement" avoids the real question: what forms men and women after the pattern of Christ into communities of faith?

I wonder if amongst those more robust responses are, for instance, the new- monastic movements, or Deep Church and a recovery of worship that relies less upon the latest sub-Christian ballad, and more upon silence, hearing Scripture, sounding lament, and preaching that is at once proclamation and pedagogy. The strategy of the Baptist Union was correct in identifying the recovery and renewal of public worship as a vital strategic goal, even if there was little notion as to how this might be achieved in the face of emotivism of a different form to MacIntyre's moral kind: the idealization of a certain romantic response to God engendered through singing as the summit of human intimacy with the divine. The masters of the spiritual life of a foregone generation would see this for the cul-de-sac that it is.

Those who lead and shape church life take on a crucial role in the developing of this more rounded and nuanced understanding of the institution of Baptist Churches, and those institutions that enable associating to take place (networks, associations, the Baptist Union, and so forth), especially where it is understood that it is a healthy church life that promotes a missionally effective community. They are those who embody the tradition, in MacIntyrean terms, as practitioners who can form others in the practice. These practitioners understand the purpose, the *telos* of discipleship through a life-time of practice, in fellowship with others, both those who are alive and those who have shaped the present by their excellence in the past. MacIntyre comments,

> Only a life whose actions have been directed by and whose passions have been disciplined and transformed by the practice of the moral and intellectual virtues and the social relationships involved in and defined by such practice will provide the kind of experience from which and about which reliable practical inferences and sound theoretical arguments about practice can be derived. But from the outset the practice of those virtues in an adequately and increasingly determined way already presupposes just those truths about the good and the best for human beings, about the *telos* for human beings, which is the object of moral and political enquiry to discover. So the only type of moral and political enquiry through which and in which success

can be achieved is one in which the end is to some significant degree presupposed in the beginning . . . [17]

This is not to dismiss the vital further transformation of Baptist ecclesial culture from one of maintenance of an institution to the re-prioritizing of evangelism and mission in its life. Without this, the overall *telos* of the building of Christian community will be unachievable. It is, however, to strengthen the connection between the witness of the community and the creation of that community through the development of its practitioners as disciples of Jesus Christ and make it a more central concern, so that mission is "a matter of being present in the world in a distinctive way such that the alluring and 'useless' beauty of holiness can be touched, tasted and tried."[18]

If this critique of Baptist missional emphases is correct, then what might be the formational priorities for those who will lead its churches? First, the personal commitment to continuing growth in discipleship, as we explored earlier in this book. This will emphasize by example a holistic approach to the mission of the church, rather than a technocratic or overly-instrumentalized one.

Secondly, the ability to shape others' lives by discipling and mentoring, together with the shaping of communities that embody values that are radically different to those of the culture in which they are embedded, while at the same time accommodating sufficiently to become "salt" or "yeast." In an era where the church is living through "exile," characterized by apparent failure and obvious decline, shallow attempts to replicate a Christian version of the surrounding consumerist culture, with some misguided notion of relevance, will fail in the long term. What is required are churches with deep roots that can cling onto the rock of faith in the teeth of indifference and opposition, and ministers who understand that and knowing what its priorities must be, can lead it accordingly. In discussing Barth's comments on the growth of the church (in *Church Dogmatics* IV (ii) chap.15) in the context of rural ministry, Percy observes,

> Barth goes some way to redeeming the notion of intensity, by suggesting that a more concentrated focus on God is at the heart of all good ministry, but that this does not necessarily lead to the kind of extensive growth one might witness in a city or suburban context. Quality of discipleship, in other words—the sheer

---

17. MacIntyre, "*Whose Justice? Which Rationality?*" in Knight, ed., *The MacIntyre Reader*, 177.

18. Stone, *Evangelism after Christendom*, 21.

faithfulness of ministries—may not necessarily lead to quantifiable results.[19]

Thirdly, the priority for forming missional ministers is growth in the two virtues that are required more than any other for mission, which are, I believe, courage and humility. Where Christian witness is most costly, then courage is required. This is true for both explicit evangelism, and witness to Christ in everyday life. Throughout 2 Timothy the writer admonishes Timothy to not be ashamed of the gospel (2 Tim 1:8) but to endure suffering (2 Tim 1:8; 2:3; 4:5) and to be ready for opposition (2 Tim 3:12.) Paul is the example of this himself in both suffering (2 Tim 1:8,12; 2:8; 4:6; 3:11) and exercising courage (2 Tim 12b; 4:7.) References to Paul's sufferings and courageous witness are scattered throughout his writings, as also Luke's Acts of the Apostles. While generally this came from those opposed to the new faith in Jesus Christ, there were occasions when suffering was at the hands of those inside the church. The courageous and humble minister should expect times when it is the church community, or elements in it, that oppose him or her, regrettable though this is. Generally, in church life, I place a premium on unity and harmony, after all it is the unity of the church for which Jesus prays as he goes to the cross in John 17. However, this is not unity at any price, harmony at all costs. Sometimes, it is the harmony of unitedly wrong. William H. Willimon observes

> Paul spends much of his pastoral time attempting to referee in congregational squabbles . . . But it is also clear that one thing Paul values even more than unity, concord, peace, and love is the gospel. Community can be demonic. Not all unified, internally loving "communities" are truthful communities. Even better than community is gospel. "Gospel," for Paul, means cross and resurrection, and perhaps predominantly, the cross. For the sake of the cruciform gospel he is willing to provoke division, call names, condemn, accuse, and judge. Paul reminds me as preacher and pastor that I must be tethered to something more than peace and harmony if I am to be faithful to my vocation.[20]

Finding some opposition from within the church for the sake of the gospel is to be expected, and is good soil in which to nurture courage and humility for the bigger battles in the wider world. The caricature of the church, in Britain at least, is polarized between communities of irredeemable "niceness," easily ignored, and to be mocked, and communities of evil

---

19. Percy, "Yeast and Salt," 49.
20. Willimon, *Calling and Character*, 96.

manipulation, sexual predation, homophobia, and misogyny. True, there are a large number of nice people in church, and there are a few whose sexual conduct is reprehensible, but the hidden middle of good, faithful, hard-working, and honorable people are largely ignored. If the church were to challenge the evils outside of itself with greater courage, perhaps it would be less marginal to the debates about the kind of society we should be. The tools of that courageous witness should never include violence, unlike some Islamic expressions of mission, but they do call for the carrying of a cross.

When it comes to mission, then, the virtues will have been borne of experience within the church first, but they should be developed in the wider world where Christ wants his name and life to be known. Where the virtues are weak, the tendency will be to seek a "technological" alternative to faithful witness: the application of some evangelistic tool or other (be that Alpha, Emmaus or similar.) Now, some of these tools are effective, and assist in telling the gospel story, applying it to the listener and sowing seeds of faith, but there is no effective alternative to personal courage and a love for people. Grow these virtues, and the tools will be helpful. Apply the tools in their absence, and the result will be disappointment.

Finally, in the process of making missional practitioners of ministry, I suggest a significant contribution is made by developing ministers as practitioners of hospitality. Not only is this a key concept in enabling intercultural mission, so that the Enlightenment virtue of tolerance is replaced by the Christian virtue of hospitality, it also provides a way of drawing nourishment from non-Western traditions where hospitality is given a very high priority, and coming closer to those biblical cultures where the missional tradition begins.

The theme of eating with sinners was characteristic of Jesus' ministry, and Luke Bretherton argues that "This table fellowship with sinners, and the refiguring of Israel's purity boundaries which this hospitality represents signifies the heart of Jesus' mission."[21] But the contribution of hospitality to formation lies not only in the practice imitates Jesus' own life, but it also plays a significant part in forming the virtues of humility and vulnerability, that we saw earlier are vital in the practice of ministry. "Hospitality involves taking the risk of sacrificing our own status and becoming genuinely humble and vulnerable."[22] Hospitality is "subversive because it undermines and challenges existing power structures and restores human dignity and respect. Moreover, the practice of hospitality protects us from the danger

---

21. Bretherton, *Hospitality as Holiness*, 128.
22. Newlands and Smith, *Hospitable God*, 5.

of abusing ownership and possession."[23] Ross recognizes the way in which this approach favors the understanding of the church as a body formed as "relationships expressed through practices, of which hospitality is a key practice and virtue."[24] Hospitality enables us to see the other as a person with dignity and value, reminding us that in Matthew 25 Jesus puts on the lips of those before the judgment seat, "Lord, when was it that we saw you hungry and gave you food, or thirsty and gave you something to drink? And when was it that we saw you a stranger and welcomed you, or naked and gave you clothes? And when was it we saw you sick or in prison and we visited you?" (Matthew 25:37–39); and that it was the *not-seeing* of the wounded man for which the priest and Levite in the Parable of the Good Samaritan avoid the duties of hospitable neighborliness, while the Samarian refuses to pass by, having seen his condition.

In this risky, demanding, practice of hospitality, we create space for the other, so vividly portrayed in the Rublev icon, where the three visitors to Abraham's tent become symbolic of the Trinity, but not enclosed to exclude the other, but, rather, at the forefront of our gaze, making space for us to enter and participate in the meal. That meal, embodying the hospitality of God, is most significantly iterated in the Eucharist, but that liturgical and sacramental expression does not exhaust by any means the many ways by which table fellowship and open home ministry both create the ecclesial culture in which mission becomes normative, and help form the virtues in those who practice it. "Creating space means allowing for a spaciousness in all our encounters. Ultimately mission really is about creating space—after all, there is a wideness in God's mercy"[25] and this points to the Great Banquet where all are invited, and reminds us of the eschatological telos of the purposes of God that ministry serves (as we saw in chapter 4). Such a perspective fills hospitality, and those who practice it, with hope, even when the outcomes of that mission are slow to appear or seem slim, "it is exactly when situations become challenging, when justice, love, and peacemaking are not quite so quick as we would wish to see enfleshed, that the thin air of hope reminds us that all is in motion even when we do not see clearly."[26]

---

23. Ross, *Hospitality*, 72.
24. Ibid., 73.
25. Ibid., 83.
26. Cimperman, *An Anthropology of Prophetic Dialogue*, 180.

16

Forming the Preacher

I trained at "The Preacher's College," not its correct title, but the nickname that it often proudly took to itself. Spurgeon's College, as it is properly called, was the product of that great nineteenth-century preacher, Charles Haddon Spurgeon. By the time I was training there it had long lost the historic link to Spurgeon's church, The Metropolitan Tabernacle at The Elephant and Castle, in South London. Its pastor deemed Spurgeon's College far too liberal to legitimize any real relationship, yet to the wider Baptist Union, and indeed, the wider church, it was still that bastion of evangelicalism that put it firmly on the right of the church's spectrum of theologies.

At the heart of its training of Baptist ministers was the preparation of thoughtful and biblically literate preachers. At the time of my training there, the vast majority of its student ministers lived in college, either on its South Norwood Hill site, or in one of its nearby houses and flats. Every student was linked to a Baptist church, but the preaching would be widely dispersed around the southern half of England, as students responded to requests to the college to have a student to take Sunday worship. I was unusual, in being a pioneer of so-called church-based training, in possession already of a call to the pastorate of a nearby church, Streatham Baptist Church, in Lewin Road, Streatham, and expected to be there on most Sundays. At the time I was "Full-time Elder," and a very naïve twenty-nine-year old, and on my acceptance by Spurgeon's College for ministerial training during a pre-ministerial year (during which I began attending lectures and taking examinations,) I became Ministerial Student at Lewin Road. When I preached, it was to my congregation at Lewin Road, whom I had known for some ten years or so, and amongst whom I ministered for most of the week. My fellow students did not have such a relationship to most of the churches in which they preached, except when they were invited to take services in the home church from which they had been sent into college. I count myself extraordinarily fortunate to have cut my teeth preaching in such a context as a familiar congregation.

What we all had in common was Sermon Class. This took place every Tuesday morning, and the whole College community was expected to be present. A student would take the whole service, and afterwards, in the critique of that service, while some reference might be made to the choice of hymns and especially the manner of public prayer, essentially the whole thing was about the sermon. A draft text would be provided to two members of college: one staff, the other a senior student. They were to lead the critique of the sermon after its delivery. The preacher would depart at the close of the service, followed by the faculty, who lingered a moment in the vestry to pray with the unfortunate soul before the long walk down the corridor to the lecture hall where sermon class would commence. Every aspect of the sermon was critiqued, the good points praised, but the weaknesses exposed, especially those of an exegetical nature.

As a church-based student (and not quite knowing what to do with me and my fellow mixed-mode student, Martin Taylor), I only preached at one Sermon Class. It was unforgettable (for me at least, and I suspect, only me). The text was my choice, and I preached on John the Baptist in the desert. Admittedly, it was a loose exposition, because what I sought to do was to explore desert spirituality, having already become attracted to forms of Christian practice and spiritual development unusual amongst Baptists, but it split the college and faculty in their assessment of its efficacy. The pastoral tutor condemned its lack of exegetical depth, while the Principal praised it as a sermon. That seemed fair to me!

What Sermon Class exposed us to week in and week out was analysis of a particular style of preaching, and the gradual formation of an ability to preach in this manner. It was said among the churches and (with some disdain perhaps,) among the other Baptist colleges, that you could always tell a Spurgeon's man (sic) by the three points he made in his sermon. It is a habit I have never really grown out of as I prepare a sermon to this day. Perhaps it did not really assist in forming preachers who could readily give an eight-minute homily at a wedding (or in the Parish Church at the annual pulpit exchange) or preach in a thematic or dogmatic way, but it did form biblical literacy and a careful attention to the text of Scripture. We were formed by the practise of a practice, and were expected to keep up that practice over a life-time. Thirty years on, I still do.

It is said of older and senior doctors that some of their opposition to the more lenient and humane way in which junior doctors are trained these days, without the days on end that lacked adequate sleep that they had endured, is borne of a spirit of "it made a doctor of me, and did me no harm!" Perhaps the decisions made after seventy-two hours without sleep might have endangered patients, but no matter: it was a rite of passage for junior housemen. Nowadays, the pressure is perhaps reduced, the lack of sleep less common and maybe the resulting training is no less rigorous, but the badge of honor with which older doctors wear their early years after graduation is undiminished. Some of us who were formed as preachers under the regime of Spurgeon's Sermon Class, feel somewhat the same. It was a rite of passage, and often a bruising one, as the sermon was torn apart after its careful crafting and hesitant delivery, so in my hesitation about newer ways of forming preachers, you should definitely bear this in mind. I am no neutral observer.

The tendency today is for feedback on sermons delivered by those in formation to be given *in situ*, since the majority of ministerial students now train as I did, in mixed-mode contexts, but without the intensity of college-based interaction with fellow students that characterized my formation. There is no time for the luxury of half a morning given over to Sermon Class every week, when that is almost twenty-five percent of the available time in college. The benefit is a more relaxed context, since the student under observation presumably knows their congregation reasonably well by the time observation happens, but maybe that very relaxing of the context weakens the rigor of the analysis, and it is limited by the feedback from only one observer, rather than over fifty people. I suspect the tendency is to be more lenient, kinder, and less aggressive in critiquing the sermon, with a corresponding weakening of the formational process.

Among Church of England clergy, historically the context in which they learned to preach was the training curacy. Following theological college, with classes in homiletics, it was the oversight of the incumbent with responsibility for training his curate/s which shaped the development of preaching. As we saw in chapter 2, prior to his ordination, Randall Davidson was apprenticed to Dr. Charles Vaughan, Master of the Temple (one of the ancient Inns of Court, comprising chambers for lawyers, primarily barristers). Vaughan had begun to train young men for the priesthood while Vicar of Doncaster, and continued the practice in London. He took young men, gave them lodgings in the Temple, and taught them the basics of theology and Scripture. Davidson writes,

> We wrote sermons for him every week, and he used to read out to the assembly one or more of these after he had carefully examined and annotated them all. I was not infrequently subjected to the rather trying ordeal of having one of my crude

productions thus set forth in all the smoothness of Vaughan's manner of speech.... Looking back at it now, I honestly think that it would have been difficult to find any other plan of preparation for Orders that would have suited me so well as Vaughan's arrangements did.[1]

Now, it is generally accepted that the sermon is a "churchly event," and so a communal event, and a formational event, in that it is a means (perhaps, for evangelicals, among others, *the* means) of forming the disciples and the community of the church. Here is the great advance made in critiquing sermons in the context in which they are normally delivered: the congregation, rather than the more artificial model of the college sermon class. This understanding is central to Hauerwas' call that the first task of the church is to be the church, and that entails learning what it means to follow Christ. He likens it to learning a new language, so that the church learns "to speak Christian"[2] and becomes God's new way of addressing the world. The "language laboratory" where we learn this new language is primarily the liturgy, and the sermon a central part of that.

The sermon, then, is primarily proclamation of the story, a call to conversion, a call to attend to this new language. Since the new language is voiced in lives that are being conformed to Christ (not just by speech, but also in actions) this will make preaching political, since the kingdom of God will challenge, and be challenged by, the prevailing culture. So, in a culture of revenge and retribution, "speaking Christian" enacts forgiveness; in a culture of unrestrained greed and consumerism, "speaking Christian" enacts self-emptying and restraint; in a culture of individualism, "speaking Christian" enacts communal concern and love. The sermon is the vehicle that calls for such language. William Willimon puts it like this, "Faithful preachers are engaged in a complex process of renarration of their congregations' lives in which they find themselves, through God's retelling of their lives, which is Scripture, living in a different linguistic world."[3]

This challenging articulation of another language is always vulnerable to distortion. The sermon can become an exercise in mere antiquarian dilettantism: full of fascinating information about the ancient world, or the meaning of this or that Hebrew or Greek word, but devoid of proclamation. The message of Scripture can be swamped by the illustrations that attempt to lighten the delivery or offer analogy, so that what is heard is not the new language, but an old one delivered with a "dialect" that mimics the

---

1. Bell, *Randall Davidson*. 28–29.
2. Hauerwas, *Learning to Speak Christian*.
3. Willimon, *Conversations with Barth on Preaching*, 206.

new. With the "new homiletics," the danger is that the sermon no longer proclaims the word of God, but expects the hearers to discover their own truth. The loss of nerve that is at the root of the problem identified by Fred Craddock[4]—a collapse of authority and loss of deference—shifts the focus of preaching away from a departure point located in Scripture and theology to one that reflects the felt concerns of the congregation. So, from confident declaration of truth to be accepted by the hearer, the move is to one of tentative questioning, avoidance of any imposition of truth claims, and helping the congregation (or, at least, individuals within it) to discover the truth for themselves as text and life collide. No longer is the world read into the text, to see how the unchanging truth of Scripture might be addressing the changing context, but the text is read into the world, hoping that it might have something to say to a postmodern culture.

Apart from the theological loss of nerve, which is really a failure to acknowledge any immediate sense that the Word revealed in the Scriptures is also revealed in the proclamation of the gospel, there is that shibboleth of "the monologue". Everywhere we are told that in the age of television and internet, the simple mechanism of a talking head is bankrupt. People lack the attention-span to cope with a fifteen-minute address, let alone the typical thirty minute Baptist sermon. Thus, combined, the style and the theological substance of the sermon are questioned, and found wanting by those who advocate the new homiletic. A half-way house, I suppose, is to accompany the sermon with a powerpoint presentation, which, at its least imaginary, is little more than a summary of the sermon plan to help those with a sort attention span. At its best, with images and music embedded, it might function for us today in the way stained glass and a Bach Cantata might aid an earlier generation – surrounding the text with alternative ways of proclamation.

All of this has presupposed a congregation versed in the medium of the sermon, and starting from a sympathetic stand-point. The problem becomes hugely more demanding when there is an attempt to proclaim the truth of the gospel in the secular market place, with little sympathy for the foundational convictions and even less for a monologue. This reality has been acknowledged by the creators of Alpha, adopting a questioning approach; an informal, food-based context and an emphasis upon relationship building. Even so, the central proclamatory element is still a talking head, either live, or Nicky Gumbel's on video. For most Christians it proves hard to let go of some attempt to proclaim truth.

---

4. Craddock, *As One without Authority*.

Stephen Holmes, in his 2009 George Beasley-Murray Memorial Lecture, *"Living like maggots": Is preaching still relevant in the 21st century?* summarizes the dilemma as,

> The one who comes today proclaiming a deposit of truth, pretending to some uncomplicated access to a privileged narration of the world, to a script that makes sense, and expecting it to command assent, is necessarily deluded. . . . Culturally, such a claim is merely risible. It seems risible to its hearers and, perhaps more importantly, it seems risible to us. No averagely intelligent and culturally aware preacher would dare to preach like this anymore.[5]

However, in demolishing this caricature of preaching, Holmes goes on to point to the rise of political rhetoric in Barak Obama's campaign for the White House, and subsequently. The more recent referendum for Scottish Independence saw that old tub-thumper Gordon Brown come out of the self-imposed shadows of the political back-benches to preach the benefits of the political Union between England, Wales and Scotland (remembering that he is the son of the manse, too) with impassioned monologues before large audiences. The style, at least, is not so utterly dead, perhaps. And any marketing man or woman worth their salt will know that a memo, or an email or a mail shot are far less effective than the impassioned and articulate presentation. It is about face-to-face human contact.

But while the deeper theological question about preaching, that it is no longer understood as an event of revelation, is harder to challenge, it may be that achieving that recovery is much more important. If preaching is not simply gifted oratory that might change a heart or mind, if it is indeed an event filled with the presence of God's Spirit, then a recovery of both gifted human endeavor and confidence in God's promises is required. Paul claims that "For since, in the wisdom of God, the world did not know God through wisdom, God decided, through the foolishness of proclamation, to save those who believe" (1 Cor. 1:21) and affirms that it is both the human act (preaching) and God's purpose (the divine power) in the salvific event that combine to bring about conversion to Christ. Confidence that God will act when we preach brings preaching close to a sacramental sign (and as we shall see in a moment, indeed, becomes sacramental) and is the Reformation answer to the question, which human words convey divine grace? Preaching for Lutherans is the event that proclaims sinners are forgiven,[6] whereas,

---

5. Holmes, "Living like maggots," 152–67.

6. *Book of Concord*, Epitome, Article V.5: "[T]he Gospel is a preaching of repentance and of the forgiveness of sins."

for the Council of Trent, it was the sacrament of penance[7] where the priest declared forgiveness after due penance, and not (contra the Reformers) in the preaching of the gospel. Both sides of the Reformation debate acknowledged that there are words that effect forgiveness, when rightly spoken: it was the location of those words that was at stake. The Second Helvetic Confession affirms what Barth developed in his Church Dogmatics, *praedicatio verbi Dei est verbum Dei*, the preaching of the Word of God is the word of God. Barth says,

> Real proclamation thus means the Word of God preached, and the Word of God preached means, in this first and outmost circle, man's language about God on the basis of an indication by God himself fundamentally transcending all human causation, and so devoid of all human basis, merely occurring as a fact and requiring to be acknowledged.[8]

And, "Finally, the Word of God—and here at last we utter the decisive word—is the event itself, in which proclamation becomes real proclamation."[9] Barth continues with the analogy of the incarnation to argue that real proclamation, real preaching as the Word of God, is both an entirely human event and a divine one, "God and the human factor are not two elements operating side by side and together. The human element is the thing created by God."

> Without depriving the human side of its freedom, its earthly substance, its humanity, without dissolving the human subject or turning its action into a mechanical event, God is the subject from whom the human action must acquire its new, true name. Its true name! Therefore, not just a title pasted on: no, the name that accrues to it, in virtue of the complete superiority of the will of its Creator and Lord, as, essentially, as primarily as possible. Where Church proclamation takes place according to this will of God, where it rests upon God's commission, where God himself gives himself to it as its object, where it is true according to his judgment, where, in short, it is the true service of God, there on the one hand its character as an event visible and audible

---

7. Council of Trent, Canon III, chapter 1 on the Sacrament of Penance: "Si quis dixerit, verba illa Domini Salvatoris: Accipite Spiritum Sanctum; arequorum remiseritus peccata, remittunter eis; et quorum retinueritis, retenta sunt: non esse intelligenda de potestate remittendi et retinendi peccata in sacramento poenitentiae, sicut Ecclesia Catholica ab initio semper intellexit; detoserit autem, contra institutionem hujus sacramenti, ad auctoritatem praedicandi evangelium: anathema sunt."

8. Barth, *Church Dogmatics*, 1/1:101.

9. Ibid., 104.

on earth is not set aside . . . But on the other hand, through the new robe of righteousness thrown over it, it becomes in this its earthly character a fresh event, the event of God speaking himself in the sphere of human events, the event of Jesus Christ's vicariate plenipotentiary . . . Therefore, real preaching means, once more the Word of God preached . . . Man's language about God, in which and through which God himself speaks about himself.[10]

Such uncompromising confidence seems arrogant today, but the hope that is ours in Christ, a hope that is completely fulfilled in Christ, must be that our words about God become God's Word about himself. This is a stronger hope than simply the preacher might make correct statements about God. The kind of preaching of truths so much beloved of an earlier generation of evangelicals misses the point entirely: it is an event whereby human words become God's Word in order, not to convince wavering minds so much as transform human hearts. Forming preachers, then, is as much about forming faith and confidence as establishing fine techniques in oratory and rhetoric.

> Preaching is, precisely, proclamation. It is speech that merely by being spoken creates a new order. As a proclamation may make a woman a queen, or free a prisoner, so the word preached changes reality. On every side of the Reformation debate this was understood. "It pleased God, through the foolishness of our preaching, to save those who believe."—and it pleases God still to do that thing.[11]

This proclamation re-narrates human existence, speaks forgiveness in place of guilt, life instead of death and hope instead of despair. Preaching that simply re-asserts the narratives current in the world, and tries to find some analogy within them that might have something to do with God, misses the point altogether. The narratives of this world need to be changed entirely by God's decisive new judgment, that Jesus Christ is Lord.

Forming preachers, as well as training them in homiletic skills, has to be accompanied by a further formational task: shaping the community that hears the sermon, and without whom the sermon ceases to be a sermon. This shaping is profoundly ethical: an exercise in formation in the virtues. It is by no means certain that at any time that community will have been sufficiently shaped by the Word and by the Spirit to welcome the disturbing message of the gospel, and so courage, a fundamental virtue for the preacher,

---

10. Ibid., 106.
11. Holmes, "*Living like maggots,*" 9–10.

will be necessary. Likewise, the virtue of patience is necessary, for it is not so much the individual sermon that changes the hearer, but rather the cumulative effect of many sermons that makes its impact upon the life of those who listen, often at a depth beyond conscious knowledge and experience. It is helpful to remember how badly Jesus' first sermon in his home town went, even though it was in the relative safety of his own synagogue congregation. Luke recalls how Jesus, returning to Galilee, full of the Spirit and fresh from the wilderness, came to his home town, Nazareth, and enters the synagogue on the Sabbath day. He takes the scroll of Isaiah, unrolls it to what we call chapter fifty-eight and reads. He then says "Today this Scripture has been fulfilled in your hearing." All well and good ("All spoke well of him and were amazed at the gracious words that came from his mouth." Luke 4:22), until he responds with the second point. Oh, if only he had stopped at the first. This illustration from 1 Kings fills them with such rage that they drove him out of town, reach the cliff and are ready to throw him off (Luke 4:29) Admittedly, Jesus had not been to homiletics class, had not learnt the arts of keeping the peace with the congregation, so that the most profound response at the door on the way out is "lovely sermon, pastor" and he had all the raw power of the untrained soap box preacher. The thing is, he never learnt those tricks that keep pastor and congregation happily colluding in avoiding the power of the gospel for them, tip-toing around the issues that will inflame and anger. He simply told it like it is, drew back the curtain on a new reality, and suffered as a consequence. Perhaps if he had put some emotional capital in the bank first, preached a few good sermons that confirmed to the congregation how good they were and how successful their strategies before hitting them with the challenging one, then things might have been better. Then with their affection assured, when Jesus preached "that sermon" they would be able to dismiss the "difficult message" and simply move on (perhaps Jesus was just having a bad day, but we know he's our sort, really . . .) and let Jesus revise his strategies for being pastor at Nazareth synagogue, with its great worship band, its Alpha courses and its comforting pot-luck suppers. In short, he would have substituted expediency for courage. But he does not, and while narrowly avoiding death on that occasion, finds it readily enough three years later.

So, to make the claim, as Scripture requires, that Jesus is the way to salvation is met in liberal, multi-ethnic and multi-faith democracies, with the demand that we make religious space for other faiths, so we do not end up killing one another. Surely, it asserts, all religions are the same really, and can all play their part in building a better community. Saying that Christianity is privileged in any way is a kind of imperialism that sits so at odds with the globalized communities in which we live that secular people will want it outlawed: the danger that others, especially those whose religion sanctions violence, will take such offence that they take up arms is too high a price to pay for gospel truth to be given its free reign. The murder of Christian migrants on a boat travelling from Libya to Italy in April 2015 by their fellow Islamist migrants, for simply being Christians, is a microcosm of the risk of religious wars that liberal democracies seek to avoid at all costs, unless dressed in the clothes of advancing the cause of a secular liberal democracy (itself, a privileged perspective, of course.) Rather, resistance to the gospel, and its contested character in the world is only a reflection of those arguments we first heard in our own hearts.

Preaching in this context calls for three virtues, especially: faithfulness to the God who has revealed himself in Jesus Christ (and thus, the God about whom we do have something to say, for he has said it first); courage to proclaim it; and humility to listen first to that word, before we speak. This latter is particularly important. Lindbeck's "experiential/expressivism" variation of religion conditions us to "think of religion as an institutional means of expressing our personal, inner innate religious experiences."[12] The different religions, on this count, are basically all the same: expressions of the human condition, and preaching draws upon human experience as the supreme source of reality, and all religions "only nominally different, culturally conditioned means of saying the same thing. This is the 'well, though you are Muslim and I am Christian, we all believe in God' school of thought. All religions have value mainly as they express various aspects of human experience of the divine. This is contemporary "spirituality" all over."[13] This tempts us to believe that the effectiveness of preaching is something that we control, by which we teach the new language of faith or enculturate a congregation to the Christian way. The virtue of humility enables us to understand, and live beneath, the truth that the gift of encounter with Christ, through the agency of the Spirit, is never at our command or entirely a fruit of our efforts, but ever and anew the work of God alone. It is God "Eastering in us" and as surely as the resurrection of Christ overwhelms the strategies of religion and state to keep Jesus silent, so preaching is God at work to dismantle this world system and declare afresh that Christ is risen.

Some elements of "old school" homiletic training still hold good. The process of long attentiveness to the text of Scripture, mulling it over during the week, is far better than the hurried writing of a sermon late on Saturday. Now, there may be times when such an extensive practice proves impossible, and the Saturday evening white-knuckle ride is all that can be attempted,

---

12. Willimon, *Conversations with Barth on Preaching*, 213.
13. Ibid.

but it should not become the norm. Reading the text, if possible in the original languages, or if not possible, through commentaries that attend to the original languages, should not be hurried. The "text" of the congregation, and its life, is read alongside the text of Scripture, together with the 'text' of the concerns that the congregation bring with them, like detritus washed up on a beach after a stormy night. I was due to preach on the Sunday following 9/11, and had my sermon ready by the eleventh, but it was torn up and re-written afterwards. How could such horror not be addressed by the sermon, or the Gospel hope not be offered in the light of that? Sadly, since I was a visiting preacher (in those days I was General Superintendent for the Baptist Union Central Area) I had little control over the remainder of the service, and it seemed that those leading were blissfully unaware of the world-changing events earlier in the week: we sang the song which included the words "walls come tumbling down" without a hint of irony, and I winced at the ineptitude of it. It fell to the sermon, then, to voice the fears and deep sadness of those who had gathered that morning in church. Even with all of the non-negotiable expectations of a college course, its fixed lecture times and its demands for completed assignments, it should still be possible to begin to form these habits of week-long preparation at seminary.

Wide reading, in part, at least, from the masters bears much fruit: Barth, Bonhoeffer, Calvin, among them. Those who preach as well as teach theology are always illuminating: Sam Wells, Stanley Hauerwas, Barbara Brown Taylor, Colin Gunton, Paul Fiddes, Fleming Rutledge, Walter Brueggemann, Tom Wright, and Rowan Williams. They help me to see how theological preaching of the scriptural text is accomplished.

It used to be said that the preacher should prepare with the Bible in one hand and the newspaper in the other, but not so many can afford to take a paper copy of a newspaper these days. However, with news information almost at overload in the digital media, including twenty-four hour rolling news coverage (with all of its limitations and shallowness), it remains possible, and vital, that the preacher is well-informed of the changing culture, context and news within which her congregation is set. Preaching that not only addresses the unchanging truths of the Christian faith, but also the fast-changing culture within which it is set, is more likely to help equip God's people to address this gospel to that culture.

A danger in this approach is, however, that the culture sets the agenda, to which the church and its preacher seeks to respond. At Streatham Baptist Church, where I was first exposed to Baptist life in the raw, the normal practice was expository preaching of books of the Bible in long series, largely ignoring the liturgical year (except a nod to Christmas and Easter) and interspersed with short series or individual sermons on contemporary topics, either reflecting changes in church life (such as the use of spiritual gifts) or wider society. The same pattern was the bread and butter of the Anglican church where I grew up, although restricted here to its mid-week Prayer and Bible Study, the Sunday sermons being drawn from the readings found in the lectionary. Imagine my surprise when attending a contemporary evangelical parish in one of our cathedral cities a while ago, and it being the First Sunday in Advent, the preacher announced they were starting a series on Philippians. "What has this to do with Advent?" I wondered (and as the sermon progressed, "very little" was my conclusion.) What hope for us Baptists, I thought, when even the Anglicans abandon the lectionary and ignore the liturgical year (and the public reading of two portions of Scripture, at least, to boot.)

During the period when I was an itinerant preacher for seventeen years, from when I previously held pastoral charge of a congregation and stood in their pulpit Sunday by Sunday, until taking up pastoral charge of a local church once more in 2015, I at first tried to discern "the relevant" text for a given congregation, and agonized over what that might be: after all, I was the Superintendent come to take Sunday service (quite possibly that most sacred of Baptist Sundays, The Church Anniversary—a Free Church equivalent of the patronal festival.) Sometimes I came away sensing, yes, that was what the church needed to hear, but mostly I was not sure. It also meant, to my shame, that I could recycle sermons and make each new one serve at least three or four outings before I got so bored with it that even I needed to hear something new (and I am sure my listeners sensed that too.) For the last decade or so, and with increasing conviction, I have abandoned that exercise in subjectivity and subjected myself to the lectionary (unless requested to preach on this or that theme by the church inviting me to their pulpit.) It has been a revelation. I cannot remember any occasion when, letting the lectionary choose my text rather than my imagination, it has not been commented that "that was really what the church needed to hear today." Now, maybe they were being kind, but I have a sense that when I choose the text, I subconsciously avoid those Scriptures that I'd rather not listen to, and certainly I consciously assess the congregation's need and try to discern what Scripture might address it. Of course, at its worst, my choosing the text simply means selecting that sermon which, with a minimum of effort, I can roll out one more time.

But the lectionary does three things: it joins me, and my hearers, to the universal church, since by far the most widely adopted texts for that Sunday throughout the world will be those taken from the lectionary; secondly, it means that I preach from what I have been *told* to preach, not what I choose to preach (and therefore places me under authority, and calls me, first of all, to obedience); and thirdly, it means that through the lectionary my hearers are connected to the liturgical year—Advent, Christmas, Epiphany, Lent, Passion-tide, Easter, Pentecost—and therefore we hear the story that forms us again and again and again. Stanley Hauerwas and William Willimon say, "That is important because it makes clear that the *story* forms us. This is the church's way of reminding itself of how it subverts the world."[14]

Forming preachers, then, is an exercise in the growth in the virtues, both those virtues the preacher needs (courage, obedience and humility), and those that she wishes to see formed in the congregation. Some will come to the task with natural gifts of intellect and rhetoric, but they are not yet a preacher. Others will come with less-developed gifts in oratory, and will need to work the harder in shaping those gifts. While powers of oratory and facility in the intellectual tasks associated with preparation, such as the ability to read complex arguments about the various interpretations of the text of Scripture, or to relate the Word to the world, certainly assist the preacher-in-formation, as they do the more-fully formed and experienced one, for preaching to be preaching, the event of revelation in the power of the Spirit is essential. That event is not restricted to the very able or more extrovert preacher, but can take place in the context of the most inept and simple of sermons. That is the way God takes human words and makes them his Word, and for that to happen, the virtues of humility, faith and prayerful waiting count for much. That is the difference between simple training and godly formation.

---

14. Hauerwas and Willimon, *Resident Aliens*, 162–63.

17

Forming the Administrator

If there is one area of ministry that polarizes its practitioners, it is administration. For some (perhaps, a few) it is their forte, but for others, probably the majority, it is the least fulfilling dimension of ministry, and seems to be the largest consumer of time and energy. What is certain is that there is no avoiding it, even if the minister is fortunate enough to have a PA or church administrator to take much of the burden of the work from their shoulders. Some find that a change from local pastoral charge to a post with wider responsibilities brings with it an even greater focus upon administrative tasks, and while I rather romantically thought of my post as the Baptist Union's Head of Ministry as one with wide pastoral challenges (mostly delegated) and national leadership responsibilities, shared with others in the leadership of a mainstream British denomination, in actuality much of my time was taken up with administration, so much so that I would describe myself at times as, essentially, an ecclesiastical bureaucrat. I guess that I am typical of many ministers: not a natural administrator, but good enough to keep my head above the administrative waters and self-organized enough to keep the chaos at bay.

Formation in the practices of administration may not sound very spiritual, but I am convinced they are essential for the conduct of effective ministry. Under this heading of administration, I want to include such disparate tasks as diary management and management of time; facilitating and chairing meetings and committees; supervision of volunteers and, sometimes, staff colleagues; correspondence; validating official forms and signing off various documents; fund-raising; and—for want of any other place to locate it—such practical tasks as present themselves day by day when the minister is the only person available (fixing the timer on the boiler, putting out chairs for a meeting and photocopying the order of service for those members of my congregation who still want such items have all figured in my ministry recently.)

There was a period in the 1980s when insights from the brave new world of management theory and organizational studies was applied to ministry. We learnt how to organize our time, distinguish between the urgent and the necessary, create work plans and delegate. The organization Christian Research ran courses on time management and vision planning, supported by books written by its director, Peter Brierley.[1] More recently Paul Beasley-Murray has discussed the management of time in his book on ministry, *Living out the Call*, itself a revision of an earlier work, *A Call to Excellence*.[2] In it he refers to a study of British clergy that revealed that in an average sixty-four-point-three hour working week, administration and committee work amounted to almost twelve hours, or a fifth of their time, second only to Sunday ministry and its preparation. Part of time management is understanding what fills such a working week, and part requires awareness of those ways in which time is used ineffectively. Certainly, the simple fact that ministers work longer hours than many others is no excuse for poor time management, and ministerial "workaholism" owes as much to low self-esteem ("I am only valued if I seem to be busy") as to a form a laziness, where ministers allow others to set their priorities and determine their workload, rather than setting that themselves. "I indolently let other people decide what I will do instead of resolutely deciding myself. I let people who do not understand the work of the pastor write the agenda for my day's work because I am too slipshod to write it myself."[3] It might also reflect a fear of being alone with oneself, so time is filled with activity. Ministers need to form good practices in planning and administration of their own time if they are to survive, and indeed, have time to pray, to listen and to be alone. Simple principles such as organizing visits rather than turning up and hoping the person might be in, being ruthless with discarding emails that are unnecessary and setting limits to activities all assist in using time well. Beasley-Murray advocates working from an office or study based on church promises, rather than at home, because it is more accessible, efficient and helps to establish boundaries between home and work, but even if the practice is to work from a home-based study, the principles of working as if this is a work-based environment, rather than home, are sound.

Creating a rhythm to the week also assists in managing time, from the pattern of sermon and service preparation, to establishing the Sabbath

---

1. Brierley, *Vision Building*; Brierley, *Priorities, Planning and Paperwork*.
2. Beasley-Murray, *Living out the Call*, 2:102–7.
3. Peterson, "The Unbusy Pastor," 71.

principle in guarding a day free from church work. For instance, if others need half a week's notice to prepare music for the Sunday service, it does them a disservice to decide on the songs and hymns on Saturday afternoon. Holding to organized deadlines so that those elements of Sunday services that involve others are prepared in time generates confidence in the minister's ability to lead with others in mind, and there is no obvious reason why the hymns cannot be chosen by Tuesday evening, even if the final draft of the sermon is not ready until early Sunday morning (after all, it involves no one else, unless a power-point is used, when the principles of consideration for others applies.) It may not be appropriate to hold to that old adage that mornings were spent in the study, afternoons in visiting and evenings in meetings, but having some structure is part of self-organizing.

Having structured a week, keeping to the various time elements involves careful use of a diary, and I am amazed at how many ministers fail to do so. There is little virtue in missing engagements because they have not been entered into a diary, and much damage to trust can result when the occasional missed meeting becomes a pattern of chaotic time management. Perhaps some ministers really do need to learn how to use a diary, and this should be an early part of initial formation, but most will find this already well-embedded in their lives from previous employment. Still, when a minister has been used to a PA or church administrator organizing their diary, and then they find themselves without that resource, perhaps in a new pastorate, it can come as a surprise to find how much depends upon good diary management.

Part of self-administration involves planning the week, but another part looks further ahead: the month or perhaps, especially, the year, as its focus. Planning ahead for annual leave, time for a study week, or a retreat, as well as recognizing the work rhythm associated with the big events and central seasons of Holy Week, pre-Christmas and the summer break, all help in managing the stresses of the role. While some find the rich mixture of tasks associated with ministry enlivening, others find it challenging. One minister remarked,

> I am appalled at what is required of me. I am supposed to move from sick-bed to administrative meeting, to planning, to supervising, to counselling, to praying, to trouble-shooting, to budgeting, to audio systems, to meditation, to worship preparation, to newsletter, to staff problems, to mission projects, to conflict management, to community leadership, to study, to funerals, to weddings, to preaching. I am supposed to be "in charge" but not *too* in charge, administrative, executive, sensitive pastor, skillful counsellor, public speaker, spiritual guide, politically

savvy, intellectually sophisticated. And I am not supposed to be depressed, discouraged, cynical, angry, hurt. I am supposed to be up-beat, positive, strong, willing, available. Right now I am not filling any of those expectations very well. And I am tired.[4]

Beasley-Murray summarizes the reasons for clergy stress[5] and divides them into long-standing pressures, such as poor remuneration, scapegoating, perfectionism, the sense that the job is never done, and powerlessness; and those more recent pressures, such as numerical decline in church attendance, the complexity of some moral issues, and the slowing down of ministerial mobility, often linked to the difficulty in moving their spouse from a job that represents the major financial contribution to the household. Some of those pressures are unavoidable, while some might be minimized by a stronger sense of self and confidence in the minister's own standing, but the self-inflicted pressures of poor organization, time management and the resulting sense of chaos that ensues are avoidable with some careful preparation and formation.

Another area of self-inflicted pressure is the tendency of some to put off to tomorrow what might best be done today: the weakness of procrastination. Now, there is an opposing weakness—that of hasty judgment, devoid of appropriate space to think things through—but on the whole, the chaos of disorganization comes from a failure to fulfil commitments and tasks in a timely fashion and at the right time. Indeed, the signs of such a tendency are often evident from early on in the formational process. The student minister who rarely submits work for marking on time, and who always seems to require an extension may be exhibiting a character trait that will diminish their effectiveness, and indeed, their trustworthiness, for the whole of their ministry, unless resolved early. This is why, perhaps, while colleges can seem harsh in failing late-submitted work, one of the formational consequences of responding robustly to procrastination is the establishment of trustworthy practices of reliability in the minister, while the consequences are a grade difference in a piece of work rather than the breakdown of trust between a minister and their congregation, and the resulting failure of ministry.

Establishing patterns of self-initiated personal organization of time and priorities brings together two of the broader formational processes—character formation and spiritual formation. There is nothing spiritually virtuous about chaos, and the building of practices that reflect reliability, the ability to discern priorities, and the effective use of time all contribute to the formation of the godly character that undergirds all ministers

4. A clergyman quoted by Gilbert, *Who Ministers to Ministers?*, 5.
5. Beasley-Murray, *Living out the Call*, 2:112–13.

do and practice. While administration may seem less glamorous than, say, preaching or spiritual direction, it can be very fruitful when seen as a set of practices that form the virtues in the minister. Small steps of courage, for instance, required to say "no" to the insistence of a demanding parishioner, or the realization that the challenges of a particularly busy day will be best met by rising an hour earlier and saying the office and praying before the business of the day begins, and thus developing faithfulness in prayer, become the building blocks for greater instances when courage and faithfulness are called for.

For those for whom such prioritizing comes with a considerable challenge, then apprenticeship models of formation, even close supervision, might prove helpful, even if initially resisted. Not every person called to ministry comes from a home background where such disciplines and habits have been formed from early years. Chaotic family contexts may contribute significantly to the abilities of some to be self-organizing and self-motivating, and so a form of reparative formation will be required, with a person exercising a supervisory role over the minister-in-training effectively replacing their experience of chaos in the home of origin with a pseudo-parental role that instils good habits.

One particular administrative challenge arises from the sheer volume of information and correspondence facilitated by the web and by email. While the telephone might ring a great deal less frequently for most ministers today compared with my early experience of ministry in the 1980s, emails have become the most used medium of conveying information, and are sometimes viewed as an alternative to a more immediate medium such as text messaging. When letters were still a relatively common means of corresponding, the post would arrive daily, but emails are posted throughout the day, and so have the ability to interrupt more frequently. The curiosity of some ministers about others' Facebook postings, the latest twenty-four-hour news bulletin and their most-read blogs can absorb far more time than the physical letter did. I have a suspicion when some ministers say they are too busy to visit, the time is taken up too much on the internet—rather than face their parishioners, they face the screen of their tablet computer or smart phone. Administrative discipline about screen time is an important aspect of ministerial formation, the ability to keep in touch with members of the church through social media notwithstanding.

For some, perhaps for most, ministers-in-training, these disciplines about time usage, the setting of priorities, and use of social media, for instance, are helped by the apprenticeship model of formation in practices discussed in chapter 7. Continuing development, however, and oversight of the practice of ministry requires other forms of professional support. Baptist ministerial formation depends quite heavily upon mentoring for the three- or four-year post-ordination period (IMF 4–6/7), and in a similar fashion, an Anglican deacon, then priest, in their first three-year appointment serves under a training incumbent who fulfils a similar, if much more intensive, role. Beyond that, however, supervision becomes more appropriate, even if the role of life-long mentoring and coaching might be more suitable at some stages. In this context, then, I will discuss briefly some aspects of supervision, although it might also be located elsewhere in this book with equal legitimacy. It is my conviction that supervision of ministry is both essential, and is likely to become normative, if not mandatory, in the main denominations that accredit or license ministry.

Supervision

The existence of supervision among other "caring professions" is commonplace: social workers, counsellors and psychotherapists consider supervision mandatory and essential. It would be almost impossible to practice social work in the statutory sector without it, and every accrediting body for counselling and psychotherapy requires those it accredits to be in regular supervision.[6] The BACP *Ethical Framework for Good Practice in Counselling and Psychotherapy* in requiring practitioners to maintain competent practice stipulate that all counsellors, psychotherapists, trainers and supervisors are required to have regular and on-going formal supervision/consultative support for their work in accordance with professional requirements.[7] Similarly, *The Association of Christian Counsellors* in its principles of ethical working states "Members . . . . Will make us of regular and adequate supervision and/or other appropriate means of professional and personal support."[8]

Yet, any form of regular supervision of pastoral practice amongst ministers remains a rarity, albeit that this is changing, and still remains mainly a support provided in the first stages of ministry. So, in addition to our discussion of Baptist mentoring for newly-accredited ministers, for Methodists, for instance (who delay ordination until the end of the formational process) "Probation is a time for the rehearsal of activities and the acquisition of

---

6. BACP accredits individuals who meet, among other criteria, an accumulation of four hundred and fifty hours of practice covered by at least one and a half hours of supervision per month.

7. BACP, *Ethical Framework for the Counselling Professions*, 2015, p. 11, sections 50–61.

8. *The Association of Christian Counsellors: Ethics and Practice*, Revised 2004, p. 2, para. 5.7.4, www.acc-uk.org.

skills by practice under supervision. Once again, acquiring during probation the habit of reflection on one's practice in a context of supervision should be seen as a support, not as a constraint to be joyfully abandoned after ordination."[9] The supervision in this case is normally provided by the circuit Superintendent. [10] For Methodists, in addition to the close supervision of pastoral practice, a mentor is appointed to be "a critical friend." This role is not that of counsellor, therapist, spiritual director or friend, but rather "the closest parallel is the model of professional coaching."[11]

These roles of pastoral supervision and mentoring of those in formation and in the early stages of ministerial practice form a significant and familiar context for the delivery of supervision. However, the growing trend is towards supervision and mentoring/coaching beyond the initial formation of a minister. Linked to principles of life-long learning, regular appraisal and Ministerial Developmental Review, continuing supervision in some form, together with life-long mentoring, and other supportive accompanying professional relationships, is beginning to figure in the kind of professional practice of pastoral ministry that many aspire to, and denominations increasingly expect.

In the wider workplace context, mentoring is helpful at some significant points in a career, neither just at its outset, nor in a life-long, permanent relationship. At points of significant change, or potential for change; returning to work after maternity or paternity leave or sabbatical leave; when starting a new project or adapting to a new role; and where current workload is overly demanding, can all be times when some time-limited mentoring is helpful. Similarly, where appraisal has shown gaps in self-knowledge, or uncertainty about strengths and weaknesses, time-limited mentoring is one useful response to these developmental needs. I believe there would great benefit in applying mentoring for a short period to each new situation in which ministry is conducted, especially where the context is quite different to the previous post (a single congregation urban setting replacing a collection of rural churches sharing a single pastor, for instance; or where a sole pastorate is replaced by a team setting—especially if the post is as team leader.)

Mentoring has also been a significant tool in wider society in developing those members of the work-force that seem to be under-represented in leadership roles: it has been used to assist women, those with disabilities

9. The Methodist Church in Britain, *Handbook for Probation*, p. 3, www.methodist.org.uk.

10. Ibid., 17. "The superintendent should ensure that there is an early meeting for supervision where the supervision contract can be agreed" (22).

11. Ibid., 26.

and those in BEM (black and ethnic minority) cultures to gain the confidence and experience to challenge a white, male able-bodied hegemony.

So, provision for both the acquisition of, and subsequent delivery of, pastoral supervision and mentoring for ministers at every stage, from initial formation in college and post-ordination practice as a new practitioner of ministry, through the mainstream stages of pastoral leadership, and, where appropriate, while holding posts of wider regional or national responsibility, is an important development.

There is considerable blurring of roles and responsibilities between supervisors, mentors, coaches and spiritual accompaniers. I would broadly differentiate them as follows for the purposes of this discussion. Supervision is the means by which pastoral practice is reflected upon by a practitioner with a skilled senior practitioner (not necessarily a minister) in pastoral care, counselling or therapy. Its focus is safe and effective delivery of pastoral care and the development of the minister's pastoral practice. Mentoring has a broader focus, and seeks to assist the practitioner in developing a rounded ministry, together with an understanding of the whole of their life as the sphere of reflection. So, a mentor will be interested in the development of the minister's work-life balance, home life, spiritual sustenance as much as pastoral practice and preaching. Coaching, on the other hand, is more focused on the development of a particular skill, or skills. Coaching might be given to improve preaching gifts, or the task of apologetics in evangelism, or the necessity for good administration.[12] Allied roles might include spiritual direction, with its focus upon "an ancient ascetical practice in which one person serves as a guide, conversation partner, and co-discerner with another who seeks to explore, reflect on, and grow in his/her spiritual life."[13]

Unlike mentoring, there is very little by way of formal supervision extant in ministry. There is, however, a form of supervision widely adopted in theological training, where ministers-in-training have placement supervision for their pastoral and missional work. This is mainly delivered by experienced ministers local to the placement, who offer this as part of their service of the wider community of churches. Their training, beyond the acquisition of wisdom that comes from experience, is minimal compared to the formal training in supervision that would be expected of a counselling supervisor.

---

12. Coaching is "a process that enables learning and development to occur and thus performance to improve. To be a successful a Coach requires a knowledge and understanding of process as well as the variety of styles, skills and techniques that are appropriate to the context in which the coaching takes place." Parsloe, *The Manager as Coach and Mentor*, 8.

13. Ruffing, "Direction, Spiritual," 243

It is the comparative lack of supervision (one might almost say its absence) in pastoral work that is shocking. Supervision of practitioners in other caring professions is mandatory, but in pastoral ministry it is almost entirely absent from both initial training and continuing practice thereafter. The churches now need to play 'catch-up' in understanding the necessity for such oversight and support.

However, the landscape of pastoral supervision is changing. Writing in 2008, Charles Hampton referred to a consultation held in Edinburgh in February 2008, sponsored by Chaplaincy Training and Development NHS Education for Scotland, and co-hosted by the UK Association for Clinical pastoral Education and the Chaplaincy Academic and Accreditation Board.[14] The aim of this consultation was to "find a way forwards common agreement on the future development of pastoral supervision in the UK."[15] The hope was to construct overarching principles that would embrace the various constituencies of chaplaincy, pastoral education, spiritual direction and psychotherapy, but the task was made complex by the differing models of pastoral supervision that each constituency held, and tensions within them about "the desired balance between spiritual, psychological, academic, and experiential elements in the practice of supervision."[16] Alert to the potential for confusion between dynamic supervision, line management, appraisal, mentoring, spiritual direction and psychological therapy, there was agreement on four functions of pastoral supervision: (i) establishing and maintaining professional and ethical norms; (ii) forming good practice through experiential learning and theoretical input; (iii) restoring good practice by differentiation, reflection and encouragement and (iv) bringing fresh perspectives to bear.

One theme kept emerging in that consultation: "the inevitability of emotional contagion when giving attention to suffering. The psychological defenses mustered to resist recognition of this fact constitute a principle obstacle to good practice. Here advocacy of supervision takes on a political—some would say even an evangelical—mission, which is of great urgency."[17] Already practiced widely in chaplaincy, where it operates in a managerial and competitive climate, the mission is to extend this to parish ministry, pastoral care in the local church and community, recognizing that

---

14. Hampton, *A National Pastoral Supervision Association?*, 159.
15. Ibid., 160.
16. Ibid.
17. Ibid., 161.

"Psychological training at theological colleges was too often a matter of tasters and tips, rather than in-depth formation."[18]

The following year, in June 2009, the (British) Association of Pastoral Supervisors and Educators (APSE) was launched.[19] This brings together the worlds of pastoral supervision and clinical education, and two of its key founders collaborated in writing the foundational text for the practice of pastoral supervision: Jane Leach and Michael Paterson, *Pastoral Supervision. A Handbook*.[20]

Donald Winnicott, pediatrician and psychoanalyst, famously coined the term "the good enough mother" to describe the mother who does not overreact to her child's tantrums and anger by perceiving it as a personal attack, nor internalize the child's inability to cope with the world by sinking into depression or anxiety. Instead, the "good enough mother" holds the child's rage and creates the safety for the child to be itself. It is difficult for a mother to be good enough, however, if she herself is not supported, argues Winnicott, and so there is forged the "nursing triad," where the mother herself is supported by the father of the child, or another adult. This analogy describes the interaction between practitioner (therapist, social worker, pastor) and their client, held by their supervisor.

The "good enough" counsellor or social worker can survive the negative attacks of their client "through the strength of being held within and by the supervisory relationship."[21] In supervision the emotional disturbance felt by the practitioner finds a safe place for expression and exploration, and the practitioner/client/supervisor relationship becomes "the therapeutic triad." A similar set of relationships is established where the pastoral task involves the minister working with demanding individuals, but it can also be helpfully enlarged to

The work of supervision is an uneasy combination of supportive assistance, quality assurance and education, and not all supervision gets the balance right. Some supervision fails to integrate these three elements, and turns supervision into a two-way case conference, quasi-counselling for the practitioner or supervisee, or approaches the task with a managerial check list to minimize risk to the institution. But at its best, supervision delivers two significant benefits: continuous learning, or life-long formation, and a lamp with which to light the shadow side of ministry.

18. Ibid.

19. For the story of its development, see *The APSE Story* at www.pastoralsupervision.org.uk.

20. Leach and Paterson, *Pastoral Supervision*.

21. Hawkins and Shohet, *Supervision in the Helping Professions*, 4.

Continuous Learning

Just as the initial training of ministers has transitioned from a primarily intellectual task (theological education) through an emphasis upon skills training (theological training) to one of personal formation (ministerial formation), so the way in which continuing education and learning has changed. Initially almost entirely absent, in any formal sense, the post second world war period saw Continuing Professional Development (CPD) become the norm. Just as the church becomes alert to this development in the wider work-place, so it has moved on to a new expression of integration of personal development and professional, especially in the helping professions. So, CPD is replaced by CPPD, Continuing Professional and Personal Development, delivered not in workshops, conferences or training courses, but embedded in the workplace. Many organizations have embraced the 70:20:10 principle: seventy percent of professional development happens on the job; ten percent by attending courses, and twenty percent by supervision or coaching that connects work-place learning and exterior training. Here the reflective cycle is enabled by supervision that enables action, reflection and reviewing to be held in balance.

This dynamic process has particular power in the context of ministry, where the increasing familiarity with the work of the formal supervision develops a heightened awareness of an "internal supervisor," giving the ability to reflect in a live interaction, and not just subsequent to it. Donald Schon[22] defines reflective practice as "the capacity to reflect on action so as to engage in a process of continuous learning," which is a defining characteristic of professional practice. Reflection-on-action (reflection after the event) develops intuition and enables the practitioner to think on their feet by reflection-in-action.

This notion of the continuing learner is deeply embedded in the Christian idea of the disciple, the one who learns. Christianity understands the role of the disciple as one of growing conformity to Christ, and this is a process of life-long learning, well beyond even any idea of continuous growth as a professional practitioner.

Supervision as a Lamp to Light the Shadow Side

Ministers all seem to enter ministry for the best of reasons: a sense of God's call, a desire to effect change for the better, a love of God's people and a

---

22. Schon, *The Reflective Practitioner*, cited in Hawkins and Schohet, *Supervision in the Helping Professions*, 16.

passion to see all things under the gracious rule of Christ. Few acknowledge that they might enter ministry to gain power over others, or because their inner world is so fragile that they need the constant reassurance of other's approval within a benign environment where positive regard is mandatory ("this is my command, that you love one another.")

However, for all of those worthy motives, and their public acknowledgment in a selection process, there lurk beneath the surface, hidden in the sub-conscious, other drivers of behavior that emerge under pressure and in conflicted situations. These hidden inner drivers include a lust for power over others, often perceived as being in conflict with an expressed sense of powerlessness over events and others. This discrepancy can be exposed in supervision, as can the need to be needed. "Just as our clients need help from us, we need our clients to want help in order to fulfil the self-esteem we gain from our ability to give help. However, we have been brought up to deny our needs but needs in themselves are not harmful. It is just that when they are denied they join the shadows of helping work and manipulate from behind as demands. Demands ask for fulfilment, needs require only expression."[23]

The need to be liked, the desire to heal, the fantasy that we are the Messiah and the fear of insignificance all hide away in the shadow side, and one way of bringing their presence to light is therapy, but even if this has been accomplished in that way, supervision will identify when their malign influence over our practice is close to the surface.

The ability to recognize these hidden "scripts" ("I am un-loveable unless I meet others' needs," "the only way to hold things together is to take control of the situation," "I cannot allow myself to fail: I must be perfect") is a shaft of light onto our core beliefs about the world and ourselves (and these are often at odds with the core beliefs we espouse as Christian doctrine, especially when it comes to grace). Supervision is a way of identifying these scripts, and learning a different way of behaving, and in the process becoming less judgmental about others, or reactive to their differing core beliefs.

Supervision, then, is most enduring of a series of supportive relationships that assist in forming the minister, and with administrative disciplines amongst the first to be addressed by it. It is likely to settle in mid-career of a minister into supervision of pastoral practice and leadership, but equally it could be applied to most areas of ministry. With it will be mentoring for specific periods, most obviously in the second phase of the initial

---

23. Hillman, *Insearch: Psychology and Religion*, 17, cited in Hawkins and Shohet, *Supervision in the Helping Professions*, 31.

ministerial formation process, when seminary training is replaced by first pastoral placement, but also beneficial in times of change and role. There may be value in coaching specific roles or applying it to specific practices, and this might well focus upon administration for those who are weak in this area (and most ministers would self-identify as not being natural administrators), while spiritual direction could be seen as a very particular form of coaching, with its accompanying role in the development of the spiritual life.

If, as I have argued, formation is a life-long process, albeit one where there is considerable weight applied in the early stages of ministry training, and if supportive relationships are helpful—even, essential—in those early stages, then the logic is to continue to apply some form of supportive relationship at every stage of the practice of ministry. There are signs that this is beginning to become expected by those denominations that accredit ministers, not least because of the risk of litigation where some liability rests with those accrediting bodies, and so will become a normal feature of formation in ministry throughout its practice.

18

Forming the Leader

First, another word of personal testimony seems appropriate. I can hardly remember a time in my teenage and adult life when I have not been a Christian leader of some sort. Aged sixteen, I was leading the church youth fellowship at my local parish church; at University I was on the Christian Union committee, for the second period as President. At the church we joined as a young married couple, we quickly became house group leaders, and then I was appointed as an elder aged (ridiculously) twenty-four. At twenty-six I was a full-time pastoral elder at that Baptist church, then by turns, ministerial student and associate pastor: I held leadership positions at Streatham Baptist Church overall for twelve years. From there I was appointed Senior Minister at Bunyan Baptist in Stevenage for seven years, then Central Area General Superintendent, with oversight of one hundred and fifty churches and their ministers, and from 2004–2014, Head of Ministry at the Baptist Union, and one of its denominational leaders. I am, as I write in 2016, minister at Abingdon Baptist Church. By most contemporary standards, I had a successful ministry as a leader in local, regional and national contexts, and all this would count as just so much boasting. It might seem odd, then, to say that I am not sure either me nor the church had really grasped what authentic leadership looks like, when modelled on Christ, rather than Bill Gates, or any other CEO of a big multi-national business. My concern with the current churchly obsession with "servant" and "missional" leadership is not borne, therefore, of envy of others who have inhabited successful leadership from which I have been excluded, but precisely from being a leader after the fashion of current models. Indeed, it is borne of a suspicion that when I have been consciously more Christ-like, I have been least approved of as the organizational leader the church had wanted.

For almost a year I held no office at all, and the perspective of being an "outsider" is only possible when you no longer hold power.

It has become commonplace to view the most significant role of the minister to be that of a leader, and no doubt there are aspects of leadership involved in ministry that are almost unavoidable. However, the view of ministry as *essentially* about the leadership of the church is a relatively modern phenomenon, and one that poses very real questions about discipleship and the nature of the church. If the church is just another institution or organization within the matrix of contemporary society, then of course, leadership assumes great significance. The church will seek those qualities in its ministers that any organization eager to find success and growth: a visionary, decisive, and vigorous person who will maximize its market share. There are plenty of such churches around, with their ministers, prophets, self-styled bishops, and "church-stars": expensively groomed and suited, ready for the show, and the pizzazz of leadership. You will detect in my tone that I do not share such a vision of what ministry is about.

The articulating of ministry as being essentially leadership has been in vogue for the past twenty years or so. The establishment of *The Foundation for Church Leadership*, with Canon Malcolm Grundy as its first Director, gave organizational presence to this trend. Grundy's own book, *Leadership and Oversight* explored this in terms of Anglican episcope,[1] but in the preceding fifteen years Richard Higginson, for instance, had written *Transforming Leadership: A Christian Approach to Management*,[2] and John Nelson edited *Leading, Managing, Ministering*,[3] while *The Leadership Institute* has compiled a bibliography of over two hundred books on leadership and the church. It is not leadership *per se* that is troublesome, but filling our understanding of leadership with an under-translated model from the world of business, commerce, and politics, with its presuppositions about the nature of success and the *telos* of the enterprise. What ensues fails to see how Christ must transform everything, if it is to be genuinely Christian. *The Faith and Leadership* resource from the Duke Divinity School Leadership Education is one seminar attempting to accomplish just such a transformed understanding, with a model of leadership that embraces failure, recognizing that "the most arresting fact about developing Christ-shaped leadership is realizing that Jesus himself was actually killed. By all normal appearances, that is, his life's work did not end in the triumphant establishment of God's reign

---

1. Grundy, *Leadership and Oversight*. Cf. Grundy, *What's New in Church Leadership?*
2. Higginson, *Transforming Leadership: A Christian Approach to Management*.
3. Nelson, ed., *Leading, Managing, Ministering*.

but in a shameful death and a scattering of his most committed workers."[4] Kavin Rowe writes in a later reflection, "[F]ailure is at the heart of what Christian leaders have to offer the world ... Leaders who want, therefore, to cultivate a Christ-shaped background must build or develop practices that teach us how to fail."[5] The three practices Rowe identifies as enabling this to be learned are forgiveness, truth-telling, and developing means of repair.

Another theological critique of leadership is the Church of England's Faith and Order Commission's report, *Senior Church Leadership*.[6] It recognizes the question that has been at the heart of this chapter thus far,

> leadership has remained a crucial area of concern within and beyond the Church of England. It has continued to provoke sharp debates among Christians, often focusing on how best to engage with a perceived "secular" discourse for understanding and developing the ministry of the church.[7]

The focus of this resource is senior leadership: that is, any leadership responsibility that extends beyond the parish (so, archdeacons, and especially, bishops, for instance.) It recognizes that the language about leadership is here to stay, and is too prevalent and deeply embedded to be easily dismissed on any theological ground. So, it discusses how this language can be used well, and how the dangers in its translation from business and public service can be recognized and avoided.

The resource commends the practice of improvisation, and the work of Begbie, Vanhoozer and Wells[8] that adopts this motif informs the Report's understanding that improvisation does not mean "making it up as we go along," but the ability to draw upon a particular tradition in order to respond creatively to a new situation. The schooling in a set of practices that deeply embed the tradition then shapes the parameters of the responses necessary.

The Report traces the history of language about leadership to the second half of the twentieth century. *The Alternative Service Book* in 1980 says that a minister "is to lead his people in prayer and worship." The Lima report, *Baptism, Eucharist and Ministry*, of 1982, speaks of ordained ministry

---

4. Rowe, "Becoming a Christ-Shaped Leader."

5. Rowe, "Failure as Christ-Shaped Leadership."

6. The Faith and Order Commission of the Church of England, Archbishops' Council, *Senior Church Leadership*, 2015, https://www.churchofengalnd.org/media/2145175/senior%20church%20leadership%20faoc.pdf.

7. Ibid., 1.

8. Begbie, *Theology, Music and Time*; Vanhoozer, *The Drama of Doctrine*; Wells, *Improvisation*.

as "loving leadership," and calls bishops to have "responsibility for leadership in the Church's mission." The Church of England's selection criteria began to articulate language of leadership in 1993, while the 1995 report on the organization of the Church of England gave prominence to leadership as a role for bishops. The church "combines leadership by bishops with governance by synods."[9] We should note here how similar this is in respect of Baptist polity, where the role of the pastor or minister is seen as leadership, shared with other lay leaders such as deacons or elders, while governance is by Church Meeting, the council of the whole membership.

The language is expressed in the many cries of despair in every denomination and church for better leadership, with greater vision, clearer teaching (of the things the critics believe in, and avoidance of those things they decry,) better motivational abilities, and a stronger voice. The almost ubiquitous appointment of worship leaders in the churches that espouse a contemporary worship style is another variant on this trope.

The resource recognizes the "widespread desire for leaders who can engage confidently and persuasively with the wider world. Descriptions of the church's uncertain voice often focus on the failure of its communication with the wider world: the lack of evangelistic passion, the lack of compelling apologetic, the task of moral leadership, the failure to speak truth to power."[10] Leadership in areas such as safeguarding, mission, and especially the creative response to change, are all seen as amongst the challenges to leadership.

The concerns about this language of leadership arises from its relative absence from the biblical record, its origins from a secular source (the work of John Adair is cited as the source of the explosion in leadership studies in the 1960s) and its adoption of whole fields of practice from management studies:

> we speak of targets, key performance indicators, behavioral competencies, competition, entrepreneurship, risk management, effectiveness, growth, and success. We can sound all but indistinguishable from our secular counterparts . . . even to the point, at times, of echoing the high-octane glitz that accompanies some secular visions of the powerful leader.[11]

Language in itself is not the problem, but rather, the practices and the relationships that the language describes, together with the prevailing

---

9. *Working as One Body*, para. 1.1.
10. *Senior Church Leadership*, 12–13.
11. Ibid., 15.

world-view within which it is embedded. The definition of leadership in the resource is itself drawn from the same understanding as this book:

> We might say that a leader is someone who assists others in the performance of a collective practice. Such a leader is not someone who himself or herself excels in the practice, though he or she certainly has to be competent in it. Rather, he or she will be good at participating in that practice in such a way as to draw others deeper into it.[12]

There needs to be care, therefore, that the activities of leadership are compatible with the church's mission and purpose. The question is whether "the rise and rise" of leadership as a dominant idea in the church has led to a failure in the ordering of our attention. Has the mission and management of the church followed a preoccupation with identifying the specific tasks of leadership as specified by a secular account?

The description of episcopal ministry in the Church of England, articulated in its Canon C 18, could equally be applied to the description of the minister in the congregational polity of the Baptists. The bishop is to be "an example of righteous and godly living," be the "chief pastor of the diocese," be a teacher who upholds "sound and wholesome doctrine," be the principal minister of the sacraments, lead God's people in prayer and praise, discern "the gifts of the Spirit in all who follow Christ," be the person responsible for discipline, and is called to "proclaim the gospel boldly, confront injustice and work for righteousness and peace in all the world." Is this a description of the generic role we now call "leadership", or should leadership be an additional task required of the bishop or the Baptist minister? The first question that arises from the focus on leadership is, therefore, whether there is a task that is distinctive and essential called "leadership", and as such, has taken pre-eminence, or is it simply a descriptor of what has traditionally been understood as the minister's role, a way of framing the tasks with a contemporary spirit?

A second question concerns the virtues being demanded of senior leaders today when those virtues are derived from the secular context. A Christian leader is first a disciple, a follower of Jesus, and the virtues that belong to that discipleship do not always sit easily with the virtues of the visionary leader: patience, kindness, gentleness, self-control, and faithfulness (Galatians 5:22–23) are not always at the top of the list of character traits of the effective leader in business. The top chef whose goal is to win that extra Michelin Star does not do so by exercising patience, gentleness, and kindness towards his staff, but generally bullies, cajoles, and swears at

---

12. Ibid., 16.

them in order to achieve the excellence of cuisine that demands the highest prices and culinary prizes.

A third question arises from the very nature of the goal of leadership where success might look more like failure. Is it a gift to be received rather than a human activity that must be achieved? This question about human and divine agency in the work of the church can seem to be replaced by a simple notion that we build the church by our own efforts (remembering that the words of Jesus are "I will build my church").

The Church of England resource also asks the question we have already raised by reference to Kavin Rowe and the Duke Faith and Leadership Forum: can the language of leadership, taken unmediated from the success-oriented world of commerce, make room for a leader who was abandoned by all his followers?

The answer to these questions will lie partly in an analysis of the biblical record, and in part in understanding how that biblical foundation has been re-shaped by tradition and history. This is not the place for such a task undertaken in full (the Church of England report we have been discussing attempts such an analysis in its third chapter). It has been completed satisfactorily elsewhere in any case, but we do need to note the following words of caution, and the summary of the current position. Any attempt to re-introduce some primitive biblical pattern of leadership, lifted without due hermeneutical care from the pages of the New Testament, is doomed to failure. There is no one pattern, but an evolving set of principles and practices. This does not make Scripture irrelevant: far from it, but it does mean that we need careful analysis rather than naïve restorationism (which tends to baptize existing power dynamics with a gloss of biblical validation.) So, it is an important theological principle to allow some flexibility and difference in interpretation, since in looking for 'the biblical pattern' of ministry (as many have sought to do) those holding to a reductionist view fail to recognize (i) the proper limits of Scripture (it is perfect in what it is meant to do, but not in other matters) and in this regard the New Testament is not laying down a blue-print for church governance or ministry (ii) the diversity of New Testament practice (iii) the passage of history and the change of culture and (iv) the inevitability of hermeneutics.

So, while there are certainly descriptions of ministry in the New Testament, there is no one systematic pattern, and those diverse patterns that we do see have to be subjected to proper hermeneutical and historical analysis. While I doubt if we can simply read off the pages of the New Testament the pattern of ministry for every current context, in general, we might say that all ministry is in its foundation a ministry of Jesus Christ: ministry that is patterned after Christ, is exercise in his name and for the fulfilling of his purposes. We are "ministers of Jesus Christ" before we are accredited ministers of the Baptist Union or licensed and ordained ministers of the Church of England.

Secondly, there are two distinct, but related, strands of thought in the New Testament. The first might be said to be ordered after the appointing of the Twelve, and the outworking of that in Jewish and Gentile contexts, changing as the time elapses from the expected return of Jesus Christ soon after his ascension. This subsequently results in a pattern of local oversight by elders (presbyters or bishops, *episkopoi*,) supported by deacons. Eventually this emerges in the three-fold pattern of bishops, presbyters (priests) and deacons. The second general strand is the charismatic anointing for "works of service" (Eph. 4:12) which may or may not be recognized by "an office." So, any disciple might prophesy, but there were also recognized prophets; there were pastors and teachers, but this role might not be restricted to those who are also called presbyters.

An older view sought to relate these two strands chronologically, with first an early "charismatic" ministry, which was derived from what the Spirit did, rather than who the person was (and so was essentially occasional), and found in the Pauline churches of the Jewish diaspora. Secondly, this was subsequently replaced by an understanding of ministry as office, where the authority of certain individuals was recognized and who exercised a permanent ministry.[13] However, since (i) a number of the key characteristics of office were already present in Pauline churches, and (ii) those parts of the New Testament where office is most prominent also emphasized charismatic empowering (Paul's encouragement of elder/bishop Timothy to stir afresh the gift of God when the other elders laid hands in him: 1 Timothy 4:13–14; 2 Timothy 1:6–7; and the elders of the Ephesian church are only overseers because of the work of the Spirit: Acts 20:28), we need to see development towards institutionalization, such as there is, being accompanied by charismatic ministry. Alastair Campbell argues that the term "elder" was not a title denoting office but rather a term denoting seniority (often linked to the householder where the church met) and this view "renders problematic the view that elders were established within Jewish-Christian churches as the alternative to Pauline charismatic ministries."[14]

Therefore, these two strands tend to cross at stages in the Pauline corpus (including the Pastorals, whether or not written by Paul.) They simply represent a complex pattern, with great provisionality and fluidity in the

---

13. For such an account, see Campenhausen, *Ecclesiastical Authority and Spiritual Power in the Churches of the First Three Centuries*.

14. Winter, "Translocal Ministry," 17.

earliest phases of the mission of the Church, reflected in charismatic ministry, gradually solidifying into an ordered pattern of Catholic ministries of bishop, priest, and deacon, but not being replaced by it until much later.

> The churches founded by Paul were "charismatic" communities, made up of individuals each of whom had received gifts of ministry to be exercised for the common good (1 Cor. 12:7, 11). Some persons were appointed directly by God to have a leadership role in the church, and their function was to equip the other members to exercise their own ministries. There is also evidence of more "official" ministries, those of bishops (overseers), elders and deacons, and of apostolic delegates as well, whose appointment was by human agency.[15]

If John's Gospel is amongst the latest of New Testament documents (the most widely held view, but note: contra. J R T. Robinson, who argues for it being the earliest,[16]) then the absence in the Johannine community of any notion of office is telling. Instead, "The spirit will guide you into all truth" (John 14:26; 16:13)

To some degree the choices made about which strand of New Testament teaching should predominate or take precedence today are as much about the reader's presuppositions as about objective evidence. Charismatics and those ill-disposed towards ordered or sacramental ministry will look to Ephesians 4 and its portrayal of "the gifts of the Risen Christ" in the form of apostles, prophets, evangelists, and pastor-teachers. The more Catholic-oriented will look to the Petrine epistles and their address to "Fellow Elders/Presbyters" and the Pastoral Epistles, and their pattern of bishops and deacons.

I tend to feel we need a range of ministerial patterns: the charisms that enable every believer to exercise their ministry; the way those will be recognized in individuals and how a particular gifting could become a recognized ministry; and the ordered pattern of those set apart for ministry and ordained by the church for ministries of pastoral leadership, oversight, and service (pastors, bishop/superintendents, and deacons.)

Croft makes the important point that the distinct orders in such a tripartite pattern are not mutually exclusive: the Archbishop, and every other bishop, remains always both a deacon and a priest; there are aspects of *episcope* that every local Parish Priest (presbyter) exercises, as well as diaconal service in the Parish, even if their focus is that of the ministry of Word

---

15. Kruse, "Ministry," 602.

16. Robinson, *Redating the New Testament*, 307. He dates the first version of the present Gospel to AD 50–55.

and Sacrament.[17] To talk thus from a Baptist perspective (which generally recognizes only two orders of ministry: that of the deacon and that of the pastor, of which regional ministry is a specific species,) we should note: (i) there are those who are not called to translocal ministry of Word and Sacrament (accredited ministry), but to service in one particular congregation (called, generally, deacons, who, like Calvin's elders, serve for a time-limited period); and (ii) we train and form much more intensively those we call "ministers," the majority of whom will be pastors in local churches. It is from those ranks, from time to time, there will be those called to the wider oversight of the churches, and which we used to call General Superintendents (General Secretary Shakespeare's 1916 "good bench of bishops"[18]) and now Regional Ministers. The use of the term "Superintendent" takes its root from *episcope*, while the "Regional Minister" terminology avoids any notion in language of a third order of ministry, even if everywhere in its exercise it assumes that it is similar to other Church Leaders such as Anglican and Catholic Bishops, Methodist District Chairs and United Reformed Church Synod Moderators.

So, there are patterns of charismatic ministry and ordered offices in the New Testament, but their exact relationship is opaque. The Baptist Union's *The Doctrine of the Ministry* (1961) reflects the conviction that terms like apostle, teacher and elder were well known in Jewish circles, whilst bishop and deacon were equally well-known in the Hellenistic world. This reflects the late nineteenth century belief that primitive Jewish religious terms were Hellenized as the church spread into those areas. This sharp distinction is no longer tenable, since even the most Jewish of Palestinian communities was already suffused with Greek thought and language by the time of Jesus.

Elders/Bishops and Presbyters

Alistair Campbell makes the case for the first expression of local leadership being the elder, and that this reflects the position held by the owner/head of the household in which the community gathered.[19] This term becomes codified by the late New Testament period, and is no longer solely tied to the person who functions as the host of the church gathering. The words *pres-*

---

17. Croft, *Ministry in Three Dimensions*, 41.

18. For the historical precedents for Baptist Superintendents, see Gouldbourne, "Messengers: Do They Have a Message for Us?," 24–32; for the origins of Shakespeare's Superintendency, see "'A Good Bench of Bishops?' Early Baptist Superintendency," in ed., Murray-Williams *Translocal Ministry*, 33–43.

19. Campbell, *The Elders: Seniority within Earliest Christianity*.

buteros and *episkopos* are variously translated "elder" or "bishop," or even "priest," in the Catholic sense. Probably the words are interchangeable and reflect the role of leadership in the local churches of the Christian diaspora: to them are entrusted the guardianship of the flock, its teaching, and care, and, increasingly, presidency at the Lord's Supper. However, some want to argue for a distinction between elders (*presbyteroi*) and bishops (*episkopoi*,) with heads of households of the early house churches having supervisory roles, and as such are designated bishops, contrasted with presbyters, who do not.[20] The parallel in Jewish synagogues of elders being community leaders, not synagogue rulers, furthers the argument to understand elders as leaders in the Christian communities, but not officials like the bishop, who held a supervisory role over the church meeting in their house.[21] This distinction might explain references to elders who "rule" (1 Tim 5:17a, προεστῶτες πρεσβύτεροι), and those who "teach" (1 Tim 3:2, 5, ἐπίσκοπον), but the argument is not strong.

The case of Jerusalem is significant and illuminating: clearly, here initially the Twelve apostles carried leadership, but in Acts 11:27-30 it is to the elders that he brings aid, and it was to the apostles and elders that the question of gentile circumcision was presented (Acts 15:2,4,6,22-23; 16:4) It was the elders, with James, the brother of the Lord (neither an apostle, nor, perhaps an elder) who seems to have assumed overall leadership of the Jerusalem church, and whom Paul greeted on his return from the third missionary journey. From all this it appears the elders were a distinct group in Jerusalem, and the equivalent to the leaders elsewhere in the Mediterranean world (where, of course, there were neither apostles, or at least not everywhere, nor a relative of Jesus.) Paul and Barnabas appointed such for the churches they founded (Acts 14:23), and some, at least, were appointed overseers (*episkopoi*) of the flock (Phil 1:1) by guidance of the Spirit, and given the responsibility of maintaining the fidelity of the church to the gospel message. Such a leading elder is Timothy, Paul's protégée.

We should note that Hebrews speaks of those "leading" the church (leaders, ἡγουμένων) and James uses the word "presbyters" for the elders who should be called to pray for the sick (James 5:14). In 1 Peter, it is as a fellow elder (presbyter) that the writer addresses the presbyters and urges them to be shepherds of the flock (1 Peter 5:1-2.) We should further note that the one use of *episkopos* outside of the Pauline corpus occurs in 1 Peter 2:25, but here refers to the Shepherd and Overseer (ἐπίσκοπον) of your

---

20. An argument made by Kruse, who is an Australian Anglican, and perhaps predisposed to see the distinction in support of his Anglican polity.

21. Giles, *Patterns of Ministry among the First Christians*; Theissen, *The Social Setting of Pauline Christianity*.

souls: that is, Christ. The author of 2 and 3 John describes himself as an elder, a presbyter (2 John 1, 3 John 1.)

So, in summary, the word *episkopos* is used only by Paul, and in Philippians 1:1 his letter is addressed to the bishops (plural,) which infers that there was perhaps more than one house church in the city, each with its overseer. The word for elder is more widely used in the New Testament, although its use in 2 and 3 John might simply confer age, if John by this time was elderly.

Among the Apostolic Fathers there is further evidence of some confusion of terminology, while also some beginnings of hierarchical differentiation. So Clement (a late first century or early second century letter addressed to the Corinthian church from Rome, where Clement is the bishop,) appears to use the words bishop and presbyter synonymously in his urging the feuding church to be subject to its leaders, as they were appointed by the apostles and their successors. (1 Clement 42:44).

The Epistles of Ignatius are the first to argue for a three-tiered hierarchy,[22] and also for monoepiscopacy (one bishop for each church). Ignatius was bishop of Syrian Antioch in the early second century, and is known from the letters he wrote to the churches of Asia Minor. Some identify him as leading the church in Antioch following Peter (and Irenaeus links his apostolic pedigree through Polycarp to the apostles, and one of Ignatius' letters is to his fellow bishop, Polycarp.) The bishop appears as the leader of the Christian community within a given city, and Ignatius urges the Christians to be subject to the bishop as to God, to the presbyters as to the council of the apostles.

Polycarp writes as bishop of Smyrna (Asia Minor) and was martyred in about 156 (the stylized account of his martyrdom is given in the *Martyrdom of Polycarp*) He writes to the Philippian church urging them to be subject to their presbyters and deacons (Phil.5:2–3)

Finally, *The Shepherd of Hermas* is a document primarily concerned with post-baptismal sin and repentance. It is a complex Christian apocalypse written from Rome in stages from AD. 90–150.[23] Its writer, a contemporary of Clement, contrasts ravenous deacons with godly and merciful bishops[24] and sees, as in a vision, a building with square white stones repre-

---

22. Ignatius, *Ephesians* 1:3; 2:1; *Magnesians* 2:1; 15:1; *Philadelphians* 11:1; *Smyrneans* 10:1. Cf. Staniforth, trans., *Early Christian Writings*, for an accessible version of all of Ignatius's letters as well as 1 and 2 Clement (albeit a translation that comes from a committed Anglican stable, so, for instance, he translates presbyters as "clergy").

23. Cf. Aune, "Hermas," in ed., Fergusson, *Encyclopaedia of Early Christianity*, 521; Jefford, "Hermas," 303.

24. Shepherd of Hermas, *Similitudes* 9.26.2; 9.27.2.

senting apostles, bishops, teachers and deacons, all of whom agreed among themselves.[25] There are also prophets ministering in the churches illustrating the continuance into the second century of charismatic ministry as well as offices.[26]

Deacons

The appointing of deacons is traditionally assumed to be recorded in Acts 6:1–6, although those appointed to wait on the tables and settle the dispute over the distribution of alms are not named as deacons, *diakonos*, but their work is described as *diakonia*, service or ministry, and that role was taken over by the elders when appointed later. Two of their number, Stephen and Philip, are no mere table functionaries. They have significant roles in witness (Stephen is the first martyr) and evangelism (accompanied by signs and wonders.) Considerable work has been done on this role by the Australian Catholic John N. Collins.[27] His original monograph, *Diakonia: Reinterpreting the Original Sources*, was a milestone forty years ago, and no discussion of *diakonia* should ignore his findings,[28] although a great many do. The implications of this seminal work are widespread and represent a "storm-center" in discussion about ministry. He challenges the assumption that the primary role of deacons today is humble service, or have a role of "social service" within State churches. This is a role much more widely distributed in European Lutheran Churches, which are often state-funded through taxation, and assumes the role that social services provide in more secular settings such as France and Britain. Even less helpful is the role of Deacon as a kind of "rookie" priest, learning the ropes for a year before being priested (and conveniently providing a role for women in Anglican polity before the priesthood was available to them.) His argument is that the New Testament word deacon, and its related word service, *diakonia*, have multiple meanings, and not least a sense of being commissioned for a task. This helps to see why among those entrusted with such service are Stephen and Philip: they are not uncharacteristic deacons (who normally serve at table), but of the essence of diaconal service as proclaimers of the Word. So, in Philippians 1:1 Paul addresses first the "saints", the holy ones, and then

---

25. Shepherd of Hermas, *Vision*, 3.5.1
26. Shepherd of Hermas, *Similitudes*, 9.15.1 and Shepherd of Hermas, *Mandates* 11:7–15.
27. Lector Emeritus, Yarra Theological Union, Melbourne, Australia.
28. Collins, *Diakonia: Reinterpreting the Original Sources*; Collins, *Diakonia Studies*. Cf. Hentschel, *Diakonia im Neuen Testament*.

the bishops (*episkopois*) and deacons (*diakonois*). This is usually interpreted as two groups of people, some bishops and some deacons. Collins argues that the term is being used synonymously: Paul is addressing one group of people, and these are 'επισκόποις καί διακόνοις', "overseers who are commissioned for service of God." The details of the arguments are beyond the scope of this book, and further reflection on the revolution set in motion by Collins is helped by reading Paula Gooders' recent paper, *Diakonia in the New Testament: A Dialogue with John N. Collins.*[29]

Deeply imbedded in the consciousness of those who serve as life-long, or permanent deacons is the theme of care, concern, and love. It characterizes the theological presuppositions of Beyer's lengthy contribution to Kittel's *Theological Dictionary of the New Testament*, and underlies the modern Catholic Permanent Diaconate movement. Since Collins' seminal re-evaluation, however (and his rather polemical style of pursuing his thesis since its publication—understandable since so much scholarship since then has refused to properly engage with it,) the idea of humble service has been accompanied by the meaning "carrying out a commissioned task,"[30] and any notion that the role of the deacon is to be a representative "icon of the self-emptying of Christ" in utter humility, and in such a way that the rest of the church can avoid such virtues or practice, has become deeply questionable.

Apostles

Even the role of Apostles seems far from straightforward. The word seems to mean "those sent forth,"[31] and its origins lie in the call of Christ (himself the One sent out by the Father) and his sending them out ("go into all the world . . .") The Twelve are those who were with Jesus from the beginning of his three-year ministry, but to that number Paul adds himself (and Luke adds Barnabas) as one "untimely born" (1 Cor. 15:8), and understands his role as in some way equivalent, although with a different audience: the gentile world. We should note that some argue for a different meaning to *apostolos* for Paul and Barnabas, one closer to "missionary." These foundational apostles are those through whom the message is transmitted from Jesus himself. Some see a sharp distinction between the Twelve and Paul and Barnabas,

---

29. Gooder, "Diakonia in the New Testament: A Dialogue with John N. Collins."

30. Thus the most recent edition of Danker, Bauer, and Arndt, *A Greek-English Lexicon of the New Testament and Other Early Christian Literature*, 3rd ed., 229–31, shifts the focus of the meaning of *diakonos* from serving and waiting at table to acting as an intermediary and functioning in the interests of a larger public service office.

31. Rengstorf, "αποστέλλω," *TDNT*, 1:398–447.

while others want a close association in function. Then, there are others who seem to be delegates, "sent ones," representing the local church. To summarize: *apostolos* is used for: (i) a local church delegate (2 Corinthians 8:23; Epaphroditus: Philippians 2:25); (ii) the Twelve who hand on the apostolic tradition because they were with Jesus; (iii) one directly commissioned by Christ, such as Paul (Romans 1:1; 11:13; 1 Corinthians 1:1;9:1; 15:9; 2 Corinthians 1:1; Galatians 1:1) Andronicus and Junia (Romans 16:7), and who exercise itinerant ministry and church planting; and (iv) apostles as foundation stones of the church, used in later New Testament texts such as 2 Peter 3:2, and who are those whose teaching and example becomes the guarantee of right doctrine.

We should note that whereas the ministry of the Apostles figures largely in the context of the question of apostolicity in most of church history, with the rise in the second half of the twentieth century of a movement calling for a full restoration of New Testament patterns of church life and witness to the contemporary Church ("Restorationism") there has been a claim that the ministry of apostles is once again restored to church life. Such (often self-appointed) "apostles" are modelled on the ministry of Paul, Barnabas and so forth (not the Twelve, who are unique). For those influenced by such movements, which includes a great many charismatic Anglicans and Baptists, a further search for identification sometimes locates the current ministry of apostleship in Bishops and Superintendent/Regional Ministers, as opposed to those from independent and Restorationist streams who are termed "apostles" by their followers.

Further, we should note that Early Baptists termed those appointed to represent the local church when gathering in association with other churches "Messengers," and their office has been seen as the predecessor of the twentieth century role of the Superintendency. Messenger has its semantic roots in the notion of the *apostolos* as representative local church delegate, while Superintendency is semantically rooted in *episcope*, overseer.

This excursus into the historical development of the patterns of ministry enables us to see that leadership is by no means a simple role from the earliest eras of the church. A direct reading of leadership from selected New Testament passages, without careful historical and exegetical attention, might seek to lend scriptural validity to current concerns, but will not bear the weight of proper hermeneutics. Meanwhile, any discussion of ministry and leadership needs to pay proper attention to the tendency to baptize current practices into biblical narratives in an attempt to give them some warrant, and such a tendency must be avoided.

We might summarize by saying that leadership begins with God's call, is heard within a communal context, to which those so called always minister, and that there is always a dynamic of service and mutual submission between leaders, those with whom they minister and the whole church. A simple managerial and hierarchical model lifted from an older kind of secular business *mileu* simply does not work in the rich and thick descriptions of relationship and ministry found in the New Testament. Various schema have been devised to give shape to that foundational experience in the early church, from Stephen Croft's "ministry in three dimensions" that interrelates diaconal, *presbyteral* and episcopal ministry at every level, to the triangulated structure described in *Senior Church Leadership* in the Church of England,[32] and the utilizing of the lens of priesthood to locate *presbyteral* ministry in a wider context of the agency of God by Graham Tomlin.[33] The biblical witness, however it is construed, must take priority over the language and concepts of effective business practice that too often are baptized relatively unreconstructed into the church (often, it must be said, at the behest of those whose primary sphere of work is in precisely that world of business, and who believe that the effectiveness of their secular work is to be translated into "running the church.")

The trouble with the current emphasis upon leadership, when defined in terms of management skills and business values, is its incongruence with the example of Jesus. When a business is failing, or the football club finds winning goals elusive, the first casualty is often the person who leads the organization: the CEO or the manager. The panacea for the ills of the organization is a new leader, a new manager—someone with the personality to turn things around (or so it is hoped.) The difficulty in church however, if Jesus Christ is the leader—the chief shepherd—is that it proves rather challenging to look for an alternative (we claim to be, after all, the church of Jesus Christ). Or so it might seem, but in actuality, seeking an alternative is precisely what churches do. Those things that Christ calls us to: costly service, walking the way of the cross, and denying self are hardly a great USP for a consumerist culture, so the church replaces authentic discipleship with cheap grace: a religion sold because it will meet our needs, help us raise our families, and support our elderly—in short, minimize our distress. This is the church that meets the secular political demand to be useful, to contribute to the public good, and above all, to recruit new members. Leaders in such churches need to be warm personalities, visionary speakers, and skillful manipulators of those many volunteers who keep the organization going.

32. *Senior Church Leadership*, 21–49.
33. Tomlin, *The Widening Circle*.

In Jesus I find none of the above. He was no great visionary speaker, but rather a teller of stories that quickly offended people by their turning of conventional wisdom on its head. He did not manipulate and cosset his disciples, but challenged them and argued with them. His message becomes harder and harder to accept, until, after 'many of his disciples heard it, they said, "This teaching is difficult; who can accept it?"' and, "because of this many of his disciples turned back and no longer went about with him." (John 6:60, 66), the pattern is set, and the numbers drop off dramatically. In the end, all who are left are three women and one disciple at the foot of a cross. Jesus would have lost his post as CEO of "Kingdom of God Enterprises" long before. In his handling of his opponents he is abrasive, and, perhaps since we are preconditioned to read into the gospel accounts a description of the loving savior we want to find, we discover even his dealings with those closest to him are at times, let us say, "difficult." I doubt he would have successfully passed out of theological college.

But we have to come to terms with the fact that it is this Jesus whom we are called to follow, and who calls us to "come after him"—that is, to walk after that pattern, to follow in those footsteps, and to live so as to describe his character by the virtues of the faith. Writing in *The Guardian* at Easter 2015, Giles Fraser wrote,

> When he was nothing but a suspended carcass, dripping with his own blood and other people's spit, there were no worshippers around clapping their hands and singing their hymns. They were long gone. At the very end, ironically at the moment of greatest triumph, he had no followers left. That says something profoundly counterintuitive about what a successful church looks like. For if the core of the Christian message—death first, then resurrection—is so existentially full-on that nobody can possibly endure it, then a church that successfully proclaims that message is likely to be empty, not full. Which is also why, quite possibly, a successful priest ought to be hated not feted. For here, as elsewhere in the Christian story, success and failure are inverted. The first shall be last and the last first. The rich are cast down and the poor are exalted. The true king is crowned with mockery and thorns not with gold and ermine. . . . Christianity, properly understood, is a religion of losers . . . There is no way one hundred top business leaders would endorse the cross. It is life without advertising, without the accoutrements of success . . . In a world where we semaphore our success to each other at every possible opportunity, churches cannot be blamed for failing to live up to this austere and wonderful message. The worst of them judge their success in entirely worldly terms, by

counting their followers... But if I am right about the meaning of Christ's passion, then a church is at its best when it fails, when it gives up on all the ecclesiastical glitter, when the weeds start to break through the floor, and when it shows others that failure is absolutely nothing of the sort. This is the site of real triumph, the moment of success. Failure is redeemed. Hallelujah.[34]

This is, generally, not what we aspire to when we form ministers and establish churches. We need something and someone altogether more comfortable, more attractive, less abrasive. And when we find it—and them—we subtly undermine the following of Jesus that is core response to the gospel. Indeed, in so many of our current ecclesial responses to the demands of a technocratic and individualistic society, we simply ape that culture: introducing organizational and human resource management techniques to improve our recruitment and retention rates (although we use the language of evangelism and pastoral care); using numerical indicators of growth or decline to promote or "let go" those we charge with the service of the church, understood as leaders; and "buy into" the myth that what the church needs to succeed in a consumerist age are better leaders and more effective managers.

Perhaps too, behind all the façade of worthy aims, such as to see more people converted to Christ, and society transformed into a better, more just, compassionate and peaceful community (all of which I would want to see in abundance), there lies that subtle god of this age: money. Denominations and local churches alike need an income to run the institution, and in a diminishing market, where competition for the "Christian pound" is fierce, maximizing the market share to enable sufficient funds to keep the show on the road can seem like the most important priority. Of course, such institutions will want ministers who will lead them in sustainable church growth. A great source of fascination each January for the past fifteen years has been to see if the Baptist Union of Great Britain had reached its Home Mission target (the amount it needed to fund its organizational programmes and

---

34. Giles Fraser, "Christianity, When Properly Understood, Is a Religion of Losers," Loose Canon, *Guardian*, 3 April 2015, 36. Of the few leader columns and comments upon the Christian faith at Easter 2015 in the main English papers, most commented upon the political fragility of Christians in the Middle East and Nigeria, or made benign comments upon the usefulness of Christianity still in our secular age. One news sheet issued by a major food retailer offered only 'spiritual journeys' as its context for this, the major Christian festival—and then described three such walks, none of which had anything to do with conventional Christianity. So, a major piece of theological comment upon the state of the church and its relation to its founding story was, to say the least, remarkable in a culture which is embarrassed by Christianity, if not outright hostile to it. Fraser's article, in of all places, *The Guardian*, stood out.

pay its staff, which included me): reaching, or even (rarely) exceeding it was success, while falling short was a cause of concern. It is no different in businesses and households the length and breadth of the land, and so there is no shame in seeking to fund what is believed to build the church. However, when it was unsuccessful, there was often a hint that "the leadership" (of which I was a part) had let us down, and if only it was more vibrant and dynamic, then we might achieve what we had failed to accomplish that year.

So, given that ambivalence about leadership, what do we think we are doing in selecting and forming ministers, and what might we need to change? First, we need to exercise greater wisdom in selection, and avoid privileging those qualities of leadership that are immediately transposed from the world of business and secular leadership. To illustrate with a minor point: in selection, we should recognize that the candidate for ministry who has been a successful business person might not have the qualities yet to be able to embrace failure, be teachable, and see humility as the foundational virtue. They might be effective, if you have an organization that needs turning around by means of secular management practices, but the church should be different. This is not to exclude such people, for in other regards they may have been profoundly transformed by the gospel of Christ's passion and resurrection. But if, by virtue of their business success alone, we see them as suited to ministry, we shall often be mistaken. They are as likely to wreck a church and its witness as foster its distinctive Christ-like way of being.

I am not sure leadership can be taught apart from those practices that we have already argued are essential for the attaining of the virtues of character, spirituality, and intellect. It is not so much that we find leaders and help them acquire the virtues, so much as those who exercise the virtues essential for ministry—gained through the steady habit-forming practices of the community of formation—become those whose leadership of the church will enable it to be conformed to the pattern of Christ. This concerns not just "the what" of leadership, but also "the where" and the "how." In what direction will the leaders of a church direct it, and towards whom? In what way will that leadership be exercised: by example and compassionate service, or by coercion and the application of the toxic mix of shame and guilt? Much of the contemporary discussion of leadership has as its context the missional church imperative: the church must be transformed into a missionally effective movement in order to reverse its decline in Western postmodern and consumerist societies. With more than a whiff of panic about it, the end can become overshadowed by the means: a misguided attempt to "sell" the church like just another commodity, and to form leaders who will be able to lead the campaigns necessary to build the market share (often at the expense, not of those in the community who have no faith, but of the churches whose consumerist Christians exercise their freedom to choose to attend a more "attractive" church.) The most exposed churches are those that are essentially self-supporting, independent, and whose finances are vulnerable to the removal of one or two key financial backers.

Given the undoubted presence of leaders in the early church, and the equally obvious necessity of their role in the contemporary church, what is needed is an inspired improvisation upon the New Testament themes and norms, rather than the insertion of an alien melody. The jazz musician can improvise on one of the pieces from The Great American Songbook because they know the original piece so well, its harmonic progression and rhythm. What does not work is the introduction of a piece of music from salsa or drum 'n base, unmediated. The original song disappears under the new rhythm, with just an echo or two of its original character. The writers of the New Testament describe a process of re-imagining, or improvising, upon given concepts of leadership, from the Jewish elder to Greek *diakonos*, borrowed from the prevailing culture; but they also show how at every stage those concepts were re-fashioned after the pattern of Christ's ministry. The primary faithfulness was always to the story of the revelation of God in Christ, using language and concepts borrowed from their culture.

There will be ways in which current management techniques and concepts, practices, and models can be borrowed by the church to enrich its understanding of the practice of leadership in our day. Countering a culture of unaccountable individualism that has often characterized the church's ministry, the utilizing of ways of careful reflection with others upon the achievements and weaknesses of ministry (ministerial appraisal or Ministerial Development Review) will do nothing but good, unless with it comes, like some parasitical virus, the language and values of "performance related remuneration" and the hiring and firing culture that takes short-term account of targets. The fundamental values are at odds with "the way of Christ," and so hijack the whole endeavor. Similarly, the development of "core competencies for ministry," such as those that I developed for Baptist ministers in the middle of the first decade of the twenty-first century, are helpful insofar as they give shape to the kinds of skills that need to be formed in and practiced by Baptist minister. However, separated from an equal emphasis upon spirituality and character, they too-easily become the way in which we conceive of ministry as about "doing" unrelated to "being." Risk-management has become an essential part of any ecclesial body, imposed by charity law and the ideas of good financial management required of its trustees. However, when improvisation that runs the risk of failure becomes subordinate to "minimizing of risk to the organization," then the church begins to march to a drum beat very different to that by which "we keep in step with the Spirit" (Galatians 5:25).[35]

So, in forming leaders, the practices that will shape leadership after the pattern of Christ will be an improvisation on biblical themes: not lording it over one another, but the greatest being the servant of all (Mark 10:41–45); being first and foremost an example, "Remember your leaders, those who spoke the word of God to you; consider the outcome of their way of life and imitate their faith" (Hebrews 13:7); and taking up a cross and denying self-interest (Mark 8:34.) Sometimes what looks like strong leadership, at closer inspection seems to be sheer self-interest, the abuse of a congregation's voluntary service in the interests of the minister's self-aggrandizement, or an inordinate concern for financial remuneration and rights that belies the Sermon on the Mount's admonition to "consider the lilies of the field,"(Matt. 6:28). The writers of *Senior Church Leadership* articulate this concern as "the temptation to isolate their own discernment from the discernment of the body, the temptation to focus on building a name or a legacy for themselves at the expense of building up the body, and the temptation to desire leadership for its own sake."[36]

The model of the lone, heroic leader must be modified to acknowledge the essential collegiality of leadership at every level of church organization, from the local congregation to diocese, regional association, or national body. Prime amongst the reasons for this is the necessity for accountability that is not regulatory but relational. "Leaders in these contexts need to exercise authority, responsibility, accountability, collegiality and prayerful discernment together in a way that seeks God's kingdom above all else and reflects the underlying pattern of the self-emptying servant leadership of Christ (Philippians 2:1–11)"[37] Thus, leadership formation must also be essentially collegial, with practices formed in company with others. This should exclude the idea that formation can be adequately undertaken by distance learning, and placements must emphasize the collegiality of leadership in those contexts.

Formation for leadership should also encompass failure, seek its redemptive purpose and understand it as an essential element in the formation of Christ-like "success." Where formation is infiltrated by a spirit of performance anxiety, where everything is evaluated and scored, and where the academy alone sets the evaluation parameters, then not only will

---

35. NIV translation of πνεύματι καὶ στοιχῶμεν; others, variously: "be guided by the Spirit" (NRSV) and "let us also walk by the Spirit" (RSV).

36. *Senior Church Leadership*, 78.

37. Ibid., 76.

experimentation and improvisation be inhibited, but the whole tenor of ministry will become subject to a kind of idolatry: that which believes the growth of the church is a function of human effort and ability evidenced by good leadership. We truly then are building something that is not the church of Jesus Christ, but a religious human institution.

The leadership that is properly formed results from the other developing practices discussed earlier in this book: the practices of preaching and spiritual guidance, pastoral care and theological reflection; leadership (a better word might be presidency) of worship and sacrament, and the practice of mission and witness. It is as the minister is faithfully exercising these roles that leadership is formed, rather than in developing skills applicable to the board room or staff meeting, whether that be insisting upon adopting their own vision or bending the will of the board to their own view by gentle means or (more likely) robust and forthright insistence.

Bibliography

Report of the Review of Selection, Formation, Funding and Continuing Ministerial Development. Didcot, UK: Baptist Union of Great Britain, 2014.
Adams, Ian. *Cave, Refectory, Road: Monastic Rhythms for Contemporary Living*. Norwich, UK: Canterbury, 2010.
Cole Ahl, Diane. *Fra Angelico*. London: Phaidon, 2008.
Anscombe, G. Elizabeth M. "Modern Moral Philosophy." *Philosophy* 33 (1958) 1–9.
Aune, David E. "Hermas." In *Encyclopaedia of Early Christianity*, edited by Everett Fergusson, 521–22. New York: Garland, 1997.
Ballard, Paul. "Theological Reflection and Providence." *Practical Theology* 1, no. 3 (2009) 285–89.
Balthasar, Hans Urs von. "Theology and Sanctity." Translated by A. V. Littledale. In *Word and Redemption: Essays in Theology 2*, 49–86. New York: Herder, 1965.
Barker, Paul A., Richard J. Condie, and Andrew S. Malone. *Serving God's Words: Windows on Preaching and Ministry*. Nottingham, UK: IVP, 2011.
Barrett, C. K. *A Commentary on the First Epistle to the Corinthians*. 2nd ed. London: A. & C. Black, 1971.
Barth, Karl. *Church Dogmatics*. Vol. 1/1, *The Doctrine of the Word of God*. Edited by Geoffrey Bromiley. Translated by G. T. Thomson. Edinburgh: T. & T. Clark, 1936.
Beadle, Ron, and Geoff Moore. "MacIntyre: Neo-Aristotelianism and Organizational Theory." In *Philosophy and Organization Theory*, edited by Haridmos Tsoukas and Robert Chia, 85–121. Research in the Sociology of Organizations 32. Bingley, UK: Emerald, 2011.
Beasley-Murray, Paul. *A Call to Excellence*. London: Hodder & Stoughton, 1995.
———. *Living out the Call*. 4 vols. Available only as an e-book. 2015.
Begbie, Jeremy S. "Created Beauty: The Witness of J. S. Bach." In *Resonant Witness: Conversations between Music and Theology*. edited by Jeremy S. Begbie and Steven R. Green, 83–108. Grand Rapids: Eerdmans, 2011.
———. *Resounding Truth: Christian Wisdom in the World of Music*. London: SPCK, 2008.
———. *Theology, Music and Time*. Cambridge: Cambridge University Press, 2000.
Bell, G. K. A. *Randall Davidson. Archbishop of Canterbury*. 2nd ed. London: Oxford University Press, 1938.
Bernard, St. *Selected Works*. Introduced by J. Leclerque. New York: Paulist, 1987.
Bertelli, Carlo. *Piero della Francesca*. London: BCA/Yale University Press, 1992.

Bloesch, Donald. *The Crisis of Piety: Essays toward a Theology of the Christian Life*. 2nd ed. Colorado Springs: Helmers and Howard, 1988.
Bonhoeffer, Dietrich. *Letters and Papers from Prison*. London: SCM, 1967.
———. *Life Together*. Translated by John W. Doberstein. London: SCM, 1972.
The Book of Common Prayer. Cambridge: Cambridge University Press, 1968.
Boulton, Matthew Myer. *Life in God. John Calvin, Practical Formation and the Future of Protestant Theology*. Grand Rapids: Eerdmans, 2011.
Bretherton, Luke. *Hospitality as Holiness: Christian Witness and Moral Diversity*. Farnham, UK: Ashgate, 2006.
Brierley, Peter. *Priorities, Planning and Paperwork*. Tunbridge Wells, UK: Marc/Monarch, 1992.
———. *Vision Building*. London: Christian Research, 1989.
Briggs, John H. Y. *The English Baptists of the Nineteenth Century*. Vol. 3 of *A History of the English Baptists*. Didcot, UK: Baptist Historical Society,1994.
Browining, Don. *A Fundamental Practical Theology: Descriptive and Strategic Proposals*. Minneapolis: Fortress, 1991.
Buber, Martin. *Between Man and Man*. Translated by R. Gregor Smith. London: Collins/Fontana, 1961.
Burrowes, G. *The Song of Songs*. London: Banner of Truth, 1963.
Calvin, John. *Institutes of the Christian Religion*. Vol. 2. Edited by John T. McNeill. Translated by Ford Lewis Battles. Library of Christian Classics 21. Philadelphia: Westminster, 1960.
Campbell, R. Alistair. *The Elders: Seniority within Earliest Christianity*. Edinburgh: T. & T. Clark, 1994.
Campenhausen, H. von. *Ecclesiastical Authority and Spiritual Power in the Churches of the First Three Centuries*. London: A. & C. Black, 1969.
Certeau, Michel de. *The Practice of Everyday Life*. Translated by Steven Rendall. Berkeley: University of California Press, 1984.
Chan, Simon. *Spiritual Theology*. Downer's Grove, IL: IVP, 1998.
Charry, Ellen. "To What End Knowledge? The Academic Captivity of the Church." In *Theology in the Service of the Church*, edited by Wallace M. Alston Jr., 73–87. Grand Rapids: Eerdmans, 2000.
Christianson, Keith, ed. *From Filippo Lippi to Piero della Francesca. Fra Carnevale and the Making of a Renaissance Master*. New Haven: Yale University Press, 2005.
Clark, Kenneth. *Piero della Francesca*. London: Phaidon, 1951.
Ciampa, Roy E., and Brian S. Rosner. *The First Letter to the Corinthians*. Pillar New Testament Commentary. Nottingham, UK: Apollos, 2010.
Cimperman, Maria. "An Anthropology of Prophetic Dialogue: Rooted in Hope." In *Mission on the Road to Emmaus. Constants, Context and Prophetic Dialogue*, edited by Cathy Ross and Stephen B. Bevans, 166–80. London: SCM, 2015.
Clebsch, W. A. and C. R. Jaeckle. *Pastoral Care in Historical Perspective*. New York: Aronson, 1975.
Clines, David J. A. *Job 21–37*. WBC. Nashville: Nelson, 2006.
Coakley, Sarah. "Deepening Practices: Perspectives from Ascetical and Mystical Theology." In *Practical Theology: Beliefs and Practices in Christian Life*, edited by Miroslav Wolf and Dorothy C. Bass, 78–94. Grand Rapids: Eerdmans, 2002.
Colledge, Edmund, and James Walsh, eds. *Julian of Norwich, Showings*. Classics of Western Spirituality. London: SPCK, 1978.

Collins, John N. *Diakonia: Reinterpreting the Original Source*. Oxford: Oxford University Press, 1990.

———. *Diakonia Studies*. Oxford: Oxford University Press, 2014.

Colwell, John E. "Mission as Ontology: A Question of Theological Grammar." *Baptist Ministers' Journal* (2006) 7–12.

Colwell, John E. *Living the Christian Story*. Edinburgh: T. & T. Clark, 2001.

Congar, Yves. *A History of Theology*. Edited and translated by Hunter Guthrie. Garden City, NY: Doubleday, 1968.

Craddock, Fred. *As One without Authority*. St Louis: Chalice, 2001.

Crenshaw, J. L. *Old Testament Wisdom: An Introduction*. Rev. and enlarged ed. Louisville: Westminster John Knox, 1998.

Croft, Stephen, and Walton, Roger. *Learning for Ministry: Making the Most of Study and Training*. London: Church House, 2005.

Cunningham, David S. *These Three Are One: The Practice of Trinitarian Theology*. Challenges in Contemporary Theology. Oxford: Blackwell, 1998.

Cupitt, Don. *Creation out of Nothing*. London: SCM, 1990.

Daniels, Harry. *Vygotsky and Pedagogy*. Abingdon, UK: RoutledgeFalmer, 2001.

———. *Vygotsky and Research*. Abingdon, UK: Routledge, 2008.

Descartes, René. *The Philosophical Works of Descartes*. Translated by E. S. Haldane and G. R. T. Ross. Cambridge, MA: Dover, 1955.

Drury, John. *Painting the Word. Christian Pictures and their Meaning*. New Haven: Yale University Press, 1999.

Eliot, T. S. "Little Gidding," V.3, from *The Four Quartets*. In *The Poems of T. S. Eliot, The Annotated Text*, 1:208. London: Faber and Faber, 2015.

Ellis, C. "Being a Minister: Spirituality and the Pastor." In *Challenging to Change: Dialogues with a Radical Baptist Theologian. Essays presented to Dr Nigel G. Wright on His Sixtieth Birthday*, edited by Peter J. Lalleman, 55–104. London: Spurgeon's College, 2009.

Ellis, R. A. "'The Leadership of Some . . .' Baptist Ministers as Leaders." In *Challenging to Change: Dialogues with a Radical Baptist Theologian. Essays presented to Dr Nigel G. Wright on His Sixtieth Birthday*, edited by Peter J. Lalleman, 71–86. London: Spurgeon's College, 2009.

Evans, Caleb. *"Elisha's Exclamation: A Sermon Occasioned by the Death of Rev. Hugh Evans, preached at Broadmead, Bristol, April 8, 1781"* (Bristol, 1781) 31. Cited in C. Ellis, "Being a Minister: Spirituality and the Pastor." In *Challenge to Change. Dialogues with a Radical Baptist Theologian. Essays presented to Dr Nigel G. Wright on his sixtieth birthday*, edited by Peter J. Lalleman, 55–104. London: Spurgeon's College, 2009

Evans, G. R. *Old Arts and New Theology: The Beginnings of Theology as an Academic Discipline*. Oxford: Clarendon, 1980.

Farley, Edward. *Theologia: The Fragmentation and Unity of Theological Education*. Philadelphia: Fortress, 1983.

Farley, Edward. *The Fragility of Knowledge. Theological Education in the Church and the University*. Philadelphia: Fortress, 1988.

Fiddes, Paul S. *Seeing the World and Knowing God: Hebrew Wisdom and Christian Doctrine in a Late-Modern Context*. Oxford: Oxford University Press, 2013.

Fiddes, Paul S., ed. *Under the Rule of Christ: Dimensions of Baptist Spirituality*. Oxford: Regent's Park College, 2008.

Foot, Philippa. *Virtues and Vices and Other Essays in Moral Philosophy*. Berkeley: University of California Press, 1978.

Ford, David. *Self and Salvation: Being Transformed*. Cambridge: Cambridge University Press, 1999.

Foster, Richard. *Streams of Living Water: Celebrating the Great Traditions of the Christian Faith*. London: HarperCollins, 1999.

Fraser, Giles. "Christianity, When Properly Understood, Is a Religion of Losers." Loose Canon, *The Guardian*, 3 April 2015, p. 36.

Gettier, Edmund. "Is Justified True Belief Knowledge?" *Analysis* 23 (1963) 121–23.

Gilbert, Barbara. *Who Ministers to Ministers? A Study of Support Systems for Clergy and Spouses*. Washington, DC: Alban 1987.

Giles, K. *Patterns of Ministry among the First Christians*. Melbourne: Collins Dove, 1989.

Ginsburg, Carlo. *The Enigma of Piero. Piero della Francesca*. London: Verso, 2000.

Goetzmann, J. "Wisdom." In *The New International Dictionary of New Testament Theology*, edited by Colin Brown, 3:1026–33. Exeter: Paternoster, 1978.

Gooder, Paula. "Diakonia in the New Testament: A Dialogue with John N. Collins." *Ecclesiology* 3, no. 1 (2006) 33–56

Goodliff, Andrew J. *"To Such as These": The Child in Baptist Thought*. Centre for Baptist History and Heritage Studies 4. Oxford: Regent's Park College, 2012.

Goodliff, Paul W. "Baptist Futures, Networks." Paper presented to Baptist Union of Great Britain's Council, Stanwick, Derbyshire, UK, March 2012.

———. *Care in a Confused Climate. Pastoral Care and Postmodern Culture*. London: Darton, Longman and Todd, 1998.

———. *Ministry, Sacrament and Representation: Ministry and Ordination in Contemporary Baptist Theology and the Rise of Sacramentalism*. Centre for Baptist History and Heritage Studies 2. Oxford: Regent's Park College, 2010.

———. *With Unveiled Face*. London: Darton, Longman and Todd, 2005.

Gouldbourne, Ruth. "Messengers: Do They Have a Message for Us?" In *Translocal Ministry*, edited by Stuart Murray-Williams, 24–32. Didcot, UK: Baptist Union of Great Britain, 2004.

Graham-Dixon, Andrew. *Caravaggio: A Life Sacred and Profane*. London: Lane, 2010.

Greenleaf, Robert. *The Power of Servant Leadership*. San Francisco: Koehler, 1988.

Gregory of Nyssa. "Catechetical Oration." In *Christology of the Later Fathers*, edited by Edward R. Hardy, 268–325. Library of Christian Classics 3. Philadelphia: Westminster, 1954.

———. *Homilies on the Song of Songs*. Translated by Richard A. Norris Jr. Society of Biblical Literature Writings from the Greco-Roman World 13. Atlanta: SBL, 2012.

———. "On Virginity." Translated by William Moore and Henry Austin Wilson. In *Nicene and Post-Nicene Fathers, Second Series*, edited by Philip Schaff and Henry Wace, 5:344–48. Peabody, MA: Hendrickson, 1994.

Grimley, Anthony, and Jonathan M. Wooding. *Living the Hours: Monastic Spirituality in Everyday Life*. Norwich: Canterbury, 2010.

Grundy, Malcolm. *What's New in Church Leadership?* Norwich: Canterbury, 2007.

———. *Leadership and Oversight: New Models for Episcopal Ministry*. London: Mowbray, 2011.

Gunton, Colin. "Christ, the Wisdom of God: A Study in Divine and Human Action." In *Where Shall Wisdom be Found? Wisdom in the Bible, the Church and the*

Contemporary World, edited by John Barton. 249–61. Edinburgh: T. & T. Clark, 1999.

Hafeman, S. J. *The God of Promise and the Life of Faith: Understanding the Heart of the Gospel*. Wheaton, IL: Crossway, 2001.

Hamill, Bruce. "Beyond Ecclesiocentricity: Navigating between the Abstract and the Domesticated in Contemporary Ecclesiology." *International Journal of Systematic Theology* (2012). doi:10.111/j.1468-2400.2011.0061.6.x.

Hampton, C., "A National Pastoral Supervision Association?" *Practical Theology* 1, no. 2 (2008) 159–62.

Harris, Brian. "Defining and Shaping an Adequate Theological Curriculum for Ministerial Training." *Perspectives in Religious Studies* 36, no. 2 (2009) 157–68.

Harrington D. J. and J. F. Keenan. *Jesus and Virtue Ethics: Building Bridges between New Testament Studies and Moral Theology*. Lanham, MD: Sheed and Ward, 2002.

Harrison, P. N. *The Problem of the Pastoral Epistles*. Oxford: Oxford University Press, 1921.

Harvey, David. *The Condition of Postmodernity: An Enquiry into the Origins of Cultural Change*. Oxford: Blackwell, 1990.

Hauerwas, Stanley. "Christian Schooling, or Making Students Dysfunctional." In *Sanctify Them in the Truth: Holiness Exemplified*, 219–26. Edinburgh: T. & T. Clark, 1998.

———. *Sanctify Them in the Truth: Holiness Exemplified*. Edinburgh: T. & T. Clark, 1998.

———. "Speaking Christian." In *On Working with Words: Learning to Speak Christian*, 84–93. London: SCM, 2011.

———. "Suffering Beauty: The Liturgical Formation of Christ's Body." In *Performing the Faith. Bonhoeffer and the Practice of Non-violence*, by Stanley Hauerwas, 151–65. London: SPCK, 2004.

Hauerwas, Stanley, and William H. Willimon. *Resident Aliens: Life in the Christian Colony*. Nashville: Abingdon, 1989.

Hauerwas, Stanley and Charles Pinches. *Christians among the Virtues: Theological Conversations with Ancient and Modern Ethics*. Notre Dame: University of Notre Dame Press, 1997.

Hawkins, P., and R. Shohet. *Supervision in the Helping Professions*. 4th ed. Maidenhead, UK: Open University Press, 2012.

Hawthorne, G. F., Ralph P. Martin, and D. G. Reid. *Dictionary of Paul and His Letters*. Leicester: IVP, 1993.

Healy, Nicholas. "Practices and the New Ecclesiology: Misplaced Concreteness?" *International Journal of Systematic Theology* 5, no. 3 (2003) 287–308.

Hentschel, Anni. *Diakonia im Neuen Testament: Studien zur Semantik unter besonderer Berucksichtigung der Rolle von Frauen*. Tubingen: Mohr/Siebeck, 2007.

Heywood, David. *Divine Revelation and Human Learning. A Christian Theory of Knowledge*. Aldershot, UK: Ashgate, 2004.

Higginson, Richard. *Transforming Leadership: A Christian Approach to Management*. London: SPCK, 1996.

Hillman, J. *Insearch: Psychology and Religion*. Dallas: Spring, 1979.

Hilton, Walter. *The Ladder of Perfection*. Translated by Leo Sherley-Price. Harmondsworth, UK: Penguin, 1957.

Holmes, Stephen. "'Living Like Maggots': Is Preaching Still Relevant in the 21st Century?" [2009 George Beasley-Murray Memorial Lecture.] In *Truth That Never Dies: The Dr. G. R. Beasley-Murray Memorial Lectures, 2002-2012*, edited by Nigel G. Wright, 152–67. London: Clarke, 2015.

Horsley, Richard A. *1 Corinthians*. Nashville: Abingdon, 1998.

———. "Gnosis in Corinth: 1 Corinthians 8:1-6." *New Testament Studies* 27 (1980) 37–39.

Hursthouse, Rosalind. "Virtue Theory and Abortion." *Philosophy and Public Affairs*, 20, no. 3 (1991) 223–46.

Hütter, Reinhard. *Suffering Divine Things: Theology as Church Practice*. Grand Rapids: Eerdmans, 2000.

Hylson-Smith, K. *Evangelicals in the Church of England, 1734–1984*. Edinburgh: T. & T. Clark, 1988.

Irigaray, Luce. "Questions to Emmanuel Levinas." In *The Irigaray Reader*, edited by Margaret Whitford, 178–89. Oxford: Blackwell, 1991.

Ivens, Michael. "The Catholic Reformation 1. Spain I. Ignatius Loyola." In *The Study of Spirituality*, edited by Cheslyn Jones, Geoffrey Wainwright, and Edward Yarnold, 357–62. London: SPCK, 1986.

Jackman, David. "Paul's Pastoral Method: Reflections on 1 Corinthians." In *Serving God's Words: Windows on Preaching and Ministry*, edited by Paul A. Barker, Richard J. Condie, and Andrew S. Malone, 75–84. Nottingham, UK: IVP, 2011.

Jefford, Clayton N. "Hermas." In *The New SCM Dictionary of Church History*, edited by Robert Benedetto, 1:303. London: SCM, 2008.

Jenson, Peter. "Teaching Doctrine as Part of the Pastor's Role." In *Interpreting God's Plan: Biblical Theology and the Pastor*, edited by R. J. Gibson, 75–90. Carlisle, UK: Paternoster, 1998.

Jewett, Robert. *Romans*. Hermeneia. Minneapolis: Fortress, 2007

Jones, Keith G. "Ministerial Formation." In *A Dictionary of European Baptist Life and Thought*, edited by John. H. Y. Briggs, 325. Milton Keynes, UK: Paternoster, 2009.

Julian of Norwich. *The Showings* 56. In *Revelations of Divine Love*, translated by Elizabeth Spearing, 133–34. Harmondsworth, UK: Penguin Classics, 1998.

Kelly, Thomas R. *A Testament of Devotion*. London: Hodder and Stoughton, 1957.

Kelsey, David H. *To Understand God Truly: What's Theological about a Theological School*. Louisville: Westminster John Knox, 1992.

Klaasen, Walter. *Anabaptism: Neither Catholic nor Protestant*. Kitchener, OT: Pandora, 2001.

Knight, K., ed. *The MacIntyre Reader*. Cambridge: Polity, 1998.

Kotva, J. J. *The Christian Case for Virtue Ethics*. Washington, DC: Georgetown University Press, 1996.

Kristjansson, Kristjan. "Ten Myths About Character, Virtue and Virtue Education—Plus Three Well-Founded Misgivings." *British Journal of Educational Studies* 61, no. 3 (2013) 269–87.

Kruse, C. G. "Ministry." In *Dictionary of Paul and His Letters*, edited by G. F. Hawthorne, Ralph P. Martin, and D. G. Reid, 602–8. Leicester, UK: IVP, 1993.

Lalleman, Pieter J., ed. *Challenging to Change*. London: Spurgeon's College, 2009.

Langmuir, Erika. *The National Gallery Companion Guide*. Rev. ed. London: National Gallery, 1997.

Lave, J., and E. Wenger. "Legitimate Peripheral Participation." In *Learners, Learning and Assessment*, edited by P. Murphy, 83–89. London: Chapman, 1999.

———. *Situated Learning: Legitimate Peripheral Participation*. Cambridge: Cambridge University Press, 1991.

Lavin, Marilyn Aronberg. *Piero della Francesca*. London: Phaidon, 2002.

Lawson, James. "Theological Formation in the Church of 'the Last Men and Women.'" *Ecclesiology* 9 (2013) 335–46.

Leach, J., and M. Paterson. *Pastoral Supervision: A Handbook*. London: SCM, 2010.

Leech, Kenneth. *Soul Friend: A Study of Spirituality*. London: Sheldon, 1977.

Levinas, E. *Otherwise Than Being: Or Beyond Essence*. Translated by A. Lingis. Pittsburgh: Dusquesne University Press, 1998.

———. "Postface: 'Transcendence and Evil.'" Translated by M. Kigel. Foreword to *Job and the Excess of Evil: With a Postface by Emmanuel Levinas*, by Philippe Nemo. Pittsburgh: Dusquesne University Press, 1998.

———. *The Theory of Intuition in Husserl's Phenomenology*. Translated by A. Orianne. Evanston, IL: Northwestern University Press, 1973.

———. *Time and Other*. Translated by R. A. Cohen. Pittsburgh: Dusquesne University Press, 1987.

Lewis, Rick. *Mentoring Matters*. Oxford: Monarch, 2009.

Lindbeck, George A. *The Nature of Doctrine. Religion and Theology in a Post-Liberal Age*. Louisville: Westminster John Knox Press, 1984.

Lumpkin, William L. *Baptist Confessions of Faith*. Rev. ed. Valley Forge, PA: Judson, 1969.

MacIntyre, Alasdair. *After Virtue: A Study in Moral Theory*. 2nd ed. London: Duckworth, 1985.

———. *Dependent, Rational Animals: Why Human Beings Need the Virtues*. London: Duckworth, 1999.

———. *Whose Justice, Which Rationality?* London: Duckworth, 1988.

Mannion, Gerard. *Ecclesiology and Postmodernity: Questions for the Church in Our Time*. Collegeville, MN: Liturgical, 2007.

Marion, Jean Luc. *God without Being*. Chicago: University of Chicago Press, 1991.

Marshall, I. Howard. *The Pastoral Epistles*. International Critical Commentary. London: T. & T. Clark, 1999.

McClendon, James Wm. *Systematic Theology*. Vol. 2, *Doctrine*. Nashville: Abingdon, 1994.

———. "The Practice of Community Formation." In *Virtues and Practices in the Christian Tradition. Christian Ethics after MacIntyre*, edited by Nancey Murphy, with Brad Kallenberg and Mark Nation, 85–110. Notre Dame: University of Notre Dame Press, 1997.

McKane, W. *Prophets and Wise Men*. London: SCM, 1965.

Ministry Division of the Archbishops' Council. *Formation for Ministry within a Learning Church*. London: Church House, 2003.

Milbank, John. *Theology and Social Theory: Beyond Secular Reason*. Signposts in Theology. Oxford: Blackwell, 1991.

Mitchell, C. W. "Tozer, A. W." In *Biographical Dictionary of Evangelicals*, edited by Timothy Larsen, 676–77. Leicester, UK: IVP, 2003.

Mollon, Phil. *The Fragile Self. The Structure of Narcissistic Disturbance*. London: Whurr, 1993.

Moore, Geoff. "Churches as Organizations: Towards a Virtue Ecclesiology for Today." *International Journal for the Study of the Christian Church* 11, no. 1 (2011) 45–65.

———. "Humanizing Business: A Modern Virtue-Ethics Approach." *Business Ethics Quarterly* 15, no. 2 (2005) 237–55.

———. "Re-imagining the Morality of Management: A Modern Virtue-Ethics Approach." *Business Ethics Quarterly* 18, no. 4 (2008) 483–511.

Moore, Geoff, and Ron Beadle. "In Search of Organizational Virtue in Business: Agents, Goods, Practices, Institutions and Environments." *Organizational Studies* 27, no. 3 (2006) 369–89.

Moseley, David J. R. S. "'Parables' and 'Polyphony': The Resonance of Music as Witness in the Theology of Karl Barth and Dietrich Bonhoeffer." In *Resonant Witness: Conversations between Theology and Music*, edited by Jeremy S. Begbie and Stephen R. Guthrie, 240–70. Grand Rapids: Eerdmans, 2011.

Murdoch, Iris. *The Sovereignty of Good*. New York: Methuen, 1970.

Murphy, Nancey. "Using MacIntyre's Method in Christian Ethics." In *Virtues and Practices in the Christian Tradition: Christian Ethics after MacIntyre*, edited by Nancey Murphy, with Brad Kallenberg and Mark Nation, 85–110. Notre Dame: University of Notre Dame Press, 1997.

Murphy, R. E. *The Tree of Life: An Exploration of Biblical Wisdom Literature*. Grand Rapids: Eerdmans, 1996.

Murray-Williams, Stuart, ed. *Translocal Ministry*. Didcot, UK: Baptist Union of Great Britain, 2004.

Nelson, John, ed. *Leading, Managing, Ministering*, MODEM. Norwich: Canterbury Press, 1999.

Newlands, G., and A. Smith. *Hospitable God: The Transformative Dream*. Farnham, UK: Ashgate, 2010.

Ngien, Dennis. *Gifted Response: The Triune God as the Causative Agency of Our Responsive Worship*. Milton Keynes, UK: Paternoster, 2008.

Nicolson, B. *The International Caravaggesque Movement: Lists of Pictures by Caravaggio and His Followers throughout Europe from 1590–1650*. Oxford: Phaidon, 1979.

Noth, M., and T. D. Winton, eds. *Wisdom Literature in Israel and the Ancient Near East*. Leiden: Brill, 1955.

O'Brien, P. *The Letter to the Hebrews, The Pillar New Testament Commentary*. Nottingham, UK: Apollos, 2010.

O'Donovan, Oliver M. T. *Resurrection and the Moral Order: An Outline for Evangelical Ethics*. Leicester, UK: InterVarsity, 1986.

Parsloe, Eric. *The Manager as Coach and Mentor*. 2nd ed. London: CIPD, 1999

Pembroke, Neil. *Divine Therapeia and the Sermon, Theocentric Therapeutic Preaching*. Eugene OR: Pickwick, 2013.

———. *Pastoral Care in Worship, Liturgy and Psychology in Dialogue*. London: T. & T. Clark, 2010.

Percy, Martyn. "Sacred Sagacity: Formation and Training for Ministry." In *Anglicanism. Confidence, Commitment and Communion*, 29–40. Farnham, UK: Ashgate, 2013.

———. "Yeast and Salt: Ministerial Formation for Rural Contexts." In *Anglicanism. Confidence, Commitment and Communion*, 41–55. Farnham, UK: Ashgate, 2013.

Peterson, Eugene H. "The Unbusy Pastor." *Christianity Today*, Leadership's Top 40, Summer 1981, http://www.christianitytoday.com/pastors/1981/summer/81l3070.html. Accessed December 19, 2016.

Phillips, Adam. *Houdini's Box*. London: Faber and Faber, 2001.
Pickard, Stephen. *Theological Foundations for Collaborative Ministry*. Farnham, UK: Ashgate, 2009.
Porter, Jean. *The Recovery of Virtue: The Relevance of Aquinas for Christian Ethics*. London: SPCK, 1990.
———. "Tradition in the Recent Work of Alasdair MacIntyre." In *Alasdair MacIntyre*, edited by Mark C. Murphy, 38–69. Cambridge: Cambridge University Press, 2003.
Br. Ramon, SSF. *Deeper into God*. Basingstoke, UK: Pickering, 1987.
Ratner, C. "Prologue." In *The Collected Works of L.S. Vygotsky*. Vol. 5, *Child Psychology*, edited by R. W. Rieber, v–xv. New York: Plenum, 1998.
Rengstorf, Karl H. "αποστέλλο." Translated by Geoffrey W. Bromiley. In *Theological Dictionary of the New Testament*, edited by Gerhard Kittel and Gerhard Friedrich, 1:398–447. Grand Rapids: Eerdmans, 1964.
Ricoeur, Paul. *The Symbolism of Evil*. Translated by E. Buchanan. Boston: Beacon, 1969.
Rignal, Charles. *Manchester Baptist College, 1866–1916*. Manchester, n.p., 1916.
Robb, Peter. *M*. London: Bloomsbury, 2000.
Roberts Robert C., and W. Jay Wood, *Intellectual Virtues: An Essay in Regulative Epistemology*. Oxford: Clarendon, 2007.
Robinson, John A. T. *Redating the New Testament*. London: SCM, 1976.
Rogoff, B. "Observing Sociocultural Activity on Three Planes: Participatory Appropriation, Guided Participation, and Apprenticeship." In *Sociocultural Studies of Mind*, edited by J. J. Wertsch, P. del Rio, and A. Alvarez, 139–64. Cambridge: Cambridge University Press, 1995.
Rolle, Richard. *The Fire of God*. Translated by Clifton Walters. Harmondsworth, UK: Penguin, 1972.
Rosenfeld, Jason, and Alison Smith. *John Everett Millais*. London: Tate, 2007.
Ross, Cathy. "Hospitality: The Church as 'A Mother with an Open Heart.'" In *Mission on the Road to Emmaus: Constants, Context and Prophetic Dialogue*, edited by Cathy Ross and Stephen B. Bevans, 67–83. London: SCM, 2015.
Rowe, C. Kavin. "Becoming a Christ-Shaped Leader." Faith and Leadership. September 12, 2011. https://www.faithandleadership.com/c-kavin-rowe-becoming-christ-shaped-leader. Accessed November 23, 2016.
———. "Failure as Christ-Shaped Leadership." Faith and Leadership. November 7, 2011. https://www.faithandleadership.com/c-kavin-rowe-failure-christ-shaped-leadership. Accessed November 23, 2016.
Ruffing, Janet K. "Direction, Spiritual." In *The New SCM Dictionary of Christian Spirituality*, edited by Philip Sheldrake, 243–45. London: SCM, 2005.
Runcorn, David. *Choice, Desire and the Will of God*. London: SPCK, 2003.
Russell, Anthony. *The Clerical Profession*. London: SPCK, 1980.
Sadgrove, Michael. *Wisdom and Ministry. The Call to Leadership*. London: SPCK, 2008.
Schleiermacher, Friedrich. *The Christian Faith*. Translated by H. R. Mackintosh and J. S. Stewart. 2nd ed. Edinburgh: T. & T. Clark, 1928.
Schon, D. *The Reflective Practitioner*. New York: Basic, 1983.
Sheldrake, Philip. *Befriending our Desires*. London: Darton, Longman and Todd, 1994.
———. "Religious Rules." In *The New SCM Dictionary of Christian Spirituality*, 549–50. London: SCM, 2005.
———. *Spirituality and Theology: Christian Living and the Doctrine of God*. London: Darton, Longman and Todd, 1998.

Shepherd, Peter. *The Making of Northern Baptist College*. Manchester: Northern Baptist College, 2004.

Smyth, Charles. *Cyril Forster Garbett: Archbishop of York*. London: Hodder and Stoughton, 1959.

Snyder, Arnold. *Following in the Footsteps of Christ: The Anabaptist Tradition*. London: Darton, Longman and Todd, 2004

Spicq, C. *Agape in the New Testament*. Vol. 2. St Louis: Herder, 1965.

Stacie, Stanley, and Alison Latham. *The Cambridge Music Guide*. Cambridge: Cambridge University Press, 1985.

Staniforth, Maxwell, trans. *Early Christian Writings*. Harmondsworth, UK: Penguin, 1968.

Steiner, G. *Real Presence: Is There Anything in What We Say?* London: Faber and Faber, 1991.

Stone, Bryan P. *Evangelism after Christendom: The Theology and Practice of Christian Witness*. Grand Rapids: Brazos, 2007.

Stone, M. "Virtue Ethics." In *The Blackwell Guide to Ethical Theory*, edited by H. LaFollette, 325–47. Oxford: Blackwell, 2000.

Stott, John R. W. *Guard the Gospel: The Message of 2 Timothy*. Bible Speaks Today. London: IVP, 1973.

Symons, Arthur. "The Lesson of Millais." *Savoy*, October 6, 1896.

Tamburello, D. E. "Bernard of Clairvaux." In *Dictionary of Major Biblical Interpreters*, edited by Donald McKim, 188–93. Downers Grove, IL: Intervarsity, 2007.

Tanner, Kathryn. *Theories of Culture: A New Agenda for Theology*. Minneapolis: Fortress, 1997.

Tanner, M. "Concordia in Piero della Francesca's *Baptism of Christ*." *Art Quarterly* 25 (1972) 1–20.

Taylor, Charles. *Sources of the Self*. Cambridge: Cambridge University Press, 1989.

———. "Overcoming Epistemology." In *After Philosophy, End or Transformation*, edited by Kenneth Baynes, James Bohman, and Thomas McCarthy, 464–88. Cambridge, MA: MIT Press, 1987.

Theissen, G. *The Social Setting of Pauline Christianity*. Edinburgh: T. & T. Clark, 1982.

Thiselton, Anthony C. *The First Epistle to the Corinthians*. New International Greek Testament Commentary. Grand Rapids: Eerdmans, 2000.

Thompson, Judith, and Ross Thompson. *Mindful Ministry*. London: SCM, 2012.

Thornton, Martin. *The Function of Theology*. New York: Seabury, 1968.

Tomlin, Graham. *The Widening Circle: Priesthood as God's Way of Blessing the World*. London: SPCK, 2014.

Torrance, Thomas F. *Royal Priesthood: A Theology of Ordained Ministry*. 2nd ed. Edinburgh: T. & T. Clark, 1993.

Treier, Daniel. *Virtue and the Voice of God: Towards Theology as Wisdom*. Grand Rapids: Eerdmans, 2006.

Vanhoozer, Kevin J. *The Drama of Doctrine: A Canonical-Linguistic Approach to Christian Theology*. Louisville: Westminster John Knox, 2005.

Vanstone, W. H. *Love's Endeavour, Love's Expense*. New ed. London: Darton, Longman and Todd, 2007.

Volf, Miroslav, and Bass, Dorothy C., eds. *Practicing Theology: Beliefs and Practices in Christian Life*. Grand Rapids: Eerdmans, 2002.

Volpe, Medi Ann. *Rethinking Christian Identity: Doctrine and Discipleship*. Chichester, UK: Wiley-Blackwell, 2013.

Vygotsky, L. S. *The Collected Works of L. S. Vygotsky*. Vol 1, *Problems of General Psychology*. Edited by R. W. Rieber and A. S. Carton. New York: Plenum, 1987.

———. "The Socialist Alteration of Man." In *The Vygotsky Reader*, edited by Rene Van der Veer and Jaan Valsiner, 175–84. Oxford: Blackwell 1994.

Warner, Robert. "The Widening Gyre: Counter-Trends in Evangelical Theology and Subculture." In *The Wisdom of the Spirit. Gospel, Church and Culture*, edited by Martyn Percy and Pete Ward, 103–18. Farnham, UK: Ashgate, 2014.

Watson, Francis. *Text, Church and World: Biblical Interpretation in Theological Perspective*. Edinburgh: T. & T. Clark, 1994.

Watts, Graham J. "Can a Baptist Believe in Sacred Space? Some Theological Reflections." In *Baptist Sacramentalism 2: Studies in Baptist History and Thought*, edited by Anthony R. Cross and Philip E. Thompson, 25:135–48. Milton Keynes, UK: Paternoster, 2008.

Webber, Robert E. *The Divine Embrace: Recovering the Passionate Spiritual Life*. Grand Rapids: Baker, 2006.

Weeks, Stuart. *Early Israelite Wisdom*. Oxford: Clarendon, 1994.

———. "Wisdom in the Old Testament." In *Where Shall Wisdom be Found? Wisdom in the Bible, the Church and the Contemporary World*, edited by Stephen Barton, 19–30. Edinburgh: T. & T. Clark, 1999.

Wells, Samuel. *Crafting Prayers for Public Worship*. Norwich: Canterbury, 2013.

———. *God's Companions: Reimagining Christian Ethics*. Oxford: Blackwell, 2006.

———. *Improvisation: The Drama of Christian Ethics*. Grand Rapids: Brazos, 2004.

Westcott, B. F. *The Epistle to the Hebrews*. London: Macmillan, 1889.

Westermann, Claus. *Genesis 1–11*. London: SPCK, 1984.

Whybray, R. N. *Wisdom in Proverbs: The Concept of Wisdom in Proverbs 1—9:45*. London: SCM, 1967.

Williams, Rowan. *The Wound of Knowledge*. London: Darton, Longman and Todd, 1990.

———. *Lost Icons: Reflections on Cultural Bereavements*. Edinburgh: Continuum, 2000.

Willimon, William H. *Calling and Character: Virtues of the Ordained Life*. Nashville: Abingdon, 2000.

———. *Conversations with Barth on Preaching*. Nashville: Abingdon, 2006.

Winter, Sean. "Translocal Ministry: New Testament Perspectives." In *Translocal Ministry*, edited by Stuart Murray-Williams, 14–23. Didcot, UK: Baptist Union of Great Britain, 2004.

Wood, Charles M. *Vision and Discernment: An Orientation in Theological Study*. Studies in Religious and Theological Scholarship. Atlanta: Scholars, 1985.

Woodwell, Anita. *On Holy Ground, Guided Prayer: A Handbook and Practical Companion*. Norwich: Canterbury, 2008.

Working as One Body: The Report of the Archbishops' Commission on the Organization of the Church of England. London: Church House, 2005.

Wright, N. G. "Inclusive Representation: Towards a Doctrine of Christian Ministry." *Baptist Quarterly* 39, no. 4 (2001) 159–74.

———. "Spirituality as Discipleship: The Anabaptist Heritage." In *Under the Rule of Christ. Dimensions of Baptist Spirituality*, edited by Paul Fiddes, 79–101. Oxford: Regent's Park College, 2008.

Wright, N. T. "Faith, Virtue, Justification and the Journey to Freedom." In *The Word Leaps the Gap: Essays on Scripture and Theology in Honor of Richard B Hays*, edited by J. Ross Wagner, C. Kavin Rowe, and A. Katherine Grieb, 472–97. Grand Rapids: Eerdmans, 2008.

———. *Virtue Reborn*. London: SPCK, 2010.

Würthwein, E. "Egyptian Wisdom and the Old Testament." In *Studies in Ancient Israelite Wisdom*, edited by J. L. Crenshaw, 113–33. New York: Ktav, 1976.

Yong, Amos. *Spirit-Word-Community: Theological Hermeneutics in Trinitarian Perspective*. Aldershot, UK: Ashgate, 2002.

Zagzebski, Linda. *Virtues of the Mind: An Enquiry into the Nature and the Ethical Foundations of Knowledge*. Cambridge: Cambridge University Press, 1996.

General Index

Abingdon Baptist Church, xii, 270
Administration, **257–69**
Adult learning, **135–37**
Adair, John. 273
anger, 48, 90, 167, 175, 208
Anscombe, E., 42, 55, 167–69, 291
Apostles, 282–83
Appraisal/Ministerial Development Review, 263, 265, 288
Apprenticeship, xvi, 25, 31–32, 47, 53, 55, **110–21**, 208, 215, 261, 299
Aquinas, Thomas, 42, 52, 74, 129, 212, 299
Annunciation, 204–7
Aristotle, 42–43, 50, 52, 55, 62, 77, 79, 84, 129, 167, 172
Athanasius, 94
Augustine of Hippo, 39, 52, 104, 154

Bach, J. S., 13–17
"Baptism of Jesus," (della Francesca) 18–22
Baptism, Eucharist and Ministry, 272–73
Baptist theological education, 31–35, 129
Baptist Union of Great Britain, xi, xii, xvi, 7, 8, 114, 126, 138, 139, 169, 227, 233, 239, 244, 254, 257, 270, 276, 278, 286, 291, 294, 298, 301
Baptist Union of Scotland, xii

Barratt, C. K., 195, 291
Barth, Karl, 185, 190, 240–41, 250, 254, 291
Barthes, R., 38
Baudrillard, J., 39
Baxter, Richard, 143
Beasley-Murray, Paul, xii, 183, 258
Begbie, Jeremy, 15–17, 190, 272, 291, 298
Benedict, 50, 108, 139, 141, 145, 147, 163
Bernard of Clairvaux, 74, **147–61**, 212, 291, 300
Bernini, 205
beauty, 15, 100, 189–92, 240
Bishops, 86, 117, 145, 271–74, **276–81**, 283
Bonhoeffer, Dietrich, 14–16, 141, 145–46, 160, 234, 254, 292, 295, 298
Bretherton, Luke, 242, 292
Bristol Baptist College, xii, 33, 56
Bruegemann, Walter, 254
burn-out, 174
Burrowes, George, 156–57, 292

Calvin, Jean, 74, 101, **103–9**, 148, 162, 211, 254, 278, 292
Capitalism, 221, 230, 236–37
Caravaggio, M., 22–27
Catherine of Sienna, 150, 203
Chaplaincy, 265, 179

character, ix, xv–xvi, 11, 15, 25–26, 34, 43–44, 56–57, 60–62, 67, 81–83, 85, 87, 89, 94, 101, 107, 112, 121, 125–30, 152, 163, **165–76**, 182, 184, 203, 231, 235–36, 260, 274, 285, 287–88, 298, 301
children, 219–23
"Christ in the House of his Parents" (Millais), 117–21
Church of England theological education, 29–30, 33, 35–37
Coakley, Sarah, 144, 292
College of Baptist Ministers, xii
Colleges, communal acts of worship, 149–50, 192–93
Collins, John N., 281–82, 293
Colmer, Geoff, xi
Colwell, John, xii, 96, 139, 237–38, 293
Communities of practice, xv, 36, **44–47**, 158
compassion, 5, 11, 40, 48, 68, 81–82, 85, 156n40, 172–74, 235–36, 286–87
Congar, Yves, 74, 293
Continuous Professional Development, 267
Craddock, Fred, 248, 293
creation, 57–61, 87
Croft, Stephen, 136, 277–78, 284, 293
"Crucifixion of St. Peter" (Caravaggio), 22–25

Davidson, Randall, 28–29, 246–47, 291
Davies, W. H., 17
Deacons, 281–82, 288
Derrida, Jacques, 38–9
desire, 97–99, 202–4
Devotio Moderna, 141
discernment, 9, 60, 75, 77–78, 85, 90–91, 107, 216, 235–36, 289, 301
Disciples/discipleship, xvi, 6, 9–12, 10n6, 20–21, 22, 24–25, 34–35, 55, 57–58, 61, 66, 81, 84, 93, **94–109**, 116, 128, 130, 136–37, 140–42, 163, 166, 169, 172–73, 198, 207–8, 222–23, 229, **231–36**, 240–41, 267, 271, 274, 284–85

Duccio, 204

Ellis, Chris, 56–57, 125–26, 143, 173n8., 293
Epistemology, 52, 75, 80, 99, **127–29**, 135, 144, 299–300
eschaton, 61–65
Eucharist / Lord's Supper, 67–68, 98, 101–2, 105, 185, 187–88, 193, 207, 243
eudaimonia, 43, 62, 168–69, 172

Face of God / Christ, 40, **65–69**, 82, 148, 154, 197, 225
Faith, 12n7, 15, 16, 51, 73, 76, 80, 90–91, 97, 107, 109, 113, 131–32, 133, 136, 140–42, 157, 165, 169, 171–73, 181, 194–95, **196–98**, 207–8, 211–13, 214–20, 227, 229, 233, 238–42, 251–3, 256, 289
Faith and Order Commission, Church of England, 272–75
Fiddes, Paul S., 37–41, 77, 81–84, 86, 140–41, 254, 293, 301
Foot, Philippa, 42, 294
Foster, Richard, 156, 162, 294
Foucault, M., 3
Fra Angelica, 204–7
Fra Carevale, 205
Francesca, Pierro della, **17–22**, 189, **196–98**, 205, 291–94, 297, 300
Franciscans, 144–45, 192
Fraser, Giles, 285–86, 294
Free Churches theological education, 31–32
friendship, 16, 50, 151, 175–76

Garbett, Cyril, Foster, 29, 183, 300
Garston-Smith, E., xi
generosity, 40, 129, 133–35, 153, 167
Gettier, E., 128
Goodliff, Andrew, 223
Gunton, Colin, 79n26, 254, 294
Gregory the Great, 203
Gregory of Nyssa, **95–101**, 203, 294
Grundy, Malcolm, 271, 294

Hampton, Charles, 265, 295
Harris, Brian, 4, 6, 295
Harvey, David, 38
Hauerwas, Stanley, 5, 24, 42, 62, 140, 181, 189, 247, 254, 256, 295
Heidegger, Martin, 39, 144
Heywood, David, 136, 295
Higginson, Richard, 271, 295
Hilton, Walter, 155–56, 295
hokmah, 77, 87
Holman Hunt, William, 190–91
Holmes, Stephen, 106, 249, 296
Hope, Christian, 57, 108, 172–73, 185, 189–96, **198–200**, 251, 254,
Horsley, Richard, 195, 296
hospitality, 50, 145, 147, 242–43, 292
Hume, David, 51, 127, 238
humility, 11, 21, 40, 79, 83, 86, 88, 104, 116, 129, 131, 133–34, 145, 161, 167, 172, 174, 202, 209, 218, 223, 225, 237, 241–42, 253, 256, 282, 287
Hursthouse, Rosalind, 43, 296
Husserl, Edmund, 38
Hütter, Reinhard, 76, 296

Ignatius Loyola, 107–8, 150, 296
Inchbold, John William, 191
Iona Community, 146
Irigaray, Luce, 40

Jesus Christ, 5, 12, 16, 25, 43, 50, 57, 62, **66–69**, 78, 80, 94–95, 101, 108, 133, 136, 144, 148, 166–67, 169, 172, 190, 191, 217, 225, 251, 275–76, **284–86**
Jesus Christ, priestly ministry, 63–64
Jesus Christ, kingship, 63–65
Jesus Christ, prophetic ministry, 63
Jenson, Philip, 217–18, 296
Jüngel, Eberhard, 185

Kelly, Thomas, 150
Kelsey, David, 76, 234, 296

laziness, 85, 92, 258
Leach, Jane, 266
leadership, xv, xvi, xvii, 4, 10–15, 20, 50, 88, 91, 93–94, 102, 111, 113–15, 117, 148, 167, 173, 176, 180–81, 187, 210, 230, 257, 259, 263–64, 268, **270–90**, 293–95, 298
Lectionary, 255–56
Leech, Kenneth, 228–29, 297
Levinas, Emmanuel, 38–41, 83, 296–97
Lindbeck, George, 75, 96–97, 253, 297
Lippi, Filippo, 204–5
liturgy, **187–93**
Luther, Martin/Lutheranism, 103, 162, 249, 281
Lyotard, JJ., 38–39

MacIntyre, Alasdair, xv–xvi, 39, 42, 44, **49–55**, 67, 76–77, 97–98, 129–31, 146, 234, 237–40, 291, 296
Management Theory, influence upon ministry, 258–59, 286
Manet, Eduard, 121
Marriage, 19, 91–92, 213, 220
McBain, Douglas, xi, 114
McClendon, James, 10, 76, 235, 297
mentoring, 263–64
Milbank, John, 95–96, 99–100, 297
Millais, John Everett, **117–21**, 191, **198–200**, 299, 300
Millard, Stephen, xii
Ministerial formation, xii, xvi, **3–27**, 31n7, 32, 34, 36–37, 43, 45–46, 53, 56–57, 69, 73, 78, 80–84, 94–95, 101, 109, 110, 125–26, 131–32, 135, 137, 149–50, 157–58, 160–61, 165–67, 168–69, 176, 204, 213, 226–27, 261–62, 268–69
Ministerial Recognition Committee / process, xii, 7, 8, 287
Ministry, New Testament origins, 275–83
Mission, xv–xvi, 3, 11-12, 26, 61, 76, 85, 92, 111, 120-21, 145, 148, 160, 165, 184, **230–43**, 264, 270, 273–74, 277, 282, 287, 290
Mollon, P., 175, 297
Monasticism, 103–5, 141, 144–46, 159–60, 163, 231, 239
Murdoch, Iris, 42, 55, 167, 298

Narcissism, 162, 175–76
Nietzsche, Friedrich, 38, 50, 52, 237
"*Noli me tangere*" (Titian), 200–204
Norris, Colin, xi
Northumbria Community, 144–45, 159, 192

O'Brien, Vivienne, xi
Order for Baptist Ministry, xi–xii, 101, 139, 147, 159, 192
Order of Mission, 145

paideia, 105, 108–9
Participation in God, 41, 81–2, 98–100, 152, 162, 234,
Pastoral care, 11, 15, 25, 31, 33, 37, 48, 64, 85, 93, 95, 113, 140, 157, 174, 176, 180, 182, 184–85, **194–209**, 213, 265, 286, 290
Paterson, Michael, 266
patience, 11, 89, 167, 252, 274
Pembroke, Neil, 184–85, 298
Percy, Martin, 215–16, 227, 231, 240, 298
Phillips, Adam, 202
phronesis, 40, 77–79, 80–81, 84
Plantinga, Alvin, 128
Postmodernism, **37–41**, 132, 200, 232, 295, 297
Post-ordination training / formation, 110–11
Poussin, 205
practices, ix, xvi, 26, 43–44, 46, 51–5, 57–58, 69, 76–77, 84, 86, 93, **94–101**, 110, 121, 130–32, 143–44, 158–59, 162–63, 165–66, 176, 180, 182, 184–86, 189, 208, 210, 216, 227, 229, 232–36, 243, 257–58, 260–61, 272–73, 275, 287–90
Prayers/prayerful, 11–13, 15–16, 26, 29, 57, 68–69, 75–77, 79–80, 85, 94, 96, 100, 102, 103, 105, 132, 139–44, 147, 148–50, 154, 156, 157–61, 162–64, 187–88, 191–93, 202, 205, 207–8, 210, 212–16, 222, 225, 227–29, 234, 245, 256, 261, 272, 274, 289

preaching, ix, 25, 47, 85, 103, 133, 136, 149, 158, 179–80, 184–85, 187, 214, 239, **244–56**, 259, 261, 264, 290
Priesthood of all believers, 102–3
Purves, Jim, xii

Rackley, John, xii
Regent's Park College, Oxford, xii, 33, 293–94, 301
"Resurrection" (Pierro della Francesca), 196–98
"Return of the Dove to the Ark" (Millais), 198–200
Rogoff, B., 46–47, 299
Rolle, Richard, 155–56, 299
Runcorn, David, 202, 229, 299
Rutledge, Fleming, 254

Sacraments/sacramentality, 15, 54, 102, 156n40., 173, 214, 232, 236, 243, 249, 277, 294, 301
sapientia, 73–75, 77, 80
Schleiermacher, Friedrich, 37, 299
sexuality, 166, 169–70, 202–203, 218–19, 226
shame, 90, 101, 175–76, 288
Sheldrake, Philip, 143, 203–4, 211, 229, 299
speech, 59–60, 63, 85, 93, 131, 206, 247, 251
Spirit, Holy, 9, 11, **15–21**, 31, 40, 44, 49, 51, 60–2, **65–69**, 77–82, 88, 95, 99–100, 108–9, 119, 120, 144, 148, 150, 152, 154–55, 162–64, 166, 171–73, 190–92, 204–6, 208, 212, 216, 228–29, 232, 238, 249, 251–53, 256, 274, 276–79, 289
spiritual direction/guidance, **210–16**, 228–29, 265
spirituality, ix, xv–vi, 13, 26, 34, 38, 57, 69, 81–82, 84, 95–96, 108–9, 126, **138–45**, 151, 160–63, 203–4, 211–14, 222, 236, 245, 253, 287–88
Spurgeon, C. H., 32, 125, 244,

Spurgeon's College, xii, xvii, 31, 33, 114, 125–26, 139, 144, 244, 293, 296
Standing, Roger, xii
Steiner, George, 39
Stom, Matthias, 224–25
Stone, Bryan, 44n10., 232–33, 235–38, 240n18., 300
Stott, John, 216, 300
Streatham Baptist Church (Lewin Road), xi, xiii, 33, 114, 126, 244, 254, 270
supervision, **262–66**

Tanner, Kathryn, 95–99, 234, 300
Taylor, Barbara Brown, 254
Taylor, Charles, 128, 144, 300
Taylor, Jeremy, 143
Taylor, Martin, xi, 245
Theological guidance, 216–29
Theresa of Avila, 150
Thiselton, Anthony C., 78, 79, 196, 300
Timothy, apostle, 116–17
Titian, 200–202
Tomlin, Graham, 284, 300
Tozer, A. W., 150
Trier, Daniel, 73–77, 80, 300

Vanstone, W. H., 229, 300
virtue ethics, xv–xvii, 8, 13, 15, 25–27, 35–6, **42–55**, 62, 86, 121, 128–32, 149, 157, 167–73, 176, 217, 233, 295–96, 298, 300
virtues, intellectual, **132–35**
Vocation / calling, 3, 8, 10n6, 11, 13, 16, 24, 53, 56–57, 60, 84, 88, 91, 94, 101–2, 105, 106–7, 145, 156, 181, 241
Volpe, Medi Ann, 94–101, 301
Vygotsky, Lev, xv, **44–49**, 293, 299, 301

Warner, Robert, 215
Watson, Francis, **57–62**, 301
Webber, Robert, 161–64, 301
Wells, Sam, 62n16, 189, 191n5, 254, 272, 301
Westcott, Brooke Fosse, 28, 172n6., 301
Wimber, John, 6
wisdom, xvi, 9, 16, 25, 34, 40, 55, **73–93**, 129, 136, 143, 145, 181, 184, 208, 211, 215–17, 249, 264, 287, 291, 293–94, 298, 300–302
Williams, Rowan, 95–99, 219–20, 254, 301
Willimon, William H., 5, 241, 247, 253, 256, 295, 301
Winnicott, Donald, 266
Wolterstorff, Nicholas, 128
Wood, Mike, xi, 114
Woodwell, Anita, 229, 301
worship, 4–5, 11, 25–26, 57, 64–65, 68–69, 105, 141–42, 147, 149–55, 158, 162, 180–81, 184–85, **187–93**, 203, 210, 214–15, 222, 232, 234–39, 244, 272, 290
Wright, Nigel G., xii, 63, 141, 301
Wright, N. Thomas, 43–44, 62–63, 129, 167–70, 254, 302

Yeames, W. F., 223–24

Zagzebski, Linda, 128, 130, 302

Ancient Document Index

Old Testament

Genesis

1:3	59
1:6	59
1:9	59
1:16	59
1:20	59
1:21	59
1:24	59
1:26	59, 60
8:8–11	199
50:24	24

Exodus

33:17–23	65n22
34:29	66n24

Job

28	87

Psalms

72:10	20

Proverbs

3:6	217
3:7	88
3:11–12	88
3:13	79
3:30	89
4:23–27	89
5	89
5:4	91
5:8–9	91
5:15–23	91
6:6–11	92
6:24–25	89
7:3	79
8:1	79
8:1–21	87
8:8	93
8:22	73
8:30	73
9:1–11	87
9:10	89
10:14	93
10:18	93
10:19	93
10:23	79
10:26	92
10:31	93
11:2	86, 88
11:5	217
12:1	88
12:15	88

Proverbs (continued)

12:17–19	93
12:18	93
12:22	93
13:3	93
14:17	90
14:23	92
14:25	95
14:29	90
15:1	89
15:12	88
15:18	90
15:19	92
15:22	88
15:23	86
15:24	91
15:25	86
15:33	88
16:18	86
16:18–19	88
16:21	90
16:25	90
16:32	90
17:14	89
17:28	93
18:2	91
18:8	93
18:12	88
19:13	91
20:4	92
21:9	91
22:3	90
22:4	88
22:24	90
23:29–35	86, 89
24:17–19	89
24:29	89
24:31	92
24:33–34	92
25:9–10	89
25:16	89
25:21–22	89
25:27	89
26:17	89
27:2	88
27:15	91
29:22	90
29:23	88

Song of Solomon

1–2	151
5:2–8	156
5:4–5	156

Isaiah

29:14	78

Jeremiah

1:4	60

Zechariah

13:6	117n7

New Testament

Matthew

5:44	90
5:46–48	40
6:28	289
16:17–18	24
16:23	24
16:24–26	24
25:37–39	243

Mark

3:13–19	116
6:6–13	116
6:30	116
8:34	289
9:37	222, 223
10:15	222
10:35–45	116

Luke

4:22	252
4:29	252
7:36–50	201
24:16	65n23

John

1:14	64
1:29	64
6:60	285
6:66	285
7:37	66n26
7:38	64
8:12	64, 66n25
10:4	11
10:15	11
11:25	64
14:6	64
14:26	277
15:15	151
16:13	277
17	96
17:3	64
20:14	65n23
21:18–19	25

Acts of the Apostles

6:1–6	281
6:4	12
9:4	60
11:27–30	279
14:27	279
15:2	279
15:4	279
15:6	279
15:22–23	279
16:1–3	116
16:4	279
16:16–40	116
18:5	116
18:22	116
19:10	116
19:21–22	116
20:28	276

Romans

1:1	283
1:20	68n31
5:1	195n4
11:13	283
12:20	89
16:7	283
16:21	116

1 Corinthians

1:1	283
1:19	78
1:21	78, 249
1:23–25	79
1:30	78
2:7–16	78
9:1	283
12:7	277
12:11	277
13:13	195
15:9	283
15:18	282

2 Corinthians

1:1	117, 283
3:13	66n24
3:18	67, 69n33
8:23	283

Galatians

1:1	283
1:13–17	60n14
5:5–6	195n4
5:22–23	166, 274

Preceding entries:

10:41–45	289
10:44–45	116

Ephesians

1:15–18	212
4:2–5	195n4
4:12	11, 276
4:13	109
4:14	90
4:15	109
4:20	109, 133
4:24	109

Philippians

1:1	117, 279
2:1–11	289
2:2	79
2:5	79
3:15	79
3:19	79
4:2	79
5:2–3	280

Colossians

1:1	117
2:25	283
3:12–14	11
3:14	167

1 Thessalonians

1:1	117
1:3	195n4
5:8	195n4

2 Thessalonians

1:1	117

1 Timothy

3:2–3	86
3:2	279
3:5	279
3:6	86
4:7	172
4:13–14	276
5:17	279
6:4	89

2 Timothy

1:6–7	276
1:8	241
1:14	216
2:3	241
2:8	241
2:8–9	217
2:15	217
2:23	217
2:24	89, 217
3:11	241
3:12	241
3:13	216
4:5	241
4:6	241
4:6–8	117
4:7	241

Titus

2:2	195n4

Hebrews

5:14	172
6:10–12	195n4
10:22–24	195n4
13:7	289

James

5:14	279

1 Peter

1:3–8	195n4
2:12	231
2:25	279
3:2	283
5:1–2	279

2 John

1	280

3 John

1	280

Revelation

1:16	66n27
21–22	57
21:3–4	63
21:4	63
21:5	63
21:24–26	64
22:1–2	64
22:3	64
22:3–4	65
22:5	63, 64
22:8	64
22:9	64
22:10	63

Early Christian Writings

1 Clement

42:44	280

Shepherd of Hermas *Mandates*

11:7–25	281n26

Shepherd of Hermas *Similitudes*

9:15.1	281n26
9:26.2	280n24
9:27.2	280n24

Shepherd of Hermas *Vision*

3:5.1	281n25

Ignatius *Letter to the Ephesians*

1:3	280n22
2:1	280n22

Ignatius *Letter to the Magnesians*

2:1	280n22
15:1	280n22

Ignatius *Letter to the Philadelphians*

11:1	280n22

Ignatius *Letter to the Smyrneans*

10:1	280n22